ESCROWS

PRINCIPLES AND PROCEDURES

Second Edition

By
Stanley S. Reyburn, D.B.A.

Anthony Schools®

Anthony Schools
Real Estate
College Level Courses

Escrows Principles and Procedures
Legal Aspects of Real Estate
Real Estate Appraisal
Real Estate Economics
Real Estate Finance
Real Estate Office Administration
Real Estate Practice
Real Estate Principles
Property Management

EDITORIAL AND
EXECUTIVE OFFICES
Anthony Schools Corporation
15942 Foothill Blvd., Suite 100
San Leandro, CA 94578

CONTINUING EDUCATION
INDEPENDENT STUDY OFFICES
Anthony Schools Corporation
15942 Foothill Blvd., Suite 200
San Leandro, CA 94578

COLLEGE-LEVEL
INDEPENDENT STUDY OFFICES
Anthony Schools Corporation
POB 18827
Irvine, CA 92713-8827

Escrows—Principles and Procedures, Second Edition

By Stanley S. Reyburn, D.B.A.
Published by Anthony Schools® Corporation
San Leandro, California 94578

ISBN 0-941833-34-8

ACKNOWLEDGEMENTS
Acknowledgment is made to the following institutions for permission to reprint forms and exhibits (endorsement not implied): California Association of Realtors®, California Escrow Association, California Federal Savings and Loan, City and County of Los Angeles, Commonwealth Escrow Company, Computer Data Control Inc., First American Title Company, Continental Lawyers Title of San Francisco, Sterling Bank, TICOR Title Insurance, Wells Fargo Bank, U.S. Internal Revenue Service and Veterans Administration.

DISCLAIMER
This material is for educational purposes only. In no way should any statements or summaries be used as a substitute for legal or tax advice.

10 9 8 7 6 5 4 3

Printed in Hong Kong

Contents

LIST OF EXHIBITS

Chapter 1
Evolution of Escrow

PREVIEW

Real Property Ownership

California Property Ownership Develops

Escrow Defined

The Escrow Process Evolves

REAL PROPERTY OWNERSHIP

Property ownership is one of the basic American constitutional rights. Federal protection of property rights is based on English common law and the U.S. Constitution. Specific constitutional references to property ownership occur in several places in the Bill of Rights:

Article III of the Bill of Rights. "No soldier shall, in time of peace, be quartered in any house, without the consent of the owner, nor in time of war, but in a manner to be prescribed by law."

Article IV of the Bill of Rights. "The right of the people to be secure in their persons, houses, papers, and effects, against unreasonable searches and seizures, shall not be violated."

Article V of the Bill of Rights. "Nor be deprived of life, liberty, or property without due process of law; nor shall private property be taken for public use without just compensation."

Property Acquisition Section 1000 of the California Civil Code states that property is acquired in California today by five methods:

- ☐ Occupancy
- ☐ Accession
- ☐ Transfer
- ☐ Will
- ☐ Succession.

In practice, these five basic types of title acquisition takes 12 different forms—title by:

- ☐ Public grant
- ☐ Private grant

- Involuntary alienation (execution sales, bankruptcy, etc.)
- Descent or succession (disposition without a will upon death of an owner)
- Devise
- Adverse possession
- Escheat (reversion to the state)
- Dedication (devoted to public use)
- Eminent domain (condemnation for public use)
- Estoppel (in the interest of justice)
- Accretion (land formation at the edge of a body of water)
- Abandonment or forfeiture (relinquishing lease or other contractual rights to real property).

CALIFORNIA PROPERTY OWNERSHIP DEVELOPS

Property ownership in California has a number of distinctive features which reflect the state's long multicultural history.

The Spanish and Mexican Period
On September 28, 1542, Juan Rodriguez Cabrillo sailed into San Diego Bay, proclaiming title to the land in the name of the king of Spain. This was the beginning of European-based land ownership systems in California.

Missions. Organized colonization by Spain evolved from the combined efforts of three Jesuit priests, Eusebio Francesco Kino, cartographer, explorer and builder of missions; Juan Maria de Salvatierra, mission builder; and Juan de Ugarte. The missionary work was assumed by 14 Franciscan friars under Father Junipero Serra, arriving at La Paz in 1768. The eventual result was 21 missions built between 1769 and 1823, from San Diego in the south to Sonoma in the north.

Spanish Land Grants. Significant secular land grants by the ten Spanish governors included the following:

Year	Grantee	Location
1784	Manuel Nieto	Majority of Los Angeles County
1784	Jose Maria Verdugo	36,000 acres in Los Angeles County
1795	The Pico family	Bean Ranches of Ventura County
1795	Jose Dario Arguello	Coastline northward from San Pedro
1810	Antonio Maria Lugo	From Lake Arrowhead to Pasadena and Los Angeles

Mexican Land Grants. In 1822, as a result of the Mexican revolution, California became part of Mexico. From 1822 to 1846, sizeable rancho grants were conferred upon Mexican citizens and foreigners who adopted Mexican citizenship. There were over 500 such grants by 1846.

California Joins the Union
On June 14, 1846, the Bear Flag Revolt set off the events by which California became a part of the United States, and on September 9, 1850, became a state.

Origins of Title. In February of 1848 the Treaty of Guadalupe Hidalgo was signed, and the following bases of title in California were recognized:

- ☐ *Mexican Grants*. Rancho and public grants conferred while California was under the jurisdiction of Spain and Mexico were confirmed.

- ☐ *State Lands*. Lands were granted by Congress to the state from the public domain, furnishing the state with funds for education, reclamation and other purposes.

- ☐ *Tidelands and Submerged Lands*. This unique form of ownership has been in a state of flux in recent years.

- ☐ *Public Lands*. All lands not included in the first three groupings became public lands of the United States.

Conflicting Claims American settlers tended to assume that much of California fell into the last category and was available for homesteading. The conflicting claims that resulted occupied the courts for decades, and are one reason escrows and title insurance are so highly developed in California.

Title Insurance and Escrows Emerge
Recording. Recording of legal documents was established by the California Constitution of 1849, and the Recorder's Office was part of the system of county and town governments organized by the legislature in 1850.

Board of Land Commissioners. In 1851 the Board of Land Commissioners was formed as authorized by the Treaty of Guadalupe Hidalgo to confirm previous grants of land throughout the state. Confirmation of ownership was by U.S. patent.

Private Examination and Search. Private title examination and search of the public records began prior to California's entry into the Union. At this stage there was no guarantee of accuracy and no insurance behind the examination.

Abstract of Title. An abstract is a written history of recorded transactions affecting a piece of land. Use of abstracts originated in first quarter of the nineteenth century in other states.

- ☐ *Legal Form*. Combined with an attorney's legal opinion as to the condition of title, the abstract was used almost exclusively in the mid-1800s.

□ *Practitioners*. Abstract company offices were usually located close to the courthouse where attorneys and records were located.

Certificate of Title. This document emerged in the early 1870s as a condensation of the more cumbersome abstract of title. A natural outgrowth of the abstract for practical use, it gave a brief summary of the condition of title. In the 1880s attorney issues of certificates were incorporated.

Formation of Title Insurance and Trust Companies. Pennsylvania has the distinction of being the first state to issue title insurance, in Philadelphia, in 1876. *Watson v. Muirhead* (Pennsylvania, 1868) was the landmark case which hastened the entry of the title insurance industry, since it established that abstractors had no liability for failure to include certain record matters in the abstract.

□ *First California Company*. In 1886, California Title Insurance and Trust Company, with offices in San Francisco, was incorporated.

□ *First California Policy*. The first title policy was issued on March 17, 1887, making California Title (later California Pacific Title Insurance Company and now TICOR) the pioneer of the title insurance business in California.

Evolution of Escrow. Escrow involving impartial representation in the sale of real property evolved as an adjunct to title insurance and appears as a formal process by the early 1890s.

ESCROW DEFINED

Escrow is formally defined in a number of statutes and treatises, and is defined in practice by the functions it fulfills in real property transfers and similar situations. (Note that although this text is written mainly with reference to California, where modern escrow procedure originated, the same principles are applicable in the eleven western states, Alaska, and Hawaii.)

Civil Code Definition According to California Civil Code § 1057: "A grant may be deposited by the grantor with a third person, to be delivered on performance of a condition, and, on delivery by the depositary, it will take effect. While in the possession of the third person, and subject to condition, it is called an escrow."

Financial Code California Financial Code § 17003 states: "Escrow means any transaction wherein one person, for the purpose of effecting the sale, transfer, encumbering, or leasing of real or personal property to another person, delivers any written instrument, money, evidence of title to real or personal property, or other thing of value to a third person to be held by such third person until the happening of a specified event or the performance of a prescribed condition, when it is to be delivered by such third person to a grantee, grantor, promisee, promisor, obligee, obligor, bailee, bailor, or any agent or employee of any of the latter."

Instrument or Transaction The treatise *Escrow Procedures* by Loren David and Arthur Bowman comments on the definition of escrow as follows:

> "The technical definition as denoting the instrument that is conditionally delivered does not entirely reflect its meaning in modern usage. Thus, when parties speak of 'an escrow' or 'going into escrow,' they generally regard the 'escrow' as a transaction wherein one party for the purpose of effecting a sale, transfer, or lease of real property, or an encumbrance upon real property, in favor of another party, delivers a written instrument, money or other thing of value to a third person, called an escrow agent or escrow holder, to be held by such third person for further delivery upon the happening of a specified event or the performance of a specified condition."

Trust *Black's Law Dictionary* defines a trust as: "A right of property, real or personal, held by one party for the benefit of another." Escrow is, in fact, a trust relationship with a multiple representation, since the escrowholder represents all principals in the transaction. Principals could be buyer and seller, borrower and lender, lessor and lessee, first party and second party, or vendor and vendee.

Purposes of Escrow **Depository.** Escrow serves as a neutral depository for documents and money. As a dual agent the escrowholder will accept deposits of both documents and money from both sides of the transaction and will hold them all in trust.

Meeting Conditions. Escrow assures conditions of transfer are met. Delivery of documents to the escrowholder is a conditional delivery. For example, the delivery of the deed from the grantor to the escrowholder does not move title. The escrowholder will assure that conditions have been met before effective delivery of the deed is effected.

Consumer Protection. Escrow provides protection to the consumer during the transfer process. Since the escrowholder holds all documents and money in trust, the transfer process is not completed until all conditions have been met.

Expertise. Escrow provides the expertise in document preparation and an understanding of the title insurance process to effect closing with a minimum of difficulty and expense.

Accounting. Escrow provides an accounting of the transfer process for income tax purposes. The escrow closing statement summarizes all the financial transactions that went through the escrow.

THE ESCROW PROCESS EVOLVES

This process of delivery to a neutral depositary has been with us for as long as history has been recorded.

Antiquity Archaeologists have unearthed tablets dating back to 2000 B.C. chronicling transactions involving money and credit. Escrow-like principles were evident in the temple banks which existed in ancient Babylonia, Greece, Egypt, and Rome.

Form. A note given by a farmer to a temple bank in exchange for a loan to purchase seeds contains the following terms:

> "Warod-Ilish, the son of Taribaum, has received from the sun-priestess, the daughter of Ibbatum, one shekel of silver by the Sun God's balance. This sum is to be used to buy sesame. At the time of the sesame harvest he will repay in sesame, at the current price, to the bearer of this instrument."

Escrow Function. In this case, the temple (bank) performed the function of an escrowholder. One condition of this transaction was the ability of the farmer to germinate his seeds and reap the harvest. This would be the only manner in which payment could be effected. An escrowholder has to be willing to accept this risk when this duty of trust has been imposed.

Biblical Reference. The Old Testament describes the prophet Jeremiah buying a piece of land, Hanameel's field, and appointing an agent, Baruch, to whom "the evidence of purchase" was given (Jeremiah 32:9-15).

Early Dictionary References Illustrations of the use of the word "escrow" and of the escrow function in Europe as early as 1598 are given in the *Oxford English Dictionary*. Many early day lawsuits involving escrows in the eastern United States are cited in *Bouvier's Law Dictionary*, the first edition of which appeared in 1839.

Derivation. The word "escrow" comes from the same early French source as the word "scroll."

Examples. Early *Oxford English Dictionary* citations include the following:

- □ *1598*. Kitchin, *Courts Leet*, "It was delivered as an Escrow upon condition."
- □ *1708*. *Termes de la Ley*, "An Escrow is a Deed delivered to a third person to be the Deed of the party upon future condition."

Modern Escrow: A Product of the West Although title insurance is accepted as an adjunct to the closing process nationwide (with the exception of Iowa where it is bootlegged), escrow processing is a distinctive commodity of the West. It is a natural result of the sheer volume of real estate and personal property transfers that emanate from this area.

Origin. Interest in California land first fueled by the gold rush of 1849 and rekindled by the land booms of the 1880s created a need for buyers, sellers, and lenders to have their transactions properly documented to protect their interests. Escrow processing has evolved on the basis of custom and usage.

Title-Escrow Relations. The title pioneer became the escrow pioneer as a natural adjunct of the process. Shortly after incorporation California Title Insurance and Trust Company began to handle escrows.

First California Escrow. Most early escrows were fairly elementary transactions and the supportive documentation equally elementary in nature. The first such transaction in southern California was recalled in the April 1928 issue of the *T.I. News*, published by Title Insurance and Trust Company. L.J. Benyon, Vice President, was quoted:

> "One day in 1895, a man came into the office of the company and left an order for a certificate of title. He said he was obliged to leave town for a few days and asked the order clerk if he would, as a matter of convenience take his executed deed, deliver it to the buyer together with the certificate, and collect and send him the sum of $1,000. This was our first escrow."

Practitioners **Title Companies**. The convenience of employing a title company to hold funds and documents and to see that disbursements and deliveries were made when the condition of title met specified requirements caused an expansion of escrow activities. Instead of representing only one side in the transaction (i.e., the grantor or lender), title companies began to represent both sides. In Northern California their procedures remained unilateral, taking separate instructions from each side of the transaction.

Banks. With the increased subdivision activity starting around 1900, it was very difficult for title companies to satisfy the demand for escrow service. In Southern California, escrow service was offered by Los Angeles County banks as a convenience to customers in the early 1900s. With the proliferation of branch banking during the 1920s, it became customary for the real estate broker to take seller and buyer to the bank nearest the property or to the broker's office and "go into escrow." Bilateral escrow instructions signed in counterparts was the form best suited to this regional process.

Independent Profession. By 1929 one Los Angeles bank claimed to have handled more than 20,000 escrows. The title companies developed continuous programs to train escrow personnel, who soon became escrow competitors in banks, savings and loan associations, and mortgage companies. The independent escrow company organized for the express purpose of handling escrows evolved naturally. In addition, law firms and real estate brokers became participants in this field.

Formal Instructions During this evolutionary period formal escrow instructions emerged together with provisions for the fulfillment of the condition of passing title as well as the disposition of deposited money. Items considered were the broker's commission, proration of taxes, rents, insurance and interest, provisions for title and fire insurance, and further disposition of deposited funds.

Geographical Differences Processing practices vary geographically, both intrastate and interstate. Through evolving local custom, escrow practices have followed different paths in Northern and Southern California. This will be discussed at length in a later chapter.

California. In Northern California escrow has been almost the exclusive province of the title companies. Only in recent years have some banks and independent escrow companies begun to offer this service. The disposition of funds as well as the responsibility for various charges differs between Northern and Southern California.

- ☐ Instruction form in Northern California is *unilateral* (Exhibit 15), in Southern California *bilateral* (Exhibit 6).

- ☐ Northern California processing completes the accumulation of data and loan approval prior to preparing instructions.

- ☐ Southern California processing finds the escrow agent more actively involved in accumulating supportive documentation as well as accounting for funds passing through the transactions.

Western States. In Oregon, as in Northern California, most escrow business is handled by title companies. Independent escrow is just beginning to be evident as a competitive business. Escrows in the state of Washington are handled by title companies, banks, independent escrow companies, real estate companies, and lawyers. Nevada procedure has evolved in a manner similar to California, since many of the escrow practitioners in that state were trained in California. There are local variations in procedure in Nevada and Arizona as well as in California.

Eastern U.S. In the eastern United States, closing concurrent with the recording of documents is common. The word escrow may not even be used. In the so-called "Eastern closing," all the parties to the transaction, or their representatives, meet in a "closing room" to effect the closing and subsequent recordation of documents. In Illinois, the recording of documents may precede the closing, the documents being "pulled back" from the recorder if problems occur in the closing process.

Outside of the United States. Closing can be a very formalized process with attorney and lender involvement. In many places forms of land registration based on Australia's Torrens Act exist in lieu of title insurance.

Chapter 1 Quiz

1. Initial European occupation of California was by:

   (A) England
   (B) France
   (C) Spain
   (D) Mexico

2. The number of missions developed between 1769 and 1823 was:

   (A) 21
   (B) 20
   (C) 17
   (D) 23

3. Mexican possession of California ceased in:

   (A) 1846
   (B) 1848
   (C) 1850
   (D) 1851

4. Official recognition of land claims predating U.S. possession came in:

   (A) The Treaty of Juarez
   (B) The Treaty of San Lorenzo
   (C) The Treaty of Guadalupe Hidalgo
   (D) Such land claims were never recognized

5. One of the disadvantages of private examination and search was:

   (A) Lack of chain of title
   (B) Lack of formal report
   (C) No insurance behind examination
   (D) Abstract and opinion

6. Which of the following provides the highest degree of protection?

   (A) Abstract of title
   (B) Title insurance policy
   (C) Certificate of title
   (D) Abstract and opinion

7. Title policies were first issued in the:

   (A) 1820s
   (B) 1850s
   (C) 1870s
   (D) 1900s

8. Escrow is:

   (A) An agent representing one party to the sale
   (B) A holder of money and/or documents involving the sale or hypothecation of real or personal property to be delivered upon conditions
   (C) A conditional transfer of property
   (D) A transfer of property interests between principals

9. The earliest form of escrow process was evident:

   (A) Around 2000 B.C.
   (B) In the 1850s
   (C) In the 1890s
   (D) Just after the turn of the 20th century

10. Escrow practices:

    (A) Are uniform throughout the country
    (B) Are uniform within a given state
    (C) Vary both intra- and interstate
    (D) Are the same on the East Coast as in California

Chapter 2
The Title and
Escrow Professions

PREVIEW

Place in Real Estate Industry

Title Insurance Personnel

Escrow Personnel

Professional Escrow Associations

PLACE IN REAL ESTATE INDUSTRY

With new technology and increasing legal requirements, title and escrow careers have expanded well beyond the escrow officer and title officer, and title and escrow now form a virtually independent industry in terms of size and specialization. Professional designations and a specialized code of ethics parallel those of the other real estate professions.

Licensee as Title and Escrow Customer The real estate licensee will encounter a whole hierarchy of professionals processing these transactions and must be able to evaluate the quality of service and recognize when specialized expertise is needed.

As Practitioner Real estate brokers may process escrows for their own sales. In addition, since the fields are closely related, real estate professionals may well find themselves working in the title and escrow fields at some point in their careers.

TITLE INSURANCE PERSONNEL

Functions in the field of title insurance range from researching and interpreting the facts of title, to making underwriting decisions, to administering and marketing the title company.

Title Searcher The "entry level" job classification is that of title searcher. Upon receiving a request for search from the title department the searcher:

Reviews. Reviews instructions for type of search required. In addition to a "normal" chain tracing sales or hypothecations (loans) involving real property, there may be a request for information on ownership of oil, easement rights, reversionary rights under a recorded deed restriction, leasehold interest, special title requirements and the like. Special policy coverages such as eminent domain (condemnation), trust deed foreclosure, subdivision and litigation guarantees require special searches. Any maps required or document copies requested are duly noted and ordered as the information becomes available to the searcher.

Retrieves. The searcher then obtains a copy of the latest title policy issued on the property under search, if available, and prepares a chain of title listing documents from the policy date to the present time. The chain of title lists the type of document, parties involved, and the appropriate recording data.

Searches. After completion of the title search, a general index search is conducted for judgments, divorces, tax liens, bankruptcies, probates, incompetencies and other general matters affecting the parties involved in the chain. The searcher develops specialized skills in using the public records of the county where he or she practices.

☐ Recorded documents are usually placed on microfilm or microfiche, and are reproduced by the searcher in preparing a chain of title. Los Angeles County recordings number thousands daily, while sparsely settled Tehama County may have just a few.

☐ Automation has revolutionized the duties performed by the title searcher. No longer are lot books hand posted and classified by legal description. The general index or name search (enhanced by Soundex) has now been automated along with the lot book. In large counties with the most recording activity, title plants shared by several companies are the order of the day.

Assembles. All documentation is assembled in date order. The search is then routed to the title engineer if a new description is required, or the opinion section for a legal opinion on a proceeding such as eminent domain or probate. If no further action of this nature is required, the search is returned to the title department.

Updates. The title searcher compiles a "date down" or "fallout" search (documents recorded on the property subsequent to search and prior to recording) either manually or by computer while the title order is active.

Skills Required **Responsibility for Facts**. Missed documents in the chain of title, such as a deed of trust, can cause considerable exposure to the title company. Clerical skills and detail orientation aid in avoiding these pitfalls. Unlike other types of casualty insurance, title insurance assures to a certain date that matters affecting title are only those shown in the title policy. Thus, title insurance insures the past. A familiarity with state history and how title evolves is helpful. In dealing with legal descriptions basic trigonometric and algebraic skills are necessary. Since compilation of title searches now uses Landex and other software applications in addition to the automated general index, basic computer knowledge is desirable.

Judgment. Decisions are constantly being made in the search and compilation process as to whether a document in the chain should be included or whether it in fact affects other property. The logical mind aids in this decision.

Career Path   **Entry.** Title secretaries often become searchers after absorbing the skills by osmosis. They have the added advantage of public relations experience in dealing with customers.

Increasing Complexity. From the entry level there is room to progress from searcher to intermediate (more complex) searching to the ultimate in skill, the long order searcher (senior searcher). At this level one gets involved with such complex matters as property resurveys, street abandonments, railroad title reversions, tideland and wetland matters, and oil searches. A skilled long order searcher can be of great value to a title company.

Title Examiner   Title insurance takes risks based upon interpretation. The principal interpreter is the title examiner (sometimes referred to as "title officer" or "T.O.") who requests the search and then distills and interprets the information compiled by the title searcher. The basic examination duties are:

Escrow Contact. The title officer works with closing (escrow) personnel in the proper dispatch of title requirements in a given transaction, and is the person who initiates a search based upon title order specifications.

Interpreting Title Search. The title examiner interprets the results of the title search through examination and inquiry. The conclusion is in the form of a written opinion known as a preliminary title report or interim binder (commitment to issue title insurance in the future).

Interpreting Title Condition. The examiner seeks advice from appropriate personnel (title advisor, attorney, etc.) or reference books if there is a question of interpretation concerning the condition of title.

Review. The examiner reviews the preliminary title report or binder as to legal description, vesting of title and encumbrances (burdens) on the land.

Examining. The title officer examines adequacy of all legal documentation prior to recording, passing on its validity to comply with instructions of closing personnel.

Administration. In addition, the title officer directs the activity of secretarial support staff.

Marketing. In practice the title examiner often operates as a "hands on" marketer in the sales and maintenance of various title products.

Complex Cases. The senior title examiner deals with specialized and complex title matters where the greatest degree of exposure exists for title insurers. This parallels the area of long order searches. These are usually the most proficient and experienced title officers in the company.

Advisory Title Officers These usually come from the ranks of senior title examiners. Title advisors resolve complex title issues and formulate underwriting decisions, i.e., whether the position taken is an acceptable insurance risk. In large title companies there may be a separately staffed underwriting department.

Title Analyst **Research**. The title research analyst supplements the work of advisory title officers when title insurers are called upon to address complex underwriting situations. Problems of Indian lands, tidelands and submerged lands, lake and river boundaries, land resurvey problems and so on may be dealt with by the title research analyst.

Development. In addition, new underwriting methods are often developed by these analysts. For example, a title insurance product developed in the 1980s is coverage for lenders who offer consumer credit secured by liens on real estate. A special endorsement was perfected to provide insurance to the lender that such advances would retain priority over most subsequent liens. Just by the development of this endorsement, a whole new market was made possible.

Title Marketer "Title reps" or marketing personnel take new products developed by the research department into the field. Under the direction of the sales or marketing manager they can be assigned on a geographic or customer basis.

Geographic. Generally title companies operate organized call programs on existing customers and new prospects, and marketing representatives are assigned to specific locations, such as the San Fernando Valley or Walnut Creek.

Type of Customer. Wholesale users of title insurance such as subdividers, fast food franchises, hotel chains and the like are assigned to experienced marketers with appropriate technical background, who are comparable to sales engineers in the high tech field.

Branch Manager As one achieves upward mobility in any organization, technical background must be complemented with managerial skills. Manager duties will include personnel selection, setting an example, training and development, expanding market share, reporting results, and personnel assessment. Skills required are adeptness in interviewing, leadership, teaching, sales, communication, and objectivity.

Executive Management The growing synergism in the financial services industry (Sears Financial Network is one familiar example, only the tip of the iceberg) means more and more administration of companies with multiple locations, dictating new and expanded duties for top executives.

Executive Duties. In title insurance as elsewhere, responsibilities at this level include understanding the big picture, placement of key personnel, knowing what is required to produce a profit, effective communication throughout the organization, and pragmatic problem solving.

Executive Skills. The title company executive must be a superior communicator, achiever of balance, outstanding projector of company image internally and externally, and creator of simple solutions to complex problems.

ESCROW PERSONNEL

Among the services provided in many title companies is escrow service. In Northern California title insurance and escrow are conducted as a cohesive unit, and the career paths are generally parallel. The escrow career path can emphasize sale escrows, loan escrows, or a combination of both. To acquire the tools of the escrow trade requires a combination of formal education and practical office experience.

Secretary-Receptionist — Because processing operations are not uniform, an entry level position may have various titles but is almost always clerical. Entry can be made from other secretarial positions as well as from clerical positions in financial organizations with real estate orientation. A basic understanding of word and data processing has now become essential.

Clerical Functions. Word transcription, whether by typewriter from a memo sheet, shorthand, stenotype, or other form, is essential to produce a well-organized escrow instruction.

Escrow Functions. Many times an escrow secretary serves as an "escrow officer without portfolio." Some offices even refer to this as a junior escrow officer position.

Escrow Officer — The escrow officer primarily needs a refinement of the skills essential for the escrow secretarial position.

Duties. Basic duties of an escrow officer include:

☐ Collecting data, interpreting and converting it into meaningful instructions, and initiating the closing process following the basic instruction to consummate the process.

☐ Taking a variety of escrows and preparing appropriate documentation.

☐ Understanding of the collateral aspects, including title and legal requirements and the role of financing in the escrow process.

☐ Training and development of subordinates and assessing the work of peers.

☐ Cost control and awareness of the productivity of the escrow unit.

Qualifications. The very essence of escrow is that it provides order in a complex, fast-moving, and often tricky transaction. Thus the escrow officer must above all be organized, efficient, and systematic.

☐ An analytical mind has the ability to assimilate data provided by the parties and reduce these requirements to a properly drafted instruction. Organization is the key to properly coordinating documentation.

☐ A paralegal background is a definite asset, due to the laws that are constantly shaping and reshaping various elements of the escrow process. Legal training of this nature is available at both private and public institutions. Formal training complements practical experience.

☐ An efficient person appreciates the quality of time and the necessity of preventing its waste. One way this can be accomplished is by reducing errors to a minimum, e.g., typing with accuracy rather than blinding speed.

☐ Mathematical skills are extremely important in the escrow process, for prorations, preparation of closing statements, computation of demands, financial statements and balancing.

☐ Tranquility under conditions of adversity is an asset to judgment, and instills customer confidence.

Loan Escrow Officer

Loan escrow work provides opportunities to specialize either in closing work or in an administrative capacity as loan underwriter.

Duties. The skills required for the escrow officer and the loan escrow officer are similar, with a few refinements. A loan officer is required to:

☐ Apply independent judgment to supervise the closing process, from initial action by the loan committee to relinquishment of the loan file to loan administration.

☐ Understand lender requirements for supporting documentation, credit criteria, title requirements, and reports.

☐ Serve as liaison between lenders and parties involved in the transaction.

☐ Appreciate variances in lender requirements for loan processing, as well as similarities, and take advantage of both.

☐ Know the legal framework that structures the lending process, from the technical requirements of consumer legislation and the needs of various regulatory agencies, to the entanglements of construction loans and the complexities of income properties pledged as security. Any potential legal problem should be brought to the attention of the loan officer by the escrow officer, who is the loan closer.

Personal Qualifications. Loan escrows tend to involve more variables and more customer contact than general sale escrow work.

☐ Superior communication skills are needed, because the loan escrow officer must establish a good working rapport with the parties involved in the transaction.

☐ Personal discipline is needed in a business that involves a constant series of peaks and valleys. Such fluctuations require personnel who can cope with difficult situations effectively and, in fact, be stimulated by them to superlative performance.

☐ Mathematical proficiency is essential for the myriad of payoffs and payment calculations required in loan work.

☐ Organization and efficiency allow a loan escrow officer to devote more time to areas which require the highest degree of experience and expertise. In many ways automation is helping this to happen. Incorporating repetitive phrases into a memory bank for later retrieval or doing searches and sorts by computer allows the loan escrow officer more time to structure each transaction and initiate business development.

Training. Like the general escrow officer, a candidate for loan escrow officer has usually already been engaged directly in loan work or in a related field. Many come from employment with:

☐ Savings and loan associations

☐ Commercial banks

☐ Mortgage bankers

☐ Insurance companies

☐ Mortgage brokers

☐ Credit unions

☐ Finance companies

☐ Other institutions involved in loan processing

Formal training programs are also important, and are offered by professional groups or by public or private educational institutions.

Escrow Manager Management of the escrow department or office is a distinct plateau in the practitioner's career path, calling for more than technical knowledge. Management is both a science and an art. A manager must exhibit:

Profit Orientation and Efficiency. In the preceding jobs emphasis was placed on specific task performance, without concern for the profits of the overall operation. Coordinating tasks in a prompt and efficient manner is the key to a profitable escrow operation. The manager must balance technical ability and business development acumen.

Tact. In any occupation dealing with people, respect is always a proper posture. A genuine concern about the people that one works with and for is a prime requisite.

Communication Skills. The ability to express ideas in speech and in writing is a hallmark of a superior manager. If a free flow of communication cannot be established within the organization and between the organization and its various publics, management's effectiveness will be severely impeded.

Teaching Ability. The conveying of new ideas and techniques is an extension of the ability to communicate. Escrow is a prime example of learning by doing and, with proper guidance, this is how new professionals are developed. Escrow mentors help to develop career aspirants by sharing their knowledge.

Marketing Ability. All the skill in the world is useless unless there are escrow files to which to apply those skills. The only way to improve a market share is an aggressive calling program. A prime sales device is knowing the services of one's company and capitalizing on those strengths. If a company has expertise in bulk sales, for example, escrow personnel should solicit brokerages that deal in business opportunities.

Objective Assessment. An ability to monitor the quality of staff work through audits and spot checks is of prime importance to a conscientious manager. Objective evaluation enables supervisors to determine weaknesses and develop appropriate training programs.

Escrow Administrator

An escrow administrator is responsible for all the interrelationships in a multi-office operation. At this point technical knowledge requirements diminish and management skills emerge as prime requisites, just as in top administration of title companies.

Managerial. All of the skills of the escrow manager are essential. In addition a thorough understanding of allocation of human resources and the effect on profitability is extremely important.

Organizational (Political). Understanding the "people power" of the organization and their interrelationships is the key to efficient administration and developing overall strength within the organization.

Problem Solving. Administration is the pinnacle of the problem solving pyramid. The main qualification of a successful administrator is the ability to solve problems.

Personal Qualifications. An ideal administrator will combine the following traits:

☐ Synergistic thinking (understanding of the parts as they affect the whole organization)

☐ Superior communication skills

☐ Organizational ability

☐ Delegatory ability

☐ Informed and impartial personnel assessment

☐ Practicality to put it all together.

PROFESSIONAL ESCROW ASSOCIATIONS

As part of a continuing dedication to professionalism, the escrow industry, from an initial local group formed in Los Angeles in 1924, has grown to the statewide California Escrow Association, formed in 1956. This group was instrumental in forming the American Escrow Association on May 1, 1980. The goals of these industry groups are as follows:

Objects and Purposes
"The objects and purposes of the California Escrow Association shall be to promote sound and ethical business practices among its members; to provide for the collection, study and dissemination of information relating to problems of and improvements in land title evidence; to promote and encourage sound legislation affecting land titles; to encourage practices which will best serve the public interest; to educate and inform the public of the integrity and stability of its members and the advantages and desirability of their services."

Education
The CEA and other professional organizations provide for continuing professional education of their members.

Training Programs. Seminars, workshops, and annual educational conferences are designed to update practitioners on the "state of the art" in escrow.

Publications. The *CEA News*, published by California Escrow Association, outlines industry trends, new legislation, timely topics, and recent court decisions. Other publications, such as *Escrow Update* and *A.E.A. News* (from American Escrow Association) provide further educational opportunities for escrow professionals.

Professional Status
Professional organizations seek to enhance the status of the profession in terms of public recognition and ethical standards.

Legislative Advocacy. Professional organizations regularly monitor laws which impact the industry.

Professional Designations Program. Through a combination of required years of experience and course work, together with completion of a supervised testing program, the following professional designations can be obtained from CEA:

☐ Certified Escrow Officer (CEO)

☐ Certified Senior Escrow Officer (CSEO)

☐ Certified Loan Escrow Officer (CLEO)*

☐ Certified Senior Loan Escrow Officer (CSLEO)*

(*designation not currently being offered.)

Code of Ethics. Like other real estate professional organizations, the CEA has its own code of ethics. Escrow agents who are also real estate brokers are also subject to the Commissioner's Code of Professional Conduct and those of their own professional organization.

CEA CODE OF ETHICS

ARTICLE I: An Escrow Officer shall keep himself informed as to legislation and laws affecting the escrow profession in order to contribute to the public thinking on matters relating to escrows, real estate, financing and other matters and questions relative to the escrow profession.

ARTICLE II: Protection of public against fraud, misrepresentation and unethical practices in the escrow profession shall be uppermost in the mind of the Escrow Officer and he shall, at all times, be ready to expose such offenses.

ARTICLE III: An Escrow Officer should expose, without fear or favor, before the proper tribunal, corrupt or dishonest conduct in the profession.

ARTICLE IV: It is the duty of an Escrow Officer to preserve his clients' confidence, including all matters surrounding an escrow, either opened or closed; he should never reveal the contents of any file to any person not entitled to such contents except where a subpoena has been issued, or to expose corrupt or dishonest practice.

ARTICLE V: An Escrow Officer shall not be a party to the naming of a false consideration in an escrow.

ARTICLE VI: An Escrow Officer shall not engage in activities that constitute the practice of law and should never hesitate recommending that a party seek legal counsel in connection with an escrow.

ARTICLE VII: An Escrow Officer shall accept escrow instructions only in writing; acceptance of instructions verbally does a disservice to the public.

ARTICLE VIII: An Escrow Officer shall deliver copies of all instructions to all parties who are affected by such instructions.

ARTICLE IX: An Escrow Officer must maintain strict neutrality as an "Unbiased Third Party" to each transaction.

ARTICLE X: An Escrow Officer should not accept an escrow which he knows is outside of his scope of knowledge unless he makes such fact first known to his principals.

ARTICLE XI: An Escrow Officer should not seek unfair advantage over his fellow Escrow Officers and should willingly share with them lessons of his study and experience.

ARTICLE XII: An Escrow Officer shall conduct his profession so as to avoid controversies with fellow Escrow Officers. In the event of a controversy between Escrow Officers, such controversy shall be arbitrated at the level of the Regional Association.

ARTICLE XIII: In the event of controversy between Escrow Officers of different Regional Associations, such controversy should be arbitrated by a board comprised of two members from each Association of members so involved.

ARTICLE XIV: An Escrow Officer shall cooperate with his fellow Escrow Officers in escrow matters which affect each mutually.

ARTICLE XV: When an Escrow Officer is charged with unethical practices, he should place all pertinent facts before the proper tribunal of Regional Association to which he belongs, for investigation and judgment.

ARTICLE XVI: An Escrow Officer shall never disparage the professional practice of a competitor, nor volunteer an opinion of a competitor's transaction. If his opinion is sought, it should be rendered with strict professional integrity and courtesy.

ARTICLE XVII: An Escrow Officer should not solicit the service of an employee in the organization of a fellow Escrow Officer without the knowledge of the employer.

ARTICLE XVIII: It is the duty of an Escrow Officer, at the outset of an escrow, to disclose to the clients all circumstances, if any, of his relationship to the parties, and any interest in or connection with the escrow which might influence one or both clients in the selection of an escrow holder.

ARTICLE XIX: It is the duty of an Escrow Officer to his clients and the public in general to be punctual and direct in the closing of his escrows.

ARTICLE XX: In the best interests of society, his associates and his own profession, an Escrow Officer shall be loyal to the California Escrow Association and the Escrow Association of his local vicinity and be active in its work, and conform to this Code of Ethics and the By-Laws of this Association.

Exhibit 1

Chapter 2 Quiz

1. Title searching:

    (A) Has a single job classification
    (B) Is a uniform task
    (C) Does not involve automation
    (D) None of the above

2. A chain of title involves:

    (A) Running the property index only
    (B) Listing documents in the general index only
    (C) Following instructions from the title department
    (D) Merely assembling documents

3. The chain of title normally begins:

    (A) Following the Board of Land Commissioners in 1851
    (B) From the date of the last recorded deed
    (C) From the temple banks
    (D) From the date of the latest title policy issued

4. A general index search involves:

    (A) A credit check of the parties involved in the title order
    (B) A listing of names similar to the principals
    (C) A search of general matters affecting the parties that would not be revealed by searching the property
    (D) A listing of the parties in order of importance

5. Title examiners:

    (A) Always have to have been title searchers previously
    (B) Interpret the results of title searches
    (C) Must be college graduates
    (D) Are not candidates for advisors or technicians

6. Detail orientation is an important quality for:

    (A) Title searchers
    (B) Escrow officers
    (C) Title examiners
    (D) All of the above

7. What characteristic is not required for an escrow officer:

    (A) Independent judgment
    (B) Obstinacy
    (C) Self starter
    (D) Communicator

8. There are few similarities in the characteristics required for loan escrow officer and escrow officer.

    (A) True
    (B) False

9. Prime requirements for an escrow administrator include:

    (A) Managerial skill
    (B) Organizational ability
    (C) Problem solving
    (D) All of the above

10. The CEA Code of Ethics encourages:

    (A) Exposing fraud or unethical practices by other practitioners
    (B) Making contents of files available whenever asked
    (C) Accepting both spoken and written escrow instructions
    (D) None of the above

Chapter 3
Practitioners and Regulatory Agencies

PREVIEW

Types of Practitioners: Financial Institutions

Insurers

Independent Escrow Companies

Real Estate Brokers

Builders

Attorneys and Others

TYPES OF PRACTITIONERS: FINANCIAL INSTITUTIONS

As noted in Chapter 1, escrow originated as a corollary to the title insurance business. Escrow services are now provided by a kaleidoscope of business enterprises which offer these services as their principal activity or as an adjunct to related activities. These services may be offered to a greater or lesser extent, depending on the needs of the employing escrowholder and the experience of the personnel within the organization. Many of the groups discussed in this chapter may also be customers of other escrows. The table on the following page lists the many entities providing escrow services in California, and their respective regulators. As it shows, financial institutions handle a large share of California's escrow business.

Commercial Banks Commercial banks are regularly involved in mortgage lending, either as principals or representing others as a mortgage banker, so escrow services are a logical extension of their operation. This service developed in the commercial banking system during the early 1900s and continues to flourish as a viable adjunct to full service banking. Many top escrow practitioners either work in the banking industry or received their initial training in banking.

Range of Escrow and Title Services. With the Garn-St. Germain Depository Institutions Act of 1982, banks and savings and loan associations now provide many similar services. Additionally, each institution is now allowed ancillary activities involving real estate. Due to the diverse nature of the commercial banking business, banks may either provide escrow business to other escrowholders or serve as escrowholders themselves.

ESCROW ENTITIES AND THEIR REGULATORS

Entity	Regulatory Body
Independent Escrow Companies	Corporations Commissioner
State Chartered Banks	State Banking Commissioner
National Banks	Comptroller of Currency
State Chartered Banks as members of Federal Reserve	Federal Reserve Board
State and National Banks	Federal Deposit Insurance Corporation
State Chartered Savings and Loan Associations	Savings and Loan Commissioner
Federally Chartered Savings and Loan Associations	Federal Home Loan Bank Board
Real Estate Brokers under exemption	Real Estate Commissioner
Builders	Corporations Commissioner
Mortgage Bankers	Corporations Commissioner
Title Insurers and Insurance Companies	Insurance Commissioner
Attorneys	California State Bar
Credit Unions	Corporations Commissioner

Commercial Lending. Today commercial banks function as the largest single source (either directly or indirectly) of funds for new construction of all types. Residential construction, involving both the sale and permanent loan escrows, plus a separate escrow for the disbursement and control of construction funds, creates extensive escrow business. In addition, escrows result from the following banking related activities:

- ☐ Real estate lending
- ☐ Installment lending
- ☐ Trust real estate
- ☐ Mortgage banking
- ☐ Joint ventures
- ☐ Real estate brokerage
- ☐ Other real estate related activities

Title Insurance. Insurance required as a result of bank transactions runs from a simple lot book report to the highest form of extended coverage (see Chapter 11). Personal property searches such as UCC-3 might be required if hypothecation of personal property is involved.

Specialized Offices. The major banks in California operate through a network of branches. Deregulation and automated teller machines have caused a dramatic reduction in both number and size of branch offices, and encouraged the development of escrow centers within the branch system, based upon size of bank, potential market, real estate orientation of management, and availability of personnel.

Regulation. Three authorities are involved in the regulation of commercial banks in California, including their escrow personnel. The State Banking Commissioner is the regulatory agency for banks operating under a state charter. State chartered banks that are members of the Federal Reserve System are regulated by the Federal Reserve Bank. Supervision of banks which are under federal scrutiny ("National Bank" or "National Banking Association") is the responsibility of the Comptroller of Currency. In addition, state and national banks are examined by the Federal Deposit Insurance Corporation (FDIC).

Savings and Loan Associations As a group, nationwide, the savings and loan industry represents the largest single investment source for one- to four-family residences, although since 1989 their share has been diminishing. California is the home of the largest federally chartered association, as well as the nation's largest association that operates under a state charter.

Escrow Services. Like commercial banks, savings and loans may process their own escrows or provide for external processing. The areas served, with the exception of trust services, are similar to those of commercial banks.

Extension of Real Estate Financing. Escrow service is a logical extension of the tremendous amount of real estate lending supplied by the savings and loan industry in California. Savings and loans also handle real estate oriented consumer lending such as property improvement loans and mobilehome financing. In order to satisfy the specialized requirements for closing these loans, people with escrow background and training are required.

Centralization. Both banks and savings and loan associations are evolving away from the concept of an escrow department in each branch, or an "escrow office on every corner." The advent of computers and wordprocessing equipment has generated a new phenomenon, the escrow center, which enables an employer to use the specialized expertise of escrow personnel in a more efficient manner.

Title Insurance. Title insurance activities are also very similar to those of commercial banks. One large California based association, interstate in scope, owns a franchised real estate network as well as a title company. This is an indication of the diversification possible in this era of deregulation.

Regulation. As with commercial banks, savings and loan associations are supervised by more than one regulator.

☐ *Federal*. Federally chartered associations operate as mutuals and cannot, theoretically, be controlled by any special group because the shareholders are the depositors. Associations that have the word *Federal* in their name are regulated by the Federal Home Loan Bank and the Office of Thrift Supervision. All of their activities, including escrow, fall within the purview of this administration.

□ ***State***. State chartered associations come under the state Savings and Loan Commissioner as well as the Office of Thrift Supervision. In recent years in California there have been some conversions from federal to state charter.

□ ***Similarity to Banks***. Since the Garn-St. Germain Act of 1982, previously mentioned, the savings and loan association operates more and more like a bank, offering interest bearing checking accounts (NOW's and IMMA's) and commercial lending capability.

□ ***Deposit Insurance and Supervision***. As a result of the savings and loan "bailout bill" of 1989, the former Federal Savings and Loan Insurance Corporation (FSLIC) was dissolved, and the insurance function was transferred to the Federal Deposit Insurance Corporation (FDIC). Supervisory functions of institutions with federal insurance were assigned to the newly created Office of Thrift Supervision (OTS). The bill also created the Resolution Trust Corporation (RTC) to take over and sell the assets of failed thrifts. The transfer of these many assets is having a significant effect on the escrowholders handling these transactions.

Mortgage Bankers

As with commercial banks and savings and loan associations, the principal activity of mortgage bankers is lending, in this case as a loan correspondent for other lenders. In connection with loan processing, loan closing escrow personnel are required to prepare and assure compliance with the lender's closing instructions.

Title and Escrow Activities. Mortgage bankers in many cases handle their own loan escrow processing in order to retain quality control over the transaction. Their investors usually have specific title insurance requirements as to coverage as well as endorsements augmenting the basic coverage.

Regulation. External audits are performed by commercial banks providing credit lines, Federal Housing Administration, Veterans Administration, and other private and public insuring and/or guaranteeing agencies who approve or supervise the lending activities of mortgage bankers. In addition, permanent lenders who are represented by the mortgage banker perform both internal and external audits on their activities.

Licensing for Expanded Activities. If escrow activity is limited to loan processing, no further licensing requirements are involved. However, if the mortgage banker wants to expand into sales and other general escrow activity, a license from the California Corporations Commissioner is required. This activity would then have the same status as that of any independent escrow company.

Credit Unions

Structure. Credit unions are thrift institutions similar to savings and loan associations and may operate under either state or federal charters. Credit unions represent employees in a specific company, public service, church, union, or some other special group. Members are referred to as shareholders and constitute the ownership of the credit union. They are represented, in turn, by a board of directors which establishes loan policy, and by a loan committee which passes upon loan requests.

Real Estate Lending. With the advent of legislation increasing maximum loan amounts and maturities for credit unions, their real estate loan activity has increased. Loan processing may be handled within the credit union, if it has the staff, or may be referred to an outside escrow agent for loan closing. Title insurance and escrow requirements are similar to other real estate lenders.

Regulation. On a state level, auditing of credit union operations is performed by the Corporations Commissioner's office. Other regulatory activity may be involved if the credit union is an approved VA or FHA lender.

Finance Companies **Real Estate Lending**. Although oriented principally toward consumer finance such as car loans, signature loans, and property improvement loans, finance companies now see real estate as a vehicle to increase the average dollar amount of loans. Normally such credit has a combination security of real and personal property, usually furniture and appliances.

Processing. Loan documentation may be processed by finance company personnel, by an escrow subsidiary, or by an escrowholder independent of the company, and title insurance requirements will vary accordingly.

Regulation. Auditing for finance companies usually falls within the purview of the Corporations Commissioner's office. Periodic audits assure proper accounting for trust moneys that flow through the transaction.

INSURERS

Both title insurers and general insurance companies are involved in real estate and escrow in various ways.

Title Insurers Title companies fall into two basic categories, those having direct financial responsibility for their underwritings, in effect, the insurers, and those having indirect responsibility for underwriting the risk.

Regulation. The companies in each category are supervised primarily by the Insurance Commissioner in the state of home office domicile, and secondarily by the insurance commissioners in states where branch offices are located. Since regulation of this activity falls under the Insurance Code, the criteria for financial responsibility, such as bonding and reserve requirements, vary from those established by the Corporations Commissioner, Banking Commissioner, and Real Estate Commissioner.

Escrow Services. In California, many title insurers also offer escrow service incidental to their issuance of title policies. In Northern California, most of the sale escrow activity is performed by title companies. In Southern California, numerous types of escrow holders engage in this activity.

Insurance Companies

Capital for Housing, 1920s-1960s. In the 1920s and early 1930s, the sunny climate of California lured capital from the eastern United States to support the housing needs of a growing state, with insurance companies as a major investor. After World War II insurance companies were important in bridging the gap caused by insufficient domestic capital for massive housing needs. Loan processing by California domiciled insurance companies became commonplace.

Changing Role, 1960s-1990s. In recent years, investments by insurance companies have shifted from single family home loans to loans on income-producing properties. This has caused a shift in the type of expertise required for loan underwriting and closing. Eastern lenders are now establishing subsidiary companies in California to generate and process new loans, which is causing a need for more processing personnel.

Regulation. Insurance companies fall under the purview of the Insurance Commissioner and are subject to the legal and financial requirements established by that department. Audits are also performed by the staff of the Insurance Commissioner. Usually these audits are financial in nature and do not delve into the intricacies of the closing process.

Title Insurance and Escrow Services Required. Although insurance companies in the main deal through correspondents or mortgage bankers, some companies deal directly with the public and engage escrowholders directly. Due to the fact that many insurance companies have extensive real estate holdings, they perform as principals in the purchase and sale of real estate as well as lending on real estate as security. They tend to be very explicit in their requirements for title insurance, usually requiring extended coverage.

INDEPENDENT ESCROW COMPANIES

Unlike the preceding institutions, an independent escrow company relies upon escrow business as its principal means of livelihood. In addition to escrow service, ancillary activities, such as acting as corporate trustee on outstanding deeds of trust and as a collection service, may be provided by the independent company.

Regulation

Experience. Unique to this type of company is a stringent experience requirement. (Although legislation has been introduced in the past to make this requirement universal, it presently applies only to independent escrow companies.) The Corporations Commissioner's regulations state that:

> "within the organization of each escrow agent corporation, either as owner, officer, or employee, there shall be one or more persons possessing a minimum of five years of responsible escrow experience. At least one such qualified person shall be stationed on duty at each business location licensed by this division during the time the location is open for business."

State Monitoring and Audits. Escrow companies are monitored closely by the state Corporations Commissioner under provisions of Division 6 of the State Financial Code and Subchapter 9 of the Code of Regulations. The Commissioner's office maintains a staff for liaison and audit of independent escrow companies, and oversees financial responsibility, ethics, and bonding requirements. Periodic audits are performed, and the escrow agent is responsible for their cost. It is obligatory that the escrow agent maintain orderly files and records.

Liquidity and Net Worth. Through legislation enacted in 1986, independent escrow agents are required to increase liquid assets to $25,000 (this can be accomplished by a certificate of deposit or surety bond) by July 1, 1988, and tangible net worth must be increased from $15,000 on July 1, 1986 incrementally in annual $5,000 increases to the new required level of $50,000 effective July 1, 1993. Branch offices impose higher net worth requirements, which reinforces the argument for escrow centers.

Bonding. Employee fidelity bonds are now provided by the Escrow Fidelity Corporation (a creation of the state legislature, governed by industry members and a casualty insurance administrator). Each independent escrow company is required to be a member of the fund and pay an annual assessment which reaches $2,250 for each location after three years. The corporation maintains a fidelity bond equal to 1% of the total escrow trust funds on deposit by independent escrows throughout the state. In addition to the annual fee of member escrows, a trust balance formula is assessed based upon the following percentages:

- $\frac{1}{2}$ of 1% of first $500,000 trust balances

- $\frac{1}{4}$ of 1% of $500,001 to $1,000,000 trust balances

- $\frac{1}{8}$ of 1% of balances exceeding $1,000,000

Example

For a company with trust balances of $2,000,000 the assessment would be:

$2,500	for the first	$500,000
$1,250	for the next	$500,000
$1,250	for the next	$1,000,000
$5000		

$5,000 = Trust balance assessment, plus $2250 annual fee = $7,250 total bonding cost

---

REAL ESTATE BROKERS

Real estate brokers are both providers and customers of escrow services, depending on the situation.

Escrow Services by Brokers

Under the provision that "any company, broker or agent licensed by the Real Estate Commissioner while performing acts in the course of or incidental to the real estate business is exempt from supervision by the Corporations Commissioner," real estate brokers may hold escrows in connection with any transaction wherein they represented the buyer or seller or both, but may not hold escrows for compensation in connection with transactions made by other brokers or by individuals acting without brokers.

Limitations on Market. The broker cannot advertise an escrow department unless it is specified that such services are only in connection with real estate brokerage. Due to the fluctuating volume in the real estate business, many broker-owned escrows have been converting to independents in order to expand their potential market.

Regulation by Real Estate Commissioner. The Real Estate Commissioner has ruled that any real estate licensee who acts as an escrowholder under this exemption provision must maintain all escrow funds in a trust account subject to inspection by the Commissioner, and keep proper records. The Commissioner maintains an investigative staff as well as auditors to assure compliance by real estate brokers in their exempted escrow operation.

Complex Duties. Provision of escrow services cannot be undertaken casually as a sideline. Even though only in-house transactions are being handled, the broker is responsible for the same level of detail, accuracy, and organization as any other escrow processor. A recent study by the DRE (see box on following page) suggests that most brokers are unable to give escrow services the same skilled attention that would be provided by a specialist escrowholder.

Using Outside Escrow and Title Services

Real estate brokers are the largest single source of residential resale business throughout the state and are a prime business source for escrowholders. Title companies often solicit real estate broker business directly, hoping that brokers will specify their services when escrow is opened for their clients. Brokers should be aware of their fiduciary responsibility of full disclosure to clients with respect to preliminary title reports from title companies, and be able to explain each item contained in the report.

"BROKER-ESCROW AUDITS REVEAL HIGH PERCENT OF VIOLATORS"

Audits of southern California real estate brokers who handled their own escrow transactions showed 86 percent of those examined were in violation of the Real Estate Law or a regulation of the Commissioner of Real Estate, according to Danio Fajardo, supervising auditor of the Department of Real Estate's Southern Regional Area Audit Section.

The audits of 30 brokers—a representative sample of brokerages known to handle escrows (broker-escrows)—were conducted by the Department of Real Estate during fiscal year 1988/89.

Formal action was recommended against 16 of the brokerages when trust account shortages and other major violations were discovered. Minor infractions or no violations at all were found in four of the audits.

Seven of the brokers account shortages ranged from $1 - $3,000; two licensees had shortages ranging from $3,001 - $10,000; four were found to have shortages from $50,001 - $100,000. Three brokers, trust accounts were short in excess of $100,000; $391,267, $178,876 and $109,952. A total of $786,027 in account shortages was found.

Corrective action letters were issued against 10 other licensees.

As a result of its initial findings, the Department of Real Estate doubled its targeted goal of broker-escrow audits for fiscal year 1989-90.

The findings of the 30 original audits revealed the licensees examined handled a total 5,397 escrows in the 12 month period prior to the audit. The number of escrows per licensee ranged from seven to 1,080. The total amount of escrow funds held in trust by the licensees at the time of audit was $5,164,922.

11 of the licensees audited brokered mortgage loans exclusively, 14 were engaged in real estate sales only and five were involved in a combination of real estate sales and mortgage lending activity.

Broker-Escrow Audits

Broker activities-related violations discovered during the examinations included:

	Regulation	No.
2950(b)	Failure to advise parties that licensee has interest as a stockholder, officer, partner or owners of the agency holding escrow	4
2950(i)	Failure to provide escrow closing statement	1
2725	Failure to review instruments	12

Trust fund handling and record keeping violations which were identified included:

	Regulation	No.
2830	Trust fund account	12
2831	Trust fund records	15
2831.1	Separate beneficiary records	13
2831.2	Reconciliation of records	7
2832	Trust fund handling	5
2832.2	Trust fund handling for multiple beneficiaries	15
2834	Trust account withdrawals	12

Reprinted from the *"Real Estate Bulletin"* (California Department of Real Estate), Spring, 1990, pp 1&7.

BUILDERS

New construction plays an important role in the western U.S. economy, particularly in California. Many large western builders try to control as many aspects of their activities as possible and so have established their own escrow companies, which are licensed by the Corporations Commissioner, to process their closings.

Subdivision Escrows Subdivision escrows involve many different legal ramifications for which legal counsel is required. Knowledge of the California Subdivision Map Act and Subdivided Lands Act is essential to proper administration of escrows involving new subdivisions. Special considerations include proper creation of protective restrictions, assurance that the preliminary public report has been delivered to all prospective purchasers, formation of homeowners' associations, and assurance that a sufficient percentage of sales are consummated to allow initial closing. (See Chapter 15.)

Specialized Providers Because the nuances of subdivision escrow require particular specialized knowledge, it is logical that large volume builders have their own escrow companies and that some of the other escrowholders mentioned in this chapter specialize in subdivision service.

Regulation In addition to the Corporations Commissioner supervising their escrow activity, builders are licensed in California by the State Contractors Licensing Board. If they build under government sponsored programs, builders are subject to limited supervision by either the Federal Housing Administration and Veterans Administration, or secondary lenders such as FHLMC or FNMA. Builders may use closing personnel for loan processing in conjunction with their lenders.

Outside Escrow and Title Services Due to the specialized nature of subdividing, many title insurance companies have established subdivision departments trained in expediting subdivision paperwork through the Department of Real Estate. These specialists are assigned to work specifically with builders and developers.

ATTORNEYS AND OTHERS

Lawyers are allowed to handle escrows for their clients and are exempted from licensing and other requirements. Their activities are monitored by the State Bar Association, which serves as a clearinghouse for complaints. As with other escrowholders, moneys are deposited in trust accounts and must be segregated by individual file. Attorneys' title insurance requirements may be very rigid.

Governmental agencies, pension funds, trusts, and various other entities may perform escrow services in accordance with their own organizational requirements, and are subject to varying forms of regulation.

Chapter 3 Quiz

1. Commercial banks offer:
   - (A) Loans and checking accounts only
   - ✓(B) An array of financial services
   - (C) Escrows for construction lending only
   - (D) Escrow services at every location

2. Savings and loan associations usually lend on all but the following:
   - (A) Residential real estate
   - (B) Property improvement loans
   - (C) Mobilehome loans
   - (D) Personal property

3. Real estate broker owned escrows that handle transactions of other brokers are governed by the:
   - ✓(A) Corporations Commissioner
   - (B) Real Estate Commissioner
   - (C) Insurance Commissioner
   - (D) Director of Finance

4. Independent escrow companies are monitored closely by the:
   - (A) Real Estate Commissioner
   - (B) Federal Reserve Board
   - (C) Corporations Commissioner
   - (D) Insurance Commissioner

5. Large builders in many cases:
   - (A) Control their own title company
   - (B) Own stock brokerage operations
   - (C) Own their own escrow companies
   - (D) Build for cash

6. Mortgage bankers operating as loan correspondents are considered:
   - (A) Mortgagors
   - (B) The same as commercial bankers
   - (C) The permanent lenders
   - ✓(D) Representatives of permanent lenders

7. Title companies:
   - (A) Insure title directly
   - (B) Are underwritten by other insurance companies
   - (C) Process escrows
   - (D) Any of the above may be true

8. Insurance companies:
   - (A) Never deal directly with customers
   - (B) Always lend directly to clients
   - (C) May use the services of mortgage bankers'
   - (D) Never deal through mortgage banker subsidiaries

9. Credit unions and finance companies:
   - (A) Lend on real and personal property
   - (B) Are principally involved in installment lending
   - (C) Are usually supervised by the Corporations Commissioner
   - (D) All of these

10. In order to act as an escrow agent, an attorney must:
    - (A) Be licensed by the Corporations Commissioner
    - (B) Refer escrows to an escrow licensee
    - (C) Be monitored by the State Bar Association
    - (D) Commingle clients' funds with personal funds

Chapter 4
Forming the Contract

PREVIEW

Contractual Relationship

Parties Involved In the Transaction

CONTRACTUAL RELATIONSHIP

As the "holder of the stakes" in a sale or loan transaction, the escrow officer, under direction of the principals, must obtain the pertinent information from which the contract of transfer and/or hypothecation in the form of an instruction will be prepared. Because an escrow instruction is contractual in nature, it requires certain basic elements.

Contract Defined A contract is "An agreement between two or more parties, preliminary step in making of which is offer by one and acceptance by other, in which minds of parties meet and concur in understanding of terms." (*Lee v. Traveler's Insurance Company*, 173 S.C. 185, 175 S.E. 429)

Promise for Promise. Most people are familiar with the principle of offer and acceptance in real estate; this concept is applicable to the entire field of contracts, in that a promise is supported by a return promise. For example, the seller (vendor) promises to transfer title to property in exchange for the purchaser's (vendee's) promise that either money or other property will be used as the consideration to consummate the transaction.

Necessary Elements. Some of the important elements in any contractual relationship are:

☐ The instrument must contain a promise.

☐ The parties to the contract must be legally capable of a contractual relationship.

☐ The agreement must be supported by consideration.

☐ This promise must be enforceable at law.

☐ There must be a meeting of the minds.

Written Instrument Most contracts involving real estate fall within the Statute of Frauds requiring a written instrument. In litigation concerning escrows, the heaviest emphasis is placed upon the written documents that form the agreement between the parties. In a typical sale transaction, there may be three or more such contracts.

Listing. Initially the seller signs a listing agreement with a real estate broker, forming the first contract.

Offer and Acceptance. Once an interested purchaser with an earnest money deposit is available, the second contract occurs. The deposit receipt initially signed by the proposed purchaser is an offer, which when executed by the seller becomes a binding sales agreement on the terms contained therein. In practice there may be counteroffers before the terms are finalized.

Escrow Instructions. At this point the parties are in a position to open escrow, which will form the third contract. (As Chapter 6 will elaborate, the timing of opening escrows varies between Northern and Southern California.)

Competent Parties
For any of these contractual relationships to be binding, it must be determined that the parties involved in the transaction have the capacity to contract.

Ownership. Parties engaging in a contract relating to a piece of property must own it, or have some other legal right to do business involving the property.

Natural Persons. Besides having title to the property, they must be able to contract by reason of age, sanity, etc. Some of the parties who do *not* have the ability to contract on real property without some form of legal representation, usually court-appointed, are minors and incompetents, whose affairs are administered by the Probate Court.

☐ *Institutionalized.* Persons committed to an institution under the provisions of Division 6 of the Welfare and Institutions Code may have instruments voided depending upon the mental condition at the time the instrument was executed.

☐ *Subsequent Determination.* Persons who are of unsound mind but not entirely without understanding, prior to determination of incapacity, may possibly create a relationship that is voidable and subject to rescission.

☐ *Acquisition of Property.* Although disposition of property is impacted by capacity, acquisition is not. Unless the acquisition is burdensome, acquisition by a minor, insane or incompetent person is considered to be beneficial. However, if the property is sold or hypothecated, guardians must be appointed by the court to act on the incompetent's behalf.

Artificial Persons. In the case of corporations, partnerships, joint ventures, and so on, investigation should be made to determine that the signing parties have the authority to act in their representative capacity.

☐ *Corporations.* Corporate authority flows from the articles of incorporation and supportive by-laws with specific resolutions duly certified by the corporate secretary to affirm a given transaction. There may be a requirement that annual franchise taxes be assessed and paid to preserve the corporate entity.

☐ *Partnerships.* Partnerships and joint ventures normally outline their powers through a formal statement which serves as the authority for purposes of transferring title to property.

Consideration   The contract must be supported by something of value.

Money. The most obvious example of consideration is money in exchange for a deed, a service, or an item of personal property. The more prevalent situation in real estate is money in the form of a downpayment plus proceeds of a new first loan in exchange for a deed.

Exchange. Consideration also exists when the parties trade deeds for deeds, personal property for a deed, or personal property for personal property.

Nominal Considerations. Consideration may also take the form of "love and affection," where the property is gratuitously given to the recipient asking nothing in exchange, or a nominal sum such as one dollar may be named.

Lawful Object   The promises and consideration must be lawful for the contract to be enforceable at law. In a state where gambling is not legal, for example, a contract involving payment of gambling debts could not be enforced. Because they rely on information from the parties, it is very difficult for escrowholders to police this aspect of the relationship.

Example

Escrow instructions involving property acquired for the express purpose of setting up a laboratory to produce LSD would not have a lawful object at the outset and such a contract could be considered void as contrary to public policy.

Mutuality   The parties' perception of the contract must coincide. Major problems evolve from the failure to establish mutuality (meeting of the minds) if the instructions prepared by the escrowholder are too vague and subject to various interpretations.

Examples

The buyer was sure that the washer and dryer and all the potted plants in the patio went with the house, while the seller isn't as sure. This must be resolved before there is a meeting of the minds on the deposit receipt concerning what personal property passes with the real estate.

Any material difference between the alleged size of a property and its actual dimensions could be serious as well as expensive. If the seller truly believed a parcel had ten acres and the purchaser's survey disclosed only eight acres, the difference would be significant enough to prevent a meeting of the minds.

Form and Content **Signature by the Charged Parties.** Whether buyer/seller, borrower/lender, vendor/vendee, assignor/assignee, lessor/lessee, or other principals, signatures of all of the parties to be charged with duties under the contract must be obtained.

Accuracy. Clarity and precise information are of extreme importance in order to preserve the contractual nature of escrow instructions. The contract should be definite and certain in its essential elements:

☐ *Subject Matter*. Transfer of title to a described parcel of real property under stated conditions.

☐ *Parties*. Buyer and seller, and trustees, mortgagors, etc.

☐ *Purchase Price*. Consideration for sale.

☐ *Time and Manner of Payment*. Proposed closing date and the nature and form of consideration being passed.

When Contract Is Incomplete. Probably the main problem that vexes practitioners is discovering whether a contract actually exists. A prime example is a transaction where instructions have been signed by one party but not by the other. Subsequent to the initial instructions, the nonsigning party has negotiated a loan that has been approved in connection with the contemplated purchase. Does a contract exist? The party who has not signed may have created an implied contract by reason of conduct which appears to assume the existence of the contract.

PARTIES INVOLVED IN THE TRANSACTION

In addition to the principals, a host of parties are involved as agents, processors, or regulators in the sale or hypothecation of real estate. Working with these diverse interests requires a clear understanding of how they fit into the process, though they may not be direct parties to the contract. Some of these parties are:

Real Estate Brokers A majority of real estate sales involve the services of real estate brokers. The escrowholder and broker must establish lines of communication that assure proper coordination of the closing.

Regional Processing Variations. The real estate broker's role varies in different areas of the state, as a result of the differing closing processes. (See Chapter 6.)

☐ *Southern*. In Southern California it is not unusual for most of the closing details to be handled by an escrow officer, including most of the communication with the new lenders and procurement of demands and/or beneficiary statements of existing lenders.

☐ *Northern*. In Northern California the broker may order the title report and stay in contact with the lender and the principals while the escrow agent, without benefit of written escrow instructions, proceeds to process the entire transaction, obtaining ratification by the principals during the final phase of the escrow. If no broker is involved, closing may be similar to the Southern California method.

Matching Escrowholder and Broker. Because customs vary from region to region and office to office, a smooth closing requires that escrowholder and broker understand each other's preference in handling such items as:

☐ Taking escrow instructions

☐ Client relations

☐ Delivery of and obtaining signatures on documents

☐ Loan processing

☐ Settlement and delivery of checks, and

☐ Communications during the course of escrow.

Disclosure. Brokers' responsibilities continue to expand in our consumer conscious society, requiring brokers to disclose known defects in one to four unit residential properties, transactions in which they are acting as principals, etc. Although outside of the basic closing process, escrowholders should be aware of this responsibility.

Title Insurance Companies
Because title insurance was the precursor of escrow activity in this state, title insurers continue to provide escrow services. Therefore, escrowholders and real estate licensees interface with title companies both as escrow agents and in their primary function of reporting on the condition of title and issuing title insurance policies.

Coordination. Since the escrow process involves the issuance of title insurance or a title binder in a majority of instances, coordination of title insurance and the escrow process is vital. If instructions and documents are not delivered to the title company in time, recordation and closing may be inhibited.

Timely Disclosure. Title matters not previously disclosed, such as additional liens, delinquent taxes and the like, are much more easily handled with early notice than if discovered just prior to closing. That is why timely and accurate title reporting is so important.

Lenders
The second principal area of communication during the escrow process is with lenders, both existing and proposed. The escrowholder should be thoroughly familiar with the documentation requirements and communicate in a timely manner with the loan administration (servicing) and loan production and closing personnel.

Termite Companies One duty of the real estate agent in a transaction that involves a "termite clearance" is to deliver the structural pest control report to the appropriate parties for approval. These reports are required for FHA-insured and VA-guaranteed loans, and may be required for conventional financing. Even if it is not a requirement of the lender, the purchaser may require such a report.

Content of Report. The report covers two basic areas:

☐ *Corrective Work*. Where actual infestation of areas has been noted, treatment is required which may consist of chemical application or wrapping the structure and treating with gas.

☐ *Preventive Work*. Where certain existing conditions may in the future cause dry rot or other deterioration that could be prevented, proper drainage, new sheet metal, or masonry work may be recommended.

State Filing. When a structural pest control report is rendered on residential property, a copy is filed with the Structural Pest Control Board in Sacramento, which regulates the industry.

Second Opinions. The party responsible for providing the termite work frequently seeks a "second opinion" in hopes of reducing the cost. When more than one report is delivered to escrow, care must be taken by the escrowholder to obtain mutual agreement on the report that is acceptable to the principals.

Escrow Information. It is important that the escrow agent be properly instructed as to the corrective and preventive work to be performed by the termite company. Work of this nature can entail considerable expense, so it is incumbent upon the escrowholder to be specific when outlining the items included and the allocation of this expense between buyer and seller.

Local Agencies Not only is escrow concerned with the multitude of rules imposed upon real estate transactions by state and federal jurisdictions; county and city governments have local ordinances that require special consideration.

Zoning Report. Many cities have ordinances that require a "zoning report" to be delivered prior to the transfer of real property interests. Generally this report indicates the type of zoning on the property, issuance of the initial building permit, and any authorized modifications of the structure since its original construction.

☐ *Purpose*. The purpose of these ordinances is to reduce the incidence of nonconforming structures that are sold without purchaser knowledge, e.g. the single-family residence with a garage conversion or the eight-unit building illegally converted to ten units but sold as conforming.

□ *Responsibility*. The responsibility of delivering this report may be imposed upon the principals to the transaction or upon the escrow agent.

Other Ordinances. Other city and county ordinances deal with safety and energy requirements, and with subdivision and map filing procedures as part of an overall planning process. Some municipalities also impose property transfer taxes or other special taxes.

Example

Mono County (California) has a "bed tax" ordinance. The operator of a condominium unit for transient purposes must register it with the county tax collector and obtain a transient occupancy registration certificate. The ordinance further states that the operator functions must be performed by a professional manager, not the owner. Even though the responsibility of informing potential investor-purchasers of this ordinance is imposed upon the real estate broker, what happens if no broker is involved? There seems to be some duty of disclosure imposed on the escrowholder.

Communication. It is important that escrowholders and licensees keep current with local legislation. In order to expedite the processing of items that require compliance it also becomes important to know the individuals in the local agencies that enforce the ordinances.

Casualty Insurance Companies

In the past, handling insurance through escrow was a simple matter. Usually the property was insured by a fire and extended-coverage policy that was either transferred with proration of the premium or simply cancelled and new insurance obtained. A lender's loss payable endorsement (Form 438 BFU) was provided for the benefit of any lienholders. Today dealing with casualty insurance agents and their companies is a necessary and important adjunct to the finance or sale of real or personal property.

Package Policies. Insurance policies now not only encompass fire and extended coverage, but are issued in a "package" of multiple coverages, which may include policyholder liability, rental loss, accidents on premises, earthquakes, flood and mudslide coverage, and hospitalization.

Exclusions. Insurance, whether it be title, fire, or another form of casualty insurance, is coverage after exclusions. A typical policy that covers damages to premises may exclude any damage caused by *force majeure* or "acts of God," such as earthquake and flood and mudslide in California. If this type of coverage is required, separate policies must be obtained.

Responsibility to Investigate. Due to the unprecedented appreciation in housing prices in the late 1970s and early 1980s, escrowholders must be extremely attentive when processing increases in insurance coverage. Even more important is to determine that there is, in fact, coverage on the property. Serious escrow losses can result from failure to investigate the status of premium payments or the insurer's ability to cover the property. This is especially true for properties covered by the California Fair Plan, which applies to properties that have high loss potential.

Working with Insurance Agents. Escrowholders should know the insurance agents in their area and each agent's scope of authority. Knowledge of the time needed to obtain the required binder, policy, or endorsement(s) enables the escrowholder to provide timely customer service.

Homeowners' Associations
In America's quest for more leisure time, maintenance-free cooperatives, condominiums, and planned unit developments are becoming common. Through the vehicle of a homeowners' group, the exterior of such premises is maintained and the upkeep costs assessed pro-rata to owners of individual units in the project.

Role in Escrow. Escrow during the sale and transfer of these units must determine that assessment liens are not in arrears and prorate the payment thereof at close of escrow.

Delivery of By-Laws. It is the responsibility of the homeowners' association to deliver a copy of the by-laws and protective restrictions, together with the most recent annual budget, to each actual or potential purchaser of a unit in a project. As a matter of convenience the delivery of these items falls on the escrow agent in many instances, but it is not the escrowholder's duty to perform this service.

Disclosure of Assessments. Maintaining communication with representatives of homeowners' associations in the service area allows the escrow agent to obtain status reports on assessments in a timely manner. Most of these liens are not fixed amounts, and increases are possible in the future. If an escrowholder finds the seller reluctant to disclose this fact, buyer inquiries should be referred to the principals, their representatives, or the homeowners' association for appropriate response.

Lien Claimants
Many times a seller may have incurred either voluntary obligations—such as a home improvement contract—or involuntary ones such as a tax lien or judgment. These liens may require either satisfaction or status reports as a condition of escrow.

Notification of Holders. It is usually the responsibility of escrow to communicate with the holders of these obligations or their legal representatives to obtain the necessary statement and supportive documentation. This is discussed further in Chapter 6.

Mechanics' Liens. Where recent improvement work has been completed on a property it is not uncommon to encounter mechanics' liens filed by contractors and/or materialmen. The escrow agent must obtain instructions from the responsible party for the disposition of such a claim.

Trust Deeds to Individuals. Many times trust deeds are held by individuals who are not sophisticated concerning their procedural responsibilities. This can be a real test of diplomacy for the escrow officer. Usually these individuals will require assistance in the preparation of the demand as well as provision of proper documents to release the lien.

State and Federal Agencies
Government agencies are deeply involved in real estate financing, and each injects its own requirements into the escrow process.

FHA. Since 1934, billions of dollars of real estate loans have been insured by the Federal Housing Administration (which is now part of the Department of Housing and Urban Development). The original purpose of FHA was to establish sound patterns for mortgage lending, to encourage wider home ownership, and to upgrade housing standards throughout the country. Although not a direct lender, FHA insurance allows approved lenders to offer excellent loan terms for minimum down payment buyers. This agency remains one of the few government units that is self-supporting, through the use of Mutual Mortgage Insurance.

VA. In 1944 Public Law 346 established a program whereby the U.S. Veterans Administration (now U.S. Department of Veterans Affairs) guarantees home loans for eligible veterans.

Uniform Federal Programs. Growing out of the FHA and VA loan programs, a pattern of loan underwriting has developed using uniform credit applications, deposit and employment verifications, and credit reporting. With the Federal Home Loan Mortgage Corporation (Freddie Mac), the Government National Mortgage Association (Ginnie Mae), and the Federal National Mortgage Association (Fannie Mae) as major secondary market sources of funds, this uniformity of underwriting procedures has extended to uniform notes for conventional loans and security instruments.

Federal Consumer Protection. With the first wave of consumer legislation in 1969 disclosure of certain aspects of the closing process has become a requirement and has become second nature to the escrow process. This is discussed in detail in Chapter 13.

Cal-Vet. California administers its own veterans' home loan program which was initiated by the Department of Veterans Affairs after World War I. This program is supported by the issuance of bonds.

Direct State Loans. Direct lending activity is governed by the ability of the Housing and Home Financing Agency of the state to sell bonds for home loans. These funds are used for low-cost housing. California Housing Finance Agency (CHFA) also provides attractive low interest rate loans for low to moderate income borrowers.

Agencies and the Escrow Process. From time to time the escrowholder may communicate with any one or all of these government agencies or other regulatory bodies which oversee various aspects of the escrow transaction. It is incumbent upon the escrowholder to be aware of the various agencies that can be involved and to develop appropriate communication channels.

Requests for Information
Each day attorneys, accountants, and other interested parties contact the escrow agent concerning active or closed files. The very foundation of the escrow process is the confidentiality of the principals' transaction, and only information authorized by the parties should be released. The one exception is a subpoena for information required by a court. An officer of a court (e.g., district attorney's office) or a government agency (FBI agent, for example) may try to extract information without a subpoena, but the escrowholder should insist upon a subpoena to protect the rights of the parties in the escrow.

Chapter 4 Quiz

1. Which of the following is *not* an essential element of a contract?

   (A) More than two parties
   (B) Lawful object
   (C) Consideration
   (D) Competent parties

2. A real estate broker:

   (A) May be a principal
   (B) May act as escrowholder
   (C) Is required to disclose residential defects
   (D) All of the above

3. Early title information is advantageous because:

   (A) Normally a title policy won't be obtained
   (B) The seller may be taking a vacation
   (C) Early detection of previously undisclosed matters facilitates their resolution
   (D) It must be recorded for a valid contract to exist

4. Package insurance policies are obtained on real property because:

   (A) They cost more
   (B) They assure no loss to the policyholder
   (C) Combined coverages cost less than if purchased separately
   (D) Even though total coverage is diluted, combined effect is convenient

5. Local ordinances involving residential property transfer usually aim at:

   (A) Delaying the transfer
   (B) Consumer protection
   (C) Inhibiting the transfer permanently
   (D) Penalties and fines imposed on the purchaser

6. Homeowners' associations are required to provide potential purchasers with:

   (A) A copy of the condo floor plan
   (B) Assurance of a minimum of two parking places per unit purchased
   (C) A list of the officers and directors of the association
   (D) Copy of CC&Rs, by-laws and annual budget

7. For the structural pest control report:

   (A) Escrowholders do nothing
   (B) Instructions are not required if a "second opinion" is obtained
   (C) It is the real estate agent's responsibility to submit to the appropriate party for approval
   (D) A copy is given to the pest control operator and escrow agent only

8. The Federal Housing Administration:

   (A) Is a direct lender
   (B) Requires at least 20% downpayment
   (C) Is not involved in building standards
   (D) Is self-supporting

9. Real estate lenders:

   (A) Have uniform requirements
   (B) Need not consider condition of title
   (C) Require prompt courteous escrow service
   (D) Do not contact escrowholders directly

10. Information in escrow files should be made available to:

    (A) All interested parties
    (B) Attorneys and accountants
    (C) Court officers with a subpoena only
    (D) Court officers with or without a subpoena

Chapter 5
From "Take Sheet"
To Escrow Instructions

PREVIEW

The Preliminary Interview

Conversion of Intent and Data to Instructions

Documentation: Requirements and Limitations

Special Considerations For Escrowholders

THE PRELIMINARY INTERVIEW

A proper escrow instruction emanates from a thorough preliminary interview. This is a process of information gathering preliminary to the instruction. It is used to prepare the "take sheet" as the framework for the instructions, assuring that the escrow contract will reflect the factual situation and the intent of the parties.

Precautions Escrowholders must be adroit and observant, tactful yet firm in retrieving the data necessary to draft instructions. Two major problems are involved in drafting meaningful instructions based upon a preliminary interview.

Third Party Information. In most cases, the escrow officer does not talk with the principals initially. The interview may be with a real estate agent at the stage of a conditional deposit, which is normally the initial deposit in escrow. This deposit is taken in the form of a third-party instruction from the agent (Exhibit 2). Depending upon the physical location of the escrow office, certain segments of the transaction may be performed by someone other than the assigned escrow officer.

Practice of Law Prohibited. The escrowholder cannot direct the parties concerning their manner of holding title, or the language to be used to protect their mutual rights, since this may be interpreted as the practice of law. Escrow employers in California entered into a series of treaties with the State Bar Association to this effect. A typical excerpt from one of these agreements is shown in Exhibit 3, sample bar treaty.

Note: Due to questions raised by the Federal Trade Commission, the State Bar of California negated all such treaties in late 1979. However, prudent escrow professionals should continue to conduct themselves in the manner prescribed by the treaty.

The Take Sheet In order to avoid many of these pitfalls a patterned interview has been developed through the use of an escrow information sheet or memorandum (Exhibit 4, Transaction Memo Data), sometimes known as the "take sheet." This sheet is designed to extract the pertinent data without dictating the terms of the transaction. Each of the elements of this transaction must be evaluated properly in order to reduce them to a mutually satisfactory instruction.

Example

The information sheet in Exhibit 4 outlines a simple sale transaction involving a 10%-down purchaser. The instructions shown in Exhibit 6, sample bilateral escrow instructions, and the commission and pest control instructions in Exhibit 7 are the final products which reflect the data obtained from the memorandum sheet.

Areas of Inquiry **Nature and Content of the Consideration.** Information must be obtained relative to sales price, trust deeds to remain and those to be paid off, any new loans to be obtained, whether the price includes any personal property, etc.

Exact Legal Description. Necessary information includes legal description together with street address of the property if improved.

Type of Property. If the property is a single family residence there may be local ordinances which require special attention, such as retrofit or zoning reports.

Names of Present and Proposed Lenders. Many escrows provide questionnaires designed for the seller to give existing loan information and the buyer or buyer's agent to provide the name of the new lender(s).

Names of Parties. Buyer/seller, borrower/lender, vendor/vendee, lessor/lessee, etc., in the transaction must be identified.

Terms of the Escrow. Terms including time limit and possession date should be spelled out. Estimating time of consummation should be realistic. Just obtaining information on the existing debt and processing a new loan will be time consuming. Don't expect a 10 day escrow unless it's all cash on clear property.

Proration Instructions. There may be many different items such as interest on existing loans, taxes, assessments, bonds, insurance, homeowners' association dues, maintenance fees, and rentals. Prorations may be on the basis of a 30-day month or an actual day month. Proration or lack of it is based upon mutual instructions of the principals and may not be traditional. Some reasons for not using the usual forms of proration include:

☐ New insurance policy being obtained

☐ Lien of supplemental taxes imposed after the transfer is effected

☐ High degree of delinquency in a rental property

☐ Other compelling reasons unique to the transaction.

Choice of Title Company. Company should be identified by name, address, etc.

Insurance. Requirements should be stated, both as to lenders and as to the parties.

Termite Reports. Establish requirements, deadlines, and responsibility for payment.

Apportionment of Charges. This is ordinarily done in accordance with local custom, but parties can agree on any division that is not in conflict with legal requirements such as those imposed by VA financing.

Information on Commission. The selling broker controls this, but may allocate to multiple listing service, selling and buying agents, etc.

Pertinent Addresses, Phone Numbers and Parties. The escrowholder needs to know whom to contact for various phases of the transaction.

Special Instructions. Procedural and housekeeping matters such as delivery of documents, special customer requirements, etc., should be spelled out.

CONVERSION OF INTENT AND DATA TO INSTRUCTIONS

After ascertaining the specific conditions of this escrow relative to the above items, the basic instruction is prepared. Instruction formats vary, but a systematic approach will insure that each item is included. It is absolutely necessary that all pertinent data be collected from the parties to fulfill the basic intent of the transaction. If errors occur through lack of attentiveness, they set the tone of the entire transaction. The ability to render quality customer service in an efficient and proficient manner is the hallmark of a skilled escrowholder.

Procedure and Timing

Time. The actual time that the escrow instructions are drafted differs according to local custom. This will be discussed in detail, with work flow charts of Northern and Southern California escrows, in Chapter 6.

Intent. Whether unilateral instructions (Northern California) or bilateral instructions (Southern California) are used it is important that the transaction is properly structured. The basic objective is to fulfill the intent of the parties.

Mechanics. The mechanics of the transaction must be established, including allocation of all charges and the documentation required.

Transaction Outline Before any document is prepared in escrow, it is important to establish intent in order to clarify what documents are needed.

TRANSACTION OUTLINE EXAMPLE

Intent. Suppose John and Mary Smith are selling to Tom and Sarah Jones for $100,000 with the Smiths taking back a $60,000 first trust deed over and above the Jones' downpayment. The Smiths have an existing loan from Independent Savings and Loan with a $25,000 balance that will be paid off in the transaction. This is a fairly simple transaction, particularly if no agent is involved.

Outline. A preliminary instruction outline would look something like this:

Downpayment	$ 40,000
Purchase Money First	60,000
Total Consideration	$100,000

Nature of Transaction: Sale.

Time limit: 60 days.

Legal: Lot 23 of Tract 17639 in the city of Hawthorne, County of Los Angeles, as per map recorded in Book 436, pages 5 to 9 of Maps

Property Address: 15021 Easy Street, Hawthorne, CA 90250

Seller: John Smith and Mary Smith

Address: 15021 Easy Street, Hawthorne, CA 90250

Buyer: Tom Jones and Sarah Jones, husband and wife, as community.

Address: 3571 Broadway, Hawthorne, CA 90250.

Financing: First Deed of Trust for $60,000, payable $600.00 or more, including interest at 10%, in favor of John Smith and Mary Smith, husband and wife as joint tenants, all due and payable in 10 years.

Trust Deed to have alienation clause.

Payoffs:

Independent Savings and Loan
17654 Victory Blvd.
Reseda, CA 91335

Loan No. 127865-4—Current balance $24,995.84, payable in monthly installments of $300.00 per month at 8% interest.

Adjustments: Taxes $1,200 annually; Insurance $450.00 annually.

Opening Deposit: $1,500

Cash Summary— The Memo Box   For the benefit of the parties, a summary list of the elements comprising the consideration is included at the head of the escrow instruction form. This "memo box" clearly defines the sources and uses of funds in the transaction. Exhibit 5 shows the contents of a typical memo box, based on the take sheet in Exhibit 4. Memo boxes of various types appear in the escrow instructions in Exhibits 6, 15, 28, 29, 36, 52, 54, 58, 63, and 69.

Money. Note that money obtained from any source, whether cash deposit or new financing, is included in the cash demand for the deed. This figure, plus or minus any fees, adjustments, or prorations, represents the actual cash that flows through the transaction.

Non-Cash Consideration. Other non-cash consideration would be accounted for below the cash demand for deed figure, such as (a) equivalent value of personal property traded, (b) purchase money encumbrance to sell, and (c) any encumbrances of record.

Exchanges. In an exchange transaction, the memo box would concern itself with the equities being transferred and the total consideration would establish equity position. This is discussed in Chapter 15.

Other Data   In a normal sale transaction basic data must be available to answer all questions that may arise in connection with the escrow instruction, the instruments of title and transfer, any new liens created by such transfer, and any that may be removed. The check sheet or "take sheet" provides guidelines to the escrowholder in obtaining complete information, which is then translated into the particular forms at hand. (Compare Exhibit 4, take sheet, and Exhibit 6, the resulting escrow instructions.)

Escrow Instructions   Based upon the preliminary information above, an escrow instruction is drawn up using the data pertinent to this specific transaction.

Basic Data. The escrow instructions form (Exhibit 6) begins with the memo box data (dollar amounts), title insurance policy liability, legal description of property, street address of property, vesting of title (in this case James Buyer and Maggie Buyer, husband and wife as community property), and conditions of title (here the purchase money deed of trust including appropriate alienation clause would be shown).

Variations. Observe that Exhibit 6 is the bilateral Southern California form, and compare other instruction forms shown in Chapters 6, 9, 10, 14, and 15. Order and wording of the items will vary, but the same basic elements are covered.

Adjustments. The next section allows escrow to adjust dates for purposes of interest collection. Additionally, the amount of consideration shown in the escrow box may be adjusted based upon any trust deed of record that might remain.

Proration. The instruction continues specifying proration of taxes, rents, loans of record, insurance, and other sales related items.

General Instructions. The text over the signatures notes the fact that the instructions signed by the parties incorporate the general provisions in the general instructions.

Buyer's and Seller's Costs. Also over the signatures are general "clean up" instructions allocating costs based upon custom in the area.

☐ *Customary Allocation.* Customary division of costs for buyers and sellers in Southern California would be:

ALLOCATION OF COSTS IN SOUTHERN CALIFORNIA	Seller	Buyer
Drawing deed	x	
Documentary transfer tax	x	
Recording deed		x
Drawing note		x
Drawing deed of trust		x
Recording trust deed		x
Notarizing deed	x	
Notarizing trust deed		x
Title policy, owner	x	
(Buyer pays in Northern California.)		
Title policy, lender	x	
Beneficiary's demand	x	
Reconveyance fee	x	
Recording reconveyance	x	
Sale escrow fees	50%	50%
Loan escrow fee		x

☐ *Additional Costs.* A new trend is emerging where cities, as well as counties, are collecting a documentary transfer tax. On a property in Hawthorne, Los Angeles county would collect $1.10 per thousand documentary tax, or $110.00 on a $100,000 transaction. If the property were 3 miles away in Redondo Beach, this city imposes an additional $2.20 per thousand of consideration or another $220.00.

Signatures and Demand. These recitals are followed by buyer's and seller's signature. The paragraph preceding the seller's signature includes the seller's demand in the form of money for the deed, less demands and costs allocated to seller's portion of the transaction.

Special Provisions. If additional pages are required to complete the instruction, they would be incorporated by reference in the first page and a signature line for buyer and seller indicating complete accord.

☐ If an alien seller is involved, the appropriate FIRPTA language is added to the instruction.

☐ Other special caveats concern immediate credit for checks, residential property reports, any retrofit requirements such as tempered glass (e.g., Los Angeles ordinance effective October 21, 1986), smoke detectors, or any other local requirements.

DOCUMENTATION: REQUIREMENTS AND LIMITATIONS

Because of restrictions regarding unauthorized practice of law, escrowholders are not always able to prepare all documentation necessary to effect the transfer of title to property. If the document goes beyond "filling in blanks" and requires legal judgment, an attorney must prepare the document. Examples would be complex leases and detailed agreements relative to property rights.

Prepared by Escrowholder Documents that are generally prepared by the escrowholder include the following, which are illustrated and discussed in detail in later chapters.

DOCUMENTS PREPARED BY ESCROWHOLDER

Escrow Instructions

Deeds. Either grant or quitclaim. Some states use the warranty deed form.

Notes. Secured by real or personal property, unless complexities are such as to require legal advice.

Deeds of Trust

Bills of Sale

Security Agreements

Financing Statements

Truth in Lending Documentation (Some practitioners will not handle this)

Closing Statements. Real Estate Settlement Procedures Act.

Insurance. Transfer and increased coverage documentation

Other Standard Forms. Forms connected with the sale or loan which would normally consist of filling in blanks.

Printed Forms And Practice of Law. There are no hard and fast rules defining the type of documentation that an escrowholder can prepare. According to the bar treaty, "The forms so used must be those in general use and of established form and be generally printed and commonly used in real or personal property transactions (including business opportunity transactions)." If strict interpretation were given to this provision the mere preparation of escrow instructions might be considered practicing law since the escrowholder must design instructions to fit each specific transaction.

Variations. Printed instruction blanks and "general instructions" (in effect, the particular company's ground rules) differ among escrowholders. A range of examples will be found in the exhibits. The reasons for these differences are threefold:

☐ *New Legislation*. Printing new instructions is expensive and legislation incessant, so it is not surprising that changes are not incorporated immediately in all companies' forms.

☐ *Responsibility*. Exculpatory or "hold harmless" language (see Exhibit 8) may be considered appropriate by one escrowholder, while another does not require or cannot use it. For example, in a loan escrow it may be difficult for the escrowholder to disclaim responsibility for violations of Title I of the Federal Consumer Protection Act—"Truth in Lending." The courts increasingly recognize an escrowholder as a person more knowledgeable in the elements of property transfer than the general public, and thus less able to disclaim responsibility.

☐ *Local Usage*. The formality or informality of instructions varies with local custom and usage.

SPECIAL CONSIDERATIONS FOR ESCROWHOLDERS

Escrow's simple basic concept continues to gain in complexity as the regulations on the process expand. Escrow instructions may include a series of "protective clauses" intended to define the escrowholder's responsibilities vis-a-vis the potentially endless complexities of taxes, code compliance, etc. (Exhibit 8 is an example).

Local Code and Assessor's Requirements

Supplemental Tax Roll. Supplemental tax billing must be addressed as bills subsequent to closing may increase or decrease the tax level imposed on the property being transferred. See paragraph 1 of Exhibit 8.

Preliminary Change of Ownership Report. This form is now required prior to closing any transfer of real property interest or in filing a memorandum of lease. Each of the 58 counties uses its own special form. The form shown in Exhibit 9 is from Los Angeles County. Paragraph 2 of Exhibit 8 refers to this requirement.

Retrofit Ordinances. State law (Health and Safety Code § 13113.8) now requires that smoke detectors must be installed in all residential properties sold and a disclosure statement given to the purchaser. In addition some municipalities require such things as tempered glass in sliding glass doors, special compliance inspections and the like. Paragraph 3 of Exhibit 8 acknowledges these matters. Exhibit 10, Application for Report of Residential Property Records ("3R Report"), indicates requirements for smoke detectors and impact hazard glazing in the city of Los Angeles, typical of the type of retrofit ordinances proliferating in the state.

Use of Funds Deposited in Escrow

Clearing. State law requires a clearing process addressed in paragraph 4 of Exhibit 8.

Interest on Deposited Money. Purchasers are extremely conscious of the earning power of deposited money. In transactions where substantial deposits may remain for extended periods of time (30 days or more), they now usually require that the escrow deposit be transferred to an interest bearing account. Exhibit 11 is a typical instruction to fulfill this purpose.

Tax Reporting

In the sample protective clauses (paragraph 5), the parties agree to assume this responsibility outside of escrow, but it may also fall to the escrowholder.

FIRPTA. The Foreign Investment in Real Property Tax Act requires that every buyer of U.S. real property must, unless an exemption applies, deduct and withhold from the seller's proceeds ten percent of the gross sales price. Withheld funds must be reported and paid to IRS within 20 days after close of escrow. The primary exemptions are:

☐ Seller's affidavit that the seller is not a "foreign person"

☐ "Qualifying statement" from IRS specifying that no withholding is necessary

☐ The buyer purchases the property for use as a personal residence and the purchase price is not over $300,000.

Cal FIRPTA, effective January 1, 1991, also requires reporting, and in some cases withholding a portion, of the sales price of California property from non-resident sellers.

Tax Reform Act of 1986. Under this law all real estate transactions must be reported to the IRS on a special Form 1099-S (Exhibit 12). The primary reporting responsibility falls to the person responsible for closing the transaction—the escrow agent, if there is one. If there is no person responsible for closing the transaction, the primary mortgage lender, or the seller's broker, or the buyer's broker, in that order, must forward copies of Form 1099-S to the buyer, seller, and IRS.

Do Escrowholders Accept all Transactions?

Escrowholders do not always handle all transactions that customers might require. Many specialize quite narrowly in order to capitalize on their strengths, while certain other transactions are likely to be avoided by most practitioners.

Common Escrows. Some of the transactions that most escrowholders commonly process are listed below:

☐ *Sale of Real Property.* The real bread and butter transactions.

☐ *Loans on Real Property.* A majority represent sales, with refinances becoming significant during periods of lower interest rates.

□ *Land Sale Contracts*. Popular during high interest rate periods. Requires more supervision than normal sale.

□ *Sale of a Trust Deed*. A popular investment device.

Specialized Areas. With specialized personnel, additional transactions may be undertaken:

□ *Builder's Control Agent*. Escrow supervises progress payments to contractors for building projects.

□ *Mobilehome Escrows*. These require familiarity with State Department of Housing and Community Development requirements and specialized transfer procedures.

□ *Bulk Sales*. Sale of a business or personal property registered with government agencies requires personnel thoroughly trained in the area.

□ *Bulk Sales with Liquor License*. A limited number of firms feel comfortable handling this type of transaction.

□ *Exchange Escrows*. Requires extensive experience in this area.

□ *Leaseholds*. Again, a very specialized area.

Risky or Illegal Transactions. These situations are not normally accepted by professional escrowholders.

□ *Depositories*. Funds held for private stock purchase, distribution of money upon performance of some condition as in an athletic contest, etc. Only a few escrowholders or attorneys will handle depositories.

□ *New Subdivision Lot Sales Prior to Map Recording*. This is an illegal transaction under the Subdivision Map Act.

□ *Unrecorded Deeds Delivered at Death of Grantor*. This fails the test of proper delivery of the document.

□ *Jewelry and Valuables, Secret Formulas*. Precious stones and safe deposit keys, personal property sealed in an envelope, so-called secret formulas or trade secrets, are very risky transactions. Know the subject matter of the escrow.

```
┌─────────────────────────────────────────────────────────────────────┐
│  _____   _____                       │
│                                                                       │
│                          Third Party                                  │
│                       ESCROW INSTRUCTIONS                             │
│                                                                       │
│                                    ESCROW NO._____              │
│                                                                       │
│  ESCROW COMPANY                                         19____        │
│  ═══════════════════════════════════════════════════════════════     │
│                                                                       │
│      I hand you herewith the sum of  $1,000 , which you are hereby    │
│                                                                       │
│      authorized and instructed to deposit immediately and use for     │
│                                                                       │
│      the account of_____John Seller and Mary Seller_____        │
│                                                                       │
│      in your above-numbered escrow at the close thereof.  In the      │
│                                                                       │
│      event of the failure to consummate said escrow, the proceeds     │
│                                                                       │
│      of said funds are to be returned to _____Broker's Realty_____    │
│                                                                       │
│      MINUS your cancellation charges.  All disbursements of funds     │
│                                                                       │
│      to be made by check of your company.                             │
│                                                                       │
│                                                                       │
│   by:                                                                 │
│                   Broker's Realty                                     │
│        SIGNATURE: George M. Broker      SIGNATURE:_____     │
│                                                                       │
│                                                                       │
│        SIGNATURE:_____        SIGNATURE:_____     │
│                                                                       │
│   These instructions may be executed in counterparts, all of which   │
│   when taken together shall be deemed to be the instrument.  I have   │
│   received a copy of these instructions as evidenced by my signature  │
│   above.                                                              │
└─────────────────────────────────────────────────────────────────────┘
```

Exhibit 2

SAMPLE BAR TREATY

". . . when acting as escrow agent, an escrow company may: . . .

(c) At the request of one or more of the principals or their agents or agent, complete legal instruments to consummate the transaction and inquire of the principals or their agents or agent concerning such instruments, if all of the following conditions are fulfilled:

(i) The completion of such instruments shall consist solely of filling in blanks in printed forms with factual information and other provisions supplied by the principals or their agents or agent or in re-typing the form with such insertions; provided however, that in completing such instruments the escrow company shall not use (or provide for the use of the principals or their agents or agent) specimen, standard, stock or usual clauses or provisions with the escrow company, for insertion in such printed instruments.

(ii) The forms so used must be those in general use and of established form and be generally printed and commonly used in real or personal property transactions (including business opportunity transactions).

(iii) The forms so used must not be of any of the following: (a) the written agreement of the parties for the purchase and sale of real property or a business or business opportunity; (b) a lease; (c) a sublease; (d) a form specially prepared by or for the escrow company.

(iv) No legal advice shall be given, including advice as to the forms to be selected and used to consummate the transaction;

(v) No charge shall be made for services in the completion of legal instruments, as herein described, other than a reasonable charge for typing and to defray the cost of purchasing the form or forms in question.

Nothing in the foregoing shall authorize the escrow company to draft, select or prepare, in the escrow instructions or otherwise, the basic agreement between the principals or the terms or conditions thereof, or the legal documents to be used and deposited in the escrow by the principals, other than as provided for herein.

As to the completion of any instrument in accord with the provisions hereof, the escrow company shall not advertise that it will prepare or complete such instruments.

8. It is not intended herein to define what is or is not practicing law. As to all matters herein specified and as to other matters which may arise, it is the intent and spirit of this instrument that every escrow company should endeavor to conduct its business so that it cannot justly be said that it is practicing law."

Note: Although this agreement has been invalidated by the State Bar of California, adherence to the principle of this document can be considered proper escrow procedure.

Exhibit 3

PROPERTY ADDRESS 1234 Easy Street, Anytown, CA _____ ESCROW NO. 0110020

TRANSACTION MEMO DATA

TITLE CO. Assurance Title Company

SELLER John Seller and Mary Seller
Borrower
_____
_____

Address: 1234 Second Street

Anytown, CA Phone: 673-5410

Legal: Lot 1 in Block 3 in Tract 3612 in

the City of Anytown, County of Anytown,

c BK 36, pg. 12 Maps

BUYER James Buyer and Maggie Buyer
Lender
h/w as community property
_____

Address: 8763 First Street

Anytown, CA Phone: 682-3651

Deliver through Escrow:

Leases___No___ Water Stock___No___

Bill of Sale___Yes*___ Termite Report DeBug Termite Co.
Range & oven, free-standing refrigerator
Adjustments and date of prorations as of_____ #6587362

Taxes___X___ Bonds___No___ Impounds___No___

Rents___No___ Interest___No___ Insurance___No-new policy*
*A sent - California Insurance Co.
Adjust principal of T.D. of record in_____No_____

(Cash)_____ (T.D. to file)_____ (Purchase Price)_____

Pay_____5___% Commission

To Anytown Board Listing No. 16710 $___850 -

Address 458 Main St. Anytown, CA

To_____R. E. Agent_____ $ 1700-

Address 1203 Broad St. Anytown, CA

To_____Broker's Realty_____ $ 1700-

Address 1819 Main St. Anytown, CA

Time Limit___60 days___

Charges Normal alloca- Documentary Stamps of Deed $ 94.05
tion of fees

Possession: close of escrow.

Paid Outside Escrow to_____ $_____

Deposit _____ 1,000

Cash through Escrow by Broker _____
Cash through Escrow by Buyer _____ 7,500

Trust Deed of Record (balance) _____
Trust Deed of Record (balance) _____

Trust Deed to file _____ 68,500
Trust Deed to file _____ 8,500

Total Consideration $ 85,500

Subject to: 2nd 1/2 taxes current fiscal year 87-88
Bonds of Record, unpaid balance $_____

(1) **Trust Deed** of record unpaid balance $ 35,782 -
monthly prin. and interest installments of
$___279.84___ including interest
at___7-1/2___% (inc.) (plus) Impounds buyer
to make payment due_____
Loan No.___6-35623___

Beneficiary: Anytown Savings & Loan
328 Third Street
Anytown, CA

(2) **Trust Deed** of record unpaid balance $ 3,287 -
monthly prin. and interest installments of
$___84.99___ including interest
at___10%___% buyer to make payment
due___All due and payable 7/1/88
Loan No.___1210

Beneficiary: J.M. Thirdparty
483 Fourth Street
Anytown, CA

LOAN Trust Deed to file in amount of $ 68,500.-
monthly prin. and interest installments of
$___547.14___ including interest
at___9___% beginning 2-1-88
Fee: $780
Beneficiary: Anytown Savings & Loan
(376-4210) 328 Third Street
Anytown, CA

PMTD Trust Deed to file in amount of $ 8,500-
monthly prin. and interest installments of
$___85.00___ including interest
at___10___% beginning 2-1-88
all due 9-1-82 Accel. Clause___Yes
Request-Notice___Yes
Beneficiary: John Seller and Mary Seller
1289 Hummingbird Lane
Anytown, CA (786-3176)

Pay off of Existing Trust Deed of Record: Amt. $_____
Name of Holder:___see (1) and (2) above

Address:_____

Loan No._____

Exhibit 4

54 *From "Take Sheet" To Escrow Instructions*

TYPICAL CONTENTS OF MEMO BOX

The undersigned buyer and seller, hereby mutually understand and agree, that the statements set forth herein shall be construed by all those concerned as unconditionally incorporated in these buyer's and seller's escrow instructions, to wit:

01.	Buyer will hand you...	$ 7,500.00
02.	....	$
03.	....	$
04.	....	$
05.	Proceeds from ____ loan to be procured by Buyer.........................	$ 68,500.00
06.	Broker will hand you, same shall be returned to Broker if this escrow is not consummated.....................................	$ 1,000.00
07.	SELLER'S CASH DEMAND FOR DEED, IN ESCROW.....................	$ 77,000.00
08.	Buyer has paid outside of this escrow, to seller (with which you are not concerned)..	$
09.	Buyer has paid outside of this escrow, to broker (with which you are not concerned)..	$
10.	Encumbrance of record, approximate unpaid balance.....................	$
11.	....	$
12.	Buyer will hand you a new purchase price encumbrance..................	$ 8,500.00
13.	....	$
14.	TOTAL CONSIDERATION...	$ 85,500.00

Exhibit 5

SALE ESCROW INSTRUCTIONS
BUYER

Escrow No. 0110020   Anytown, California   11-15 , 19 88

Notice is hereby given that the escrow holder is a subsidiary of   Company.

The undersigned Buyer and Seller, hereby mutually understand and agree, that the statements set forth herein shall be construed, by all those concerned, as unconditionally incorporated in these Buyer's and Seller's escrow instructions, to-wit:

1. Buyer will hand you .prior to c/e.	$	7,500
2.	$	
3.	$	
4.	$	
5. Proceeds from conventional loan to be procured by Buyer	$	68,500
6. Broker will hand you, same shall be returned to Broker if this escrow is not consummated.	$	1,000
7. SELLER'S CASH DEMAND FOR DEED, IN ESCROW		$77,000
8. Buyer has paid outside of this escrow, to seller (with which you are not concerned)	$	
9. Buyer has paid outside of this escrow, to broker (with which you are not concerned)	$	
10. Encumbrance of record, approximate unpaid balance	$	
11.	$	
12. Buyer will hand you a new purchase price encumbrance	$	8,500
13.	$	
14. TOTAL CONSIDERATION		$85,500

and Buyer will deliver to you any instruments and/or funds required from Buyer to enable you to comply with these instructions, all of which you are authorized to use and/or deliver pursuant to obtaining on or before 1-15-89 a standard Policy of Title Insurance, with the Title Company's exceptions, provided that said policy has a liability of at least the amount of the above total consideration, (new title policy to be delivered to lien holder) covering the property in the City of Anytown and County of Anytown, State of California, described as follows:

Lot 1 Block 3 of Tract 3612 recorded in Book 36 page 12.

insuring title vested in: James Buyer and Maggie Buyer, h/w as community property

SUBJECT TO: 2nd 1/2,   installment(s) of General and Special County, and City (if any), Taxes, including any special district levies, payments for which are included therein and collected therewith, for current fiscal year, not delinquent, including taxes for the ensuing year, if any, a lien but not yet payable.

(N/A) Assessments and bonds, of record, unpaid balance $

(X) Conditions, restrictions, reservations, covenants, rights, rights of way, easements and the exception of minerals, oil, gas, water, carbons and hydrocarbons on or under said land, now of record, and in deed to file, if any, affecting the use and occupancy of said property.

( ) Deed of Trust, now of record, and note secured thereby approximate unpaid balance of $ as per their terms; further approval of which is hereby waived through this escrow by Buyer and Seller, except that principal and interest repayable in monthly installments of $ including interest at   % per annum.

(X) Deed of Trust, (loan) to file, and note secured thereby for $ 68,500   as per their terms. You are authorized and instructed to comply with lender's requirements, further approval of which is hereby waived through this escrow by Buyer and Seller, the proceeds of which shall be used to apply on purchase price, to be payable in monthly installments of $ including interest at   % per annum.

(X) Deed of Trust, to file, as a part of the purchase price, on Form handed you, executed by above Vestee(s), to secure one Note, for $ 8,500 , in favor of John Seller and Mary Seller, h/w dated 11/15/88 , with interest at 10 percent, per annum from close of escrow payable at where holder designates principal and interest payable in installments of $ 85.00 , or more each, on the 1st day of each calendar month beginning 2/1/89

NOTE and Trust Deed to contain the following clause: If the maker hereof sells, conveys, or alienates the property described in the deed of trust securing this note, or any part thereof, or any interest therein, any indebtedness or obligation secured hereby, irrespective of the maturity date expressed herein, at the option of the holder hereof, and without demand or notice, shall immediately become due and payable. (See attached)

in accordance with the manner specified under "GENERAL INSTRUCTIONS", the following are to be adjusted or pro-rated to . . . .

(X) Taxes   (N/A) Interest on Encumbrance of Record   (X) Interest on Purchase Money Note
(X) Fire Insurance on Property   (Yes) Impounds held by Beneficiary, if any   (N/A) Rentals

If unpaid balance on Trust Deed of record, based on statement of beneficiary, or his agent, is more or less than the sum(s) stated above on lines 10 and/or 11, adjust said difference as follows: ( ) in cash   ( ) thru Deed of Trust to file.

In addition to the aforementioned sum Buyer will hand you, before the date of recording, sufficient funds to cover adjustments and pro-rations as hereinbefore set out, also for your buyer's service charge and my proper recording fees.

Exhibit 6.1

As a matter of record only between Buyer and Seller, property address is known as: 1234 Easy Street   Anytown, CA

The foregoing terms, conditions and instructions, as well as the "GENERAL INSTRUCTIONS" as set forth on the reverse hereof, have been read and are understood and agreed to by each of the undersigned, and are hereby concurred in, approved and accepted in their entirety, as if fully set forth in this paragraph.

James Buyer	8763 First Street, Anytown, CA			682-3651
Buyer	Present Address	City	Zone	Phone
Maggie Buyer	1234 Second Street Anytown, CA			487-1320
Buyer	Mailing Address After close of Escrow	City	Zone	Phone

SELLER

The foregoing terms, conditions and instructions, as well as the "GENERAL INSTRUCTIONS" attached hereto, have been read and are understood and agreed to by each of the undersigned, and are hereby concurred in, approved and accepted in their entirety, as if fully set forth in this paragraph.

The undersigned Seller will hand you all instruments and/or funds necessary to enable you to comply therewith, including deed(s) to the herein described property, all of which you are authorized to use and/or deliver, pursuant to your obtaining in this escrow for the account of the undersigned party(ies) within the time limit as above provided for, the monies, being the total on line 7, page 1 hereof plus or minus above pro-rations and adjustments, and instruments called for under these instructions. From said monies, together with any necessary funds I hand you, you shall deduct and pay your seller's escrow, drawing and recording fees, also for evidence of title called for above, Documentary Transfer Tax stamps as required on Deed to property I am conveying; and you are authorized to pay off any bonds, assessments and/or taxes, also any encumbances of record, plus accrued interest, charges and bonus, if any, to show title as called for above and/or necessary to comply with same. Instruct the title company to begin search of title at once.

John Seller	1234 Second Street Anytown, CA			673-4510
Seller	Present Address	City	Zone	Phone
Mary Seller	7547 Taft Avenue, Anytown, CA			824-3637
Seller	Mailing Address After close of Escrow	City	Zone	Phone

(These instructions consist of two pages, the herein being Page 1 thereof.)

attachment

As a matter of record only with which escrow is not to be concerned, sale price includes free standing range and oven, together with refrigerator serial #6587362. No bill of sale will be required and escrow is relieved of any liability concerning delivery or condition of the personal property described.

Seller is to furnish Buyer through escrow with a current report in writing from a licensed pest control operator covering an inspection of visible and accessible areas of house and garage. If the report should disclose any debris under the house, termites, dry rot, or other infection, the seller is to eliminate it and all work recommended in said report to repair damage caused by infestation or infection of wood-destroying pests or organisms found and all work to correct conditions that caused such infestation or infection shall be done at the expense of seller and funds shall be held in escrow and disbursed upon receipt in escrow of certificate of completion by the structural pest control operator, or upon close of escrow, whichever occurs later.

Exhibit 6.2

General Information

(a)   Escrow Holder shall not be held liable for the sufficiency or correctness as to form, manner of execution, or validity of any instrument deposited in this escrow, not as to the identity, authority, or right of any person executing the same, nor for failure to comply with any of the provisions of nay agreement, contract, or other instrument filed herein or referred to herein and the duties of Escrow Holder hereunder shall be limited to the safekeeping of such money, instruments or other documents received by Escrow Holder and for the disposition of the same in accordance with the written instructions accepted by Escrow Holder. Your knowledge of matters affecting the property, provided such facts do not prevent compliance with these instructions, does not create any liability or duty in addition to your responsibility under these instructions.

(b)   Should Escrow Holder before or after the close of escrow receive or become aware of any conflicting demands or claims with respect to this escrow or the rights of any of the parties hereto, or of any money or property deposited herein or affected hereby, Escrow Holder shall have the right to discontinue any or all further acts on its part to be performed until such conflict is resolved to the satisfaction of Escrow Holder, and Escrow Holder shall have the further right to commence or defend any action or proceedings for the determination of such conflict. The parties hereto jointly and severally agree to pay all costs, damages, judgments and expenses, including reasonable attorney's fees, suffered or incurred by Escrow Holder in connection with, or arising out of this escrow, including, but without limiting the generality of the foregoing, any suit and interpleader brought by Escrow Holder. In the event that Escrow Holder shall file any action and interpleader in connection with this escrow, Escrow Holder shall automatically be released and discharged from all obligations further to perform any and all duties or obligations imposed upon Escrow Holder by the terms hereof.

(c)   Escrow Holder shall not be concerned with the giving of any disclosures required by federal or state law including, but not limited to, any disclosures required under Regulation Z promulgated pursuant to the Federal Consumer Credit Protection Act, which may or should be given outside of this escrow, or the effect of any zoning laws, ordinances or regulations affecting any of the property transferred hereunder. The undersigned jointly and severally agree to save and hold Escrow Holder harmless by reason of any misrepresentation or omission by either party hereto or their respective agents or the failure of any of the parties hereto to comply with the rules and/or regulations of any governmental agency, state, federal, county, municipal or otherwise.

(d)   The parties to this escrow have satisfied themselves outside of this escrow that the transaction covered hereby is not in violation of the Subdivision Map Act or any other law relating to land division, and Escrow Holder is relieved of all responsibility and/or liability in connection therewith, and is not to be concerned with the enforcement of said laws.

(e)   Escrow Holder shall as agent for the parties hereto, assign any fire and other insurance of the parties hereto handed you or policies of insurance that the beneficiaries thereof inform Escrow Holder that they hold.

(f)   All proration shall be made on the basis of a 30-day month. All deposits made by the parties hereto in connection with this transaction shall be deposited by Escrow Holder in an account designated as "Escrow Fund Account" with any local bank, without any liability for interest. All disbursements shall be made by check of Escrow Holder drawn on said account.

(g)   Escrow Holder shall mail all fire and other insurance policies to the respective holders of first encumbrances, if any. All policies of title insurance shall be mailed to the holders of existing encumbrances provided there is to be a substitution of liability thereon; otherwise, to the respective holders of the prior encumbrances recorded concurrently with the documents herein or, if there is no such encumbrance, then to the respective grantees. Other documents and checks in favor of each of the parties hereto shall be mailed, unregistered, to the addresses of the respective parties hereinbelow set forth.

(h)   Escrow Holder shall be under no obligation or liability for the failure to inform the parties hereto regarding any sale, loan, exchange, or other transaction, or facts within the knowledge of Escrow Holder, even though the same concern the property described herein, provided they do not prevent the compliance of Escrow Holder with these instructions.

(i)   These instructions may be executed in counterparts, each of which so executed shall, irrespective of the date of its execution and delivery, be deemed an original and said counterparts together shall constitute one and the same instrument. Any amended and/or supplemental instructions hereto must be in writing, executed by all of the parties hereto, and deposited with Escrow Holder.

(j)   Any policy of title insurance called for under these instructions will be subject to the exceptions and conditions contained in the standard from of the company issuing such insurance including, but not limited to, the exception that said company will not insure against loss by reason of the reservation or exception of any water rights, claims or title to water.

(k)   Your company is authorized to destroy or otherwise dispose of any and all documents, papers, instructions, correspondence and other material pertaining to this escrow at the expiration of five (5) years from the date of these instructions, regardless of the date of any subsequent amendments hereto, additional or supplemental instructions or the date of the close of escrow, without liability and without further notice to the undersigned.

(l)   The parties hereto hereby authorize the recordation of any instruments delivered through this escrow, if necessary or proper in the issuance of the policy of title insurance called for, and in connection therewith, funds and/or instruments received in this escrow may be delivered to, or deposited with, any title company situated in the county in which any of the property covered hereby is situated for the purposes of complying with the terms and conditions of these escrow instructions.

(m)   In the event that it may be necessary or proper for the consummation of this escrow, you are authorized to deposit or have deposited funds or documents, or both, with any bank, trust company, title insurance company, savings and loan association, building and loan association, industrial loan company, credit union, insurer or licensed escrow agent, subject to your order pursuant to closing this escrow, and such deposit shall be deemed a deposit in accordance with the meaning of these instructions.

(n)   The signature of the undersigned or any documents and instructions pertaining to this escrow indicates their unconditional acceptance and approval of the same, and the undersigned hereby acknowledge the receipt of a copy of these instructions.

_____   _____

_____   _____

Exhibit 6.3

COMMISSION AND PEST CONTROL INSTRUCTIONS

Escrow Instructions to:

Escrow No. __0110020_____ Escrow Officer __Jane D. Holder__ Date __11-15-1989_____

You are advised that the commission be paid for services in connection with this transaction is the sum of $ __4,250.00_____
Said amount is to be paid as follows:

$ __1,700.00__ to __R. E. Agent_____ Lic. #_____

             address __1203 Broad Street_____ Phone _____

$ __1,700.00__ to __Broker's Realty_____ Lic. #_____

             address __1819 Main Street_____ Phone _____

$ __850.00__ to __Anytown Realty_____ Lic. #_____

             address __458 Main Street_____ Phone _____

$ _____ to _____ Lic. #_____

             address _____ Phone _____

I have read and hereby approve the foregoing, and you will pay said commission at the close of this escrow and charge my account with the amount thereof, or if necessary, I will hand you funds required to pay the same.

_____

PAGE _____

Escrow Instructions to:

Escrow No. __0110020_____ Escrow Officer __Jane D. Holder__ Date __11-15-1989_____

The seller herein agrees to furnish, at his expense, an inspection report by a licensed structural pest control operator and a notice that all measures recommended in the report have been completed. Such report is to affect the premises known as _____
_____1234 Second Street, Anytown CA_____

Escrow holder is instructed to deliver, as soon as possible, a copy of the structural pest control inspection report to the buyer(s) herein prior to the close of escrow. Also, if the completion report is received by the escrow holder prior to the close of escrow, you are instructed to deliver, as soon as possible, a copy of said completion report to the buyer(s) herein prior to the close of escrow.

Delivery means delivery in person to any one of the buyers (if there is more than one buyer) or mailing, by ordinary mail, at least two working days prior to the close of escrow, to any one of the buyers.

From the seller's funds you are authorized to pay, upon presentation, invoices purporting to be from a licensed structural pest control operator for the inspection, report and recommended work.

Exhibit 7

SAMPLE PROTECTIVE CLAUSES

PAGE . . . .

Escrow Instructions to: **STERLING BANK** — 3287 Wilshire Boulevard, Los Angeles, California 90010, (213) 384-4444

Escrow No. . . . . Escrow Officer . . . . Date . . . .

Prorate taxes on the basis of $_____ for one year, which is the tax information presently available, and it is satisfactory that the title policy reflect same. You are not to be concerned with any supplemental bills which either party may receive after the close of escrow.

Unless buyer furnishes you with a Preliminary Change of Ownership Report to attach to the grant deed prior to close of escrow, you are to charge buyer and pay the additional $20 fee for recording said deed.

City or County Ordinances requiring special reports or inspections, if any, will be handled outside of escrow and you are not to be concerned.

The parties are aware that Sections 12413 and 12413.5 of the California Insurance Code, which became effective January 1, 1985, provide that funds deliverable through or by a title insurance company, underwritten title company or controlled escrow company shall not be disbursed until such funds have cleared. You are relieved of all liability and responsibility in the event that close of escrow is delayed pending clearance of said funds.

The parties acknowledge that they are aware of Section 1445 of the Tax Reform Act of 1984 and will comply with same outside of escrow, and you are not to be concerned in any way.

Signature _____   Signature _____

Signature _____   Signature _____

ESC-803 (7/86)

Exhibit 8

JOHN J. LYNCH
COUNTY ASSESSOR
COUNTY OF LOS ANGELES
500 West Temple Street
Los Angeles, California 90012-2770

THIS SPACE FOR RECORDER'S USE

PRELIMINARY CHANGE OF OWNERSHIP REPORT
THIS REPORT IS NOT A PUBLIC DOCUMENT

(To be completed by transferee (buyer) prior to transfer of the subject property in accordance with Section 480.3 of the Revenue and Taxation Code.)

SELLER/TRANSFEROR: _____

BUYER/TRANSFEREE: _____

ASSESSOR'S IDENTIFICATION NUMBER(S): _____
Map Book   Page   Parcel

PROPERTY ADDRESS OR LOCATION: _____
No   Street

_____
City   State   Zip Code

MAIL TAX INFORMATION TO:

NAME: _____

ADDRESS: _____
Street No   City   State   Zip Code

FOR ASSESSOR'S USE ONLY

Cluster _____

OC1 _____ OC2 _____

DT _____ INT _____

RC _____ SP $ _____

DTT $ _____ # Pcl _____

A Preliminary Change in Ownership Report must be filed with each conveyance in the County Recorder's office for the county where the property is located; this particular form may be used in all 58 counties of California.

The property which you acquired may be subject to a supplemental assessment in an amount to be determined by the Los Angeles County Assessor. For further information on your supplemental roll obligation, please call the Los Angeles County Assessor at (213) 974-3211

PART I: TRANSFER INFORMATION   Please answer all questions.

YES NO

☐   ☐   A. Is this transfer solely between husband and wife? (Addition of a spouse, death of a spouse, divorce settlement, etc.)

☐   ☐   B. Is this transaction only a correction of the name(s) of the person(s) holding title to the property? (For example, a name change upon marriage)

☐   ☐   C. Is this document recorded to create, terminate, or reconvey a lender's interest in the property?

☐   ☐   D. Is this transaction recorded only to create, terminate, or reconvey a security interest (e.g., cosigner)?

☐   ☐   E. Is this document recorded to substitute a trustee under a deed of trust, mortgage, or other similar document?

☐   ☐   F. Did this transfer result in the creation of a joint tenancy in which the seller (transferor) remains as one of the joint tenants?

☐   ☐   G. Does this transfer return property to the person who created the joint tenancy (original transferor)?

          H. Is this transfer of property:

☐   ☐   1. to a trust for the benefit of the grantor, or grantor's spouse?

☐   ☐   2. to a trust revocable by the transferor?

☐   ☐   3. to a trust from which the property reverts to the grantor within 12 years?

☐   ☐   I. If this property is subject to a lease, is the remaining lease term 35 years or more including written options?

Please provide any other information that would help the Assessor to understand the nature of the transfer.

_____

_____

IF YOU HAVE ANSWERED "YES" TO ANY OF THE ABOVE QUESTIONS, PLEASE SIGN AND DATE ON THE BACK SIDE.
IF YOU HAVE ANSWERED "NO" TO ALL OF THE ABOVE QUESTIONS, PLEASE COMPLETE BALANCE OF THE FORM.

PART II: OTHER TRANSFER INFORMATION

A. Date of transfer if other than recording date _____

B. Type of transfer. Please check appropriate box.

☐ Purchase   ☐ Foreclosure   ☐ Gift   ☐ Trade or Exchange

☐ Contract of Sale – Date of Contract _____

☐ Inheritance – Date of Death _____ ☐ Other: Please explain: _____

☐ Creation of a lease;   ☐ Assignment of a lease;   ☐ Termination of a lease

Date lease began _____

Original term in years (including written options) _____

Remaining term in years (including written options) _____

C. Was only a partial interest in the property transferred?   ☐ Yes   ☐ No

If yes, indicate the percentage transferred _____ %.

SBE-ASD AH 502-A FRONT (3-6-85) (REV. 5-7-86) ASSR-70

Exhibit 9.1

PRELIMINARY CHANGE OF OWNERSHIP REPORT

Please answer, to the best of your knowledge, all applicable questions, sign and date. If a question does not apply, indicate with "N/A."

PART III: PURCHASE PRICE & TERMS OF SALE

A. CASH DOWN PAYMENT OR Value of Trade or Exchange (excluding closing cost)   Amount $ _____

B. FIRST DEED OF TRUST @ _____ % interest for _____ years. Pymts./Mo. = $ _____ (Prin. & Int. only) Amount $ _____

   ☐ FHA   ☐ Fixed Rate   ☐ New Loan
   ☐ Conventional   ☐ Variable Rate   ☐ Assumed Existing Loan Balance
   ☐ VA   ☐ All Inclusive D.T. ($_____ Wrapped)   ☐ Bank or Savings & Loan
   ☐ Cal-Vet   ☐ Loan Carried by Seller   ☐ Finance Company
   Balloon Payment   ☐ Yes   ☐ No   Due Date_____   Amount $ _____

C. SECOND DEED OF TRUST @ _____ % interest for _____ years Pymts./Mo. = $ _____ (Prin. & Int. only) Amount $ _____

   ☐ Bank or Savings & Loan   ☐ Fixed Rate   ☐ New Loan
   ☐ Loan Carried by Seller   ☐ Variable Rate   ☐ Assumed Existing Loan Balance
   Balloon Payment   ☐ Yes   ☐ No   Due Date _____   Amount $ _____

D. OTHER FINANCING: Is other financing involved not covered in (b) or (c) above?   ☐ Yes   ☐ No   Amount $ _____

   Type _____ @ _____ % interest for _____ years. Pymts./Mo. = $ _____ (Prin. & Int. only)
   ☐ Bank or Savings & Loan   ☐ Fixed Rate   ☐ New Loan
   ☐ Loan Carried by Seller   ☐ Variable Rate   ☐ Assumed Existing Loan Balance
   Balloon Payment   ☐ Yes   ☐ No   Due Date _____   Amount $ _____

E. IMPROVEMENT BOND   ☐ Yes   ☐ No   Outstanding Balance: Amount $ _____

F. TOTAL PURCHASE PRICE (or acquisition price, if traded or exchanged, include real estate commission if paid.)

                                                Total Items A through E $ _____

   Please explain any special terms of financing and any other information that would help
   the Assessor understand the purchase price and terms of sale.

   _____

   _____

PART IV: PROPERTY INFORMATION

A. IS PERSONAL PROPERTY INCLUDED IN THE PURCHASE PRICE?
   (other than a mobilehome subject to local property tax)?   ☐ Yes   ☐ No
   If yes, enter the value of the personal property included in the purchase price $ _____ (Attach itemized list of personal property)

B. IS THIS PROPERTY INTENDED AS YOUR PRINCIPAL RESIDENCE?   ☐ Yes   ☐ No
   If yes, enter date of occupancy _____ / _____ , 19 _____ or intended occupancy _____ / _____ , 19 _____
                                  Month   Day   Month   Day

C. TYPE OF PROPERTY TRANSFERRED:
   ☐ Single-Family residence   ☐ Agricultural   ☐ Timeshare
   ☐ Multiple-Family residence (no. of units: _____)   ☐ Co-op/Own-your-own   ☐ Mobilehome
   ☐ Commercial/Industrial   ☐ Condominium   ☐ Unimproved lot
   ☐ Other (Description: _____)

D. DOES THE PROPERTY PRODUCE INCOME?   ☐ Yes   ☐ No

E. IF THE ANSWER TO QUESTION D IS YES, IS THE INCOME FROM:
   ☐ Lease/Rent   ☐ Contract   ☐ Mineral rights   ☐ Other–explain: _____
   Enter here, or on an attached sheet, any other information that would assist the Assessor in determining value of the property such as the physical condition of the property,
   restrictions, etc.

   _____

   _____

I certify that the foregoing is true, correct and complete to the best of my knowledge and belief.

Signed _____ Date _____
      (New Owner/Legal Representative/Corporate Officer)

Please Print Name of New Owner/Legal Representative/Corporate Officer _____
Phone No. where you are available from 8:00 a.m. – 5:00 p.m. ( ) _____

                       (NOTE: The Assessor may contact you for further information)

If a document evidencing a change of ownership is presented to the recorder for recordation without the concurrent filing of a PRELIMINARY CHANGE OF OWNERSHIP REPORT, the recorder may charge an additional recording fee of twenty dollars ($20). The additional fee shall not be charged if the document is accompanied by an affidavit that the transferee is not a resident of California.

AFFIDAVIT OF NONRESIDENT TRANSFEREE

The Transferee (buyer) named above is a resident of _____ and not a resident of the State of California.
                                             State

Signed: _____ Date: _____
      (New Owner/Legal Representative/Corporate Officer)

SBE-ASD AH 502-A BACK (3-6-85) (REV 5/7/86)

Exhibit 9.2

9a

City of Los Angeles

APPLICATION FOR REPORT OF RESIDENTIAL PROPERTY RECORDS AND PENDING SPECIAL ASSESSMENT LIENS

B & S B-9a (R 8/86)

INSTRUCTIONS: COMPLETE NUMBERED ITEMS AND MAIL CHECK OR MONEY ORDER FOR $31.00 PAYABLE TO DEPARTMENT OF BUILDING AND SAFETY, RESIDENTIAL PROPERTY RECORDS, ROOM 460F, 200 N. SPRING ST., LOS ANGELES, CA 90012-4869 SUBMIT A SEPARATE CHECK WITH EACH APPLICATION. **DO NOT SEND CASH. Phone (213) 485-2216**

1 | STREET NUMBER | STREET NAME (BLVD., AVE., ST., PLACE, ETC.) | POST OFFICE CITY

2 LEGAL DESCRIPTIONS OF PROPERTY AS SHOWN ON GRANT DEED. ATTACH ANY LONG LEGAL DESCRIPTIONS AND INCLUDE A COPY OF THE TITLE INSURANCE POLICY MAP.

FROM COUNTY TAX BILL

LOT	BLOCK	TRACT	MAP BOOK	PAGE	PARCEL

Mail Completed Report To

3 NAME

7 Description of Property Being Sold
- ☐ VACANT LOT
- ☐ ONE FAMILY DWELLING
- ☐ OTHER RESIDENTIAL BLDG.

4 ADDRESS

5 | CITY | STATE | ZIP CODE | ESCROW NO.
8

6 PERSON TO CONTACT FOR ADDITIONAL INFORMATION: | NAME | PHONE NO.

9 I declare that the following statement is true and correct: in the residential building for which this report is sought, smoke detectors in compliance with Section 91.1210 and sliding glass door impact hazard glazing in compliance with Section 91.5406(e):

A. ☐ Smoke Detectors ☐ Impact Glazing/Approved Film **have been installed, or,**

☐ Smoke Detectors ☐ Impact Glazing/Approved Film **will be installed prior to** entering into an agreement of sale or contracting for an exchange of said residential building or, where an escrow agreement has been executed in connection therewith, prior to close of escrow and that within 10 days after installation I will so advise, in writing, the Department of Building and Safety, Residential Property Records, Room 460F, 200 N. Spring St., Los Angeles, CA. 90012-4869.

☐ Impact Hazard Glazing Ordinance does not apply

Signature of Owner _____

B. ☐ Smoke Detectors ☐ Impact Glazing/Approved Film **will be installed within** 30 days after entering into an agreement of sale or contracting for an exchange of said residential building, or where an escrow agreement has been executed in connection therewith, within 30 days after close of escrow and that within 10 days after installation I will so advise, in writing, the Department of Building and Safety, Residential Property Reocrds, Room 460F, 200 N. Spring St., Los Angeles, CA. 90012-4869.

Signature of Buyer _____

Section 96.300 L.A.M.C. requires that the seller of Residential Property within the City of Los Angeles shall apply to the City for a Report of Residential Property Records and Pending Special Assessment Liens and deliver such report to the buyer prior to entering an agreement of sale or exchange of the Residential Property or prior to close of escrow in connection therewith. There is a fee of $31.00 for this service.

Residential Property is defined as:
1. Any real property improved with one or more buildings or structures which in whole or in part are used for or are legally permitted to be used for dwelling unit or guest room purposes.
2. Any vacant real property located in a zone wherein dwelling units or guest rooms are legally permitted.

A Report is **not** required in the following cases:
1. Property exempt from taxation under the Documentary Transfer Tax Act of the State of California.
2. The first sale of a residential building located in a subdivision whose final map has been approved and recorded in accordance with the Subdivision Map Act not more than two years prior to the first sale (except for condominium conversions).

No new Report need be obtained by an owner for a period of six months after the issuance of a Report on a Residential Property. However, the seller must still deliver a copy of the previously issued Report to the buyer prior to sale or exchange of the Residential Property or prior to close of escrow.

ATTACH CHECK HERE

FOR DEPARTMENTAL USE ONLY		
DATE	1)	2)
CONTROL NUMBER	1)	2)

NOTE: Before you buy or sell your home, you may want to determine whether the building complies with City requirements for existing residential buildings. If so, you may request that it be inspected and a Certificate of Compliance issued by the Building Department when it complies. For information on Building Inspection Service call (213) 485-7037.

Exhibit 10.1

THIS SIDE FOR DEPARTMENTAL USE ONLY

ADDRESS (Check box)

☐ O.K.,
USE STAMP # 2,
_____ Address on map is one lot away
_____ Address is not on map
☐ OTHER
(See below)

LEGAL (Check box)

☐ O.K.,
☐ USE STAMP # 1,
(Lot split not on map)
☐ OTHER
(See below)

ZONE	OTHER	RESEARCHER'S NAME
R1-1 RA-1		
RS-1 R5-1		DATE

OTHER ADDRESSES ON PROPERTY   **FORMER STREET NAMES**

☐ OTHER REASONS FOR REFERRAL OF APPLICATION

---------------a) Address does not match legal description
---------------b) Address and legal description are not in the City of L.A.
---------------c) Incorrect legal description
---------------d) Incomplete legal description
---------------e) Legal description does not match tax parcel number
---------------f) Other

1) INITIALS & DATE	2) INITIALS & DATE	3) INITIALS & DATE

RESEARCH COMMENTS:

Exhibit 10.2

DEPOSIT INTEREST INSTRUCTIONS

Escrow Instructions to: **STERLING BANK** — 3287 Wilshire Boulevard, Los Angeles, California 90010, (213) 384-4444

Escrow No. .... Escrow Officer .... Date ....

The undersigned hereby agree:

1. That the sum of $_____ delivered, or to be delivered, to you by _____ _____ in subject escrow shall be deposited in an interest bearing Money Market Account in your office, in the name of _____ by STERLING BANK, as Escrow Agent;

2. That interest earned on said Money Market Account, if any, shall be reported as required by governmental regulations. For reporting of such interest Bank shall use the social security number or taxpayer identification number of _____ _____;

3. That the sum of $10 shall remain on deposit in said Account through the end of the satement cycle period within which this escrow closes;

4. That the Account shall be governed by applicable banking laws, customs and rules printed pertaining to Money Market Accounts, and the undersigned shall execute such additional authorizations or other documents that may be required by Bank;

5. That the Account shall be handled by you in accordance with your usual procedures for holding funds deposited with you as an escrow agent, and you are to disburse the funds in said Account as directed herein and in joint escrow instructions delivered to you by the undersigned. It is hereby agreed that you are to hold any evidence of deposit and you shall have exclusive authority to withdraw or otherwise handle such funds until you have made all disbursements;

6. That when you make disbursements you are to pay all interest earned on the deposit to _____. This instruction is not subject to change with respect to any amounts that Bank has reported to tax authorities as required by law or regulation;

7. That the deposit shall be subject to Bank's rules and regulations and pricing structure for insured Money Market Accounts, as provided in the disclosure statement delivered to the undersigned, receipt of which is hereby acknowledged;

8. That federal regulations also permit the Bank to require 7 days prior written notice for any withdrawal or transfer, and, Bank rules provide that interest accumulated during a statement cycle period is lost if the account is closed prior to the end of the period. You shall have no responsibility for any delay in closing escrow arising from imposition of the 7-day notice requirement, nor for any loss of interest arising from closing escrow and making disbursements prior to the end of a statement cycle period; and

9. That funds deposited pursuant to this instrument shall at all times be considered deposited in this escrow subject to all prior or amended escrow instructions, except that this instrument may not be amended or changed without the Bank's written consent.

Date_____   _____   _____
                                                (Buyer)   SS or ID #

Date_____   _____   _____

Date_____   _____   _____
                                                (Seller)   SS or ID #

Date_____   _____   _____

Exhibit 11

7575 ☐ VOID ☐ CORRECTED For Official Use Only

| Type or machine print FILER'S name, street address, city, state, and ZIP code | | OMB No. 1545-0997 | **Proceeds From Real Estate Transactions** |
| | | 19**90** Statement for Recipients of | |

FILER'S Federal identification number	TRANSFEROR'S identification number	1 Date of closing (MMDDYY)	2 Gross proceeds $	**Copy A** **For Internal Revenue Service Center**
Type or machine print TRANSFEROR'S name (first, middle, last)		3 Address or legal description		For Paperwork Reduction Act Notice and instructions for completing this form, see Instructions for Forms 1099, 1098, 5498, 1096, and W-2G.
Street address				
City, state, and ZIP code				
Account number (optional)		4 Check here if the transferor received or will receive property or services as part of the consideration . . . . ▶ ☐		

Form **1099-S**　　　　　　　　　　　　　　　Department of the Treasury - Internal Revenue Service

---

☐ VOID ☐ CORRECTED

| FILER'S name, street address, city, state, and ZIP code | | OMB No. 1545-0997 | **Proceeds From Real Estate Transactions** |
| | | 19**90** Statement for Recipients of | |

FILER'S Federal identification number	TRANSFEROR'S identification number	1 Date of closing	2 Gross proceeds $	**Copy B** **For Transferor**
TRANSFEROR'S name (first, middle, last)		3 Address or legal description		This is important tax information and is being furnished to the Internal Revenue Service. If you are required to file a return, a negligence penalty or other sanction will be imposed on you if this item is required to be reported and the IRS determines that it has not been reported.
Street address				
City, state, and ZIP code				
Account number (optional)		4 Check here if the transferor received or will receive property or services as part of the consideration . . . . ▶ ☐		

Form **1099-S**　　　　　　　　　　　　　　　Department of the Treasury - Internal Revenue Service

---

Instructions for Transferor

Generally, persons responsible for closing a real estate transaction must report the real estate proceeds to the Internal Revenue Service and must furnish this statement to you. If the real estate transferred was your main home, file **Form 2119,** Sale of Your Home, with your income tax return even if you sold at a loss or you did not replace your home. If the real estate transferred was not your main home, report the transaction in the applicable parts of **Form 4797,** Sales of Business Property, **Form 6252,** Installment Sale Income, and/or **Schedule D** (Form 1040), Capital Gains and Losses.

Box 1.—Shows the date of closing.

Box 2.—Shows the gross proceeds from a real estate transaction. Gross proceeds include cash and notes payable to you and notes assumed by the transferee (buyer). This does not include the value of other property or services you received or are to receive.

Box 3.—Shows the address of the property transferred or a legal description of the property.

Box 4.—If you received or will receive property (other than cash) or services as part of the consideration for the property transferred, this box should be checked. The value of any property (other than cash) or services is not included in Box 2.

Copy C For Filer

Exhibit 12

Chapter 5 Quiz

1. Escrow processing is uniform throughout the state of California:

   (A) True
   (B) False -

2. Since rescission of the bar treaties, brokers and escrow agents may answer clients' legal questions as long as they relate only to the specific transaction being processed.

   (A) True
   ✓(B) False

3. To insure accurate information, the preliminary interview is always conducted by the assigned escrow officer, face-to-face with the principals.

   (A) True
   ✓(B) False

4. Escrowholders' legal and practical responsibilities are defined by:

   (A) Protective clauses
   (B) Case law
   (C) Bar treaties
   (D) All of the above

5. The preliminary interview:

   (A) Is performed to obtain all the details on a new loan
   (B) Is used to revise the deposit receipt
   ✓(C) Is a device used to properly prepare escrow instructions
   (D) Screens out unqualified clients

6. The memo box:

   (A) Is an area where the escrow officer takes notes
   (B) Is a suggestion box for the escrow office
   (C) Is a place to deposit messages in the escrow office
   (D) Provides a summary of the consideration

7. The check sheet:

   (A) Lists all the checks written in an escrow
   (B) Is an orderly presentation of the information required in an escrow instruction
   (C) Is used for ordering supplies
   (D) Is seldom used in a sale escrow

8. Escrow agents can draw all documents required in any given transaction:

   (A) True
   (B) False

9. Of the following, which transaction may not be acceptable to an escrowholder?

   (A) Loan escrow
   (B) Sale escrow
   (C) Secret formula in a sealed envelope
   (D) Sale of a trust deed

10. Which of the following does not represent a normal responsibility of escrow?

    (A) Preparing a deed
    (B) Foreign Investment in Real Property Tax Act (FIRPTA) reporting
    (C) Giving legal advice
    (D) Investing deposited funds

Chapter 6
Overview of Processing— Regional Variations

PREVIEW

Principles Are Universal But Processing Varies

Northern California—Focus on Title Report

Southern California—Focus on Financing

PRINCIPLES ARE UNIVERSAL BUT PROCESSING VARIES

Regardless of geographical area, escrow involves gathering the required information and performing the closing process, in order to transfer or hypothecate real or personal property and provide the accounting for the transaction.

Basic Principles The escrow agent will:

Prepare the Escrow Instruction. This establishes the contractual agreement of the parties. Escrow is a *limited agency*, being limited to the duties conferred by the parties to the transaction. Escrowholders are not held to the full disclosure requirements of a general agent. They are responsible only for carrying out the duties contained in the escrow instructions.

Assemble Documentation. Deeds, notes, bills of sale, trust deeds, security agreements, UCC (Uniform Commercial Code) forms, such as financing statements, information requests, termination statements, assignments of trust deeds, etc., must be gathered or prepared. Certain documents require preparation by attorneys. The bar treaty (Exhibit 3) indicates the type of documents an escrow agent would not draft.

Obtain Title Report. Based upon information provided in the title report, the escrow agent will proceed to eliminate such items as existing trust deeds, unpaid taxes, judgment or tax liens, etc., as required by the parties to complete the transaction.

Finalize and Carry Out Instructions. This includes authorizing broker's commission if a broker is involved, allocation of charges, prorations, contingencies, etc.

☐ *Bilateral Instructions*. Prevalent in Southern California, these are prepared early in the process, and are likely to be amended as closing approaches.

☐ *Unilateral Instructions*. Used in Northern California, these are drafted late in the process, in more or less final form.

Authorize Recording. When escrow is complete, the transfer is recorded. Complete escrow implies:

☐ All required documents, signed instructions, and amendments thereto have been deposited and are in the possession of the escrowholder.

☐ Good funds have been received and are in the possession of the escrowholder.

☐ All conditions to the completion of the contract have been satisfied.

Follow Up Recordation. Disbursement of funds, transmittal of funds, and delivery of documents is carried out. Additionally, information relative to the closing is transmitted to the fire insurance companies and existing lenders and any other interested parties. A closing statement is prepared and transmitted to the parties summarizing all financial transactions.

Regional Variations The difference between Northern and Southern California procedures concerns the division of duties and responsibilities between the real estate agent and the escrow officer, the form of the escrow instructions, the role of bank or title company, and the apportionment of fees. This chapter will trace both versions of the escrow process, looking in detail at title matters in the Northern California example, and at loan processing in the discussion of Southern California.

NORTHERN CALIFORNIA—FOCUS ON TITLE REPORT

In Northern California, escrow procedure is closely related to the title insurance process. Real estate broker involvement in the closing process is greater than in the south, and the preparation of instructions occurs as one of the last items in the closing procedure. Exhibit 13 outlines the typical steps involved in the closing process in Northern California. Unilateral instructions are used. Each step of the procedure is now examined in detail.

Broker or Client Opens the Order Usually the real estate broker begins by contacting the title company for a preliminary title report. This is initiated through the escrow department of the title company, although no instructions are drawn at this time.

Order Preliminary Report The escrow department then contacts the title department to initiate the second step in the closing process. In order to perform a title search on the subject property the following information should be available:

Complete Legal Description. Title records are normally retrieved by legal description, e.g., assessor's block and parcel number.

Current Parties in Title. The title insurance company can provide better service if they have complete information on the parties involved. Identity statements are provided for this purpose. (See Exhibit 33)

Prospective Parties in Title. Names and forms of ownership to be assumed should be indicated.

Type and Amount of Title Insurance Required. Standard or extended coverage should be specified.

Name and Address of New Lenders. A copy of the report will be forwarded to them.

Miscellaneous. Any special requirements relative to copies of covenants, conditions and restrictions, special endorsements, or inspections should be added.

Preliminary Report Received

A preliminary title report, as shown in Exhibit 14, outlines the condition of title and is usually reviewed by the broker to ascertain what is required to deliver title in the condition outlined in the deposit receipt. Each aspect of the preliminary title report should be examined in detail.

Estate and Interest. In this example the property has a fee estate coupled with an easement appurtenant to the fee title interest. Other interests covered could be equitable interests, life estates, leasehold estates, and remainders. Only the dominant tenement of the legal description may have been provided to open title. Any easements are normally described as a matter of course by the title insurer.

Vesting. The current ownership should be compared with the seller's name on the original deposit receipt; if the names do not agree, several possibilities exist and must be resolved:

□ An incorrect legal description is shown,

□ The parties are equitable owners under an unrecorded contract, or

□ Some misrepresentation has occurred.

Legal Description. The legal description should be compared with information originally submitted. Lot dimensions should be examined on the plot map to determine that they are essentially in accordance with those shown on the original listing. This is particularly important where FHA/VA financing is involved. Since an easement for ingress and egress shown as parcel 2 in our description has been added, it should be determined that this in fact allows parcel 1 access to a dedicated street.

Exceptions or Encumbrances. Several matters require special attention.

□ *Taxes.* Are there any taxes or assessments to be paid? Who is responsible for their payment? Are these items to be prorated? With the introduction of supplemental tax rolls, adjustments by the parties may be performed outside of the escrow, since billing rates may be raised or lowered.

□ *Easements*. Verify type and location. For example, the easement shown in Exhibit 14 as Exception Item 3 appears to be within the boundaries of parcel 1.

□ *CC&Rs*. Covenants, conditions, and restrictions shown as Exception 4 may require further examination by any lender if new construction or change of use is planned by the purchaser. Note the language deleting any racial restrictions.

□ *Loans*. The existing loan (Item 5) must be dealt with, ordering a beneficiary statement if assumption (formally assuming the obligation) or "subject to" (taking title subject to the loan without a formal agreement with the existing lender) is contemplated. If a new first lien is involved, a demand for payoff must be obtained. In either case the responsibility is usually assumed by the escrowholder based upon information supplied by the broker.

□ *Judgments*. A lien like Item 6 would normally have to be eliminated. In order to accomplish this, a demand would be ordered from the judgment creditor or the legal representative of such creditor. If there is any question concerning the identity of the debtor, e.g., if the debtor merely has a name similar to one of the principals, step D Statement of Identity (below) will clarify the issue.

□ *Holds on Funds*. Item 7 is to remind escrow that under state law, as of January 1, 1990, escrow and title insurance companies cannot disburse deposited funds before the deposit check has cleared the financial institution from which it was issued. Funds may be disbursed the following business day if the deposit is in the form of a cashier's check, certified check or teller's check.

□ *Change of Ownership Report*. Item 8 is a reminder that the change of ownership form (Exhibit 9) is required when an interest in property is conveyed.

Order Statements of Identity Title companies solicit Statement of Identity (or Statement of Information—Exhibit 33) forms from each principal in order to determine if certain general index (G.I.) matters such as judgments, tax liens, insanities, paroles, attorneys in fact, guardianship proceedings, bankruptcies, probates, and other legal matters relating to capacity or financial responsibility affect the principals. A personal signature is required on these forms, since one of the assurances given by the title policy will be protection against forgery.

Demands If existing liens are to be paid off, written request is made to lienholders for their demand for payment in full, together with supportive documents necessary for release.

Review Demands. Notify client upon receipt of the demand for payment. The figures should be reviewed with the seller to determine that the payoff amount is in agreement with the seller's records. Many institutional first trust deeds secure notes that call for prepayment of six months' interest on the unpaid principal balance of the note that they secure. This could amount to a sizable sum; if buyer and seller have agreed to share this cost, their concurrence on the amount is imperative.

Beneficiary Statement If client wishes liens to remain, a written request is made of the present lienholder to provide a beneficiary statement. It indicates the following, which should be reviewed with the client:

☐ The current balance of the lien

☐ Terms of payment

☐ Insurance data, and

☐ Information required for loan assumption and how this assumption will affect loan terms in the future.

Alienation (Acceleration) Clause. Most institutional first trust deeds provide for acceleration of loan maturity upon sale of the property. The reason is simple; the lender wants to be assured that the purchaser is financially qualified to purchase the property. Also it allows the lender to adjust the yield on the existing loan to current lending terms. The Garn-St. Germain Depository Institutions Act of 1982 affirmed the legality of acceleration clauses, with a final assumption window period which expired October 15, 1985.

Acceptance of New Loan Terms. Once new terms have been provided by the current lienholder, the buyer must be consulted to determine if these terms are satisfactory.

New Financing. If new financing were involved, during this period the purchasers would have completed a loan application and provided credit information to the lender, and an appraisal would have been initiated to provide substantiating property valuation for loan purposes. This sequence is illustrated in the Southern California example, below.

Miscellaneous Billings Bills from termite company, roofer, appliance inspection company, home warranty companies, and the like are forwarded to the escrow office at the direction of the client. The escrowholder becomes a clearinghouse for many workers and materialmen who perform corrective or preventive work on the property.

Example

In the structural pest control report, items of both corrective and preventive nature are usually shown; it may be the desire of the parties that only corrective work be performed. It is not unusual for the mechanical system (gas, plumbing, and electrical) to be warranted as in operating order; home warranty programs may allow the parties to obtain an extension of this warranty for one year after purchase.

Loan Documents Received from Lender Work on a new loan may have been under way during the other stages of the process. Upon approval by the lender's loan committee and the terms being communicated and accepted by the buyer, supportive documentation is forwarded to the escrowholder for completion of the closing process.

Initiation of Escrow At this point the Northern California escrowholder prepares the escrow instructions and completes the closing process. This is one of the principal geographic differences.

Real Estate Agent's Role. After the initiation of the escrow the real estate agent is usually involved in communications as to status, delivery of documents, instructions, and the like, and has minimal participation in the closing process.

Amendments to Instructions. In the north, instructions are prepared with almost 100% assurance of closing; few amendments to instructions are necessary because all the terms of closing are known. In the south instructions are prepared earlier in contemplation of closing, and often involve several amendments prior to the receipt of loan documents.

Prepare Escrow Instructions This includes buyer's and seller's instructions and all pertinent documents. Exhibit 15 illustrates unilateral instruction forms for seller and buyer in Northern California. In the case of the seller's instructions, a deed is being delivered in return for money. Conversely, in the buyer's instructions, money is being delivered in return for the deed. Charges are assessed to each side on the basis of their initial agreement. Any specific terms of the transaction that require verification are obtained from the brokers or principals. Note that these instructions, like the bilateral instruction form in Exhibit 6, include general provisions on the reverse.

Receive Signed Instructions Buyer's and seller's instructions and documents are executed and returned with depository funds. In Northern California all documents other than loan documentation may be prepared and signed immediately prior to closing, the receipt of any new loan documents being the final catalyst in the process leading toward recording and consummation of the sale.

Review File The process is reviewed to date to determine that all conditions have been met and all documents properly executed, notarized, and good funds received. This is a preliminary file audit to clear any possible deficiencies concerning documentation or funds prior to consummation of the transaction. If all items appear to be in order, documents are forwarded to the party at the title company who is responsible for recording them, with instructions to hold the documents until advised. Concurrently loan funds are requested from the new lender, if applicable.

Do Policy Writeups This step illustrates the dual role of a title company escrow officer in Northern California. In addition to being responsible for documents and money, the escrow officer establishes the format for the final title policy. (See Chapter 11.)

Funds Received Usually the last stage in the process is the receipt of the balance of funds from the purchaser and/or the purchaser's lender to complete the payment. In rare instances the funds for closing may be obtained from the seller. After clearance of funds, the closing process enters its final stages.

Audit and Recording After sufficient closing moneys have been deposited and the cleared, the closing figures are double checked to determine that the escrow statement is in balance and no additional funds are required. The escrow file is then checked to verify that all required signatures have been obtained and all necessary instructions are in the file. Upon completion of this final audit, recording of documents is requested and the file proceeds to final settlement and disposition.

Closing Statements and Disbursements; Close File Upon confirmation of recording, the closing process is officially consummated. The closing statements are then typed for buyer and seller, checks are cut for payment to the respective parties, and delivery of the funds initiated. As other closing documents such as title insurance policies, recorded documents, and insurance endorsements are received they are forwarded to the appropriate parties. When all have been accounted for, the file on this escrow is closed.

SOUTHERN CALIFORNIA—FOCUS ON FINANCING

Exhibit 16 outlines the sequence of operations in Southern California. The escrow agent becomes involved at a very early stage of the transaction. Communication with the lender begins concurrently with other early stages of the process. The bilateral instructions are more elaborate, containing considerable exculpatory language, as described in Chapter 5, and because they are prepared early they are often subject to amendment. Most of the same steps take place as in Northern California, though in somewhat different order; the following outline looks mainly at the areas of difference.

Prepare Escrow Institutions The instructions (Exhibit 6), together with any required deeds, purchase money encumbrances, and notes, are prepared and delivered to the appropriate parties for signatures. Note that in the bilateral procedure, buyer's and seller's instructions are the same document. Delivery may be by mail, in person, or through an agent representing the respective parties.

Obtain Signed Instructions No contract exists until the instructions are executed by both sides. Upon signature of the respective parties on the instructions and/or their counterparts, the escrow contract is formed. If a loan is involved, two separate activities commence at this point. One concerns getting title in a position for closing; the other concerns processing the loan.

Prepare Title for Closing **Order Title Search.** Now that the instructions are signed and an escrow contract is formed, a preliminary title report (Exhibit 14) is ordered to ascertain the condition of title.

Receive and Review Preliminary Title Report. Upon receipt of the preliminary title report, the matters contained therein must be made to conform with the conditions of transfer. For example, if the property is to be sold free and clear of any liens, the existing deed(s) of trust or other liens must be paid.

Review Liens. The escrowholder requests demands (if any), requests clarification of other liens (if any), and reviews taxes on the preliminary title report. After examination for existing liens, the escrow agent solicits demands for payment with a request for supportive documents. Tax status must also be examined at this point to see if it conforms with the agreement of the parties and satisfies the requirements of any new lender.

Example

Escrow is scheduled for recording on December 15, and the parties agree to show the title subject to the second installment of taxes, requiring only the first installment to be paid. However, the lender requires the second installment to be paid, which becomes the buyer's responsibility if a sale is involved, or the borrower's in a refinancing transaction.

Demands. Escrow receives demands and enters them into the file. Since escrow is already open, care should be given to the payoff amounts shown in the demands, to determine that these amounts conform with the understanding of the parties. Any inordinate prepayment amounts, excessive late charges, or large variance in the principal balance (amounts vary with company policy—over $500 is a good measuring standard) should be brought to the attention of the party responsible for payment of the lien. Approval should be secured prior to payment of such a demand.

Process Financing Parallel with title review and clearance is the process of qualifying the buyer for a new loan or the assumption of existing financing.

Existing Loans **Assumption or "Subject To".** Assumption of an existing loan entails the execution of a formal agreement which may or may not alter the existing loan terms. If the parties take "subject to" the loan, no personal liability is assumed by the parties as under an assumption agreement.

Request Beneficiary Statement. This procedure will initiate action by the existing lender if an acceleration provision (immediate payoff) is applicable. Usually a loan counselor is assigned to provide documentation with the statement, in the form of a factual report prepared by the purchasers to qualify their credit.

Receive Beneficiary Statement and Enter Into File. After reviewing the terms of transfer and the current payment status, the escrow agent determines if prior approval is necessary to record. The lender will request certain information; completion of this documentation may or may not be a condition of transfer. The party responsible for the debt must keep loan payments current during the course of escrow.

New Financing At the same time that the escrow agent is obtaining the information required to clear existing liens, new financing is processed. Concurrent activity allows an orderly closing process. In order for loan approval to proceed with minimum delay, care should be taken to provide complete and accurate information to the new lender.

New Loan Application. Most conventional loan applications are of the uniform Federal Home Loan Mortgage Corporation (Freddie Mac/Fannie Mae) form (Exhibit 17). The VA and FHA forms request similar information. As lenders strive for uniformity in underwriting, the trend is toward verification of employment and assets. Thorough attention to detail and the provision of any required exhibits, such as financial statements, tax forms, or special verifications, will expedite processing. After credit verification and appraisal of the property by the lender, the loan package is ready for the approval process.

Obtain Loan Approval. If the application meets the lender's requirements, approval is obtained from the loan committee and a loan commitment letter is issued. The lender will want to approve the preliminary title report, and indicate the items that are satisfactory.

Example

In reviewing the report shown in Exhibit 14, the lender might approve title as follows:

"Preliminary title report dated October 3, 1986, is approved as to the following:

"Legal Description and items 3 and 4. The title policy will show title vested in Mike Buyer and Shirley Buyer, husband and wife as joint tenants with endorsements 100 and 116 verifying street address as 1325 Sutter St., San Francisco, CA."

This implies, by omission, that the lender requires that assessment item 2 and the liens shown as items 5 and 6 be paid. In addition, if the transaction closes after November 1, item 1 will have to be paid in full.

Review Loan Terms. The escrow agent will examine the loan terms and whether or not they conform with the original escrow instructions, and secure the approval and acceptance of the buyers for any modified loan conditions.

Example

The instructions may indicate that buyer is to obtain a loan for a term of 30 years in the amount of $100,000 at a rate not to exceed $9\frac{1}{2}$% and the fee not to exceed $1\frac{1}{2}$% plus $100. The best obtainable actual loan may be a 30-year loan for $98,000 at $9\frac{3}{4}$% with the loan fee indicated.

Review File The escrow agent determines that all conditions have been met, that all documents have been drawn, and that all documents are correct and available for signature. If the file is found to be complete the file is figured for closing, and any additional signatures required are obtained. Three activities then complete the closing process:

Forward Documents to Title Company. In Southern California, the majority of escrows are processed outside of the title company so the closing documents must be forwarded to the title insurer for examination and recording upon further instructions.

Obtain Funds From Buyer. Based upon closing calculations, funds are requested in an amount that provides sufficient leeway to prevent a need for future requests. In rare instances closing moneys are required from the seller.

Return Loan Documents. Usually the note, the signed disclosure statements, and the instructions are forwarded to the lender. The deed of trust is included with the enclosures forwarded to the title company.

Request Loan Funds If no complication occurs in the three procedures outlined above, funds are requested from the lender, and upon their receipt by the escrow agent or by the title company the escrow is usually in a position to record. From this point on, the closing process parallels Northern California procedure, through auditing, recording, disbursement, and closing.

Regional Differences As the escrow reaches this final stage, northern and southern procedures have a high degree of similarity. Minor variations center around the fact that many escrow activities in the north merge with the title insurance process and therefore certain title insurance functions, such as preparing the policy writeup, are performed by the escrowholder.

Preference. Neither procedure is superior; each has its singular advantages. The bilateral instruction used in Southern California reduces the possibility of disagreement between the parties about the terms of the transaction. The fact that Northern California processors do not prepare instructions until nearly all the terms of the transaction are known reduces the possibility of cancellations as well as the innumerable amendments that occur in Southern California transactions.

Distribution. Due to the increased activity of Southern California based financial institutions, bilateral instructions are making considerable inroads in Northern California.

"EFFECTS OF THE DIFFERENT ESCROW PRACTICES"

The two alternative escrow practices have different effects on both the consumer and on the real estate industry in general. In the paragraphs below, we describe several of these effects.

Effects on Consumers

There appear to be several effects which the different escrow practices have on the consumer. One effect appears to be the relatively higher escrow fee paid by the consumer for a bilateral (front-end) escrow possibly due at least in part to the increased involvement in the transaction of the escrow officer. However, because of regional practices, consumers rarely have the opportunity to select which escrow procedure to use in their transaction and often probably do not know that alternative escrow practices even exist.

Another effect of the different escrow practices on the consumer appears to be the ease with which the transaction closes. When escrow instructions are signed up front, the buyer and seller usually have sufficient time to closely read all the provisions contained in the escrow instructions prior to signing them. In addition, neither party has to be present at closing and both parties can assume escrow *will not* close unless all conditions have been met. However, when the escrow instructions are signed at the end of a transaction, there is somewhat more pressure exerted on both the buyer and the seller to sign the instructions quickly.

A third effect on the consumer relates to the ease with which funds are disbursed should the transaction fall out of escrow. In bilateral (up-front) escrow transactions, the escrow instructions usually contain a clause as to (1) how the funds will be disbursed if the transaction fails, and (2) the amount of the cancellation fee to be paid to the escrow agent. In unilateral (back-end) escrows, the purchase contract (which functions as the escrow instructions until the end of the transaction) generally does not contain a provision for cancellation fees to be paid to the escrow agent. So if the transaction falls out of escrow, the escrow agent has a difficult time collecting a cancellation fee for work completed prior to termination of escrow.

Effects on the Real Estate Industry

One effect on the real estate industry of the different escrow practices is the level of involvement required of a real estate agent. In bilateral (up-front) escrows, the responsibility of making sure all conditions have been met prior to the close of escrow rests primarily with the escrow agent. All amendments to the escrow instructions must be completed by the escrow agent and signed by both parties. With unilateral (back-end) escrows, primary responsibility rests with the real estate broker to ensure that all necessary requirements have been met, and the broker must amend the purchase contract for any changes both parties have agreed on. Thus, real estate agents are relatively more involved in real estate transactions using unilateral (back-end) escrow instructions.

Another effect on the real estate industry relates to the pressure placed on the escrow agent by the lender. Most lenders place a constraint on the length of time for which a loan package is approved. With unilateral (back-end) escrows, the lender exerts pressure on the escrow agent to complete the escrow instructions and have them signed quickly while the loan is still approved. For bilateral (front-end) escrows, the escrow instructions are already completed and signed prior to the buyer obtaining financing, so the lender does not need to exert as much pressure on the escrow agent to complete the escrow instructions.

Average Settlement or Closing Fee on the Sale of a $160,000 Single-family, Residential Home		
	Northern	Southern
Independent Escrow Companies	$464	$792
Title Companies	$351	$635
Real Estate Brokers	$400	$624
Lending Institutions	$425	$729

As shown by in the table above, the highest settlement or closing fees are charged by escrow service providers in Southern California. This may be partially due to the different escrow practices with the two regions and/or the different costs of operating a company in the two regions. In addition, independent escrow companies charge the highest fee in each region, which could be due in part to the additional costs of having to adhere to the requirements of the Escrow Law and regulations promulgated by the Department of Corporations.

Reprinted from *"Analysis of California's Escrow Industry as it Affects Real Estate Licensees,"* a study conducted by Arthur Young under a grant from the California Department of Real Estate, December 31, 1988.

NORTHERN CALIFORNIA PROCESSING

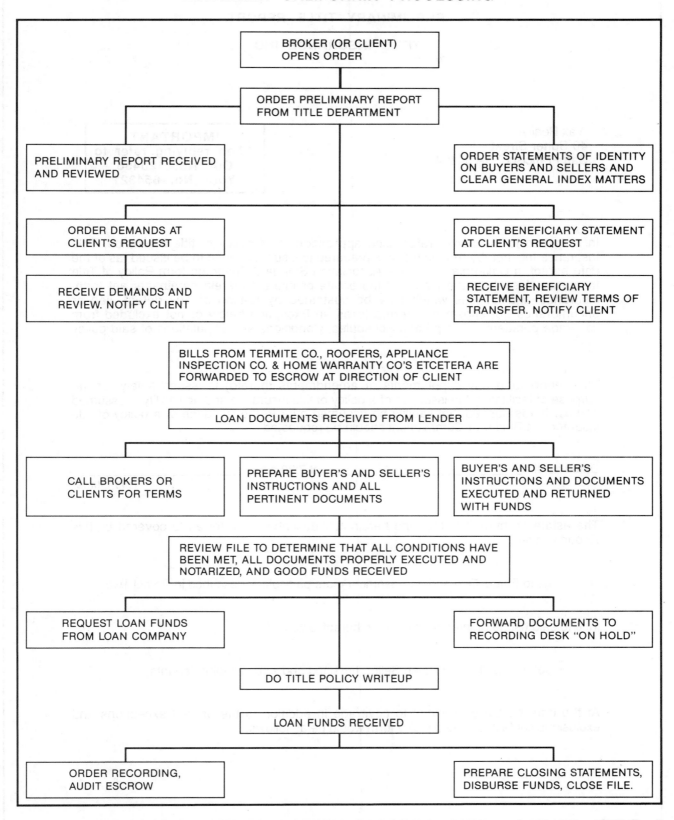

Exhibit 13

PRELIMINARY TITLE REPORT

TITLE INSURANCE INC.

Ajax Realty
40 Sutter Street
San Francisco, CA 94104

| **IMPORTANT** |
| When replying refer to |
| Our No. 123456 |
| Your No. 654321 |

In response to the above referenced application for a policy of title insurance, Title Insurance Inc. hereby reports that it is prepared to issue, or cause to be issued, as of the date hereof, a California Land Title Association Standard Coverage form Policy of Title Insurance describing the land and the estate or interest therein hereinafter set forth, insurance against loss which may be sustained by reason of any defect, lien or encumbrance not shown or referred to as an Exception below or not excluded from coverage pursuant to the printed Schedules, Conditions and Stipulations of said policy form.

This report (and any supplements or amendments thereto) is issued solely for the purpose of facilitating the issuance of a policy of title insurance and no liability is assumed hereby. If it is desired that liability be assumed prior to the issuance of a policy of title insurance, a Binder or Commitment should be requested.

Dated as of _____ , _____ , at 7:30 a.m. _____
Title Officer

The estate or interest in the land hereinafter described or referred to covered by this Report is a fee,

      as to Parcel One and an Easement more particularly described in Parcel Two

Title to said estate or interest at the date hereof is vested in:

      John C. Seller and Helen Seller, husband and wife, as Joint Tenants.

At the date hereof exceptions to coverage in addition to the printed exceptions and exclusions contained in said policy form would be as follows:

Exhibit 14.1

Exceptions   Our Number 123456

1. General and special City and County Taxes for the Fiscal Year 1988-1989, including
    personal property tax, if any:

    Total Amount: $500.00
    First Installment: $250.00
    Personal Property: None
    In the Amount of: None
    Second Installment: $250.00

2. Assessment No.:   456

    Bond No.:   250
    Series No.:   70-3
    For: Sewers
    Became a lien on: December 1, 1983
    Original Amount: $4,000.00
    Unpaid Balance: $1,600.00

    All installments principal have been paid to: January 2, 1988
    Interest has been paid to: July 2, 1988

    a. The lien of supplemental taxes, if any, assessed pursuant to the provisions of
        Chapter 3.5 (commencing with Section 75) of the Revenue and Taxation Code of
        the State of California.

3. An Easement affecting the portion of said land and for the purpose stated herein, and
    incidental purposes:

    In favor of: City and County of San Francisco
    For: Storm Drains
    Recorded: December 10, 1971 in Book B100, page 215, Official Records
    Instrument No: 3000
    Affects: The north 10 feet of Parcel One of said land.

4. Covenants, Conditions, and Restrictions in the Declaration of Restrictions:

    Executed by: First Development Company
    Recorded: December 20, 1972 in Book B103, page 200, Official Records
                            which provide that a violation thereof shall not defeat or render
                            invalid the lien of any Mortgage or Deed of Trust made in Good
                            Faith and For Value. Restrictions, if any, based on race, color,
                            religion, or national origin are deleted.

Exhibit 14.2

5. A Deed of Trust to secure an indebtedness of the amount stated herein:

Dated:	July 1, 1975
Amount:	$30,000.00
Trustor:	John C. Seller and Helen Seller, his wife
Trustee:	Title Insurance and Trust Company, a California Corporation
Beneficiary:	Western Mortgage Company, a California corporation
Recorded:	July 27, 1975 in Book B300, page 17, Official Records
Instrument No:	2750

6. An Abstract of Judgment for the amount herein stated and any other amounts due:

Case No:	1000, Municipal Court, City and Count of San Francisco
Debtor:	John C. Seller
Creditor:	San Francisco Credit Association
Amount:	$2,000.00
Entered:	August 3, 1984
Recorded:	August 25,1984
Document No:	3500

Note: Title of the Vestee herein was acquired by Deed recorded prior to six months from the date hereof.

7. In the event the company receives funds, other than wired funds, from an out of state bank, or receives a draft issued by a California Bank, we will only be able to disburse when funds have been collected by our bank, pursuant to Sections 12413 and 12413.5 of the California Insurance Code.

8. In accordance with Section 480.3 of the Revenue and Taxation Code, it will be necessary to attach the form entitled "Preliminary Change of Ownership Report" to any of those certain instruments which convey an interest (or partial interest) in, or perfect title to, real property prior to recording such instrument.

Exhibit 14.3

The land referred to herein is described as follows:

All of the real property situated in the City and County of San Francisco, State of California, described as follows:

Parcel One:

Lot 34 as shown on the map entitled "Sutter Acres," which map was filed January 1, 1968 in book 15 of Maps, page 73 in the Office of the County Recorder of said City and County.

Parcel Two:

A non-exclusive Easement for ingress and egress, appurtenant to Parcel One above, over the west 10 feet which map was filed January 1, 1968 in book 15 of Maps, page 73 in the Office of the County Recorder of said City and County, as granted to John C. Seller and Helen Seller, his wife, by Deed dated January 1, 1970 recorded January 15, 1974 in book B500, page 295, Official Records.

Exhibit 14.4

PRELIMINARY TITLE REPORTS

ITEM	ENTER	SPECIAL INSTRUCTIONS
Space For Address	Name and address of customer to whom report is to be mailed.	In some counties, reports are not mailed out but are sent directly from the Title Department to the Escrow Department. In that case, nothing will appear in this space.
Our Number	Order number.	Number assigned by title company for reference purpose.
Your Number	Customer's reference number.	Number used by customer for reference purposes.
Dated As Of . . .	Month-day-year and time.	This is the date and time to which the public records have been examined.
Space For Signature	Signature of title officer.	This is the signature of the title officer most familiar with the content of the preliminary report
The Estate . . . Is A:	Fee, easement, leasehold, life estate, as applicable.	This paragraph shows the degree (type) of ownership being reported on. The word "fee" is printed but will be modified to show desired information.
Title . . . Is Vested In:	The name(s) of the owner(s) of the estate or interest being reported on, together with the status and the manner of holding title.	This is the name(s) of the vested owner(s) as it appears of record together with marital status and manner of holding title, e.g., community property, joint tenants, tenants in common, etc.; or corporate status in the case of a corporation; partnership status in the case of a partnership, etc.
At the date Hereof Exceptions . . . As Follows:	Typed exceptions.	Any matters which will be exceptions to policy coverage unless paid, released or otherwise eliminated before policy is issued, are typed here, e.g., taxes, Assessments, easements, rights of way, covenants, conditions and restrictions, deeds of trust, liens, etc.
The Land . . . Described As Follows:	The legal description of the property being reported on.	Legal description must be sufficient to enable land described to be physically located.

Exhibit 14.5

First American Title Guaranty Company

ESCROW INSTRUCTIONS

☐ SELLER'S   ☐ LENDER'S   DATE

Order Number

To: FIRST AMERICAN TITLE GUARANTY COMPANY

I/We hand you herewith

☐ Deed from _____ To _____

☐ Approved copy of Note   ☐ Request for Notices

☐ Approved copy of Deed of Trust   ☐ _____

     which you are authorized to deliver and/or record when you have   ☐ _____

     received for my account the following:

☐ Balance of sale proceeds as per following statement.

☐ Original promissory note corresponding to attached copy.   Interest to commence _____ .

     First payment due _____ .   Maturity date _____ .

☐ Evidence of Fire Insurance

☐ _____

     and when you can issue your standard coverage form policy of title insurance with a liability of $_____

     on the property described as in your preliminary report No. _____ , commonly known as:

     _____ , _____ , California

     showing title vested in _____

Subject to:

1. Printed exceptions and conditions in said policy.
2. ☐ all   ☐ 2nd half   General and special taxes for fiscal year   19   19
3. Assessments and/or bonds not delinquent.
4. Exceptions numbered   as shown in your preliminary title report

     dated _____ , 19_____ issued in connection with the above order number.

Upon consummation of this escrow, you are authorized to disburse in accordance with the attached statement.

As of _____ prorate on the basis of a 30 day month:

☐ Taxes (Based on the most recent information obtainable in the office of the proper taxing authorities.)

☐ Fire Insurance Premiums (If acceptable to Buyer)   ☐ Interest on Existing Loan   ☐ F.H.A. Mortgage Insurance

☐ Credit Existing Loan Trust Funds, if any, to Seller.   ☐ Rents   ☐ Homeowners Assoc. Dues

☐ _____

These instructions are effective until the "time limit date" of _____ 19_____ unless revoked by written demand and authorization satisfactory to you. If no demand for cancellation is made, you will proceed to close this escrow when the principals have complied with the escrow instructions. Incorporated herein and made a part hereof by reference are the "General Provisions" appearing on the reverse side of this page.

Signed _____   Signed _____

Address _____   Address _____

City _____ Phone _____   City _____ Phone _____

Signed _____   Signed _____

Address _____   Address _____

City _____ Phone _____   City _____ Phone _____

Received: _____ , 19

First American Title Guaranty Company

By _____

FORM 4015 (REV. 11/84)

Exhibit 15.1

First American Title Guaranty Company

ESCROW INSTRUCTIONS

☐ BUYER'S   ☐ BORROWER'S   DATE

Order Number

To: FIRST AMERICAN TITLE GUARANTY COMPANY

I/We hand you herewith

☐ Executed loan documents—First loan   ☐ _____
☐ Executed loan documents—Second loan   ☐ _____
☐ Balance of funds to close   ☐ _____
☐ _____   ☐ _____

  which you are authorized to deliver and/or record when you have
  received for my account the following:

☐ Grant Deed
☐ _____
☐ _____

  and when you can issue your standard coverage form policy of title insurance with a liability of $_____
  on the property described as in preliminary report No. _____, commonly known as:
  _____ , _____ , California,
  showing title vested in _____
  _____
  _____
  _____
  _____

Subject to:

1. Printed exceptions and conditions in said policy.
2. ☐ all ☐ 2nd half   General and special taxes for fiscal year 19   19
3. Assessments and/or bonds not delinquent.
4. Exceptions numbered   as shown in your preliminary title report
    dated _____ , 19___ issued in connection with the above order number.

Upon consummation of this escrow, you are authorized to disburse in accordance with the following statement.

As of _____ prorate on the basis of a 30 day month:
☐ Taxes (Based on the most recent information obtainable in the office of the proper taxing authorities.)
☐ Fire Insurance Premiums (If acceptable to Buyer)   ☐ Interest on Existing Loan   ☐ F.H.A. Mortgage Insurance
☐ Credit Existing Loan Trust Funds, if any, to Seller.   ☐ Rents   ☐ Homeowner's Assoc. Dues
☐ _____

These instructions are effective until the "time limit date" of _____ 19_____ unless revoked by written demand
and authorization satisfactory to you. If no demand for cancellation is made, you will proceed to close this escrow when the principals
have complied with the escrow instructions. Incorporated herein and made a part hereof by reference are the "General Provisions"
appearing on the reverse side of this page.

Signed _____   Signed _____

Address _____   Address _____

City _____ Phone _____   City _____ Phone _____

Signed _____   Signed _____

Address _____   Address _____

City _____ Phone _____   City _____ Phone _____

Received: 19
First American Title Guaranty Company

By _____

FORM 4014

Exhibit 15.2

GENERAL PROVISIONS

DEFINITION

The expression "close of escrow" means the date on which the instruments referred to herein are filed for record. The letters "COE" wherever used in these instructions mean 'close of escrow'.

WRITTEN INSTRUCTIONS

Any amendments of or supplements to any instructions affecting this escrow must be in writing. I will hand you any funds and instruments required to complete this escrow. These escrow instructions constitute the entire escrow between the escrow holder and the principals hereto.

Upon receipt of any conflicting instructions, you are to take no further action in connection with this escrow until consistent instructions are received from the principals or final order of a court of competent jurisdiction is issued.

INSURANCE ENDORSEMENTS

Where applicable, you are to request necessary endorsements to fire insurance policies from agent and deliver said policies and endorsements to the principals entitled hereto. In all acts in this escrow relating to fire insurance you shall be fully protected in assuming that each policy is in force and that the necessary premium therefor has been paid.

AUTHORIZATION TO FURNISH COPIES

You are instructed to furnish copies of all instructions, amendments, and statements to any broker, lender, or attorney identified with this transaction, upon request.

FEES AND CHARGES

The principals hereto agree to pay any charges, billings, advances, and expenses, including cancellation fees, that are properly chargeable to them. The principals herein agree that in the event First American Title Guaranty Company agrees to "hold funds" for any purpose, there may be a "service charge" of $25.00 per calendar month. Said service charge may be charged from said funds for each and every calendar month or any portion thereof during which said funds are held.

DEPOSITS AND DISBURSEMENTS

All funds received in this escrow shall be deposited in one or more of your general escrow accounts with any bank or banks doing business in the State of California. All disbursements shall be made by your check. You are authorized not to close escrow or disburse until "good funds" have been confirmed in escrow.

CANCELLATION

Any principal instructing you to cancel this escrow shall file written notice of cancellation in your office. You shall thereupon notify each of the other principals to this escrow. Unless written objection to cancellation is filed in your office by a principal within ten (10) days after date of such notification, you are authorized to comply with such notice and demand payment of your cancellation charges as provided in this agreement. If written objection is filed, you are authorized to hold all money and instruments in this escrow and take no further action until otherwise directed, either by the principal's mutual written instructions, or final order of a court of competent jurisdiction.

INTERPLEADER

The principals hereto acknowledge that you, as escrow holder, have the absolute right at your election to file an action in interpleader requiring the principals to answer and litigate their several claims and rights among themselves. You are authorized to deposit all documents and funds held in this escrow with the clerk of the court. In the event such action is filed, the principals jointly and severally agree to pay your cancellation charges, costs, expenses, and reasonable attorney's fees which you are required to expend or incur in such interpleader action — the amount thereof to be fixed and judgement therefor to be rendered by the court.

TIME

If there is no action taken on this escrow within six (6) months after the "time limit date" as set forth in the escrow instructions or written extension(s) thereof, your agency obligation shall terminate at your option and all documents, monies, or other items held by you shall be returned to the principals depositing same.

Exhibit 15.3

SOUTHERN CALIFORNIA PROCESSING

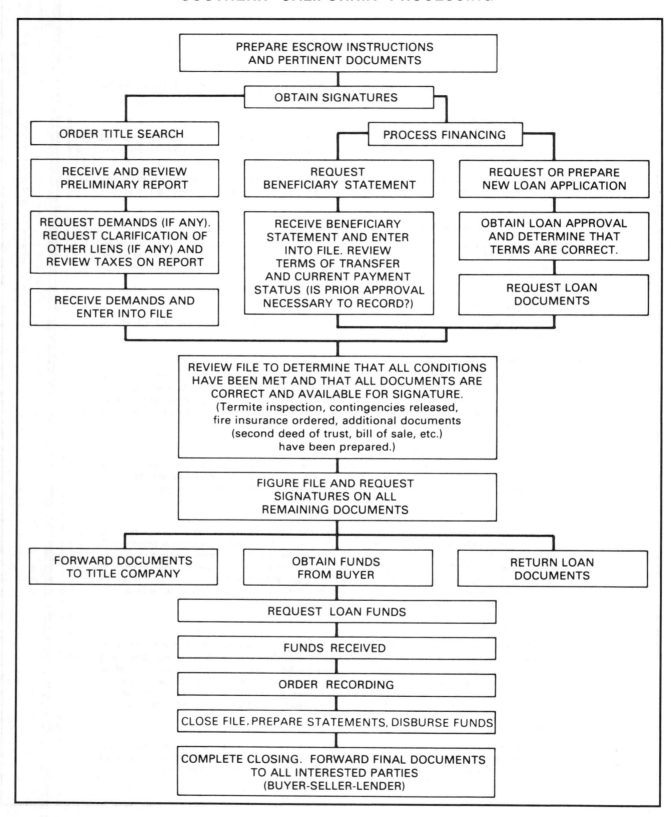

PREPARE ESCROW INSTRUCTIONS AND PERTINENT DOCUMENTS

OBTAIN SIGNATURES

ORDER TITLE SEARCH

PROCESS FINANCING

RECEIVE AND REVIEW PRELIMINARY REPORT

REQUEST BENEFICIARY STATEMENT

REQUEST OR PREPARE NEW LOAN APPLICATION

REQUEST DEMANDS (IF ANY). REQUEST CLARIFICATION OF OTHER LIENS (IF ANY) AND REVIEW TAXES ON REPORT

RECEIVE BENEFICIARY STATEMENT AND ENTER INTO FILE. REVIEW TERMS OF TRANSFER AND CURRENT PAYMENT STATUS (IS PRIOR APPROVAL NECESSARY TO RECORD?)

OBTAIN LOAN APPROVAL AND DETERMINE THAT TERMS ARE CORRECT.

RECEIVE DEMANDS AND ENTER INTO FILE

REQUEST LOAN DOCUMENTS

REVIEW FILE TO DETERMINE THAT ALL CONDITIONS HAVE BEEN MET AND THAT ALL DOCUMENTS ARE CORRECT AND AVAILABLE FOR SIGNATURE. (Termite inspection, contingencies released, fire insurance ordered, additional documents (second deed of trust, bill of sale, etc.) have been prepared.)

FIGURE FILE AND REQUEST SIGNATURES ON ALL REMAINING DOCUMENTS

FORWARD DOCUMENTS TO TITLE COMPANY

OBTAIN FUNDS FROM BUYER

RETURN LOAN DOCUMENTS

REQUEST LOAN FUNDS

FUNDS RECEIVED

ORDER RECORDING

CLOSE FILE, PREPARE STATEMENTS, DISBURSE FUNDS

COMPLETE CLOSING. FORWARD FINAL DOCUMENTS TO ALL INTERESTED PARTIES (BUYER-SELLER-LENDER)

Exhibit 16

RESIDENTIAL LOAN APPLICATION

MORTGAGE APPLIED FOR	☐ Conventional ☑ ☐ VA ☐	☐ FHA	Amount $	Interest Rate %	No. of Months	Monthly Payment Principal & Interest $	Escrow/Impounds (to be collected monthly) ☐ Taxes ☐ Hazard Ins. ☐ Mtg. Ins. ☐ _____

Prepayment Option

<table>
<tr><td rowspan="11">SUBJECT PROPERTY</td></tr>
<tr><td colspan="6">Property Street Address   City   County   State   Zip   No. Units</td></tr>
<tr><td colspan="6">Legal Description (Attach description if necessary)   Year Built</td></tr>
<tr><td colspan="6">Purpose of Loan: ☐ Purchase   ☐ Construction-Permanent   ☐ Construction   ☐ Refinance   ☐ Other (Explain)</td></tr>
<tr><td colspan="6">Complete this line if Construction-Permanent or Construction Loan ☑   Lot Value Data   Original Cost   Present Value (a)   Cost of Imps. (b)   Total (a + b)   ENTER TOTAL AS PURCHASE PRICE IN DETAILS OF PURCHASE.</td></tr>
<tr><td colspan="6">Year Acquired ____ $ ____ $ ____ $ ____ $ ____</td></tr>
<tr><td colspan="6">Complete this line if a Refinance Loan   Purpose of Refinance   Describe Improvements [ ] made [ ] to be made</td></tr>
<tr><td colspan="6">Year Acquired | Original Cost | Amt. Existing Liens   Cost: $</td></tr>
<tr><td colspan="6">$ $</td></tr>
<tr><td colspan="6">Title Will Be Held In What Name(s)   Manner In Which Title Will Be Held</td></tr>
<tr><td colspan="6">Source of Down Payment and Settlement Charges</td></tr>
</table>

This application is designed to be completed by the borrower(s) with the lender's assistance. The Co-Borrower Section and all other Co-Borrower questions must be completed and the appropriate box(es) checked if ☐ another person will be jointly obligated with the Borrower on the loan, or ☐ the Borrower is relying on income from alimony, child support or separate maintenance or on the income or assets of another person as a basis for repayment of the loan, or ☐ the Borrower is married and resides, or the property is located, in a community property state.

BORROWER				CO-BORROWER			
Name		Age	School Yrs ____	Name		Age	School Yrs ____
Present Address No. Years ____ ☐ Own ☐ Rent				Present Address No. Years ____ ☐ Own ☐ Rent			
Street				Street			
City/State/Zip				City/State/Zip			
Former address if less than 2 years at present address				Former address if less than 2 years at present address			
Street				Street			
City/State/Zip				City/State/Zip			
Years at former address ☐ Own ☐ Rent				Years at former address ☐ Own ☐ Rent			
Marital Status ☐ Married ☐ Separated ☐ Unmarried (incl. single, divorced, widowed)		DEPENDENTS OTHER THAN LISTED BY CO BORROWER NO / AGES		Marital Status ☐ Married ☐ Separated ☐ Unmarried (incl. single, divorced, widowed)		DEPENDENTS OTHER THAN LISTED BY BORROWER NO / AGES	
Name and Address of Employer		Years employed in this line of work or profession? ____ years Years on this job ____ ☐ Self Employed*		Name and Address of Employer		Years employed in this line of work or profession? ____ years Years on this job ____ ☐ Self Employed*	
Position/Title	Type of Business			Position/Title	Type of Business		
Social Security Number***	Home Phone	Business Phone		Social Security Number***	Home Phone	Business Phone	

GROSS MONTHLY INCOME				MONTHLY HOUSING EXPENSE**			DETAILS OF PURCHASE	
Item	Borrower	Co-Borrower	Total		PRESENT	PROPOSED	Do Not Complete If Refinance	
Base Empl. Income	$	$	$	Rent	$	$	a. Purchase Price	$
Overtime				First Mortgage (P&I)		$	b. Total Closing Costs (Est.)	
Bonuses				Other Financing (P&I)			c. Prepaid Escrows (Est.)	
Commissions				Hazard Insurance			d. Total (a + b + c)	$
Dividends/Interest				Real Estate Taxes			e. Amount This Mortgage	( )
Net Rental Income				Mortgage Insurance			f. Other Financing	( )
Other† (Before completing, see notice under Describe Other Income below.)				Homeowner Assn. Dues			g. Other Equity	( )
				Other:			h. Amount of Cash Deposit	( )
				Total Monthly Pmt.	$	$	i. Closing Costs Paid by Seller	( )
				Utilities			j. Cash Reqd. For Closing (Est.)	$
Total	$	$	$	Total	$	$		

DESCRIBE OTHER INCOME		
▷ B – Borrower C – Co-Borrower	NOTICE: † Alimony, child support, or separate maintenance income need not be revealed if the Borrower or Co-Borrower does not choose to have it considered as a basis for repaying this loan.	Monthly Amount $

IF EMPLOYED IN CURRENT POSITION FOR LESS THAN TWO YEARS COMPLETE THE FOLLOWING

B/C	Previous Employer/School	City/State	Type of Business	Position/Title	Dates From/To	Monthly Income
						$

THESE QUESTIONS APPLY TO BOTH BORROWER AND CO-BORROWER

If a "yes" answer is given to a question in this column, explain on an attached sheet.	Borrower Yes or No	Co-Borrower Yes or No		Borrower Yes or No	Co-Borrower Yes or No
Have you any outstanding judgments? In the last 7 years, have you been declared bankrupt?	____	____	Are you a U.S. citizen?	____	____
Have you had property foreclosed upon or given title or deed in lieu thereof?	____	____	If "no," are you a resident alien?	____	____
Are you a co-maker or endorser on a note?	____	____	If "no," are you a non-resident alien?	____	____
Are you a party in a law suit?	____	____	Explain Other Financing or Other Equity (if any).		
Are you obligated to pay alimony, child support, or separate maintenance?	____	____			
Is any part of the down payment borrowed?	____	____			

*FHLMC/FNMA requires business credit report, signed Federal Income Tax returns for last two years; and if available, audited Profit and Loss Statement plus balance sheet for same period.
**All Present Monthly Housing Expenses of Borrower and Co-Borrower should be listed on a combined basis.   Conforms to FHLMC 65 and FNMA 1003. Rev. 10/86
***Optional for FHLMC

Exhibit 17.1

This Statement and any applicable supporting schedules may be completed jointly by both married and unmarried co-borrowers if their assets and liabilities are sufficiently joined so that the Statement can be meaningfully and fairly presented on a combined basis; otherwise separate Statements and Schedules are required (FHLMC 65A/FNMA 1003A). If the co-borrower section was completed about a spouse, this statement and supporting schedules must be completed about that spouse also. ☐ Completed Jointly   ☐ Not Completed Jointly

ASSETS		LIABILITIES AND PLEDGED ASSETS			
Indicate by (*) those liabilities or pledged assets which will be satisfied upon sale of real estate owned or upon refinancing of subject property.					
Description	Cash or Market Value	Creditors' Name, Address and Account Number	Acct. Name if Not Borrower's	Mo. Pmt. and Mos. left to pay	Unpaid Balance
Cash Deposit Toward Purchase Held By	$	Installment Debts (include "revolving" charge accts)		$ Pmt./Mos.	$
				/	
Checking and Savings Accounts (Show Names of Institutions/Acct. Nos.)				/	
				/	
Stocks and Bonds (No./Description)				/	
				/	
Life Insurance Net Cash Value Face Amount ($)		Other Debts Including Stock Pledges		/	
SUBTOTAL LIQUID ASSETS	$				
Real Estate Owned (Enter Market Value from Schedule of Real Estate Owned)		Real Estate Loans			
Vested Interest in Retirement Fund					
Net Worth of Business Owned (ATTACH FINANCIAL STATEMENT)					
Automobiles (Make and Year)		Automobile Loans		/	
Furniture and Personal Property		Alimony, Child Support and Separate Maintenance Payments Owed To		/	
Other Assets (Itemize)					
		TOTAL MONTHLY PAYMENTS		$	
TOTAL ASSETS	A $	NET WORTH (A minus B) $		TOTAL LIABILITIES	B $

SCHEDULE OF REAL ESTATE OWNED (If Additional Properties Owned Attach Separate Schedule)

Address of Property (Indicate S if Sold, PS if Pending Sale or R if Rental being held for income)	◇	Type of Property	Present Market Value	Amount of Mortgages & Liens	Gross Rental Income	Mortgage Payments	Taxes, Ins. Maintenance and Misc.	Net Rental Income
			$	$	$	$	$	$
TOTALS →			$	$	$	$	$	$

LIST PREVIOUS CREDIT REFERENCES

◇ B - Borrower C – Co-Borrower	Creditor's Name and Address	Account Number	Purpose	Highest Balance	Date Paid
				$	

List any additional names under which credit has previously been received _____

AGREEMENT: The undersigned applies for the loan indicated in this application to be secured by a first mortgage or deed of trust on the property described herein, and represents that the property will not be used for any illegal or restricted purpose, and that all statements made in this application are true and are made for the purpose of obtaining the loan. Verification may be obtained from any source named in this application. The original or a copy of this application will be retained by the lender, even if the loan is not granted.   The undersigned ☐ intend or ☐ do not intend to occupy the property as their primary residence.

I/we fully understand that it is a federal crime punishable by fine or imprisonment, or both, to knowingly make any false statements concerning any of the above facts as applicable under the provisions of Title 18, United States Code, Section 1014.

_____ Date _____   _____ Date _____
Borrower's Signature   Co-Borrower's Signature

INFORMATION FOR GOVERNMENT MONITORING PURPOSES

The following information is requested by the Federal Government for certain types of loans related to a dwelling, in order to monitor the lender's compliance with equal credit opportunity and fair housing laws. You are not required to furnish this information, but are encouraged to do so. The law provides that a lender may neither discriminate on the basis of this information, nor on whether you choose to furnish it. However, if you choose not to furnish it, under Federal regulations this lender is required to note race and sex on the basis of visual observation or surname. If you not wish to furnish the above information, please check the box below. [Lender must review the above material to assure that the disclosures satisfy all requirements to which the Lender is subject under applicable state law for the particular type of loan applied for.]

Borrower: ☐ I do not wish to furnish this information   Co-Borrower: ☐ I do not wish to furnish this information
Race/National Origin: Race/National Origin:
☐ American Indian, Alaskan Native ☐ Asian, Pacific Islander   ☐ American Indian, Alaskan Native ☐ Asian, Pacific Islander
☐ Black ☐ Hispanic ☐ White   ☐ Black ☐ Hispanic ☐ White
☐ Other (Specify): _____   ☐ Other (Specify): _____
Sex: ☐ Female ☐ Male   Sex: ☐ Female ☐ Male

TO BE COMPLETED BY INTERVIEWER

This application was taken by:
face to face interview
by mail
by telephone

Interviewer	Name of Interviewer's Employer
Interviewer's Phone Number	Address of Interviewer's Employer

Conforms to FHLMC 65 and FNMA 1003   Rev. 10/86   **REVERSE**

Exhibit 17.2

Quiz Chapter 6

1. In Southern California escrow instructions are prepared:

   √(A) In bilateral form
   (B) In unilateral form
   (C) Sequentially
   (D) Under duress

2. In Northern California escrow instructions are prepared:

   (A) In bilateral form
   (B) In unilateral form
   (C) Sequentially
   (D) Under duress

3. Real estate brokers are more active in the closing process in:

   (A) Northern California
   (B) Southern California
   (C) Hawaii
   (D) No difference

4. A dominant tenement is:

   (A) The biggest home on the block
   (B) The main tenant in a building
   (C) The property served by an appurtenant easement
   (D) An overbearing landlord

5. Compared to the deposit receipt, the vesting shown on the title report:

   (A) Always agrees
   (B) Must agree
   (C) Has no relation
   (D) Must be resolved if it does not agree

6. An encumbrance:

   (A) Refers to liens only
   (B) Refers to any burden or title exception
   (C) Refers to easements only
   (D) Refers to covenants, conditions, and restrictions only

7. A statement of identity:

   (A) Is an invasion of the principals' privacy
   (B) Is used to prosecute principals
   (C) Is used by the title insurer to properly identify principals
   (D) Is used to verify that the principals are incompetent

8. A demand is:

   (A) A written statement indicating the conditions under which an existing loan can be paid in full
   (B) A statement to escrow which prevents its closing
   (C) A threat to the escrow officer
   (D) A statement of loan condition from an existing lender, when a loan is being assumed

9. A beneficiary statement is:

   (A) A written statement indicating the conditions under which an existing loan can be paid in full
   (B) A statement to escrow which prevents its closing
   (C) A threat to the escrow officer
   √(D) A statement of loan condition from an existing lender, when a loan is being assumed

10. Loan processing involves:

   (A) Arranging assumption or payoff
   (B) Requesting beneficiary statements
   (C) Qualifying the borrower
   (D) All of the above

Chapter 7
Compliance with Instructions— Title and Consideration

PREVIEW

Role of Instructions

Title: The Grant Deed

Notes

Deeds of Trust

Consideration: The Closing Statement

ROLE OF INSTRUCTIONS

The escrow instructions are the basic document guiding the sale, loan, or other transaction to an orderly close. The escrowholder follows these instructions to the letter, step by step, never losing sight of the underlying purpose and nature of the transaction.

Directed by Principal The escrowholder does not direct the transaction, the principals do. The escrow officer reacts to instructions which represent the mutual agreement of the parties.

Disposition of Property Escrow instructions concern themselves with the disposition and/or hypothecation (pledging) of real or personal property. In the context of this text, personal property is usually incidental to a real estate transaction.

Two Objects There are two aspects to a majority of escrow transactions: *title* and *consideration*. The first requires preparation of the instruments of transfer and/or hypothecation, and the second involves allocation of proceeds together with the proper accounting thereof.

Documents of Title Three basic documents serve as the focal point of sale and loan escrows: the grant deed, note, and deed of trust. Preparation of each will be discussed in detail. There are other documents that are the subject of escrows such as security agreements, financing statements, bills of sale, disclosure forms (more fully discussed in Chapter 13), and documents required in specialized escrows (outlined in Chapter 15), but the three discussed here are basic.

TITLE: THE GRANT DEED

The principal document of transfer in a real estate transaction is a deed. Typical escrow instructions (Exhibits 6, 15) state that the seller will provide "any instruments or funds" necessary to consummate the transaction. This authorizes the escrowholder to prepare a deed effecting transfer. The essential elements of a deed (Exhibits 18 and 19) relate to form and content, delivery and acceptance, and recording.

Form and Content

Written Instrument. The Statute of Frauds requires deeds to be in writing.

Competent Grantor. This means a party who has the capacity to convey without necessity for a court appointed representative.

Operative Words of Conveyance. The instrument, whether deed, note, or trust deed, requires some form of language creating a moving force in the document. Here the operative words are "Grant(s) to . . . ," describing the objective of the document.

Grantee Capable of Acquiring Title. As with the grantor, rules apply concerning competency and/or capacity of the grantee. However, they are less strict; for example, a minor may acquire title to property without need for guardianship.

Property to be Conveyed. A deed must contain a sufficient and adequate description (e.g., a legal description) of the property and all property interests to be transferred.

Due Execution by the Grantor. The party conveying interest must execute (sign) in the manner title is held.

☐ *Variant Names.* Any variation should be covered by a grantor caption like "John P. Jones and Mathilda Jones, who acquired title as John Paul Jones and Mathilda M. Jones."

☐ *Fictitious Persons.* In the case of legal entities like corporations, partnerships, trusts, joint ventures and so forth, special consideration must be given to proper execution by the appropriate representatives, together with documentation supporting the individual signatories' capacity to sign on behalf of the entity.

☐ *Vesting.* Strict compliance with the escrow instructions concerning the names of the grantor(s) and grantee(s) and how title is to be held is of extreme importance. Community property does not mean joint tenancy and vice versa. Escrowholders under no circumstances should advise clients concerning methods of holding title, as mode of taking title may affect tax status and giving such advice may be considered practice of law.

Delivery and Acceptance

Delivery to Grantee. The preceding items complete the validity of the deed on paper, but delivery and acceptance are also essential for the deed to become effective, that is, to move title.

☐ Physical possession of the deed by the grantee is presumptive evidence of delivery.

☐ The deed in the possession of the grantor presumes non-delivery.

☐ Recordation is a presumption of delivery to the grantee although conflicting presumptions may prevail if the recorded deed is in the possession of the grantor. Each of these presumptions is rebuttable.

Acceptance. Normally recordation would also be presumed to effect acceptance. In addition, grants to minors or incompetents may have presumed acceptance if a beneficial conveyance is created by the grant. In the case of governmental units, there must be a positive act of acceptance on the part of the agency.

Recording

The items listed under content and delivery represent the elements essential for a valid and effective deed which would be operative between the parties. In order for the parties' rights to be protected, however, the deed must be recorded. Recording confers constructive notice of the existence and contents of this document. Acknowledgment of all executing parties is required for recording. Recording also triggers certain tax-related requirements. Civil Code Section 1189 is modified, effective January 1, 1991, to establish a uniform acknowledgment form.

Assessor's Parcel Number. This identification is required the by county recorder, as an aid in updating the assessor's rolls for tax collection purposes.

Documentary Transfer Tax. The amount depends on the amount of equity conveyed in the transaction. Documentary transfer tax is based upon $.55 per $500 of equity or fraction thereof. Thus, a $100,000 sale results in a transfer tax liability of $110.

☐ Some cities in California impose further documentary tax requirements.

☐ Leases are also subject to imposition of a documentary tax.

Change of Ownership Report. This report (Exhibit 9) is required any time an instrument affecting property ownership is recorded. This not only applies to conveyances, but also to any memorandum of lease on real property. Failure to provide this form with the conveyance can result in a penalty for late filing.

Special Interests. Deeds may be drawn to convey any type of interest, burden or encumbrance, in addition to fee simple title. For example:

☐ Easements appurtenant to the fee parcel being conveyed

☐ Rights of the grantor under leasehold interest (reciprocal or otherwise) created by prior contractual arrangement

☐ Water rights involved in a mutually controlled pumping plant in agricultural areas

☐ Mineral rights

☐ Riparian rights

☐ Other rights incidental or appurtenant to the parcel being conveyed

☐ Covenants, conditions and restrictions imposed by incorporating general plan restrictions

☐ Rights that may be reserved by the grantor as part of the transfer process.

Grant Deed When the word "grant" is used in any conveyance of a fee simple estate (unless excluded or restrained by an express term), it implies certain covenants on the part of the grantor:

☐ That the *grantor* has not already conveyed the same estate or any interest therein to any other person;

☐ That the estate is free from undisclosed encumbrances made by the *grantor*, or any person claiming under grantor.

Thus, a grant deed by a private party, which is the form commonly used, is presumed by law to convey a fee simple title (i.e., absolute ownership) unless it appears from the wording of the deed itself that a lesser estate was intended. Moreover if a grantor subsequently acquires any title or claim of title to the real property which grantor had purported to grant in fee simple, that after-acquired title passes by operation of law to the grantee or grantee's successors, ordinarily. (Exhibit 18)

Interspousal Transfer A modified grand deed is commonly used for an interspousal transfer in order to make it clear that the transfer is not subject to the documentary transfer tax. This deed is usually labeled Interspousal Transfer Grant Deed. (Exhibit 19)

NOTES

Most transfers of real property involve the *hypothecation* of real estate, usually evidenced with a note secured by a deed of trust. A note (Exhibit 20) serves as an evidence of indebtedness and represents an amount due to the previous owner, an institutional lender, or a private financing source. The note and deed of trust securing it are interrelated and, in many cases, require the same or similar language to be effective.

Types of Notes   Escrowholders are now faced with a variety of loan products from institutional lenders as well as sources such as Federal Home Loan Mortgage Corporation (Freddie Mac) and Federal National Mortgage Association (FNMA).

Fixed Payment Amortized Note. This traditional instrument provides for payment in full by means of a series of equal payments of principal and interest over a fixed period of time (commonly 30 years) Today it has been augmented with various forms of alternative financing.

Graduated Payment Notes. Low payments graduate in stair steps, over usually the first five years, to the eventual payment level.

Adjustable Rate Notes or Mortgages—ARMs. Riders lay down the ground rules concerning the index used to calculate the rate, payment ceilings, rate ceilings, dates that rate and/or payment will change, how the change is calculated and other pertinent disclosure information.

Other. Specialized notes may be a combination or modification of these.

Standard Forms   In the case of FNMA/FHLMC, VA or FHA notes, the closer is dealing with standard forms. In many cases documentation services using word processing programs can work from a memo sheet or "laundry list" (see Chapter 12) to prepare a complete set of documentation.

Specialized Preparation   Where principals have special requirements relating to conditions within the note and deed of trust, the preparer may address some or all of the following issues. With the abrogation of the state bar treaty, whether or not a note may be prepared by escrow personnel is somewhat moot. However, escrowholders should continue to adhere to the basic intent of the bar agreement, and avoid anything which might be interpreted as practice of law.

Type of Lender. Who is the lender/client?

☐ An institution (under what regulatory?)

☐ An individual?

☐ Does it fall within the loan categories of the Business and Professions Code involving real estate licensees?

☐ Is it a loan falling within the purview of state usury law or is it just purchase money to a seller or other private-party loan?

Terms. Loan terms must be clarified.

☐ *Principal.* Is there to be one note for the principal amount or a combination of notes secured by one deed of trust?

□ *Interest Rate.* Fixed or variable? If the rate is variable, do decisions have to be made regarding 1) the time elements involved in rate change? 2) the appropriate index? 3) interest to be deferred and/or added to the principal payment? 4) any unusual methods of accrual, etc.?

□ *Payments—Fixed or Variable.* Or a combination of the two, as in the FHA 245 and other graduated payment plans in which the monthly payment increases $7\frac{1}{2}\%$ annually for the first five years of the loan. In today's market a fixed monthly payment may be insufficient to cover interest. If this is the case, the note must state how the deferred interest is to be accrued and how future payments are to be applied.

□ *Balloon Payments.* Considerable care should be exercised with balloon payments, particularly in those loans arranged under the Business and Professions Code sections applying to licensee-arranged loans, since no balloon payment is allowed until the 73rd month on a single-family, owner-occupied residence. Under current California law, holders of indebtedness containing a balloon payment must remind payors no sooner than 150 days nor later than 90 days from maturity that the loan is due.

□ *Place of Payment.* If a location outside of the state of California is described as the place of payment, the usury laws of that state may apply to the note.

□ *Late Charges.* A myriad of regulations apply in this area, dependent upon the institutional regulator or applicable sections of the Business and Professions Code.

□ *Prepayment Penalty.* As with late charges, applicable regulations must be determined and complied with.

□ *Alienation Clauses.* These so-called acceleration clauses must be contained in both the deed of trust and the note secured thereby. The nature and composition of these recitals is complex. An escrowholder who is not a lawyer should never volunteer a "sample" clause.

□ *Note Selection.* Straight notes should be used in an "interest only" situation, while an installment note, interest included, should be used where principal is amortized. There may be cases where a level monthly payment of principal is required. In those cases, an installment interest extra note could be used.

□ *Identification of Collateral.* Sometimes more than one property is used to secure the obligation. In this case, an appropriate notation should be made on the note that it is collateralized by two separate deeds of trust. When one deals in metes and bounds descriptions involving two or more contiguous parcels, a contiguity endorsement for the lender's title policy should be considered.

Other Special Provisions. Many individual lenders want to protect their tax positions in installment sales and may restrict principal reductions in the note. Certain lenders, such as insurance companies, may prevent prepayment entirely for a specified period through the use of a "lock-in" clause. Other special provisions may include partial release clauses for subdivision property, additional loan advances, extension of loan accommodation, willingness to subordinate in the future, renegotiation of rates at specific intervals, and so on.

- □ *Subdivisions*. Under the Subdivided Lands Act and the Subdivision Map Act:

  - ◻ Foreclosure of a lien on more than four lots in a subdivision may require the issuance of a new white report from the Department of Real Estate, and

  - ◻ If a deed of trust is created dividing an existing lot, it may be a violation of the Subdivision Map Act creating an illegal division of the parcel without filing of a parcel map, record of survey, or tract map for such division.

- □ *Stated Beneficiary*. Recently, due to certain legislation involving community real property, trustees have required an assignment by the non-named spouse in situations where a married person is described holding the note "as separate property"

DEEDS OF TRUST

Uniformity has also crept into the documentation of deeds of trust. A discussion of pertinent provisions of the FNMA/FHLMC uniform deed of trust will cover most types. A sample of this form is shown in Exhibit 21. The operative words are "irreversibly grants and conveys to trustee, in trust, with power of sale." Specific numbered provisions cover a variety of rights and obligations of the parties.

Contents **Payment of Principal and Interest.** This provision relates the deed of trust to the note it secures.

Funds for Taxes and Insurance. The trust deed allows the lender to impound payment for these items.

Application of Payments. The trust deed contains a reaffirmation of note provisions on this subject.

Charges and Liens. It is the responsibility of borrower to pay obligations set forth in paragraph 2, which might place the lender's position in jeopardy if left unpaid.

Hazard Insurance. The trust deed states the requirements for property insurance coverage and application of insurance proceeds.

Preservation and Maintenance of Property. Compliance with lease provisions may also be included. This is the so-called "waste" provision as a cause of default, which was supported in the *Wellenkamp* decision of 1978.

Protection of Lender's Security. The lender is able to take action upon borrower's nonperformance.

Inspection. Lender has reasonable access to the property for this purpose.

Condemnation. The trust deed outlines disposition of funds in case of eminent domain proceedings.

Borrower Not Released. Forbearance by the lender is not a waiver. This means that although the lender may provide certain concessions during the life of the trust, the borrower is not entitled to expect the same concessions in the future.

Successors and Assigns. Language regarding joint and several liability and co-signers extends borrower's obligation to all successors in interest, and lender's rights to its successors in interest.

Loan Charges. Compliance with legal limits is stated.

Legislation Affecting Lender's Rights. Language in the trust deed provides for an acceleration clause in case the agreement is invalidated.

Notice. Mailing addresses of borrower and lender are stated.

Governing Law; Severability. The laws of the state supersede any conflicting provisions of the uniform document.

Borrower's Copy. This is a consumer protection provision.

Transfer of the Property. Potential acceleration upon transfer is addressed. If assumption is allowed, original trustor(s) would still be secondarily liable for the indebtedness.

Borrower's Right to Reinstate. The instrument outlines methods to cure default.

Acceleration, Remedies (Non-Uniform Covenants). This section discusses matters constituting default and the right to pursue foreclosure under the provisions of § 2924 of the Civil Code.

Assignment of Rents. This section allows the lender in a default or abandonment situation to appoint a receiver and collect rents from the occupants to protect its position.

Reconveyance. Conditions for release of the deed of trust are outlined.

Substitute Trustee. A new trustee may be substituted at lender option.

Request for Notices. Notification of default must be mailed to the borrower at the property address.

Riders. Provision may be made for special conditions such as adjustable rates or condominium ownership. (FNMA/FHLMC uniform instruments are available.)

Statement of Obligation. This clause allows for collection of a fee for rendering a beneficiary's statement.

Precautions Two important caveats apply to deeds of trust.

Misuse of Document. A document is not always used in its conventional form of application. For example, if John Jones deeds property to James Smith for $60,000 to be resold to John Jones upon repayment of that sum plus 12% interest, this is, in effect, not a sale but a security instrument. If similar homes in the area are selling for $92,000, there is a potential tax fraud which might place the escrow in jeopardy in a legal sense, as well as the possibility of negating title insurance on the transaction.

Junior Lenders. As of July 1, 1985, the law places a burden upon senior lenders to inform holders of junior indebtedness if the senior indebtedness is more than four months delinquent. The intent is to aid junior lenders in protecting their position.

CONSIDERATION: THE CLOSING STATEMENT

Once the signed documents are obtained, adequate collected moneys are on deposit and instructions are in full compliance, a "complete" escrow is created, capable of recording documentation and distributing the proceeds. This will complete the exchange of title for consideration. A closing statement (Exhibit 22) serves as the accounting summary of an escrow.

Based on Instructions Escrowholder must determine that the allocation of charges shown in this statement is authorized by appropriate instructions, to wit:

Total Consideration (Sales Price). Is this amount as shown in the memo box? Has it been amended?

Deposits. Were instructions obtained governing the use of deposited moneys from buyers, sellers, lenders, or third party?

Trust Deeds of Record. Have statements been obtained verifying the balance, interest rate, and terms? Are there instructions concerning proration of interest?

Payment of Existing Indebtedness. Demands, as a matter of precaution, should be approved by the seller. This is particularly important due to the prevalence of prepayment charges and other lender fees which may not meet with the seller's approval.

Impounds. Are there instructions to transfer impounds as existing loans by crediting seller and debiting buyer?

New Loans. Has the buyer agreed to all the terms and the amount of the new loan as well as all charges incidental thereto? Has the seller agreed to defray a portion or all of the buyer's loan charges?

Prorations. Have instructions been obtained for proration of:
☐ Interest on existing debt
☐ Homeowners' association fees
☐ Taxes
☐ Insurance
☐ Rents?

Association Transfer Fee. Do instructions authorize its payment and other matters involving property owners' association, if applicable?

Supplemental Tax Provisions. The assessor issues supplemental bills for property which is reassessed during the tax year because of change of ownership or completion of new construction. Do escrow instructions provide for payment?

Commission. Has the commission instruction been obtained with seller authorization? Is the commission to be taken in the form of a deed of trust? In this case, instructions must be obtained from the buyer.

Fees. Is each of the fees incurred covered by specific instruction as to the obligation of either seller or buyer?

Incidental Charges. Any other charges which may require instructions of seller or buyer, such as judgments, tax liens, credit card payoffs, private note payments, purchase of personal property, etc.

Outside of Escrow. Are instructions obtained outlining moneys passing outside of escrow? Take extreme care if any of buyer's moneys deposited in escrow are authorized to be transferred to seller prior to closing.

Remaining Balance. Usually it is the balance due the seller or a small refund to the buyer. If there is a negative balance due the buyer, the escrow is short and the transaction is not in a position to record.

Proper Accounting Mechanics of preparing closing statements and figuring prorations are discussed in the next chapter.

Regional Variations Northern California processing typically calls for an estimated closing statement to be issued as part of the escrow instructions, showing, for example, the estimated net proceeds to the seller and the estimated funds needed to close for the buyer in a sale escrow. Southern California processing allows the broker's net sheet to serve the same purpose, providing the closing statements only at settlement.

RECORDING REQUESTED BY

AND WHEN RECORDED MAIL TO

Name
Street
Address
City &
State

MAIL TAX STATEMENTS TO

(1)

Name
Street
Address
City &
State

SPACE ABOVE THIS LINE FOR RECORDER'S USE

(2) DOCUMENTARY TRANSFER TAX $..............
COMPUTED ON FULL VALUE OF PROPERTY CONVEYED,
OR COMPUTED ON FULL VALUE LESS LIENS AND
ENCUMBRANCES REMAINING AT TIME OF SALE.

Signature of Declarant or Agent determining tax.   Firm Name

(1)   IN WRITING   **Grant Deed**

FOR A VALUABLE CONSIDERATION, receipt of which is hereby acknowledged,   (2) GRANTOR

(3)   hereby GRANT(S) to   (4)   GRANTEE

(5)   the following described real property in the
County of   , State of California:

ESSENTIALS

FOR VALIDITY	TO EFFECTIVELY CONVEY TITLE
(1) IN WRITING	1. VALID DEED
(2) COMPETENT GRANTOR	
(3) GRANTING CLAUSE	2. DELIVERY WITH INTENTION
(4) CAPABLE GRANTEE	TO CONVEY THE TITLE
(5) ADEQUATE DESCRIPTION	
(6) SIGNED BY GRANTOR	3. ACCEPTANCE BY GRANTEE

---

(6)   /s/ GRANTOR

Dated _____

STATE OF CALIFORNIA (3)
COUNTY OF_____   }ss.
On _____ before me, the under-
signed, a Notary Public in and for said State, personally appeared
_____
_____
_____
_____, known to me
to be the person____whose name_____ subscribed to the within
instrument and acknowledged that_____executed the same.
WITNESS my hand and official seal.

Signature _____

Name (Typed or Printed)

FOR RECORDING

(1) ADDRESS FOR TAX STATEMENT

(2) DOCUMENTARY TRANSFER TAX

(3) GRANTOR'S ACKNOWLEDGMENT
(in presence of a notary)

(This area for official notarial seal)

Title Order No._____ Escrow or Loan No._____

MAIL TAX STATEMENTS AS DIRECTED ABOVE

Exhibit 18

Order No. _____
Escrow No. _____

WHEN RECORDED MAIL TO:

SPACE ABOVE THIS LINE FOR RECORDER'S USE

MAIL TAX STATEMENTS TO:

DOCUMENTARY TRANSFER TAXS . . No Consideration
Computed on the consideration or value of property conveyed; OR Computed on the consideration or value less liens or encumbrances remaining at time of sale.
is exempt from imposition of the Documentary Transfer Tax pursuant to Revenue and Taxation Code § 11927(a), on transfering community, quasi-community, or quasi-marital property, assets between spouses, pursuant to a judgment, an order, or a written agreement between spouses in contemplation of any such judgment or order.

_____
Signature of declaring grantor or grantee

Assessor's Lot _____ Block _____

INTERSPOUSAL TRANSFER GRANT DEED
(Excluded from reappraisal under California Constitution Article 13 A § 1 et. seq.)

This is an interspousal Transfer and not a change in ownership under § 63 of the Revenue and Taxation Code and Grantor(s) has (have) checked the applicable exclusion from reappraisal:

☐ A transfer to a trustee for the beneficial use of a spouse, or the surviving spouse of a deceased transferor, or by a trustee of such a trust to the spouse of the trustor.
☐ A transfer to a spouse or former spouse in connection with a property settlement agreement of decree of dissolution of a marriage or legal separation, or
☐ A creation, transfer, or termination, solely between spouses, of any co-owner's interest.
☐ The distribution of a legal entity's property to a spouse or former spouse in exchange for the interest of such spouse in the legal entity in connection with a property settlement agreement or a decree of dissolution of a marriage or legal separation.
☐ Other _____

FOR VALUABLE CONSIDERATION, receipt of which is hereby acknowledged,

    Ken Richards

hereby GRANTS(S) to

    Setsuko Richards

the real property in the City of   San Francisco   , County of   San Francisco
State of California, described as:

It is the interest of the Grantor to divest himself of any and all interest community or otherwise in and to the above described property and to vest title in the Grantee as her sole and separate property.

Dated _____   X _____

STATE OF CALIFORNIA
COUNTY OF _____   _____

on _____   _____

before me, the undersigned, a Notary Public in and for said
State, personally appeared

_____
_____
_____

personally know to me (or proved to me on the basis of satisfactory evidenced
to be the person(s) whose name(s) is/are subscribed to the within instrument
and acknowledged to me that he/she/they executed the same

WITNESS my hand and official seal

(This area for official notarial seal)

Signature _____

MAIL TAX STATEMENTS AS DIRECTED ABOVE   1004 (5/64)

Exhibit 19

NOTE

19

(City)   (State)

(Property Address)

1. BORROWER'S PROMISE TO PAY

In return for a loan that I have received, I promise to pay U.S. $ _____ (this amount is called "principal"), plus interest, to the order of the Lender. The Lender is

I understand that the Lender may transfer this Note. The Lender or anyone who takes this Note by transfer and who is entitled to receive payments under this Note is called the "Note Holder."

2. INTEREST

Interest will be charged on unpaid principal until the full amount of principal has been paid. I will pay interest at a yearly rate of _____ %.

The interest rate required by this Section 2 is the rate I will pay both before and after any default described in Section 6(B) of this Note.

3. PAYMENTS

(A) Time and Place of Payments

I will pay principal and interest by making payments every month.

I will make my monthly payments on the _____ day of each month beginning on _____ , 19 ____ . I will make these payments every month until I have paid all of the principal and interest and any other charges decribed below that I may owe under this Note. My monthly payments will be applied to interest before principal. If, on _____ , I still owe amounts under this Note, I will pay those amounts in full on that date, which is called the "maturity date."

I will make my monthly payments at _____

or at a different place if required by the Note Holder.

(B) Amount of Monthly Payments

My monthly payment will be in the amount of U.S. $ _____

4. BORROWER'S RIGHT TO PREPAY

I have the right to make payments of principal at any time before they are due. A payment of principal only is known as a "prepayment." When I make a prepayment, I will tell the Note Holder in writing that I am doing so.

I may make a full prepayment or partial prepayments without paying any prepayment charge. The Note Holder will use all of my prepayments to reduce the amount of principal that I owe under this Note. If I make a partial prepayment, there will be no changes in the due date or in the amount of my monthly payment unless the Note Holder agrees in writing to those changes.

5. LOAN CHARGES

If a law, which applies to this loan and which sets maximum loan charges, is finally interpreted so that the interest or other loan charges collected or to be collected in connection with this loan exceed the permitted limits, then: (i) any such loan charge shall be reduced by the amount necessary to reduce the charge to the permitted limit; and (ii) any sums already collected from me which exceeded permitted limits will be refunded to me. The Note Holder may choose to make this refund by reducing the principal I owe under this Note or by making a direct payment to me. If a refund reduces principal, the reduction will be treated as a partial prepayment.

6. BORROWER'S FAILURE TO PAY AS REQUIRED

(A) Late Charge for Overdue Payments

If the Note Holder has not received the full amount of any monthly payment by the end of _____ calendar days after the date it is due, I will pay a late charge to the Note Holder. The amount of the charge will be _____ % of my overdue payment of principal and interest. I will pay this late charge promptly but only once on each late payment.

(B) Default

If I do not pay the full amount of each monthly payment on the date it is due, I will be in default.

(C) Notice of Default

If I am in default, the Note Holder may send me a written notice telling me that if I do not pay the overdue amount by a certain date, the Note Holder may require me to pay immediately the full amount of principal which has not been paid and all the interest that I owe on that amount. That date must be at least 30 days after the date on which the notice is delivered or mailed to me.

(D) No Waiver By Note Holder

Even if, at a time when I am in default, the Note Holder does not require me to pay immediately in full as described above, the Note Holder will still have the right to do so if I am in default at a later time.

(E) Payment of Note Holder's Costs and Expenses

If the Note Holder has required me to pay immediately in full as described above, the Note Holder will have the right to be paid back by me for all of its costs and expenses in enforcing this Note to the extent not prohibited by applicable law. Those expenses include, for example, reasonable attorneys' fees.

7. GIVING OF NOTICES

Unless applicable law requires a different method, any notice that must be given to me under this Note will be given by delivering it or by mailing it by first class mail to me at the Property Address above or at a different address if I give the Note Holder a notice of my different address.

Any notice that must be given to the Note Holder under this Note will be given by mailing it by first class mail to the Note Holder at the address stated in Section 3(A) above or at a different address if I am given a notice of that different address.

8. OBLIGATIONS OF PERSONS UNDER THIS NOTE

If more than one person signs this Note, each person is fully and personally obligated to keep all of the promises made in this Note, including the promise to pay the full amount owed. Any person who is a guarantor, surety or endorser of this Note is also obligated to do these things. Any person who takes over these obligations, including the obligations of a guarantor, surety or endorser of this Note, is also obligated to keep all of the promises made in this Note. The Note Holder may enforce its rights under this Note against each person individually or against all of us together. This means that any one of us may be required to pay all of the amounts owed under this Note.

9. WAIVERS

I and any other person who has obligations under this Note waive the rights of presentment and notice of dishonor. "Presentment" means the right to require the Note Holder to demand payment of amounts due. "Notice of dishonor" means the right to require the Note Holder to give notice to other persons that amounts due have not been paid.

10. UNIFORM SECURED NOTE

This Note is a uniform instrument with limited variations in some jurisdictions. In addition to the protections given to the Note Holder under this Note, a Mortgage, Deed of Trust or Security Deed (the "Security Instrument"), dated the same date as this Note, protects the Note Holder from possible losses which might result if I do not keep the promises which I make in this Note. That Security Instrument describes how and under what conditions I may be required to make immediate payment in full of all amounts I owe under this Note. Some of those conditions are described as follows:

Transfer of the Property or a Beneficial Interest in Borrower. If all or any part of the Property or any interest in it is sold or transferred (or if a beneficial interest in Borrower is sold or transferred and Borrower is not a natural person) without Lender's prior written consent, Lender may, at its option, require immediate payment in full of all sums secured by this Security Instrument. However, this option shall not be exercised by Lender if exercise is prohibited by federal law as of the date of this Security Instrument.

If Lender exercises this option, Lender shall give Borrower notice of acceleration. The notice shall provide a period of not less than 30 days from the date the notice is delivered or mailed within which Borrower must pay all sums secured by this Security Instrument. If Borrower fails to pay these sums prior to the expiration of this period, Lender may invoke any remedies permitted by this Security Instrument without further notice or demand on Borrower.

WITNESS THE HAND(S) AND SEAL(S) OF THE UNDERSIGNED.

_____ (Borrower)   _____ (Borrower)

_____ (Borrower)   _____ (Borrower)
                                          (Sign Original Only)

MULTISTATE FIXED RATE NOTE—Single Family—**FNMA/FHLMC UNIFORM INSTRUMENT**   **Form 3200 12/83**
                                                                                           MC 0306 C

Exhibit 20

SPACE ABOVE THIS LINE FOR RECORDER'S USE

DEED OF TRUST

THIS DEED OF TRUST ("Security Instrument") is made on   19   The trustor is

("Borrower").

The trustee is

("Trustee").

The beneficiary is

which is organized and existing under the laws of   , and whose
address is

("Lender").

Borrower owes Lender the principal sum of

Dollars (U.S. $). This debt is evidenced by Borrower's note dated the same date as this Security Instrument ("Note"), which provides for monthly payments, with the full debt, if not paid earlier, due and payable on   This Security Instrument secures to Lender: (a) the repayment of the debt evidenced by the Note, with interest, and all renewals, extensions and modifications; (b) the payment of all other sums, with interest, advanced under paragraph 7 to protect the security of this Security Instrument; and (c) the performance of Borrower's covenants and agreements under this Security Instrument and the Note. For this purpose, Borrower irrevocably grants and conveys to Trustee, in trust, with power of sale, the following described property located in   County, California:

which has the address of   (Street)

                  , California   ("Property Address");
          (City)   (Zip Code)

TOGETHER WITH all the improvements now or hereafter erected on the property, and all easements, rights, appurtenances, rents, royalties, mineral, oil and gas rights and profits, water rights and stock and all fixtures now or hereafter a part of the property. All replacements and additions shall also be covered by this Security Instrument. All of the foregoing is referred to in this Security Instrument as the "Property."

BORROWER COVENANTS that Borrower is lawfully seised of the estate hereby conveyed and has the right to grant and convey the Property and that the Property is unencumbered, except for encumbrances of record. Borrower warrants and will defend generally the title to the Property against all claims and demands, subject to any encumbrances of record.

THIS SECURITY INSTRUMENT combines uniform covenants for national use and non-uniform covenants with limited variations by jurisdiction to constitute a uniform security instrument covering real property.

CALIFORNIA—Single Family—FNMA/FHLMC UNIFORM INSTRUMENT   Form 3005 12/83
                                                                  MC 0420 C

Exhibit 21.1

UNIFORM COVENANTS. Borrower and Lender covenant and agree as follows:

1. Payment of Principal and Interest; Prepayment and Late Charges. Borrower shall promptly pay when due the principal of and interest on the debt evidenced by the Note and any prepayment and late charges due under the Note.

2. Funds for Taxes and Insurance. Subject to applicable law or to a written waiver by Lender, Borrower shall pay to Lender on the day monthly payments are due under the Note, until the Note is paid in full, a sum ("Funds") equal to one-twelfth of: (a) yearly taxes and assessments which may attain priority over this Security Instrument; (b) yearly leasehold payments or ground rents on the Property, if any; (c) yearly hazard insurance premiums; and (d) yearly mortgage insurance premiums, if any. These items are called "escrow items." Lender may estimate the Funds due on the basis of current data and reasonable estimates of future escrow items.

The Funds shall be held in an institution the deposits or accounts of which are insured or guaranteed by a federal or state agency (including Lender if Lender is such an institution). Lender shall apply the Funds to pay the escrow items. Lender may not charge for holding and applying the Funds, analyzing the account or verifying the escrow items, unless Lender pays Borrower interest on the Funds and applicable law permits Lender to make such a charge. Borrower and Lender may agree in writing that interest shall be paid on the Funds. Unless an agreement is made or applicable law requires interest to be paid, Lender shall not be required to pay Borrower any interest or earnings on the Funds. Lender shall give to Borrower, without charge, an annual accounting of the Funds showing credits and debits to the Funds and the purpose for which each debit to the Funds was made. The Funds are pledged as additional security for the sums secured by this Security Instrument.

If the amount of the Funds held by Lender, together with the future monthly payments of Funds payable prior to the due dates of the escrow items, shall exceed the amount required to pay the escrow items when due, the excess shall be, at Borrower's option, either promptly repaid to Borrower or credited to Borrower on monthly payments of Funds. If the amount of the Funds held by Lender is not sufficient to pay the escrow items when due, Borrower shall pay to Lender any amount necessary to make up the deficiency in one or more payments as required by Lender.

Upon payment in full of all sums secured by this Security Instrument, Lender shall promptly refund to Borrower any Funds held by Lender. If under paragraph 19 the Property is sold or acquired by Lender, Lender shall apply, no later than immediately prior to the sale of the Property or its acquisition by Lender, any Funds held by Lender at the time of application as a credit against the sums secured by this Security Instrument.

3. Application of Payments. Unless applicable law provides otherwise, all payments received by Lender under paragraphs 1 and 2 should be applied: first to amounts payable under paragraph 2; second to interest; and last to principal.

4. Charges; Liens. Borrower shall pay all taxes, assessments, charges, fines and impositions attributable to the Property which may attain priority over this Security Instrument, and leasehold payments or ground rents, if any. Borrower shall pay these obligations in the manner provided in paragraph 2, or if not paid in that manner, Borrower shall pay them on time directly to the person owed payment. Borrower shall promptly furnish to Lender all notices of amounts to be paid under this paragraph. If Borrower makes these payments directly, Borrower shall promptly furnish to Lender receipts evidencing the payments.

Borrower shall promptly discharge any lien which has priority over this Security Instrument unless Borrower: (a) agrees in writing to the payment of the obligation secured by the lien in a manner acceptable to Lender; (b) contests in good faith the lien by, or defends against enforcement of the lien in, legal proceedings which in the Lender's opinion operate to prevent the enforcement of the lien or forfeiture of any part of the Property; or (c) secures from the holder of the lien an agreement satisfactory to Lender subordinating the lien to this Security Instrument. If Lender determines that any part of the Property is subject to a lien which may attain priority over this Security Instrument, Lender may give Borrower a notice identifying the lien. Borrower shall satisfy the lien or take one or more of the actions set forth above within 10 days of the giving of notice.

5. Hazard Insurance. Borrower shall keep the improvements now existing or hereafter erected on the Property insured against loss by fire, hazards included within the term "extended coverage" and any other hazards for which Lender requires insurance. This insurance shall be maintained in the amounts and for the periods that Lender requires. The insurance carrier providing the insurance shall be chosen by Borrower subject to Lender's approval which shall not be unreasonably withheld.

All insurance policies and renewals shall be acceptable to Lender and shall include a standard mortgage clause. Lender shall have the right to hold the policies and renewals. If Lender requires, Borrower shall promptly give to Lender all receipts of paid premiums and renewal notices. In the event of loss, Borrower shall give prompt notice to the insurance carrier and Lender. Lender may make proof of loss if not made promptly by Borrower.

Unless Lender and Borrower otherwise agree in writing, insurance proceeds shall be applied to restoration or repair of the Property damaged, if the restoration or repair is economically feasible and Lender's security is not lessened. If the restoration or repair is not economically feasible or Lender's security would be lessened, the insurance proceeds shall be applied to the sums secured by this Security Instrument, whether or not then due, with any excess paid to Borrower. If Borrower abandons the Property, or does not answer within 30 days a notice from Lender that the insurance carrier has offered to settle a claim, then Lender may collect the insurance proceeds. Lender may use the proceeds to repair or restore the Property or to pay sums secured by this Security Instrument, whether or not then due. The 30-day period will begin when the notice is given.

Unless Lender and Borrower otherwise agree in writing, any application of proceeds to principal shall not extend or postpone the due date of the monthly payments referred to in paragraphs 1 and 2 or change the amount of the payments. If under paragraph 19 the Property is acquired by Lender, Borrower's right to any insurance policies and proceeds resulting from damage to the Property prior to the acquisition shall pass to Lender to the extent of the sums secured by this Security Instrument immediately prior to the acquisition.

6. Preservation and Maintenance of Property; Leaseholds. Borrower shall not destroy, damage or substantially change the Property, allow the Property to deteriorate or commit waste. If this Security Instrument is on a leasehold, Borrower shall comply with the provisions of the lease, and if Borrower acquires fee title to the Property, the leasehold and fee title shall not merge unless Lender agrees to the merger in writing.

7. Protection of Lender's Rights in the Property; Mortgage Insurance. If Borrower fails to perform the covenants and agreements contained in this Security Instrument, or there is a legal proceeding that may significantly affect Lender's rights in the Property (such as a proceeding in bankruptcy, probate, for condemnation or to enforce laws or regulations), then Lender may do and pay for whatever is necessary to protect the value of the Property and Lender's rights in the Property. Lender's actions may include paying any sums secured by a lien which has priority over this Security Instrument, appearing in court, paying reasonable attorneys' fees and entering on the Property to make repairs. Although Lender may take action under this paragraph 7, Lender does not have to do so.

Exhibit 21.2

Any amounts disbursed by Lender under this paragraph 7 shall become additional debt of Borrower secured by this Security Instrument. Unless Borrower and Lender agree to other terms of payment, these amounts shall bear interest from the date of disbursement at the Note rate and shall be payable, with interest, upon notice from Lender to Borrower requesting payment.

If Lender required mortgage insurance as a condition of making the loan secured by this Security Instrument, Borrower shall pay the premiums required to maintain the insurance in effect until such time as the requirement for the insurance terminates in accordance with Borrower's and Lender's written agreement or applicable law.

8. Inspection. Lender or its agent may make reasonable entries upon and inspections of the Property. Lender shall give Borrower notice at the time of or prior to an inspection specifying reasonable cause for the inspection.

9. Condemnation. The proceeds of any award or claim for damages, direct or consequential, in connection with any condemnation or other taking of any part of the Property, or for conveyance in lieu of condemnation, are hereby assigned and shall be paid to Lender.

In the event of a total taking of the Property, the proceeds shall be applied to the sums secured by this Security Instrument, whether or not then due, with any excess paid to Borrower. In the event of a partial taking of the Property, unless Borrower and Lender otherwise agree in writing, the sums secured by this Security Instrument shall be reduced by the amount of the proceeds multiplied by the following fraction: (a) the total amount of the sums secured immediately before the taking, divided by (b) the fair market value of the Property immediately before the taking. Any balance shall be paid to Borrower.

If the Property is abandoned by Borrower, or if, after notice by Lender to Borrower that the condemnor offers to make an award or settle a claim for damages, Borrower fails to respond to Lender within 30 days after the date the notice is given, Lender is authorized to collect and apply the proceeds, at its option, either to restoration or repair of the Property or to the sums secured by this Security Instrument, whether or not then due.

Unless Lender and Borrower otherwise agree in writing, any application of proceeds to principal shall not extend or postpone the due date of the monthly payments referred to in paragraphs 1 and 2 or change the amount of such payments.

10. Borrower Not Released; Forbearance By Lender Not a Waiver. Extension of the time for payment or modification of amortization of the sums secured by this Security Instrument granted by Lender to any successor in interest of Borrower shall not operate to release the liability of the original Borrower or Borrower's successors in interest. Lender shall not be required to commence proceedings against any successor in interest or refuse to extend time for payment or otherwise modify amortization of the sums secured by this Security Instrument by reason of any demand made by the original Borrower or Borrower's successors in interest. Any forbearance by Lender in exercising any right or remedy shall not be a waiver of or preclude the exercise of any right or remedy.

11. Successors and Assigns Bound; Joint and Several Liability; Co-signers. The covenants and agreements of this Security Instrument shall bind and benefit the successors and assigns of Lender and Borrower, subject to the provisions of paragraph 17. Borrower's covenants and agreements shall be joint and several. Any Borrower who co-signs this Security Instrument but does not execute the Note: (a) is co-signing this Security Instrument only to mortgage, grant and convey that Borrower's interest in the Property under the terms of this Security Instrument; (b) is not personally obligated to pay the sums secured by this Security Instrument; and (c) agrees that Lender and any other Borrower may agree to extend, modify, forbear or make any accommodations with regard to the terms of this Security Instrument or the Note without that Borrower's consent.

12. Loan Charges. If the loan secured by this Security Instrument is subject to a law which sets maximum loan charges, and that law is finally interpreted so that the interest or other loan charges collected or to be collected in connection with the loan exceed the permitted limits, then: (a) any such loan charge shall be reduced by the amount necessary to reduce the charge to the permitted limit; and (b) any sums already collected from Borrower which exceeded permitted limits will be refunded to Borrower. Lender may choose to make this refund by reducing the principal owed under the Note or by making a direct payment to Borrower. If a refund reduces principal, the reduction will be treated as a partial prepayment without any prepayment charge under the Note.

13. Legislation Affecting Lender's Rights. If enactment or expiration of applicable laws has the effect of rendering any provision of the Note or this Security Instrument unenforceable according to its terms, Lender, at its option, may require immediate payment in full of all sums secured by this Security Instrument and may invoke any remedies permitted by paragraph 19. If Lender exercises this option, Lender shall take the steps specified in the second paragraph of paragraph 17.

14. Notices. Any notice to Borrower provided for in this Security Instrument shall be given by delivering it or by mailing it by first class mail unless applicable law requires use of another method. The notice shall be directed to the Property Address or any other address Borrower designates by notice to Lender. Any notice to Lender shall be given by first class mail to Lender's address stated herein or any other address Lender designates by notice to Borrower. Any notice provided for in this Security Instrument shall be deemed to have been given to Borrower or Lender when given as provided in this paragraph.

15. Governing Law; Severability. This Security Instrument shall be governed by federal law and the law of the jurisdiction in which the Property is located. In the event that any provision or clause of this Security Instrument or the Note conflicts with applicable law, such conflict shall not affect other provisions of this Security Instrument or the Note which can be given effect without the conflicting provision. To this end the provisions of this Security Instrument and the Note are declared to be severable.

16. Borrower's Copy. Borrower shall be given one conformed copy of the Note and of this Security Instrument.

17. Transfer of the Property or a Beneficial Interest in Borrower. If all or any part of the Property or any interest in it is sold or tranferred (or if a beneficial interest in Borrower is sold or transferred and Borrower is not a natural person) without Lender's prior written consent, Lender may, at its option, require immediate payment in full of all sums secured by this Security Instrument. However, this option shall not be exercised by Lender if exercise is prohibited by federal law as of the date of this Security Instrument.

If Lender exercises this option, Lender shall give Borrower notice of acceleration. The notice shall provide a period of not less than 30 days from the date the notice is delivered or mailed within which Borrower must pay all sums secured by this Security Instrument. If Borrower fails to pay these sums prior to the expiration of this period, Lender may invoke any remedies permitted by this Security Instrument without further notice or demand on Borrower.

18. Borrower's Right to Reinstate. If Borrower meets certain conditions, Borrower shall have the right to have enforcement of this Security Instrument discontinued at any time prior to the earlier of: (a) 5 days (or such other period as applicable law may specify for reinstatement) before sale of the Property pursuant to any power of sale contained in this Security Instrument; or (b) entry of a judgment enforcing this Security Instrument. Those conditions are that Borrower: (a) pays Lender all sums which then would be due under this Security Instrument and the Note had no acceleration occurred; (b) cures any default of any other covenants or agreements; (c) pays all expenses incurred in enforcing this Security Instrument, including, but not limited to, reasonable attorneys' fees; and (d) takes such action as Lender may reasonably require to assure that the lien of this Security Instrument, Lender's rights in the Property and Borrower's obligation to pay the sums secured by this Security Instrument shall continue unchanged. Upon reinstatement by Borrower, this Security Instrument and the obligations secured hereby shall remain fully effective as if no acceleration had occurred. However, this right to reinstate shall not apply in the case of acceleration under paragraphs 13 or 17.

Exhibit 21.3

NON-UNIFORM COVENANTS. Borrower and Lender further covenant and agree as follows:

19. Acceleration; Remedies. Lender shall give notice to Borrower prior to acceleration following Borrower's breach of any covenant or agreement in this Security Instrument (but not prior to acceleration under paragraphs 13 and 17 unless applicable law provides otherwise). The notice shall specify: (a) the default; (b) the action required to cure the default; (c) a date, not less than 30 days from the date the notice is given to Borrower, by which the default must be cured; and (d) that failure to cure the default on or before the date specified in the notice may result in acceleration of the sums secured by this Security Instrument and sale of the Property. The notice shall further inform Borrower of the right to reinstate after acceleration and the right to bring a court action to assert the non-existence of a default or any other defense of Borrower to acceleration and sale. If the default is not cured on or before the date specified in the notice, Lender at its option may require immediate payment in full of all sums secured by this Security Instrument without further demand and may invoke the power of sale and any other remedies permitted by applicable law. Lender shall be entitled to collect all expenses incurred in pursuing the remedies provided in this paragraph 19, including, but not limited to, reasonable attorneys' fees and costs of title evidence.

If Lender invokes the power of sale, Lender shall execute or cause Trustee to execute a written notice of the occurrence of an event of default and of Lender's election to cause the Property to be sold. Trustee shall cause this notice to be recorded in each county in which any part of the Property is located. Lender or Trustee shall mail copies of the notice as prescribed by applicable law to Borrower and to the other persons prescribed by applicable law. Trustee shall give public notice of sale to the persons and in the manner prescribed by applicable law. After the time required by applicable law, Trustee, without demand on Borrower, shall sell the Property at public auction to the highest bidder at the time and place and under the terms designated in the notice of sale in one or more parcels and in any order Trustee determines. Trustee may postpone sale of all or any parcel of the Property by public announcement at the time and place of any previously scheduled sale. Lender or its designee may purchase the Property at any sale.

Trustee shall deliver to the purchaser Trustee's deed conveying the Property without any covenant or warranty, expressed or implied. The recitals in the Trustee's deed shall be prima facie evidence of the truth of the statements made therein. Trustee shall apply the proceeds of the sale in the following order: (a) to all expenses of the sale, including, but not limited to, reasonable Trustee's and attorneys' fees; (b) to all sums secured by this Security Instrument; and (c) any excess to the person or persons legally entitled to it.

20. Lender in Possession. Upon acceleration under paragraph 19 or abandonment of the Property, Lender (in person, by agent or by judicially appointed receiver) shall be entitled to enter upon, take possession of and manage the Property and to collect the rents of the Property including those past due. Any rents collected by Lender or the receiver shall be applied first to payment of the costs of management of the Property and collection of rents, including, but not limited to, receiver's fees, premiums on receiver's bonds and reasonable attorneys' fees, and then to the sums secured by this Security Instrument.

21. Reconveyance. Upon payment of all sums secured by this Security Instrument, Lender shall request Trustee to reconvey the Property and shall surrender this Security Instrument and all notes evidencing debt secured by this Security Instrument to Trustee. Trustee shall reconvey the Property without warranty and without charge to the person or persons legally entitled to it. Such person or persons shall pay any recordation costs.

22. Substitute Trustee. Lender, at its option, may from time to time appoint a successor trustee to any Trustee appointed hereunder by an instrument executed and acknowledged by Lender and recorded in the office of the Recorder of the county in which the Property is located. The instrument shall contain the name of the original Lender, Trustee and Borrower, the book and page where this Security Instrument is recorded and the name and address of the successor trustee. Without conveyance of the Property, the successor trustee shall succeed to all the title, powers and duties conferred upon the Trustee herein and by applicable law. This procedure for substitution of trustee shall govern to the exclusion of all other provisions for substitution.

23. Request for Notices. Borrower requests that copies of the notices of default and sale be sent to Borrower's address which is the Property Address.

24. Statement of Obligation. Lender may collect a fee, not to exceed the maximum amount permitted by law for furnishing the statement of obligation as provided by Section 2943 of the Civil Code of California ($50.00).

25. Riders to this Security Instrument. If one or more riders are executed by Borrower and recorded together with this Security Instrument, the covenants and agreements of each such rider shall be incorporated into and shall amend and supplement the covenants and agreements of this Security Instrument as if the rider(s) were a part of this Security Instrument. [Check applicable box(es)]

☐ Adjustable Rate Rider   ☐ Condominium Rider   ☐ 2-4 Family Rider
☐ Graduated Payment Rider   ☐ Planned Unit Development Rider
☐ Other(s) [specify]

BY SIGNING BELOW, Borrower accepts and agrees to the terms and covenants contained in this Security Instrument and in any rider(s) executed by Borrower and recorded with it.

_____ Borrower   _____ Borrower

_____ Borrower   _____ Borrower

_____ **[Space Below This Line Reserved For Acknowledgement]** _____

State of California,   County ss:

On this _____ day of _____, 19___, before me, the undersigned, a Notary Public in and for said State, personally appeared _____

known to me, or proved to me on the basis of satisfactory evidence to be the person(s) whose name(s) _____ subscribed to the foregoing instrument and acknowledged that _____ executed the same.

Witness my hand and official seal.

Signature _____

(Reserved for official seal)

_____
Name (typed or printed)

My commission expires:

REQUEST FOR RECONVEYANCE

TO TRUSTEE:

The undersigned is the holder of the note or notes secured by this Deed of Trust. Said note or notes, together with all other indebtedness secured by this Deed of Trust, have been paid in full. You are hereby directed to cancel said note or notes and this Deed of Trust, which are delivered hereby, and to reconvey, without warranty, all the estate now held by you under this Deed of Trust to the person or persons legally entitled thereto.

Dated: _____   _____

Exhibit 21.4

First American Title Guaranty Company

SELLERS ESCROW SETTLEMENT SHEET

Estimated COE:_____ Escrow Officer:_____ Escrow No._____

	DEBITS	CREDITS
Sales Price		
Deposit Retained (paid outside of escrow)		
Encumbrance of Record		
Loan Trust Fund		
Deed of Trust ☐ 1st ☐ 2nd ☐ 3rd		
Pay Demand of		
Principal to $		
Interest @ fr. to $		
Interest @ fr. to $		
Prepayment Charge $		
Reconveyance Fee $		
Forwarding Fee $		
Less Loan Trust Fund $ $		
TOTAL		
Pay demand of		
Loan Discount Fee (points)		
Fees and charges required by:		
☐ Pay Taxes		
☐ Pay Assessments or Bonds		
☐ Prorate Mtg. Ins. Prem. fr. to on $		
☐ Prorate Homeowner's Assoc. Dues fr. to on $		
☐ Prorate Taxes fr. to on $		
☐ Prorate Fire Ins. fr. to on $		
☐ Prorate Int. @ % to on $		
☐ Prorate Int. @ % to on $		
☐ Prorate Rent fr. to on $		
☐ Prorate to on $		
☐ Prorate to on $		
☐ Prorate to on $		
Pay Commission		
☐ Pay Termite Inspection Fee		
☐ Pay Termite Repair		
Transfer Tax City County		
Reconveyance Fee		
Draw Doc.		
Notary Fee		
Title Prem. Std. $ ALTA $		
Escrow Fee		
Recording		
Balance to Seller ☐ Mail ☐ Will Call		
TOTALS		

PLEASE REMIT ALL FUNDS IN THE FORM OF A CASHIER'S OR CERTIFIED CHECK.

The balance shown is an estimated amount based on the closing date indicated above. If the closing date changes, adjustments will be made prior to close.

_____   _____

Exhibit 22

Quiz Chapter 7

1. Which of the following is not an essential element for an effective deed?

   (A) Parties—grantor/grantee
   (B) Delivery and acceptance
   √(C) Recording
   (D) Legal description

2. Recordation is a presumption of delivery.

   √(A) True
   (B) False

3. A minor may not acquire title to property without the benefit of a court appointed representative.

   (A) True
   √(B) False

4. Documentary transfer tax is applied exclusively to deeds.

   (A) True
   (B) False

5. The preliminary change of ownership form is:

   (A) Restricted to deeds only
   (B) Used for leases only
   (C) Optional
   (D) Accepted subsequent to recording with a penalty charge

6. Another word for burdens is:

   (A) Impositions
   (B) Distractions
   (C) Encumbrances
   (D) Deletions

7. A note is:

   (A) A promise to pay
   (B) Evidence of an obligation
   (C) An indication of amount due another
   (D) All of the above

8. A deed of trust

   (A) Means the property is not transferable
   (B) Secures a note or notes
   (C) Imposes no responsibilities on the borrower
   (D) Is the same as a deed

9. Instructions concerning payment of an existing loan must be:

   √(A) Cognizant of any unusual lender charges
   (B) Ambiguous
   (C) In the ballpark of the figure shown on the original instrument
   (D) Within $5,000 of the amount being paid off

10. All charges in connection with any new financing are to be paid by the buyer only.

    (A) True
    (B) False

Chapter 8
Preparing to Close—
Accounting and Prorations

PREVIEW
The Closing Statement
Proration

THE CLOSING STATEMENT

Various obligations and responsibilities for payments are assumed by the parties involved in an escrow transaction. It is the job of the escrowholder to reflect these mutual obligations properly in the form of a closing statement prepared for each party. This statement outlines the flow of consideration through escrow as well as listing the adjustments and authorized disbursements for payment of obligations.

Example

A representative sale is reflected in the ledger sheet shown as Exhibit 23. Escrow statements for the seller and buyer are shown in Exhibits 24 and 25 respectively. This transaction involves a sale for $90,000.00 with a ninety percent conventional private mortgage insured loan for $81,000.00. The transaction requires the payment of an existing loan, and proration of taxes, homeowners' association dues, and fire insurance.

The Ledger Sheet The initial process involves proper accounting for money actually deposited and disbursed through escrow, which is reflected on the escrow ledger sheet (Exhibit 23). These deposits and disbursements are then reflected in the supporting escrow statements, which will summarize the entire consideration.

Content. Except in an all cash sale, although the entire consideration and adjustments will be subject to an accounting, the actual total dollar amounts will not flow through the transaction in the form of checks.

Rationale. Loan proceeds and the payment of demands may flow through a sub-escrow at the title company with only a net amount disbursed to the escrow agent. In the example, total consideration is $90,000, but only $10,613.96 actually passes through the sale escrow.

Seller's Statement The closing statement form (Exhibit 24) usually shows debit and credit columns headed seller/borrower and buyer/lender, marked by the user to differentiate between a sale and loan transaction. This in-house worksheet will be translated at closing into a HUD-1 Settlement Statement annotated to conform to the Real Estate Settlement Procedures Act. (See Exhibit 50, Seller's Statement. Refer to Exhibit 24, page 122)

Credits **Demand for Deed**. $90,000.00 represents the total consideration outlined in the escrow instructions. Note corresponding debit to buyer marked (1) in Exhibit 25.

Taxes. Credit for first installment of $448.00 from 12-16-88 to 1-1-89—$37.34—represents 15 days of tax prepaid by the seller. A corresponding debit for this amount is reflected on the buyer's statement marked (2) in Exhibit 25.

Prepaid Monthly Homeowners' Association Dues. For 15 days at the rate of $50.00 per month—$25.00, marked (3)—shown as debit on the buyer's statement.

Impound Balance. $210.00. This amount represents a refund from impounds collected monthly for payment of taxes and/or insurance. Marked (8) on seller's statement only.

Total Credits. $90,272.34.

Debits **Rental**. From 12-16-88 through 12-31-88, calculated per escrow instructions—$300.00 marked (4), with corresponding credit to buyer.

Charges Attributable to Payoff. Existing S&L first trust deed lien (5, 6):

Principal balance	$57,395.84
Interest at 10% from 12-1-86 to	
12-16-86 (date of receipt)	239.15
Prepayment penalty	———
Forwarding fee and late payment	———
	————
Total S&L demand	$57,684.99*

*Note: Payment of this figure would be less the $210.00 shown in seller's credits and discussed in d. above.

Commission. $4,800.00, representing 5.3% of the sales price, marked (9), covered by seller's separate instruction.

Termite Report. $150.00, marked (10), covered by sale escrow instruction that seller will furnish buyer with this item.

Payments to Title Company. All items that deal with transferring satisfactory title to the seller.

Title policy (11)	$448.50
Reconveyance fee (7)	50.00
Documentary transfer tax (12)	99.00
Title company handling fee (sub-escrow)	—
Recording fee (reconveyance) (13)	3.00
Total title company payment	$600.50

Custom and usage in various parts of California may cause some of the above to be charged to the purchaser instead.

Balance. Seller's proceeds, marked (14) $26,786.85

Debits to Seller. Balancing corresponding credits $90,272.34

Buyer's Statement Exhibit 25 is a sample buyer's statement. Some items balance or parallel the seller's statement, while some are unique to the buyer.

Credits Deposits totaling $2,700.00 on buyer's statement. These amounts (15) represent best estimate of money required to close in excess of new loan amount.

New Loan Amount. $81,000 (16) on buyer's statement. This represents the principal balance of the new trust deed note.

Rental Credit. $300 corresponding to buyer's debit (4).

Total Credits. Including $8,872.89 due from buyer (21), $92,872.89.

Debits **Offsets.** Amounts (1) through (3), in the sum of $90,062.34, represent adjustment offsets to corresponding credits for the same amounts on seller's escrow statement.

New Loan Fees and Impounds. Fees connected with preparing the new loan, totaling $2257.50. These represent either charges or advance collections associated with the new loan.

Title-Related Payments. Totaling $253.05 (19, 20).

Total Debits to Buyer. Balancing corresponding credits—$92,872.89.

Allocation and Proration The allocation of the charges is the result of agreement between the parties and is reflected in the escrow instructions. Due to the use of a 365-day or a 360-day year, and the number of decimal places used, the prorations may vary slightly between escrowholders. In this example proration is computed on a 360-day year and a 30-day month.

PRORATIONS

Tables are available (Exhibit 26) for computing the prorated amount of accrued items, such as rents, taxes, and insurance; financial calculators and software are also available. However, it is important to know the principles used to derive the percentage or dollar figure shown on the proration tables, as well as to know how to calculate simple prorations directly (Exhibit 27).

Time Period The first step in proration is to establish the appropriate time period. For proration purposes, the day of closing is not included. In order to perform the prorata calculations the time is converted to a day factor, either as an amount per day or as a percentage of the total time period.

Taxes. The usual time span is 180 days or six months.

Insurance. The usual policy is for one year.

Rents. One month or 30 days.

Tax Computations Proration is based on the lien dates (due dates) of the various taxes involved.

Lien of the Tax. In general every tax on real property is a lien on the property assessed (Rev. & Tax. Code, Section 2187). The lien of the tax is removed only when the tax is paid, legally cancelled, or sale of the property for nonpayment is made to a private purchaser or to the state (Rev. & Tax. Code, Section 2194).

Lien Date. The lien of the tax attaches annually as of noon on March 1st preceding the fiscal year for which the taxes are levied (Rev. & Tax. Code, Section 2192), regardless of the date the assessment is made. The fiscal year is from July 1 to the following June 30. The lien of a municipal tax may, by statute or by charter, attach at a different date.

Improvements. Taxes on improvements are a lien on the taxable land on which they are located, if they are assessed to the same person to whom the land is assessed (Rev. & Tax. Code, Section 2188). Where improvements are owned by a person other than the owner of the land, the owner of the land or the owner of the improvements may file a written statement attesting separate ownership and request separate assessment (Rev. & Tax. Code, Section 21838).

Lien Priority. The liens of real property taxes and assessments of all taxing agencies have priority over all other liens on the real property, regardless of the time of creation (Rev. & Tax. Code, Section 2192.1).

Enforcement of the Lien. Real property and secured personal property taxes are enforced by sale of the property subject to the lien (Rev. & Tax. Code, Sections 2189, 21839, and 21841).

Collection and Payment of Tax

Jurisdiction. In general, Section 51501 of the Government Code provides that the legislative body of a city may transfer the assessment and collection duties to county officers.

Time of Payment. Most real property is assessed on the secured roll. One-half the taxes on the secured roll are due November 1 and become delinquent December 10. The second half of real property taxes are due February 1 and become delinquent April 10.

Personal Property. Rev. & Tax. Code, Section 2700 authorizes the county board of supervisors, by resolution, to provide for payment of one-half personal property taxes with each installment of real property taxes; however, absent such resolution, all personal property taxes on the secured roll are payable with the first installment of real property taxes. Taxes on the unsecured roll are due on the lien date of March 1st and are delinquent August 31.

Delinquencies

After April 10th of each year a delinquent roll is prepared showing all property on the secured roll upon which taxes are delinquent. Annually before June 8 a delinquency list of real property taxes is published stating a date upon which delinquent real property will be "sold to the state."

Sale to the State. Pursuant to Rev. & Tax. Code, § 3436 et seq., on or before June 30, at the date stated in the published notice of delinquency by operation of law and by declaration of the tax collector, all property on the published delinquency list upon which taxes and penalties have not been fully paid is deemed to have been "sold to the state."

Definition. The term "sold to the state" does not refer to a sale in the sense that there was an auction, bids, and the issuance of a deed to a successful purchaser. It refers to a bookkeeping transaction which establishes the beginning of a five year statutory redemption period during which time the owner has an absolute right to redeem the property by paying all delinquent taxes, costs, penalties, and interest.

Treatment During Redemption Period. During the five-year redemption period the taxpayer retains legal title to the property and enjoys the right of possession. The property is assessed for taxes for each of the ensuing five years; however, there is no subsequent "sale to the state" for tax delinquencies while a prior "sale to the state" is in effect.

Supplemental Tax Roll

Supplemental taxes may be the result of either the sale transaction itself or work of improvement recently performed or to be performed. Under most circumstances the impact of supplemental taxes should be a matter of agreement between the parties, and the escrowholder should not volunteer to prorate such items.

Sales. If the sale price exceeds the current assessed valuation, there will be a supplemental tax bill rendered by the tax collector based upon reassessment by the county assessor in keeping with the new sale price.

Improvements. Another trigger for a supplemental tax billing is work of improvement that is completed during the tax billing period (usually before November 1st). After assessment of the value of the added improvement by the tax assessor, the tax collector will render a billing on a prorated basis.

Amount. This new tax amount is usually based upon 1% of the market value, or sales price. It is then imposed as a prorated supplemental tax based on the closing date (or recording) of the transaction. There may be occasions where the new annual taxes are in excess of 1% due to special assessments on the property.

Reassessment Up or Down. Property values do not necessarily go up and in certain instances actually are reduced. In these cases there would be no supplemental tax billing and the subsequent tax bill would reflect a lowered assessment and lowered tax.

Escrow. Normally the parties to a sale will handle adjustments for the supplemental tax billing outside of escrow.

Tax Proration Example

Escrow is closing on 10-25-88. Taxes for six months on the subject property amount to $980.00. Calculate the charge to the seller for the yet unpaid first installment 1988-89 taxes and the corresponding credit to the buyer.

Time Span. The first step is to calculate the number of days:

Year	Month	Day
1988	10	25 (Escrow closes)
1988	$\frac{7}{3}$	$\frac{1}{24}$ (Start of tax year)

Monthly (Percentage) Method. Based upon a 30-day month the seller owes for 114 days out of a potential 180, which works out to 63.33%; this percentage figure when applied to the property tax gives us a proration charge of $620.63.

Per Diem Method. To calculate on a per diem basis we divide the property tax by 180 to arrive at $5.44 per day and multiply by 114. Using this per diem method provides a proration charge of $620.16, which differs slightly from the percentage method result due to rounding.

Insurance

In addition to basic fire insurance, other types of policies are now common.

"Package" Policies. Not only are the structure and its contents covered for fire, but other acts of damage can be covered. Future legal liability can be included in homeowner's policy coverage. Many of these complex policies are no longer assigned in escrow, and proration problems become academic.

Special Coverage Requirements. Principally imposed by lenders, these special policies may or may not be prorated. Earthquake and especially flood insurance have received increased attention from lenders, due to requirements of the Department of Housing and Urban Development.

☐ Earthquake

☐ Flood insurance

☐ Course of construction—a 39-month policy prorated on the basis of the last 36 months

☐ Plate glass coverage, usually on commercial properties.

Calculation Prorations may be appropriate in each instance above. Consider a three-year policy with a premium of $1200 effective May 13, 1987, to be prorated to the closing date of October 25, 1989, assuming a 30- day month/360-day year.

Time Span. The first procedure is to convert dates into days:

	Year	Month	Day	Total
October 25, 1989	89	10	25	
May 13, 1987	87	5	13	
subtracting,	2	5	12	
	x360	x30	x1	
	720	150	12	882

Percentage. The total number of days in three years is 1080, and this figure is used to divide 882, to determine the percentage of premium used, or 81.67%. Based upon this proration percentage, $980.04 of the premium has been used. The seller would get $219.96 credit for the unused portion and the buyer would be debited a like amount.

Per Diem Method. When calculating on a per diem basis, multiplying the daily premium ($1200/1080 days, or $1.11) by 882 yields a different result of $979.00, due to rounding.

Time Conversions. It is sometimes necessary to convert years to months, and so on. Consider an insurance policy commencing December 28, 1990, with the closing date October 25, 1992. The calculations are:

	Year	Month	Day	Total
October 25, 1992	1992	10	25	55
December 28, 1990	1990	12	28	
borrowing and subtracting,	1	9	27	
	x360	x30	x1	
converting to days,	360	270	27	657

The procedure is to borrow days from months and months from years. From the later date you borrow one month (30 days) to have sufficient days to subtract, and decrease the month figure by one. A year is borrowed from the later date, adding 12 to the months column. After subtracting, months are multiplied by 30 and years by 360, and the answer of 657 days is derived. Calculation methods may vary among practitioners: the important thing is the result.

Rents Rental proration is normally upon a 30-day month. Rents differ from loan payments in that they are usually collected in advance instead of in arrears. Sample calculations using the same closing date of October 25, 1991 follow.

Apartment No.	Monthly Rental	Paid To
A	$185	11-1-91
B	$215	11-1-91
C	$195	11-1-91

	Year	Month	Day
November 1, 1991	1991	11	1
October 25, 1991	1991	10	25
	-0-	-0-	-6-

It is usually better to calculate each rental individually for the six days rental credit to the buyer, although it can be done collectively since the payment date is the same. Both methods are illustrated.

```
┌─────────────────────────────────────────────────────────────┐
│                  Method  1—Individually                       │
│                                                               │
│   $185 per month = $6.16 per day for 6 days =      $36.96    │
│                                                               │
│   $215 per month = $7.16 per day for 6 days =       42.96    │
│                                                               │
│   $195 per month = $6.50 per day for 6 days =       39.00    │
│   Totals                                           $118.92    │
│                                                               │
│                  Method  2—Collectively                       │
│                                                               │
│   $595 per month = $19.83 per day for 6 days =     $118.98   │
│                                                               │
└─────────────────────────────────────────────────────────────┘
```

The two results differ a few cents due to rounding. In setting up the proration it is important that the basis for rental collection be established (arrears or advance), and that any other credits to be transferred to the buyer, such as security deposits, cleaning deposits, and key deposits, are fully indicated in the rent statement provided by the seller.

Loan Assumptions— Payoffs   If not handled correctly this can result in substantial losses to the escrowholder. It is extremely important to observe the provisions of the beneficiary statement in the case of an assumption and the demand statement in the case of a payoff. Some of the more important items of consideration are:

Frequency of Payment. Most of us assume that loan payments are on a monthly basis. Although this is generally true, some loans are payable quarterly, semi-annually, or even annually. This is especially true in agricultural loans.

Current or Delinquent Status. Many principals feel that once they are "in escrow" no need exists for continuance of timely payments on existing debts against the property. Such impressions should be dispelled, and the importance of keeping obligations current should be emphasized. Because of this requirement for current status, the escrowholder should not order statements of loan condition prematurely.

Impounds Involved. In the case of impounds, especially where the payoff of a land contract is involved, it must be determined which party is entitled to the impound credit. In the case of a new loan the amount of additional funds required from the buyer to establish an impound account must be determined.

Amortized or Interest Only. Some loans require "interest only" payments while others are partially or fully amortized.

Prepayment Penalties. Assumption fees, or other charges. It should be determined and agreed what parties are to be responsible for such fees.

Calculations for Assumptions/Payoffs. Consider a typical loan payoff where the payment is being made in arrears. An important item when computing payoff is to determine whether the lender requires payment to the date of closing or to the date of receipt of the funds. This could change the amount of money required for closing. With graduated payment loans, adjustable mortgage loans and other modern instruments of real estate finance, extreme care must be taken to properly allocate interest between buyer and seller.

Example

Consider a loan with a current principal balance of $54,986.25. Interest is imposed at the rate of 9% per annum, with monthly payments including both principal and interest. The October 1 payment has been made, and closing date is October 25.

	Year	Month	Day
October 25, 1991	1991	10	25
October 1, 1991	1991	10	1
	0	0	24

In order to calculate the 24 days' interest, a per diem rate is established by multiplying the principal balance by 9% and dividing the result by 360, giving $13.74 per day. The per diem figure multiplied by 24 provides the debit to the seller of the yet unpaid interest due on the loan, $329.76.

Other Proration Matters Recently parties to property transfers have been demanding precise adjustment of such items as homeowners' association assessments, personal property taxes, and other debts that have been prepaid by the seller or that have become the buyer's obligation. Escrowholders should be aware of this sensitivity and be willing to accommodate it.

ESCROW SETTLEMENT LEDGER SHEET

Escrow Company   ESCROW NO. 12345

ESCROW SETTLEMENT

RECEIPTS

DATE	DEPOSITED BY	RECEIPT No.	AMOUNT
10-25-88	James and Maggie Buyer	878	500 00
12-13-88	James and Maggie Buyer	903	2 200 00
12-16-88	Their Title Company	924	7 913 96
			10 613 96

DISBURSEMENTS

DATE	DISBURSEMENTS	CHECK No.	AMOUNT	
12-16-88	TITLE #38240	4031	239 00	
	F & C	drawn	211 00	
	Comm. to Selling Broker	4032	1 440 00	
	Listing Broker	4033	2 400 00	
	Salesperson	4034	960 00	
	Homeowners Association	4035	25 00	
	ABC Termite Co. - report	4036	150 00	
	John and Mary Seller (sellers)	4037	4 783 96	
	Tie-In Lender (MGIC prem.& fee)	4038	405 00	

Below is pencil memo space for items to close escrow.

Exhibit 23

SELLER'S CLOSING STATEMENT

ESCROW STATEMENT

LOT _____ TRACT _____

ESCROW NO. __12345__

(SELLER) BORROWER

BUYER-LENDER

	DEBITS		CREDITS		PROPERTY:	DEBITS		CREDITS	
					DEPOSIT				
					DEPOSIT				
(1)			90,000	00	TOTAL CONSIDERATION Demand for Deed				
					FIRST TRUST DEED BALANCE				
					SECOND TRUST DEED BALANCE				
					PRORATIONS MADE AS OF				
(2)			37	34	TAXES ON $ 448 FOR 6 MONTHS PAID TO 1-1-89				
					INTEREST $ @ % PAID TO				
(3)			25	00	Association Dues				
					INSURANCE PREMIUM $ 1 YR. PAID TO				
					FHA MMI PREMIUM $ 1 YR. PAID TO				
(4)	300	00			RENT @ $ 600 PER mo. PAID TO 12-31-88				
					IMPOUND ACCOUNT BALANCE				
					LENDER'S LOAN TRANSFER FEE				
					LENDER'S SERVICE FEE				
					NEW FIRE INSURANCE POLICY PREMIUM				
					NEW LOAN FEE				
					INTEREST ON LOAN @ FROM TO				
					TAX SERVICE CONTRACT				
					CREDIT REPORT				
					APPRAISAL FEE				
					IMPOUND ACCOUNT DEPOSIT				
					DISCOUNT POINTS				
					PHOTOS, INSPECTIONS & DOCUMENTS				
(5)	57,395	84			PRINCIPAL OF NOTE: DEMAND OF Your Federal S & L				
(6)	239	15			INTEREST @ 10%, 12-1 to 12-15				
					PREPAYMENT PENALTY				
					FORWARDING FEE				
(7)	50	00			RECONVEYANCE FEE				
(8)			210	00	IMPOUND ACCOUNT CREDIT				
					PRINCIPAL OF NOTE: DEMAND OF				
					INTEREST @				
					RECONVEYANCE FEE				
(9)	4,800	00			COMMISSION				
(10)	150	00			TERMITE REPORT AND/OR WORK				
					COUNTY TAX COLLECTOR				
(11)	448	50			TITLE INSURANCE POLICY with escrow services				
					LENDER'S TITLE POLICY				
(12)	99	00			DOCUMENTARY TRANSFER TAX				
					SUB-ESCROW FEE				
(13)	3	00			RECORDING FEES Reconveyance				
					ESCROW FEE				
					LOAN TIE-IN ESCROW FEE				
					DRAWING OF DOCUMENTS				
					HANDLING LENDERS STATEMENTS/DEMANDS				
					BALANCE DUE THIS ESCROW				
(14)	26,786	85			BALANCE DUE YOU				
	90,272	34	90,272	34	TOTALS				

DATE __12-16-88__

BY_____
ESCROW OFFICER

PLEASE RETAIN THIS STATEMENT FOR INCOME TAX PURPOSES

Exhibit 24

BUYER'S CLOSING STATEMENT

ESCROW STATEMENT

LOT _____ TRACT _____

ESCROW NO. 12345

SELLER·BORROWER				BUYER·LENDER	
DEBITS	**CREDITS**	**PROPERTY:**		**DEBITS**	**CREDITS**
		DEPOSIT			500 00 } (15)
		DEPOSIT			2,200 00
		TOTAL CONSIDERATION Demand for deed		90,000 00	(1)
		FIRST TRUST DEED BALANCE			81,000 00 (16)
		SECOND TRUST DEED BALANCE			
		PRORATIONS MADE AS OF 12-16-88			
		TAXES ON $ 448 FOR 6 MONTHS PAID TO 1-1-89		37 34	(2)
		INTEREST $ @ % PAID TO			(3)
		Association Dues		25 00	(17)
		INSURANCE PREMIUM $ 1 YR. PAID TO			
		FHA MMI PREMIUM $ 1 YR. PAID TO			
		RENT @ $ 600 PER mo. PAID TO 12-31-88			300 00 (4)
		IMPOUND ACCOUNT BALANCE			
		LENDER'S LOAN TRANSFER FEE			
		LENDER'S SERVICE FEE			
		NEW FIRE INSURANCE POLICY PREMIUM $300/yr. pd. to 12-15-89		300 00	(17)
		NEW LOAN FEE		810 00	
		INTEREST ON LOAN @ 10% FROM 12-16 TO 12-31-88		337 50	
		TAX SERVICE CONTRACT		25 00	
		CREDIT REPORT		20 00	
		APPRAISAL FEE		150 00	(18)
		IMPOUND ACCOUNT DEPOSIT Taxes - 6 months		450 00	
		Insurance - 2 months		25 00	
		DISCOUNT POINTS			
		PHOTOS, INSPECTIONS & DOCUMENTS		35 00	
		MGIC		405 00	
		PRINCIPAL OF NOTE: DEMAND OF			
		INTEREST @			
		PREPAYMENT PENALTY			
		FORWARDING FEE			
		RECONVEYANCE FEE			
		IMPOUND ACCOUNT CREDIT			
		PRINCIPAL OF NOTE: DEMAND OF			
		INTEREST @			
		RECONVEYANCE FEE			
		COMMISSION			
		TERMITE REPORT AND/OR WORK			
		COUNTY TAX COLLECTOR			
		TITLE INSURANCE POLICY			
		LENDER'S TITLE POLICY		242 05	(19)
		DOCUMENTARY TRANSFER TAX			
		SUB-ESCROW FEE			
		RECORDING FEES Deed and Trust Deed		11 00	(20)
		ESCROW FEE			
		LOAN TIE-IN ESCROW FEE			
		DRAWING OF DOCUMENTS			
		HANDLING LENDERS STATEMENTS/DEMANDS			
		BALANCE DUE THIS ESCROW			8,872 89 (21)
		BALANCE DUE YOU			
		TOTALS		92,872 89	92,872 89

DATE 12-16-88   BY _____

ESCROW OFFICER

PLEASE RETAIN THIS STATEMENT FOR INCOME TAX PURPOSES

Exhibit 25

TAX ADJUSTMENT TABLE

DAY	JAN. JULY	FEB. AUG.	MAR. SEPT.	APR. OCT.	MAY NOV.	JUNE DEC.
1	.0000	.1667	.3333	.5000	.6667	.8333
2	.0056	.1722	.3389	.5056	.6722	.8389
3	.0111	.1778	.3444	.5111	.6778	.8444
4	.0167	.1833	.3500	.5167	.6833	.8500
5	.0222	.1889	.3556	.5222	.6889	.8556
6	.0278	.1944	.3611	.5278	.6944	.8611
7	.0333	.2000	.3667	.5333	.7000	.8667
8	.0389	.2056	.3722	.5389	.7056	.8722
9	.0444	.2111	.3778	.5444	.7111	.8778
10	.0500	.2167	.3833	.5500	.7167	.8833
11	.0556	.2222	.3889	.5556	.7222	.8889
12	.0611	.2278	.3944	.5611	.7278	.8944
13	.0667	.2333	.4000	.5667	.7333	.9000
14	.0722	.2389	.4056	.5722	.7389	.9056
15	.0778	.2444	.4111	.5778	.7444	.9111
16	.0833	.2500	.4167	.5833	.7500	.9167
17	.0889	.2556	.4222	.5889	.7556	.9222
18	.0944	.2611	.4278	.5944	.7611	.9278
19	.1000	.2667	.4333	.6000	.7667	.9333
20	.1056	.2722	.4389	.6056	.7722	.9389
21	.1111	.2778	.4444	.6111	.7778	.9444
22	.1167	.2833	.4500	.6167	.7833	.9500
23	.1222	.2889	.4556	.6222	.7889	.9556
24	.1278	.2944	.4611	.6278	.7945	.9611
25	.1333	.3000	.4667	.6333	.8000	.9667
26	.1389	.3056	.4722	.6389	.8056	.9722
27	.1444	.3111	.4778	.6444	.8111	.9778
28	.1500	.3167	.4833	.6500	.8167	.9833
29	.1556	.3222	.4889	.6556	.8222	.9889
30	.1611	.3278	.4944	.6611	.8278	.9944

HOW TO USE PRORATION TABLES

TAX ADJUSTMENT TABLE

Multiply tax amount by percentage figure shown in table on proration date. Example: Second half taxes $140 not paid; documents recorded March 15. Multiply $140 by .4111 = $57.55. Debit seller and credit buyer.

INSURANCE TABLE

Multiply **paid-up** policy premium by percentage figure shown in table. Example: Premium $80; on proration date policy has 15 months, 10 days to run. Multiply $80 by .4259 = $34.07. Credit seller and debit buyer.

(Note: Insurance tables shown apply to 36-month policies only. For 39-month policies, follow same procedure and multiply result by .9231.)

RENTAL TABLE

Only a few sample rents can be shown on a table. For a rent that is not easily related to one of those listed, the last column expresses number of days as a percent of the 30-day month. The monthly rent is multiplied by this percentage to find the prorated amount.

Exhibit 26.1

INSURANCE TABLE
9 to 17 Months (3-YEAR POLICIES)

DAYS	9	10	11	12	13	14	15	16	17
0	.2500	.2778	.3056	.3333	.3611	.3889	.4167	.4444	.4722
1	.2509	.2787	.3065	.3343	.3620	.3898	.4176	.4454	.4731
2	.2519	.2796	.3074	.3352	.3630	.3907	.4185	.4463	.4741
3	.2528	.2806	.3083	.3361	.3639	.3917	.4194	.4472	.4750
4	.2537	.2815	.3093	.3370	.3648	.3926	.4204	.4481	.4759
5	.2546	.2824	.3102	.3380	.3657	.3935	.4213	.4491	.4769
6	.2556	.2833	.3111	.3389	.3667	.3944	.4222	.4500	.4778
7	.2565	.2843	.3120	.3399	.3676	.3954	.4231	.4509	.4787
8	.2574	.2852	.3130	.3407	.3685	.3963	.4241	.4519	.4796
9	.2583	.2861	.3139	.3417	.3694	.3972	.4250	.4528	.4806
10	.2593	.2870	.3148	.3426	.3704	.3981	.4259	.4537	.4815
11	.2602	.2880	.3157	.3435	.3713	.3991	.4269	.4546	.4824
12	.2611	.2889	.3167	.3444	.3722	.4000	.4278	.4556	.4833
13	.2620	.2898	.3176	.3454	.3731	.4009	.4287	.4565	.4843
14	.2630	.2907	.3185	.3463	.3741	.4019	.4296	.4574	.4852
15	.2639	.2917	.3194	.3472	.3750	.4028	.4306	.4583	.4861
16	.2648	.2926	.3204	.3481	.3759	.4037	.4315	.4593	.4870
17	.2657	.2935	.3213	.3491	.3769	.4046	.4324	.4602	.4880
18	.2667	.2944	.3222	.3500	.3778	.4056	.4333	.4611	.4889
19	.2676	.2954	.3231	.3509	.3787	.4065	.4343	.4620	.4898
20	.2685	.2963	.3241	.3519	.3796	.4074	.4352	.4630	.4907
21	.2694	.2972	.3250	.3528	.3806	.4083	.4361	.4639	.4917
22	.2704	.2981	.3259	.3537	.3815	.4093	.4370	.4648	.4926
23	.2713	.2991	.3269	.3546	.3824	.4102	.4380	.4657	.4935
24	.2722	.3000	.3278	.3556	.3833	.4111	.4389	.4667	.4944
25	.2731	.3009	.3287	.3565	.3843	.4120	.4398	.4676	.4954
26	.2741	.3019	.3296	.3574	.3852	.4130	.4407	.4685	.4963
27	.2750	.3028	.3306	.3583	.3861	.4139	.4417	.4694	.4972
28	.2759	.3037	.3315	.3593	.3870	.4148	.4426	.4704	.4981
29	.2769	.3046	.3324	.3602	.3880	.4158	.4435	.4713	.4991

INSURANCE TABLE
27 to 35 Months (3-YEAR POLICIES)

DAYS	27	28	29	30	31	32	33	34	35
0	.7500	.7778	.8056	.8333	.8611	.8889	.9167	.9444	.9722
1	.7509	.7787	.8065	.8343	.8620	.8898	.9176	.9454	.9731
2	.7519	.7796	.8074	.8352	.8630	.8907	.9185	.9463	.9741
3	.7528	.7806	.8083	.8361	.8639	.8917	.9194	.9472	.9750
4	.7537	.7815	.8093	.8370	.8648	.8926	.9204	.9481	.9759
5	.7546	.7824	.8102	.8380	.8657	.8935	.9213	.9491	.9769
6	.7556	.7833	.8111	.8389	.8667	.8944	.9222	.9500	.9778
7	.7565	.7843	.8120	.8398	.8676	.8954	.9231	.9509	.9787
8	.7574	.7852	.8130	.8407	.8685	.8963	.9241	.9519	.9796
9	.7583	.7861	.8139	.8417	.8694	.8972	.9250	.9528	.9806
10	.7593	.7870	.8148	.8426	.8704	.8981	.9259	.9537	.9815
11	.7602	.7880	.8157	.8435	.8713	.8991	.9269	.9546	.9824
12	.7611	.7889	.8167	.8444	.8722	.9000	.9278	.9556	.9833
13	.7620	.7898	.8176	.8454	.8731	.9009	.9287	.9565	.9843
14	.7630	.7907	.8185	.8463	.8741	.9019	.9296	.9574	.9852
15	.7639	.7917	.8194	.8472	.8750	.9028	.9306	.9583	.9861
16	.7648	.7926	.8204	.8481	.8759	.9037	.9315	.9593	.9870
17	.7657	.7935	.8213	.8491	.8769	.9046	.9324	.9602	.9880
18	.7667	.7944	.8222	.8500	.8778	.9056	.9333	.9611	.9889
19	.7676	.7954	.8231	.8509	.8787	.9065	.9343	.9620	.9898
20	.7685	.7963	.8241	.8519	.8796	.9074	.9352	.9630	.9907
21	.7694	.7972	.8250	.8528	.8806	.9083	.9361	.9639	.9917
22	.7704	.7981	.8259	.8537	.8815	.9093	.9370	.9648	.9926
23	.7713	.7991	.8269	.8546	.8824	.9102	.9380	.9657	.9935
24	.7722	.8000	.8278	.8556	.8833	.9111	.9389	.9667	.9944
25	.7731	.8009	.8287	.8565	.8843	.9120	.9398	.9676	.9954
26	.7741	.8019	.8296	.8574	.8852	.9130	.9407	.9685	.9963
27	.7750	.8028	.8306	.8583	.8861	.9139	.9417	.9694	.9972
28	.7759	.8037	.8315	.8593	.8870	.9148	.9426	.9704	.9981
29	.7769	.8046	.8324	.8602	.8880	.9157	.9435	.9713	.9991

Exhibit 26.2

30-DAY RENTAL TABLE
PER MONTH

DAY	33.00	34.00	35.00	36.00	37.00	37.50	38.00	39.00
1	1.10	1.13	1.17	1.20	1.23	1.25	1.27	1.30
2	2.20	2.27	2.33	2.40	2.47	2.50	2.53	2.60
3	3.30	3.40	3.50	3.60	3.70	3.75	3.80	3.90
4	4.40	4.53	4.67	4.80	4.93	5.00	5.07	5.20
5	5.50	5.67	5.83	6.00	6.17	6.25	6.34	6.50
6	6.60	6.80	7.00	7.20	7.40	7.50	7.60	7.80
7	7.70	7.93	8.17	8.40	8.63	8.75	8.87	9.10
8	8.80	9.07	9.33	9.60	9.87	10.00	10.13	10.40
9	9.90	10.20	10.50	10.80	11.10	11.25	11.40	11.70
10	11.00	11.33	11.67	12.00	12.33	12.50	12.66	13.00
11	12.10	12.47	12.83	13.20	13.57	13.75	13.93	14.30
12	13.20	13.60	14.00	14.40	14.80	15.00	15.20	15.60
13	14.30	14.73	15.17	15.60	16.03	16.25	16.46	16.90
14	15.40	15.87	16.33	16.80	17.27	17.50	17.73	18.20
15	16.50	17.00	17.50	18.00	18.50	18.75	19.00	19.50
16	17.60	18.13	18.67	19.20	19.73	20.00	20.26	20.80
17	18.70	19.27	19.83	20.40	20.97	21.25	21.53	22.10
18	19.80	20.40	21.00	21.60	22.20	22.50	22.80	23.40
19	20.90	21.53	22.17	22.80	23.43	23.75	24.06	24.70
20	22.00	22.67	23.33	24.00	24.67	25.00	25.33	26.00
21	23.10	23.80	24.50	25.20	25.90	26.25	26.60	27.30
22	24.20	24.93	25.67	26.40	27.13	27.50	27.86	28.60
23	25.30	26.07	26.83	27.60	28.37	28.75	29.13	29.90
24	26.40	27.20	28.00	28.80	29.60	30.00	30.40	31.20
25	27.50	28.33	29.17	30.00	30.83	31.25	31.66	32.50
26	28.60	29.47	30.33	31.20	32.07	32.50	32.93	33.80
27	29.70	30.60	31.50	32.40	33.30	33.75	34.20	35.10
28	30.80	31.73	32.67	33.60	34.53	35.00	35.46	36.40
29	31.90	32.87	33.83	34.80	35.77	36.25	36.73	37.70

30-DAY RENTAL TABLE
PER MONTH

DAY	47.00	47.50	48.00	49.00	50.00	100.00	PERCENTAGE	
1	1.56	1.58	1.60	1.63	1.67	3.33	.0333	1
2	3.13	3.17	3.20	3.27	3.33	6.67	.0667	2
3	4.70	4.75	4.80	4.90	5.00	10.00	.1000	3
4	6.26	6.33	6.40	6.53	6.67	13.33	.1333	4
5	7.73	7.92	8.00	8.17	8.33	16.67	.1667	5
6	9.40	9.50	9.60	9.80	10.00	20.00	.2000	6
7	10.96	11.08	11.20	11.43	11.67	23.33	.2333	7
8	12.53	12.67	12.80	13.07	13.33	26.67	.2667	8
9	14.10	14.25	14.40	14.70	15.00	30.00	.3000	9
10	15.66	15.83	16.00	16.33	16.67	33.33	.3333	10
11	17.23	17.42	17.60	17.97	18.33	36.67	.3667	11
12	18.80	19.00	19.20	19.60	20.00	40.00	.4000	12
13	20.36	20.58	20.80	21.23	21.67	43.33	.4333	13
14	21.93	22.17	22.40	22.87	23.33	46.67	.4667	14
15	23.50	23.75	24.00	24.50	25.00	50.00	.5000	15
16	25.06	25.33	25.60	26.13	26.67	53.33	.5333	16
17	26.63	26.92	27.20	27.77	28.33	56.67	.5667	17
18	28.20	28.50	28.80	29.40	30.00	60.00	.6000	18
19	29.76	30.08	30.40	31.03	31.67	63.33	.6333	19
20	31.33	31.67	32.00	32.67	33.33	66.67	.6667	20
21	32.90	33.25	33.60	34.30	35.00	70.00	.7000	21
22	34.46	34.83	35.20	35.93	36.67	73.33	.7333	22
23	36.03	36.42	36.80	37.57	38.33	76.67	.7667	23
24	37.60	38.00	38.40	39.20	40.00	80.00	.8000	24
25	39.05	39.58	40.00	40.83	41.67	83.33	.8333	25
26	40.73	41.17	41.60	42.47	43.33	86.67	.8667	26
27	42.30	42.75	43.20	44.10	45.00	90.00	.9000	27
28	43.86	44.33	44.80	45.73	46.67	93.33	.9333	28
29	45.43	45.92	46.40	47.37	48.33	96.67	.9667	29

Exhibit 26.3

PRORATIONS

When a property is sold, on the settlement date various items are usually adjusted between the buyer and seller. Property taxes, mortgage interest, insurance, rental income, and utilities are among the most common adjustments prorated at the close of escrow (commonly the day escrow closes is "the buyer's day;" that is, the buyer pays items as of that day and thereafter, and is entitled to the rents for that day and thereafter). Prorations are usually calculated using the "banker's rule": 360 days per year, 30 days per month.

To Prorate Property Taxes
The home you sold is to have an escrow closing date of April 21st. The $1,440 tax bill for the year has already been paid by the seller. What is the amount of taxes to be reimbursed to the seller by the buyer?

Calculate the daily tax charge: $1,440 ÷ 360 days = $4 per day
Calculate time buyer will own the home in the tax year: 4/21 through 6/30 = 70 days
Multiply the 70 days by the daily rate: 70 days x $4/day = $280 (debit to buyer, credit to seller)

To Prorate Mortgage Interest
Escrow closes on August 16th. Buyers are assuming the loan of $63,280 at 10.5% interest paid to and including August 3rd. How much interest should be credited to the buyers?

Calculate the interest on the unpaid loan balance: $63,280 x .105 = $6,644.40 per year
Calculate the daily interest: $6,644.40 ÷ 360 days = $18.457 per day
Determine the number of days of accrued interest: 15 days elapsed — 3 days paid = 12 days accrued
Multiply the daily charge by the number of days: 12 days x $18.457 = $221.48 (debit to seller, credit to buyer)

To Prorate Insurance
An insurance company allowed the buyer to assume a three-year fire insurance policy that cost the seller $217.08 on March 20, 1989. What rebate is the seller entitled to if he sells on January 10, 1990?

Calculate the monthly insurance premium: $217.08 ÷ 36 months = $6.03 per month
Calculate time buyer will own home for remainder of policy: 1/10/90 to 3/20/92 = 2 years, 2 months, 10 days = $26\frac{1}{3}$ months
Multiply the monthly charge by the number of months: $6.03 x $26\frac{1}{3}$ = $158.79 (debit to buyer, credit to seller)

To Prorate Rental Income
A duplex was sold on the twenty-first day of April. Rents are due in advance on the first day of the month. The seller has collected $1,692 of rent. How much of the rent is due the buyer?

Calculate the daily rental income: $1,692 ÷ 30 days = $56.40 per day
Calculate days buyer will own home for remainder of month: 30 days — 20 days = 10 days due buyer
Multiply the daily rental income by number of days due buyer: $56.40 x 10 days = $564.00 (due buyer) (debit to seller, credit to buyer)

Exhibit 27

Quiz Chapter 8

1. If taxes were paid when due, and close of escrow was October 1, the prorated property taxes would be a _____ to the seller and a _____ to the buyer.

   (A) Debit, debit
   (B) Credit, credit
   ✓(C) Debit, credit
   (D) Credit, debit

2. The tax year begins:

   (A) June 30
   (B) July 1
   (C) November 1
   (D) March 1

3. Tax impound balances are credited to:

   (A) Buyer
   (B) Seller
   (C) Lender
   (D) Escrowholder

4. Prorations of prepaid insurance premiums are credits to the_____at close of escrow.

   (A) Insurance agent
   (B) Homeowners' association
   (C) Buyer
   (D) Seller

5. Rents are paid to the first of the month. Escrow closes on the 16th. Credit for_____days:

   ✓(A) Buyer, 15
   (B) Seller, 16
   (C) Buyer, 16
   (D) Seller, 15

6. Homeowner's insurance policies:

   ✓(A) In many cases are not prorated
   (B) Are always prorated in escrow
   (C) Are always assumed in escrow
   (D) Do not provide fire insurance coverage

7. Trust deed payments are normally:

   (A) Collected in advance
   (B) Payable quarterly
   ✓(C) Collected in arrears
   (D) Collected by automatic charge to borrower's bank account

8. Impounds are:

   (A) For taxes only
   (B) For insurance only
   (C) Not applicable to all real estate loans
   (D) Applicable to all real estate loans

9. The escrow ledger sheet and buyer's/seller's closing statements:

   (A) Must both account for the entire consideration
   (B) Will differ only in an all cash sale
   ✓(C) Will probably differ due to sub-escrow involving loan funds
   (D) Make it possible to shelter cash payments from the IRS

10. For escrow to close, each debit on the buyer's statement must be reflected by a corresponding credit to the seller.

    (A) True
    ✓(B) False

Chapter 9
Documentation—
The Key to a Smooth Closing

PREVIEW

Intent and Implementation

Document Transmittal

Final Audit for Compliance

Closing and Recordation

INTENT AND IMPLEMENTATION

As closing approaches, the escrowholder should go back to the original take sheet, outline, and instructions to make sure that all requirements have been correctly stated and met, double checking all of the following.

- ✔ Legal description of the property
  Current ownership data

- ✔ Special conditions of transfer (subject to sale of purchaser's current home, subject to loan approval, etc.)

- ✔ Trust deeds to be assumed:
    - ✔ Are impounds involved?
    - ✔ Is the obligation current?
    - ✔ Will a formal assumption be required?

- ✔ Insurance requirements
- ✔ Charges
- ✔ Instructions to pay commission

- ✔ For loans other than purchase money encumbrances, separate loan escrow instructions should be prepared.

- ✔ Exact name(s) of purchaser(s) and method of holding title (vesting)

- ✔ Personal property involved: Clearly identify any free-standing appliances or other furnishings included in the sale.

- ✔ Trust deeds to be created:
  Terms, conditions, and responsibilities imposed by lender

- ✔ Structural pest control
- ✔ Prorations
- ✔ Other special requirements of the parties.

Instructions and Amendments   As noted in Chapter 6, processing variations produce different types of instructions in specific geographic areas. As closing approaches, these differences affect the number and types of amendments and pitfalls encountered.

Unilateral Instructions   In Northern California, the use of a separate seller's instruction in conjunction with a buyer/borrower's instruction is common practice (Exhibit 28; compare Exhibit 15).

Prepared Near Closing. A unilateral instruction actually represents consummation of the transfer process which has been handled by the escrowholder for some time prior to the preparation of the instructions. The instruction serves to recapitulate the transaction and provide an allocation of responsibility for closing costs of the respective parties. At this point, all that is required usually is the provision of funds from the parties.

Contents. The difference between the seller's and the buyer/borrower's instruction is that the seller's instruction provides the necessary documents of transfer in exchange for some consideration, whether it be monetary or a combination of money and obligations on the part of the buyer. The buyer's instruction provides that consideration is to be given when escrow is in a position to transfer title.

Meeting of the Minds. The inherent problem that may evolve from using unilateral instructions is that there may not be a meeting of the minds between buyer and seller. A problem may arise if the nature of the consideration changes between the two instructions. For example, the seller's instruction might provide for all cash or "cash through escrow," but the buyer's instruction provide for a purchase money trust deed in favor of the seller instead of the bank as originally indicated. Further instructions from the seller, who would have a vested interest in this change, would be required, if the buyer had changed the instructions in this manner.

Ratification. Unilateral escrow instructions in Northern California are typically a ratification of what escrow has been doing in the form of instructions "to escrow" from the principals and do not necessarily create the subsequent contract between the principals.

☐ *Steps Completed.* Demands have been obtained, title reports rendered, the amount of structural pest control work ascertained, and new loans, if any, have been approved.

☐ *Closing Statement.* The principal ingredient of unilateral instructions is a pro forma closing statement, which, in most cases, will be the same as the statement rendered as of the anticipated closing date.

Bilateral Instructions In a bilateral instruction (Exhibit 29), the mutual promises of buyer and seller are combined into one instruction. Much of the information is either sketchy or nonexistent when the original instructions are prepared. The conditions of the buyer's purchase along with printed general instructions make up most of the body of this instruction. The seller further agrees to those items necessary to place title in a position to meet the terms of the transfer.

General Instructions. General escrow instructions vary due to escrow administrators' different philosophies about the extent and degree of protective clauses required in the instructions, and the different regulations applying to different types of escrowholders. Typical provisions include:

☐ *Completion Time*. Many times it is not possible to close within the time prescribed. A provision in the general instruction allows the transaction to continue past the proposed closing date if no objections are raised by either party.

☐ *Recordkeeping*. Escrowholders licensed by the Corporations Commissioner in California must retain escrow files for five years from date of closing. Most general instructions of such escrow companies permit the destruction of files after this five-year period.

Amendments and Special Instructions. With bilateral instructions, various types of amendment are common as the transaction develops. Sometimes parties other than the principals become involved in a transaction, and special instructions are required relative to the provision of documents, demand, and/or funds into escrow.

☐ *Third Party Instructions*. To assert or disavow a financial interest in the transaction, parties other than the principals may execute a third-party instruction similar to that shown in Exhibit 2, Chapter 5. A typical example is the authorization by the paying party to pay a broker's commission from the proceeds of the sale. Other examples where third-party instructions might be used are:

  ☐ Instructions for an interspousal transfer grant deed from one spouse to another without consideration (Exhibit 19).

  ☐ Lender's instructions relating to payoff or assumption (subject to existing loans).

  ☐ Other documents such as release of mechanics' liens, judgments, tax liens, etc. together with the corresponding instructions for their use.

☐ *Amendments*. Since escrow instructions are a binding contract between parties, any modification of the terms of transfer stated in the original instruction requires a formal modification of the contract. These modifications are referred to as amendments, and they constitute substituted terms of transfer upon execution by all parties in interest.

□ *Newly Disclosed Facts*. For example, say a bond for $2,000 against the property is disclosed by the title report, and the lender requires that this bond be paid in full. An agreement may be made between buyer and seller either to adjust the price or to split the cost of the bond payment. Whatever the choice, an amendment is required to establish the "meeting of the minds."

□ *Continuing Negotiations*. In areas where bilateral instruction is used, the tendency is to open an escrow if a transaction appears at all "warm." From opening on there is usually a parade of amendments, perhaps ending with a cancellation instruction because there was never a true meeting of minds. To this extent the unilateral instruction has its advantages.

Transfer and Financing Documents

Once instructions are complete, the contract is formed. Prior to this time, the three basic documents discussed in Chapter 7 will have been prepared for signature of the parties, and will be returned with the escrow instructions, properly executed. These documents, like the escrow instructions, vary in form. Note the differences between the examples shown here and the equivalent documents in Chapter 7.

Grant Deed. The grant deed (Exhibit 18) is a notarized statement granting title, prepared in accordance with instructions by the parties. It is important to verify that this document has been prepared in exact conformance with instructions. The following areas require particular care.

□ *Taxes*. Box in upper right relates to city transfer tax (as in Redondo Beach), documentary transfer tax ($110 on a $100,000 sale) and survey monument preservation fund (assessed in many counties). The documentary tax is computed on the consideration or value of the property conveyed, or on consideration or value less remaining encumbrances. Thus on this form the first statement is checked if the entire existing encumbrance is being paid off.

□ *Assessor's Parcel Number*. In order for the recorder to accept the document for recording, the assessor's parcel *must* be identified.

□ *Form and Content*. Common reasons for document rejection are:

□ Notary seal not adequate for reprographics

□ Improperly prepared notarization or expiration of notary commission

□ Missing or questionable signatures

□ Attaching poor photocopies of legal descriptions to deed

□ Property not in that county

□ Sale to government body without appropriate acceptance.

Installment Note. The note (Exhibit 30) shows exact terms of the loan, including any acceleration (alienation) clause contracted by the parties. Since this is the principal obligation of the buyers, it is extremely important that it properly reflect their mutual agreement. For example, both sides must be clear that they are undertaking a $60,000 lien, payable monthly at payments of $600 per month, including interest, with a balloon payment due in 10 years.

Deed of Trust. The trust deed (Exhibit 31) secures the debt evidenced by the note, by creating a lien and naming a trustee and beneficiary. It incorporates the terms of the acceleration clause and describes the amount of debt and the property subject to the lien. A short form deed of trust is generally used, to avoid the paperwork and expense of recording the general provisions. This is done by incorporating a previously recorded fictitious (master) deed of trust. (In Los Angeles County, for example, this is found in Book T-3878, page 574 of the official records.)

Documents Required for Closing In order to close this transaction, the remaining elements are the title related documents necessary to release the trust deed of record and a statement of the amount to pay it off in full. Therefore, upon receipt of the contract (escrow instructions) and supporting documents, the next steps involve:

Ordering Preliminary Title Report. See Exhibit 32. The preliminary title report (Exhibit 14, Chapter 6) is to be reviewed for liens or other complications, or discrepancies from the escrow instructions.

Examples

What is to be done if the report shows delinquent taxes? The escrowholder has general instructions to pay, but as a matter of courtesy would discuss the matter with the seller to determine if they had been recently paid. Or the report might show a mortgage in favor of the County of Los Angeles. These mortgages are a general lien on present or future property ownership of the grantor, usually contracted for the cost of health care at a county hospital. Specific instructions must be obtained approving payment in full of this or any other lien discovered at this stage.

Ordering Demands. Demands are ordered at this point from lienholders, for example:

☐ Independent Savings and Loan—for payoff of old loan

☐ County of Los Angeles—for taxes, fees, and liens if any.

Document Transmittal

At this stage various documents require review and processing by the title company and assessor.

Deed The deed, properly acknowledged, is forwarded to the title insurance company to review its adequacy for recording and to verify correct placement of title (names, form of ownership, etc.).

Example

If a sale was begun by John and Mary Smith, and title were shown on the title report as John Clark Smith and Mary Forbes Smith, husband and wife, and Jeffrey Lynn Smith, a single man, their son, all as joint tenants, additional instructions would be required.

☐ A third party (without consideration) instruction from the son (provided he is not a minor) together with a quitclaim deed would have to be made in favor of the buyers.

☐ If the son was a minor, a guardian would have to be appointed and a court order obtained authorizing the deed.

☐ In addition, a statement would have to be added to the grantor section of the deed from the Smiths as follows: "Who acquired title as John Clark Smith and Mary Forbes Smith . . . ."

Deed of Trust Upon receipt from the buyer, the acknowledged deed of trust is sent to the title company for examination and retention for further instruction.

Statement of Information Title insurers require this data to establish the identity of the parties with certainty and clear general index items such as abstracts of judgment. Customers can be sensitive about this information—note the explanatory statement on the sample form. (Exhibit 33)

Preliminary Change of Ownership Report If the form is not prepared at closing, it is required to be filed with the assessor subsequent to closing along with a $20 penalty for separate recording. (See Exhibit 9, Chapter 5)

Final Audit for Compliance

Since escrow transactions can become cumbersome and complex, a final check list can help determine full compliance with the wishes of the parties. A transaction audit using the audit check sheet shown as Exhibit 34 is one suggested approach.

Escrow Instructions Signed Have all parties that have a vested interest in the subject matter of the instruction been included in the instruction? Additionally, have all parties signed the original or its counterparts?

Supplemental Instructions Signed Do all subsequent modifications, amendments, and supplementary exhibits to the initial instructions bear the signatures of the necessary parties?

Disbursements Authorized Does escrowholder have the commission authorization, payoff approval, approvals for loan escrow, title fees, termite work, withholding of funds for work to be performed, bills to be presented, and so on?

Legal Description Correct This seemingly insignificant item can cause title to the wrong property to pass and considerable liability to be incurred by the parties responsible for the oversight. It should be checked carefully.

Escrow Instructions Followed This includes not only the original instructions but the addenda, supplements, and amendments as well. Many times the essence of a transaction has been changed by amendment. It is very important to note the modifications of the original instructions in order to determine compliance.

Lender's Requirements Met Each lending institution has its own requirements relative to documentation, title matters, taxes, structural pest control reports, credit matters, and insurance requirements. It is important that the lender's instruction letter and the loan escrow instructions prepared in accordance therewith be fully understood and followed (see Chapter 14). Any deviation from the instruction requires further approval.

Fire Insurance OK? Not only must coverage be sufficient, but in some cases the insurance company must be approved. Many lenders accept only those fire insurers that they deem financially able to meet their requirements.

Correct Names on Documents Does the seller's name agree with the ownership indicated on the preliminary title report? Have the purchaser's name and status been properly reflected on all appropriate documents?

Sufficient Funds There must be sufficient funds to close the file from the seller and buyer. This is a critical item, especially if funds are required from the seller to close. In order to draw any funds against the money deposited in escrow, the deposit must consist of "good funds."

Checks Cleared Prior to closing, cashier's checks or certified checks should have been requested. Even then the moneys must be collected through the clearing process. If personal checks are given, sufficient time must be allowed for them to clear prior to closing. In addition, out of state and bank proceeds checks may be held for an extended period of time. By law, title companies cannot use funds remitted from escrows for payoff until they are physically deposited.

Tax Reporting Have funds been withheld or exemption filed in compliance with the Foreign Investment in Real Property Tax Act, and Form 1099-S filed? In the case of alien sellers, buyers are required to have escrowholders retain a percentage of the sale proceeds for the benefit of the Internal Revenue Service in single family residential sales exceeding $300,000 and transactions other than residential in excess of $50,000, unless affidavits of exemption have been provided by the parties. The IRS also requires a 1099-S in every seller's name showing the tax I.D. number and stating the amount of consideration passing in the transaction (Exhibit 12, Chapter 5).

Termite Compliances Done Has all remedial work been completed? If preventive work has been authorized, is the work performed, or have instructions been obtained to withhold sufficient funds?

Documents at the Title Company Are all documents at the title company? It is very embarrassing to the escrowholder to discover that the grant deed and trust deed(s) are still in the escrow file when they should have been forwarded to the title company two weeks prior to closing time, or when the title company advises that the documents are improperly executed or that the form of acknowledgment is incorrect.

Ready to Record Satisfactory completion of the foregoing items places the file in a position to record. Prior to ordering the recording it is helpful if the next procedure, pre-settlement, is completed to avoid possible shortages.

Pre-Settlement It is advisable to figure the file prior to closing, to determine that sufficient collected moneys are on deposit to meet all of the obligations of the parties. Closing "short" with insufficient funds is not an acceptable escrow practice.

CLOSING AND RECORDATION

By careful attention to detail a fairly simple escrow reaches a smooth conclusion with this last three step process. Upon completion of all correspondence and disbursement of funds, the file is then considered closed.

Deposit of Funds By Buyer Some of this deposit might, for example, be transmitted to the title company to pay off any liens of record through a sub-escrow.

Final Audit Escrowholder verifies once more that all instructions are fulfilled and there are adequate funds.

Order Recording Escrowholder arranges for recording of the deed, trust deed, note, change of ownership report, and miscellaneous documents such as release of liens.

UNILATERAL ESCROW INSTRUCTIONS

SELLERS INSTRUCTIONS

To: Insurance Trust Company

Date: April 25, 1989 ____ Escrow Officer: E. O. Smith ____ Escrow No.: 510234 ____

I/We ____ hand you: (X) A deed in favor of Joseph Buyer and Mary Buyer, his wife, as Community Property
( ) Signed and approved rental statement
( ) Existing fire insurance ☐ to be cancelled ☐ to be transferred to buyer
( ) ____

covering the real property described in your preliminary title report No. 510234 ____ dated 4/15-89 ____ a copy of which I/We have read and approved. All of which you may deliver and/or record when you have collected for my/our account the balance due as shown below in the form of (X) Check

( ) Note and ☐ 1st ☐ 2nd Trust Deed for $____ dated ____
payable to ____ at $____
or more per month ☐ plus ☐ including interest at ____ % per annum from ____ . First payment
due ____ . ☐ Note and Trust Deed in form attached hereto as Exhibit A and B for $____
( ) You may complete said note and Trust Deed upon close of escrow.
( ) ____

And when you can issue your CLTA Form Title Insurance Policy (and ALTA Policy if required by Buyer's Lender) with liability in the amount of $ 50,000 ____ , as indicated below, on the real property described in said report showing title vested in Joseph Buyer and Mary Buyer, his wife, as community property ____

SUBJECT TO: County and/or City taxes not delinquent; covenants, conditions, restrictions, rights of way, easements and reservations of record;
(X) Preliminary report items numbered 2, 3, 4, & 5 ____
(X) Trust Deed to record in favor of Bank of America ____
( ) ____

PRORATE AS OF
C.O.E.
(X) Taxes (based on latest available tax bill)
( ) Prepaid fire insurance premium
( ) Interest on existing loan
( ) Rents (based on statement provided by Seller)
( ) ____
( ) ____

You are authorized to make deductions, adjustments and disbursements in accordance with the following statement. Estimated amounts may be adjusted dependent upon date of close of escrow.

ESTIMATED STATEMENT	DEBITS	CREDITS
PURCHASE PRICE		$50,000.00
DEPOSIT RETAINED BY:		
EXISTING LOAN BALANCE		
EXISTING LOAN TRUST FUNDS		
EXISTING LOAN TRANSFER FEE		
NEW TRUST DEED ( ) 1st ( ) 2nd		
NEW TRUST DEED ( ) 1st ( ) 2nd		
TAXES PRO-RATA (62.00/mo) C.O.E. to 7/1/89		124.00
FIRE INSURANCE PRO-RATA		
INTEREST PRO-RATA		
RENT PRO-RATA		
ASSESSMENT INTEREST PRO-RATA		
RENT DEPOSIT		
TITLE INSURANCE PREMIUM		
ESCROW FEE		
RECONVEYANCE FEE	20.00	
RECORDING Reconveyance	3.00	
DOCUMENT PREPARATION $ 5.00 PLUS NOTARY FEE $ 2.00	7.00	
TRANSFER TAX	55.00	
PAY TAXES AND ASSESSMENTS ☐ COUNTY ☐ CITY ☐ OTHER		

	OF John & Mary Jones	PRINCIPAL $	8,500.00	
PAY DEMAND	INT. AT 10% FROM 4/1/89 TO C.O.E.	$	70.84	
	PREPAYMENT CHARGE	$		
	RECON/FORWARDING FEE	$		
		$		
	LESS LOAN TRUST FUND	$ (	)	
		TOTAL	8,570.84	

	DEBITS	CREDITS
COMMISSION TO: Ajax Realty	3,000.00	
PAY: XYZ Termite Control -- upon presentation of the Standard Notice of Work Completed	65.00	
BALANCE DUE ☐ THIS ESCROW ☒ SELLER	38,403.16	
TOTALS	$50,124.00	$50,124.00

The GENERAL PROVISIONS printed on the reverse side of this page of these instructions are by reference thereto incorporated herein and made a part hereof and have been read and are hereby approved by the undersigned.

Time is of the essence of these instructions. If this escrow is not in condition to close by the "time limit date" of May 1, 1989 ____ , and demand for cancellation is received by you from any principal to this escrow after said date, you shall act in accordance with Paragraph 7 of the General Provisions printed on the reverse side hereof. If no demand for cancellation is made, you will proceed to close this escrow when the principals have complied with the escrow instructions.

Any amendments of or supplements to any instructions affecting this escrow must be in writing. I will hand you any funds and instruments required to complete this escrow.

All documents, balances and statements due the undersigned are to be mailed to the address shown below.

SIGNATURE John Seller ____ ADDRESS ____ TELEPHONE ____

SIGNATURE Helen Seller ____ CITY ____ STATE ____ ZIP ____

Exhibit 28.1

BUYERS AND/OR BORROWERS INSTRUCTIONS

To: Insurance Trust Escrow Company

Date: April 25, 1989   Escrow Officer: E. O. Smith   Escrow Number: 510234

I/We _____ hand you: (X) Balance due, as indicated below, in the form of cash/cashier's check

(   ) Note and ☐ 1st ☐ 2nd Trust Deed for $_____, dated _____, payable to _____ at $_____

or more per month ☐ plus ☐ including interest at _____% per annum from _____, First payment due _____, ☐ Note and Trust Deed in form attached hereto as Exhibit A and B for $_____

(X) Note and Trust Deed in favor of Bank of America for $25,000.00

(   ) You may complete said Note(s) and Trust Deed(s) upon close of escrow

(') _____

All of which you may deliver and/or record when you obtain for my/our account a Deed to the real property described in your preliminary report no. 510234 dated 4/15/89 , a copy of which I/we have read and hereby approve.

And when you can issue your CLTA Form Title Insurance Policy (and ALTA Policy if required by Buyer's Lender) with liability in the amount of $ 50,000.00 ', as indicated below, on the real property described in said report showing title vested in Joseph Buyer and Mary Buyer, his wife, as community property

SUBJECT TO: County and/or City taxes not delinquent; covenants, conditions, restrictions, rights of way, easements and reservations of record;

(X) Preliminary report items numbered 2,3,4, & 5

(X) Trust Deed to record in favor of Bank of America

(   ) _____

PRORATE AS OF
C.O.E.

{
(X) Taxes (based on latest available tax bill)
(   ) Prepaid fire insurance premium
(   ) Interest on existing loan
(   ) Rents (based on statement provided by Seller)
(X) See reverse side for additional instructions.
(   ) _____
}

You are authorized to make deductions, adjustments and disbursements in accordance with the following statement. Estimated amounts may be adjusted dependent upon date of close of escrow.

ESTIMATED STATEMENT	DEBITS	CREDITS
PURCHASE PRICE:	$50,000.00	
DEPOSIT PAID BY BUYER TO:		$ 1,000.00
DEPOSIT RETAINED BY:		
EXISTING LOAN BALANCE:		
EXISTING LOAN TRUST FUNDS:		
LOAN TRANSFER FEE		
1st DEED OF TRUST: Bank of America		25,000.00
2nd DEED OF TRUST:		
NEW LOAN CHARGES OF Bank of America		
FHA MTG. INS. $ INS. RESERVE $		
TAX RESERVE $ 150.00 RECON. FEE $		
CREDIT REPORTS $ 5.00 TAX SERVICE $		
LOAN FEE $ 250.00 APPRAISAL FEE $ 25.00		
INT. AT 6 % FROM C.O.E. TO 6/1/89== $125.00		
TOTAL LOAN CHARGES	555.00	
TAX PRO-RATA ($62.00/mo) C.O.E. to 7/1/89	124.00	
FIRE INSURANCE ( ) PRO-RATE (x) NEW Allstate Insurance	150.00	
INTEREST PRO-RATA		
RENT PRO-RATA		
ASSESSMENT INTEREST PRO-RATA		
RENT DEPOSIT		
TITLE INSURANCE PREMIUM CLTA $260.00: ALTA $44.75	304.75	
ESCROW FEE	104.00	
RECORDING Deed and Deed of Trust	6.00	
DOCUMENT PREPARATION $ _____ PLUS NOTARY FEE $ 2.00	2.00	
TRANSFER TAX		
XYZ Termite Control (Inspection Fee)	50.00	
BALANCE DUE ☒ THIS ESCROW ☐ BUYER		25,295.75
TOTALS	$51,295.75	$51,295.75

The GENERAL PROVISIONS printed on the reverse side of this page of these instructions are by reference thereto incorporated herein and made a part hereof and have been read and are hereby approved by the undersigned.

Time is of the essence of these instructions. If this escrow is not in condition to close by the "time limit date" of May 1, 1989 and demand for cancellation is received by you from any principal to this escrow after said date, you shall act in accordance with Paragraph 7 of the General Provisions printed on the reverse side hereof. If no demand for cancellation is made, you will proceed to close this escrow when the principals have complied with the escrow instructions.

Any amendments of or supplements to any instructions affecting this escrow must be in writing. I will hand you any funds and instruments required to complete this escrow.

All documents, balances and statements due the undersigned are to be mailed to the address shown below.

SIGNATURE Joseph Buyer

SIGNATURE Mary Buyer

ADDRESS 1721 Homewood Place   TELEPHONE 854-7777

CITY Woodside,   STATE CA   ZIP 94069

Exhibit 28.2

GENERAL PROVISIONS

1. **Deposit of Funds**

   All funds received in this escrow shall be deposited with other escrow funds in a general escrow account or accounts of Title Insurance and Trust Company, with any state or national bank, and may be transferred to any other such general escrow account or accounts. All disbursements shall be made by check of Title Insurance and Trust Company.

   Any commitment made in writing to Title Insurance and Trust Company by a bank, trust company, insurance company, or savings and loan association to deliver its check or funds into this escrow may, in the sole discretion of Title Insurance and Trust Company, be treated as the equivalent of a deposit in this escrow of the amount thereof.

2. **Prorations and Adjustments**

   All prorations and/or adjustments called for in this escrow are to be made on the basis of a thirty (30) day month unless otherwise instructed in writing.

   The phrase "close of escrow" (COE or CE) as used in this escrow means the date on which documents are recorded and relates only to proration and/or adjustments unless otherwise specified.

3. **Recordation of Instruments**

   Recordation of any instruments delivered through this escrow, if necessary or proper for the issuance of the policy of title insurance called for, is authorized.

4. **Authorization to Furnish Copies**

   You are authorized to furnish copies of these instructions, supplements, amendments, or notices of cancellation and closing statements in this escrow, to the real estate broker(s) and lender(s) named in this escrow.

5. **Authorization to Execute Assignment of Hazard Insurance Policies**

   You are to execute, on behalf of the principals hereto, form assignments of interest in any insurance policy (other than title insurance) called for in this escrow; forward assignment and policy to the agent requesting that insurer consent to such transfer and/or attach a loss payable clause and/or such other indorsements as may be required; and, forward such policy(s) to the principals entitled thereto.

6. **Personal Property Taxes**

   No examination or insurance as to the amount or payment of personal property taxes is required unless specifically requested.

7. **Right of Cancellation**

   Any principal instructing you to cancel this escrow shall file notice of cancellation in your office, in writing. You shall within two (2) working days thereafter mail, by certified mail, one copy of such notice to each of the other principals at the addresses stated in this escrow. Unless written objection to cancellation is filed in your office by a principal within ten (10) days after date of such mailing, you are authorized to comply with such notice and demand payment of your cancellation charges as provided in this agreement. If written objection is filed, you are authorized to hold all money and instruments in this escrow and take no further action until otherwise directed, either by the principals' mutual written instructions, or final order of a court of competent jurisdiction.

   The principals hereto expressly agree that you, as escrow holder, have the absolute right at your election to file an action in interpleader requiring the principals to answer and litigate their several claims and rights among themselves and you are authorized to deposit with the clerk of the court all documents and funds held in this escrow. In the event such action is filed, the principals jointly and severally agree to pay your cancellation charges and costs, expenses and reasonable attorney's fees which you are required to expend or incur in such interpleader action, the amount thereof to be fixed and judgment therefor to be rendered by the court. Upon the filing of such action, you shall thereupon be fully released and discharged from all obligations to further perform any duties or obligations otherwise imposed by the terms of this escrow.

8. **Termination of Agency Obligation**

   If there is no action taken on this escrow within six (6) months after the "time limit date" as set forth in the escrow instructions or written extension thereof, your agency obligation shall terminate at your option and all documents, monies or other items held by you shall be returned to the parties depositing same.

   In the event of cancellation of this escrow, whether it be at the request of any of the principals or otherwise, the fees and charges due Title Insurance and Trust Company, including expenditures incurred and/or authorized shall be borne equally by the parties hereto (unless otherwise agreed to specifically).

9. **Conflicting Instructions**

   Upon receipt of any conflicting instructions other than cancellation instructions, you are no longer obligated to take any further action in connection with this escrow until further consistent instructions are received from the principals to this escrow except as provided in Paragraph 7 of these General Provisions.

ADDITIONAL INSTRUCTIONS

Sellers are to provide the Buyers with a Standard Notice of Work Completed

prior to "Close of Escrow" covering Inspection Report from XYZ Termite Control,

dated March 30, 1989, Items 2 and 3 only. Sellers are to Pay XYZ Termite Control

$65.00 for this repair.

Exhibit 28.3

BILATERAL SALE ESCROW INSTRUCTIONS

S T E R L I N G   B A N K

3287 Wilshire Boulevard   Los Angeles, California 90010   (213) 384-4444

SALE ESCROW INSTRUCTIONS   Escrow No._____

ESCROW OFFICER   Date_____

On or before   I/We will hand you

Paid outside of escrow	$_____
Cash through escrow	$_____
Encumbrance of records	$_____
Encumbrance of records	$_____
New encumbrance	$_____
	$_____
	$_____
	$_____
Total Consideration	$_____

and any funds and instruments necessary for me to comply with these instructions, which you are to use provided you can have issued a CLTA policy of title insurance with the liability for the total consideration.

COVERING the following described real property in the

County of

SHOWING TITLE VESTED IN

FREE FROM ENCUMBRANCES EXCEPT

(1) General and special county taxes, if any, together with special district levies, if any, included and collected with tax bill, not delinquent.

(2) Covenants, conditions, restrictions, reservations, rights, rights of way, easements and exceptions of minerals, oils, gas, water, carbons and hydrocarbons on or under said land, now of record, and in deed to file, if any, affecting the use and occupancy of said property.

If above encumbrance is a purchase money trust deed, endorse interest on note as of date of recording deed.
In event unpaid balance of trust deed(s) of record are more or less than the sum(s) set forth above, adjust difference ( ) in cash ( ) thru trust deed to file
Prorations and adjustments to be made as of_____

( ) Taxes	( ) Impounds
( ) Rents	( ) Interest on Trust Deed of Record
( ) Fire Insurance Premiums	( ) Mortgage Insurance Premium
( ) Homeowners Assoc. Dues	( )
( ) Buyer will furnish new fire insurance in form and amount satisfactory to lender, on property known as:	

I, Seller agree to the foregoing terms, conditions and instructions hereby concurred in, approved and accepted. I will hand you all instruments and money necessary of me to enable you to comply herewith which you are authorized to use and/or deliver when you hold in this escrow for my account the funds, prorata adjustments and instruments deliverable to me under these instructions. I agree to pay your usual escrow charges, except those the buyer agreed to pay, my recording fees, charges for assurance of title, beneficiaries' statement(s) and/or demand(s) together with any amounts necessary to place title in condition called for. Pay Documentary Transfer Tax as required.

BUYER AND SELLER HAVE READ AND AGREE TO THE GENERAL PROVISIONS PRINTED ON THE REVERSE.

Sellers _____   Buyers _____

_____   _____

_____   _____

_____   _____

Address _____   Address _____

_____   _____
        (TELEPHONE)   (TELEPHONE)

ESC-801 (7/86)   (OVER)   RE-3/11

Exhibit 29.1

GENERAL PROVISIONS

1. If the conditions of this escrow have not been complied with prior to the date stated on Line 1, or any extension thereof, you are nevertheless to complete the escrow as soon as the conditions, except as to time have been complied with, unless written demand shall have been made upon you not to complete it.

2. To pay on demand, whether or not this escrow closes, any charges incurred by you on our behalf and your usual escrow fees and charges.

3. Fees and charges will be paid as follows: (a) By Buyer — for recording deed, filling in, acknowledging and recording trust deed, any documents necessary on his part, lender's assumption or change of records fee, and buyer's escrow fee; and (b) By Seller — for title policy, beneficiaries' statements and/or demands, documentary transfer tax on deed, filling in, acknowledging and recording any documents necessary on his part, and seller's escrow fee.

4. Use your usual instrument forms and insert dates and terms on instruments in this escrow to the real estate broker, any lender, lender's agent, FHA or VA, upon their request.

5. You are authorized to deliver copies of all instructions and closing statements in this escrow to the real estate broker, any lender, lender's agent, FHA or VA, upon their request.

6. This escrow affords no protection against possible conditional sales contracts, if any, affecting the property acquired or any fixtures or equipment in connection therewith.

7. As escrow holder you shall deposit funds paid into this escrow with other escrow funds in a general escrow fund account. The aggregate of all such funds so on deposit in all banks shall constitute one general escrow fund. All disbursements may be made by check of **STERLING BANK**, checks not promptly presented for payment are subject to service charges in accordance with your bank's schedule in effect from time to time.

8. It is agreed by the parties hereto that so far as your rights and liabilities are concerned, this transaction is an escrow and not any other legal relation and you are an escrow holder only on the terms expressed herein, and you shall have no responsibility of notifying me or any of the parties to this escrow of any sale, resale, loan, exchange, or other transaction involving any property herein described or of any profit realized by any person, firm or corporation (broker, agent, and parties to this and/or any other escrow included) in connection therewith, regardless of the fact that such transaction(s) may be handled by you in this escrow or in another escrow.

9. The policy of title insurance to be delivered through this escrow will be issued subject to exceptions and conditions set out in the title company's printed form, which exceptions and conditions are hereby approved. No Bill of Sale, chattel or security interest search is required covering personal property, if any, being transferred through this escrow. Bill of Sale if any required, is to be delivered unrecorded at the close of escrow. If a structural pest control report and/or notice of work completed are handed into escrow, when received a copy thereof is to be delivered to buyer.

10. Obtain beneficiary statement to verify the encumbrance principal balance; make adjustments and prorations required based on the figures therein set forth.

11. "Trust deed" shall mean mortgage; "encumbrance" shall mean either of the previous, as well as liens of any type whatsoever; the singular, the plural word or visa versa, "close of escrow" shall mean the day instruments are recorded. Make each proration on the basis of a 30 day month.

12. Prorate taxes and levies on the basis of the current year's figures, except during the period they are not available you are to use the immediately prceding year's figures; as furnished you by the title company. Seller will pay outside of escrow and prior to delinquency any taxes on property not being conveyed herein, which taxes are a lien on the real property conveyed.

13. Prorate rents and charge seller and credit buyer with any deposits paid in advance on the basis of a statement furnished by seller. Seller represents that he will collect all rents which fall due prior to the close of escrow. Make no adjustment against buyer on uncollected rents.

14. Prorate premiums on fire insurance policies on improvements, which seller hands you or which beneficiary informs you he holds; assign policies if premium to be prorated; request insuror's agent to transfer the policy to buyer, and issue mortgagee clauses. Transfer and prorate all other insurance policies, if approved by Buyer. Seller represents that the policies are in force, not hypothecated, and premiums paid. You are relieved of all responsibility and/or liability as to the correctness of the street address or other description shown in insurance policies handed to you.

15. Mail policy of title insurance to the holder of prior encumbrance recorded concurrently with documents herein, if any, with a copy to the Buyer; otherwise the original to the Buyer. Mail fire insurance policies to holder of first encumbrance, if any, otherwise to buyer; other instruments in favor of buyer or seller to their address stated on Page 1. Deed to file is to provide that tax statements be mailed to the address set forth.

16. When property being conveyed is held in joint tenancy any cash derived therefrom in this escrow shall be joint tenancy funds.

17. Should you, before or after close of escrow, receive or become aware of any conflicting demands or claims with respect to this escrow or the rights of any of the parties hereto, or any money or property deposited herein or affected hereby, you shall have the right to discontinue any or all further acts on your part until such conflict is resolved to your satisfaction, and you shall have the further right to commence or defend any court proceedings for the determination of such conflict. Buyer and seller jointly and severally agree to pay all costs, damages, judgments and expenses, including reasonable attorney's fees, with regard to any such proceedings or otherwise suffered or incurred by you in connection with or arising out of this escrow.

18. You are not to be held liable for the sufficiency or correctness as to form, manner of execution, or validity of any instrument deposited in this new escrow, nor as to identity, authority, or rights of any person executing the same, nor for failure to comply with any of the provisions of any agreement, contract, or other instrument filed herein, and your duties hereunder shall be limited to the safekeeping of such money, instruments, or other documents, received by you as escrow holder, and for the dispostion of same in accordance with the written instructions accepted by you in this escrow.

19. These instructions may be executed in counterparts, each of which so executed shall, irrespective of the date of its execution and delivery be deemed an original, and said counterparts together shall constitute one and the same instrument.

20. Any amended, supplemental, or additional instructions given shall be subject to the foregoing conditions.

PAGE 2

Exhibit 29.2

INSTALLMENT NOTE

(INTEREST INCLUDED)

(This note contains an acceleration clause)

$_____   _____ , California,_____

In installments and at the times hereinafter stated, for value received_____

promise____ to pay to

or order, at_____

the principal sum of_____Dollars,

with interest from_____ on the amounts of principal remaining from time to time

unpaid, until said principal sum is paid, at the rate of_____per cent, per annum. Principal and interest due

in monthly installments of_____Dollars,

($_____), or more on the_____day of each and every month, beginning on the _____day

of_____, 19_____

and continuing until said principal sum and the interest thereon has been fully paid. AT ANY TIME, THE PRIVILEGE IS RESERVED TO PAY MORE THAN THE SUM DUE. Each payment shall be credited first, on the interest then due; and the remainder on the principal sum; and interest shall thereupon cease upon the amount so credited on the said principal sum. Should default be made in the payment of any of said installments when due, then the whole sum of principal and interest shall become immediately due and payable at the option of the holder of this note.

If the trustor shall sell, convey or alienate said property, or any part thereof, or any interest therein, or shall be divested of his title or any interest therein in any manner or way, whether voluntarily or involuntarily, without the written consent of the beneficiary being first had and obtained beneficiary shall have the right, at its option, to declare any indebtedness or obligations secured hereby, irrespective of the maturity date specified in any note evidencing the same, immediately due and payable.

Should suit be commenced to collect this note or any portion thereof, such sum as the Court may deem reasonable shall be added hereto as attorney's fees. Principal and interest payable in lawful money of the United States of America. This note is secured by a certain DEED OF TRUST to the FIRST AMERICAN TITLE INSURANCE COMPANY, a California corporation, as TRUSTEE.

_____   _____

_____   _____

_____   _____

Exhibit 30

SHORT FORM DEED OF TRUST

```
Order No.
Escrow No.
Loan No.

WHEN RECORDED MAIL TO:
```

───────────────────────────────── SPACE ABOVE THIS LINE FOR RECORDER'S USE ─────────────────────────────────

DEED OF TRUST WITH ASSIGNMENT OF RENTS
(This Deed of Trust contains an acceleration clause)

This DEED OF TRUST, made   , between

                                                                                          herein called TRUSTOR,

whose address is

| (Number and Street) | (City) | (State) |

FIRST AMERICAN TITLE INSURANCE COMPANY,   a California corporation, herein called TRUSTEE, and

                                                                    , herein called BENEFICIARY,

WITNESSETH: That Trustor grants to Trustee in Trust, with Power of Sale, that property in the

County of   , State of California, described as:

If the trustor shall sell, convey or alienate said property, or any part thereof, or any interest therein, or shall be divested of his title or any interest therein in any manner or way, whether voluntarily or involuntarily, without the written consent of the beneficiary being first had and obtained, beneficiary shall have the right, at its option, except as prohibited by law, to declare any indebtedness or obligations secured hereby, irrespective of the maturity date specified in any note evidencing the same, immediately due and payable.

Together with the rents, issues and profits thereof, subject, however, to the right, power and authority hereinafter given to and conferred upon Beneficiary to collect and apply such rents, issues and profits.

For the Purpose of Securing (1) payment of the sum of $ with interest thereon according to the terms of a promissory note or notes of even date herewith made by Trustor, payable to order of Beneficiary, and extensions or renewals thereof, and (2) the performance of each agreement of Trustor incorporated by reference or contained herein (3) Payment of additional sums and interest thereon which may hereafter be loaned to Trustor, or his successors or assigns, when evidenced by a promissory note or notes reciting that they are secured by this Deed of Trust.

To protect the security of this Deed of Trust, and with respect to the property above described, Trustor expressly makes each and all of the agreements, and adopts and agrees to perform and be bound by each and all of the terms and provisions set forth in subdivision A, and it is mutually agreed that each and all of the terms and provisions set forth in subdivision B of the fictitious deed of trust recorded in Orange County August 17, 1964, and in all other counties August 18, 1964, in the book and at the page of Official Records in the office of the county recorder of the county where said property is located, noted below opposite the name of such county, namely:

COUNTY	BOOK	PAGE	COUNTY	BOOK	PAGE	COUNTY	BOOK	PAGE	COUNTY	BOOK	PAGE
Alameda	1288	556	Kings	858	713	Placer	1028	379	Sierra	38	187
Alpine	3	130-31	Lake	437	110	Plumas	166	1307	Siskiyou	506	762
Amador	133	438	Lassen	192	367	Riverside	3778	347	Solano	1287	621
Butte	1330	513	Los Angeles	T-3878	874	Sacramento	5039	124	Sonoma	2067	427
Calaveras	185	338	Madera	911	136	San Benito	300	405	Stanislaus	1970	56
Colusa	323	391	Marin	1849	122	San Bernardino	6213	768	Sutter	655	585
Contra Costa	4684	1	Mariposa	90	453	San Francisco	A-804	596	Tehama	457	183
Del Norte	101	549	Mendocino	667	99	San Joaquin	2855	283	Trinity	108	595
El Dorado	704	635	Merced	1660	753	San Luis Obispo	1311	137	Tulare	2530	108
Fresno	5052	623	Modoc	191	93	San Mateo	4778	175	Tuolumne	177	160
Glenn	469	76	Mono	69	302	Santa Barbara	2065	881	Ventura	2607	237
Humboldt	801	83	Monterey	357	239	Santa Clara	6626	664	Yolo	769	16
Imperial	1189	701	Napa	704	742	Santa Cruz	1638	607	Yuba	398	693
Inyo	165	672	Nevada	363	94	Shasta	800	633			
Kern	3756	690	Orange	7182	18	San Diego SERIES 5 Book 1964, Page 149774					

shall inure to and bind the parties hereto, with respect to the property above described. Said agreements, terms and provisions contained in said subdivision A and B, (identical in all counties, and printed on the reverse side hereof) are by the within reference thereto, incorporated herein and made a part of this Deed of Trust for all purposes as fully as if set forth at length herein, and Beneficiary may charge for a statement regarding the obligation secured hereby, provided the charge therefor does not exceed the maximum allowed by law.

The undersigned Trustor, requests that a copy of any notice of default and any notice of sale hereunder be mailed to him at his address hereinbefore set forth.

```
STATE OF CALIFORNIA           }                          Signature of Trustor
COUNTY OF_____      }ss.
On_____             _____

before me, the undersigned, a Notary Public in and for said State, per-
sonally appeared_____     _____
_____

personally known to me (or proved to me on the basis of satisfactory
evidence) to be the person(s) whose name(s) is/are subscribed to the
within instrument and acknowledged to me that he/she/they executed
the same.

WITNESS my hand and official seal.
                                              (This area for official notarial seal)   1192 (6/82)
Signature_____
```

Exhibit 31.1

DO NOT RECORD

The following is a copy of Subdivisions A and B of the fictitious Deed of Trust recorded in each county in California as stated in the foregoing Deed of Trust and incorporated by reference in said Deed of Trust as being a part thereof as if set forth at length therein.

A.   To protect the security of this Deed of Trust, Trustor agrees:

(1)   To keep said property in good condition and repair; not to remove or demolish any building thereon; to complete or restore promptly and in good and workmanlike manner any building which may be constructed, damaged or destroyed thereon and to pay when due all claims for labor performed and materials furnished therefor; to comply with all laws affecting said property or requiring any alterations or improvements to be made thereon; not to commit or permit waste thereof; not to commit, suffer or permit any act upon said property in violation of law; to cultivate, irrigate, fertilize, fumigate, prune and do all other acts which from the character or use of said property may be reasonably necessary, the specific enumerations herein not excluding the general.

(2)   To provide, maintain and deliver to Beneficiary fire insurance satisfactory to and with loss payable to Beneficiary. The amount collected under any fire or other insurance policy may be applied by Beneficiary upon any indebtedness secured hereby and in such order as Beneficiary may determine, or at option of Beneficiary the entire amount so collected or any part thereof may be released to Trustor. Such application or release shall not cure or waive any default or notice of default hereunder or invalidate any act done pursuant to such notice.

(3)   To appear in and defend any action or proceeding purporting to affect the security hereof or the rights or powers of Beneficiary or Trustee; and to pay all costs and expenses, including cost of evidence of title and attorney's fees in a reasonable sum, in any such action or proceeding in which Beneficiary or Trustee may appear, and in any suit brought by Beneficiary to foreclose this Deed.

(4)   To pay: at least ten days before delinquency all taxes and assessments affecting said property, including assessments on appurtenant water stock; when due, all incumbrances, charges and liens, with interest, on said property or any part thereof, which appear to be prior or superior hereto; all costs, fees and expenses of this Trust.

Should Trustor fail to make any payment or to do any act as herein provided, then Beneficiary or Trustee, but without obligation so to do and without notice to or demand upon Trustor and without releasing Trustor from any obligation hereof, may: make or do the same in such manner and to such extent as either may deem necessary to protect the security hereof, Beneficiary or Trustee being authorized to enter upon said property for such purposes; appear in and defend any action or proceeding purporting to affect the security hereof or the rights or powers of Beneficiary or Trustee; pay, purchase, contest or compromise any incumbrance, charge or lien which in the judgment of either appears to be prior or superior hereto; and, in exercising any such powers, pay necessary expenses, employ counsel and pay his reasonable fees.

(5)   To pay immediately and without demand all sums so expended by Beneficiary or Trustee, with interest from date of expenditure at the amount allowed by law in effect at the date hereof, and to pay for any statement provided for by law in effect at the date hereof regarding the obligation secured hereby any amount demanded by the Beneficiary not to exceed the maximum allowed by law at the time when said statement is demanded.

B.   It is mutually agreed:

(1)   That any award of damages in connection with any condemnation for public use of or injury to said property or any part thereof is hereby assigned and shall be paid to Beneficiary who may apply or release such moneys received by him in the same manner and with the same effect as above provided for disposition of proceeds of fire or other insurance.

(2)   That by accepting payment of any sum secured hereby after its due date, Beneficiary does not waive his right either to require prompt payment when due of all other sums so secured or to declare default for failure so to pay.

(3)   That at any time or from time to time, without liability therefor and without notice, upon written request of Beneficiary and presentation of this Deed and said note for endorsement, and without affecting the personal liability of any person for payment of the indebtedness secured hereby, Trustee may: reconvey any part of said property; consent to the making of any map or plat thereof; join in granting any easement thereon; or join in any extension agreement or any agreement subordinating the lien or charge hereof.

(4)   That upon written request of beneficiary stating that all sums secured hereby have been paid, and upon surrender of this Deed and said note to Trustee for cancellation and retention or other disposition as Trustee in its sole discretion may choose and upon payment of its fees, Trustee shall reconvey, without warranty, the property then held hereunder. The recitals in such reconveyance of any matters or facts shall be conclusive proof of the truthfulness thereof. The Grantee in such reconveyance may be described as "the person or persons legally entitled thereto."

(5)   That as additional security, Trustor hereby gives to and confers upon Beneficiary the right, power and authority, during the continuance of these Trusts, to collect the rents, issues and profits of said property, reserving unto Trustor the right, prior to any default by Trustor in payment of any indebtedness secured hereby or in performance of any agreement hereunder, to collect and retain such rents, issues and profits as they become due and payable. Upon any such default, Beneficiary may at any time without notice, either in person, by agent, or by a receiver to be appointed by a court, and without regard to the adequacy of any security for the indebtedness hereby secured, enter upon and take possession of said property or any part thereof, in his own name sue for or otherwise collect such rents, issues, and profits, including those past due and unpaid, and apply the same, less costs and expenses of operation and collection, including reasonable attorney's fees, upon any indebtedness secured hereby, and in such order as Beneficiary may determine. The entering upon and taking possession of said property, the collection of such rents, issues and profits and the application thereof as aforesaid, shall not cure or waive any default or notice of default hereunder or invalidate any act done pursuant to such notice.

(6)   That upon default by Trustor in payment of any indebtedness secured hereby or in performance of any agreement hereunder, Beneficiary may declare all sums secured hereby immediately due and payable by delivery to Trustee of written declaration of default and demand for sale and of written notice of default and of election to cause to be sold said property, which notice Trustee shall cause to be filed for record. Beneficiary also shall deposit with Trustee this Deed, said note and all documents evidencing expenditures secured hereby.

After the lapse of such time as may then be required by law following the recordation of said notice of default, and notice of sale having been given as then required by law, Trustee, without demand on Trustor, shall sell said property at the time and place fixed by it in said notice of sale, either as a whole or in separate parcels, and in such order as it may determine, at public auction to the highest bidder for cash in lawful money of the United States, payable at time of sale. Trustee may postpone sale of all or any portion of said property by public announcement at such time and place of sale, and from time to time thereafter may postpone such sale by public announcement at the time fixed by the preceding postponement. Trustee shall deliver to such purchaser its deed conveying the property so sold, but without any covenant or warranty, express or implied. The recitals in such deed of any matters or facts shall be conclusive proof of the truthfulness thereof. Any person, including Trustor, Trustee, or Beneficiary as hereinafter defined, may purchase at such sale.

After deducting all costs, fees and expenses of Trustee and of this Trust, including cost of evidence of title in connection with sale, Trustee shall apply the proceeds of sale to payment of: all sums expended under the terms hereof, not then repaid, with accrued interest at the amount allowed by law in effect at the date hereof; all other sums then secured hereby; and the remainder, if any, to the person or persons legally entitled thereto.

(7)   Beneficiary, or any successor in ownership of any indebtedness secured hereby, may from time to time, by instrument in writing, substitute a successor or successors to any Trustee named herein or acting hereunder, which instrument, executed by the Beneficiary and duly acknowledged and recorded in the office of the recorder of the county or counties where said property is situated, shall be conclusive proof of proper substitution of such successor Trustee or Trustees, who shall, without conveyance from the Trustee predecessor, succeed to all its title, estate, rights, powers and duties. Said instrument must contain the name of the original Trustor, Trustee and Beneficiary hereunder, the book and page where this Deed is recorded and the name and address of the new Trustee.

(8)   That this Deed applies to, inures to the benefit of, and binds all parties hereto, their heirs, legatees, devisees, administrators, executors, successors and assigns. The term Beneficiary shall mean the owner and holder, including pledgees, of the note secured hereby, whether or not named as Beneficiary herein. In this Deed, whenever the context so requires, the masculine gender includes the feminine and/or neuter, and the singular number includes the plural.

(9)   That Trustee accepts this Trust when this Deed, duly executed and acknowledged, is made a public record as provided by law. Trustee is not obligated to notify any party hereto of pending sale under any other Deed of Trust or of any action or proceeding in which Trustor, Beneficiary or Trustee shall be a party unless brought by Trustee.

DO NOT RECORD   REQUEST FOR FULL RECONVEYANCE

TO FIRST AMERICAN TITLE INSURANCE COMPANY, TRUSTEE:

The undersigned is the legal owner and holder of the note or notes, and of all other indebtedness secured by the foregoing Deed of Trust. Said note or notes, together with all other indebtedness secured by said Deed of Trust, have been fully paid and satisfied; and you are hereby requested and directed, on payment to you of any sums owing to you under the terms of said Deed of Trust, to cancel said note or notes above mentioned, and all other evidences of indebtedness secured by said Deed of Trust delivered to you herewith, together with the said Deed of Trust, and to reconvey, without warranty, to the parties designated by the terms of said Deed of Trust, all the estate now held by you under the same.

Dated _____

_____

_____

Please mail Deed of Trust,
Note and Reconveyance to _____

Do not lose or destroy this Deed of Trust OR THE NOTE which it secures. Both must be delivered to the Trustee for cancellation before reconveyance will be made.

Exhibit 31.2

144   _Documentation—The Key to a Smooth Closing_

ORDER FOR PRELIMINARY TITLE REPORT

TITLE COMPANY			COUNTY (Office)		If in connection with order already opened, please check here	
DATE	ESCROW OR LOAN NUMBER	TITLE OFFICER		ORDER NUMBER		NEW

Please enter
THIS CONFIRMS } order for policy or policies of title insurance as checked below:

CLTA OWNER'S/LENDERS ..... Standard Coverage Form ..... [ ] with liability in the amount of .... $ _____

CLTA JOINT PROTECTION ..... Standard Coverage Form ..... [ ] with liability in the amount of .... $ _____

ALTA LENDERS ..... American Land Title Association Form .... [ ] with liability in the amount of .... $ _____

CLTA ENDORSEMENT .... [ ] _____

———————→ IF ALTA POLICY IS REQUESTED   [ ] SINGLE RESIDENCE [ ] MULTIPLE RESIDENCE [ ] COMMERCIAL
THIS INFORMATION WILL EXPEDITE YOUR REPORT—→   [ ] STREET ADDRESS _____

The property to be covered is described as

Present Owner's Name _____

We Enclose the Following:

Deed from _____ To _____ D.T.T. $ _____

Deed from _____ To _____ D.T.T. $ _____

Deed of Trust by _____ Amount $ _____

Deed of Trust by _____ Amount $ _____

Deed of Trust by _____ Amount $ _____

Recon _____ Item _____ of your report dated _____

Note _____ Deed of Trust _____ Request for Recon _____ Item _____ of your report dated _____

Miscellaneous _____

Statement of Information _____ Buyer _____ Recent Owner _____

UPON FURTHER AUTHORIZATION you will record all instruments without collection when you can VEST TITLE IN:

Subject to:
1. [ ] All   [ ] 2nd ½   [ ] None   General and Special Taxes for fiscal year 19 _____ 19 _____.
2. Bonds and/or Assessments _____
3. Covenants, conditions, restrictions, reservations, easements and rights of way of record.
4. Items numbered _____ as shown on preliminary report dated _____
5. Deed of Trust of record - to record for $ _____
6. _____
7. _____

Additional Instructions:

Send _____ copies of report to _____   COMPANY   **Sterling Bank**
_____   3287 Wilshire Boulevard
_____   Los Angeles, CA 90010
Street _____   (213) 384-4444
City _____ Zip _____
Order Tax Service: _____ Type _____ Years
Please Forward: (check items requested, if any.)
[ ] 1. _____ Copies of covenants, conditions and restrictions.
[ ] 2. _____ Copies of plat map.   BY _____
[ ] 3. Amount of _____ taxes for proration purposes

Exhibit 32

STATEMENT OF INFORMATION

TO: Ticor Title Insurance Company of California   Order No.

To expedite the completion of your escrow, please fill out and return this form at your earliest convenience. This information is for confidential use by Ticor Title Insurance Company of California in searching the land records in connection with the order number shown above. Further explanation of the need for this information is printed on the reverse side of this form.

PERSONAL IDENTIFICATION

Please Print all information
Name _____

    FIRST NAME   FULL MIDDLE NAME—IF NONE, INDICATE   LAST NAME

Year of Birth _____   Birthplace _____   Social Security No. _____

                 Wife
Full name of Husband _____
                FIRST NAME   FULL MIDDLE NAME—IF NONE, INDICATE   LAST NAME

Year of Birth _____   Birthplace _____   Social Security No. _____

Are you a citizen of the United States?   By Birth ☐   By Naturalization ☐   When _____

IF NOT, what citizenship do you hold? _____

We were married on _____ at _____
                      DATE   CITY AND STATE

Wife's maiden name _____

RESIDENCES DURING PAST 10 YEARS

NUMBER AND STREET	CITY	FROM (DATE)	TO (DATE)
NUMBER AND STREET	CITY	FROM (DATE)	TO (DATE)
NUMBER AND STREET	CITY	FROM (DATE)	TO (DATE)

(If more space is needed, use reverse side of form)

OCCUPATIONS DURING PAST 10 YEARS

Husband's

OCCUPATION	FIRM NAME	STREET AND CITY	FROM (DATE) TO (DATE)
OCCUPATION	FIRM NAME	STREET AND CITY	FROM (DATE) TO (DATE)
OCCUPATION	FIRM NAME	STREET AND CITY	FROM (DATE) TO (DATE)

Wife's

OCCUPATION	FIRM NAME	STREET AND CITY	FROM (DATE) TO (DATE)
OCCUPATION	FIRM NAME	STREET AND CITY	FROM (DATE) TO (DATE)

(If more space is needed, use reverse side of form)

FORMER MARRIAGE(S), IF ANY

If no former marriages, write "None" _____ Otherwise, please complete the following:

Name of former wife _____

Deceased ☐   Divorced ☐   When _____   Where _____

Name of former husband _____

Deceased ☐   Divorced ☐   When _____   Where _____

(If more space is needed, use reverse side of form)

Buyer intends to reside on the property in this transaction   Yes ☐   No ☐

Exhibit 33.1

THIS PORTION IS TO BE COMPLETED BY THE SELLER

The Street Address of the property in this transaction is _____
(LEAVE BLANK IF NONE)

The land is unimproved ☐   or improved with a structure of the following type;

IMPROVEMENTS: ☐ SINGLE RESIDENCE OR 1–4 FAMILY   ☐ MULTIPLE RESIDENCE   ☐ COMMERCIAL
OCCUPIED BY: ☐ OWNER   ☐ LESSEE   ☐ TENANTS
ANY PORTION OF NEW LOAN FUNDS TO BE USED FOR CONSTRUCTION
IMPROVEMENTS, REMODELING OR REPAIRS TO THIS PROPERTY HAVE BEEN MADE WITHIN THE PAST SIX MONTHS ☐ YES ☐ NO
HAVE ALL COSTS FOR LABOR AND MATERIALS ARISING IN CONNECTION THEREWITH BEEN PAID IN FULL? ☐ YES ☐ NO

The undersigned declare, under penalty of perjury, that the foregoing is true and correct.

DATE _____   _____

HOME
PHONE _____

BUSINESS
PHONE _____   (IF MARRIED, BOTH HUSBAND AND WIFE SHOULD SIGN)

THERE REALLY IS A REASON

We don't like to ask you to fill out this statement of information. We don't want you to think we are unnecessarily interested in your personal affairs. We are not. We have been asked to insure the title to real property in which you are interested, and if you will give us the information called for, it will help us do our job accurately and expedite the closing of your transaction.

California is the most populous state in the nation with some 20,000,000 residents. Please think for a moment how many of those residents have the same or similar names. In searching the public records relating to your title we will probably encounter judgments, bankruptcies, divorces and income tax liens involving persons with names very similar to yours. Such items cloud the title until eliminated by personal identification information showing you are not the person involved in these matters. Therefore, we need to know something about you—and, because of California's community property laws, something about your husband or wife, too, if you are married—so that we may eliminate reference to all matters not affecting the title to property you now own or may acquire.

By filling out this form in full, you are helping to make it possible for us to give you the prompt service we are sure you would like to receive.

**TICOR
TITLE INSURANCE**

CAT. NO. NN00057
TO 91 CA (2–86)

Exhibit 33.2

CLOSING AUDIT CHECK SHEET—ESCROW NO. _____

PRE-RECORDING AUDIT

	ITEM VERIFIED	
	DATE	BY
ALL ESCROW INSTRUCTIONS SIGNED BY ALL PARTIES _____		
ALL SUPPLEMENTAL ESCROW INSTRUCTIONS SIGNED BY ALL PARTIES _____		
ALL DISBURSEMENTS HAVE BEEN AUTHORIZED IN WRITING _____		
LEGAL DESCRIPTION IS CORRECT _____		
ALL REQUIREMENTS OF ESCROW INSTRUCTIONS HAVE BEEN MET _____		
ALL LENDER'S REQUIREMENTS HAVE BEEN MET _____		
FIRE INSURANCE—OK? _____		
NAMES ARE CORRECT ON ALL DOCUMENTS _____		
THERE ARE SUFFICIENT FUNDS TO CLOSE THE FILE FROM THE BUYER ( ) SELLER ( ) _____		
TAX REPORTING/WITHHOLDING _____		
TERMITE COMPLIANCES DONE _____		
ALL DOCUMENTS ARE AT THE TITLE COMPANY _____		
AFTER THE ABOVE IS COMPLETED, ORDER RECORDING. RECORDING ORDERED _____		
SHOULD RECORD ON _____		

PRE-SETTLED BY _____ ON _____

CLOSING PROCESS

	ACTION COMPLETED	
	DATE	BY
DOCUMENTS RECORDED ON _____		
BALANCE FILE _____		
CHECK ESCROW STATUS REPORT—DO FIGURES AGREE? _____		
RUN TAPES ON ALL ACCOUNTING AND ATTACH TAPES ONTO FACE SHEET OF FILE _____		
DRAW DRAFT _____		
PREPARE CLOSING STATEMENTS _____		
RUN TAPES ON CLOSING STATEMENTS *AND* ON ALL CHECK COPIES & RECEIPT COPIES _____		
INSURANCE—TRANSFER AND LENDER'S LOSS PAYABLE _____		
SELLER'S CLOSING LETTER _____		
BUYER'S CLOSING LETTER _____		
BROKER'S CLOSING LETTER _____		
LENDER'S CLOSING LETTER _____		
BORROWER'S CLOSING LETTER _____		
FILE IS NOW AUTHORIZED TO BE CONSIDERED CLOSED. BY _____		

Exhibit 34

1. Before any instructions or documents are prepared, it is important to establish which of the following:

   (A) Existence of an escrow
   (B) Intent
   (C) Status of the parties
   (D) None of the above

2. Amendments to escrow instructions:

   (A) Are more common with unilateral than bilateral instructions
   (B) Are more common in Southern California procedure than in Northern California
   (C) Are not permitted once escrow has formally opened
   (D) Are not considered formal modifications of the contract

3. Unilateral and bilateral escrow instructions differ in:

   (A) Time of preparation
   (B) Likelihood that amendments will be needed
   (C) Region where they are used
   (D) All of the above

4. Grantors shown on a deed:

   (A) Can be shown in the approximate manner they held title
   (B) Need not be recited exactly as shown in a Preliminary Report
   (C) Must be identified by the exact name in which title is held
   (D) Have no bearing on the title report

5. The final audit of an escrow should verify:

   (A) Authorization of disbursements
   (B) Legal description of property
   (C) Clearance of checks
   (D) All of the above

6. Any addenda to the original page require:

   (A) No further signatures, as they are incorporated to the first page
   (B) Initials by the parties for any typographical errors
   (C) Signatures of all parties
   (D) No further attention by the parties

7. Deeds in order to be accepted by the county recorder must:

   (A) Be acknowledged
   (B) Be capable of reprographics
   (C) Contain the assessor's parcel number
   (D) All of the above

8. A promissory note is:

   (A) The security for the debt
   (B) An obligation of the seller
   (C) Evidence of the debt
   (D) Not required to be in writing

9. A deed of trust is:

   (A) The security for the debt
   (B) An obligation of the seller
   (C) Evidence of the debt
   (D) Not required to be in writing

10. Demands for payment are:

    (A) A part of the language of the seller's instructions
    (B) Obtained from lienholders
    (C) Both of the above
    (D) Neither of the above

Chapter 10
The Sale Escrow—
Fallouts and Variants

PREVIEW

Contingencies and Cancellations

Related Transactions

CONTINGENCIES AND CANCELLATIONS

Each escrow is opened in anticipation of closing successfully. Unfortunately many "fallouts" result, often from provisions in the original instructions which serve as obstructions to closing.

General Principles   **Terms of Contract.** When the instructions have been signed by the parties to the escrow, neither party may unilaterally change the content in the forms binding the other principal. However, by mutual agreement between both parties to the escrow the instructions may be changed at any time and one party may waive the performance of certain conditions if in doing so the waiver does not act as a detriment to the other parties to the transaction.

Agent's Role. An escrow agent is customarily held liable for violating the instructions of the parties to the escrow. However, the escrowholder is really only a stakeholder and not legally concerned with controversies between the parties and is entitled to join such parties in an action of interpleader to require them to litigate controversies between themselves.

Liquidated Damages   There is an increased pressure upon escrowholders to insert liquidated damages provisions in the instructions. These are usually damages due the seller if the transaction fails to consummate.

Complicates Escrow. Most escrowholders discourage this insertion because the deposit receipt (a separate contract in the chain of transfer) already provides for this item. If there is such a clause and it is acted upon, the matter usually ends up in an involved and expensive interpleader action.

Deposit Receipt   In California, legislation enacted in 1978 established the liquidated damages language in paragraph 10 of the deposit receipt form (see Exhibit 35). As currently designed, the form has become an instrument of consumer protection in addition to its original purpose of orchestrating the conditions of sale.

Contents. The deposit receipt reflects the expanded responsibilities of the real estate licensee in the area of disclosure, paralleling those of the escrowholder. Not only does the deposit receipt outline the conditions of sale, including its details, but also outlines extensive consumer information relative to the premises and the transaction.

☐ Foreign Investment in Real Property Tax Act (FIRPTA) disclosure

☐ Warranty of fitness of mechanical systems; waiver or acceptance of a home protection plan on mechanical systems for the first year

☐ Fixture and structural modification disclosure

☐ Physical and geological inspection provisions

☐ Warranty of property condition and that property is not presently in violation of government or agency requirements

☐ Smoke detector installations

☐ Flood hazard and special studies zone disclosures

☐ Energy conservation retrofit

☐ Condominium disclosure.

Role in Escrow. Acceptance of a copy of the deposit receipt by escrow agents is a controversial issue and reflects company policy of the escrow agent. Acceptance will insure that escrow has all needed information required to prepare instructions and documents, but the danger is in the interpretation of that contract by the escrow agent and the possible liability placed on escrow by the courts.

Contingencies

Obstructions in the closing process may evolve from contingencies imposed by parties to the transaction. For example, typically the buyer's performance is predicated upon the ability to obtain new financing on the property. In some cases the contingencies become so onerous that the escrow is, in effect, an option.

Procedure. The preferable vehicle in such situations would be an option allowing sufficient time to work out each of the contingencies. Then it would be appropriate to open the sale escrow free of these burdens, and closing would be expedited.

Application. Contingencies are particularly common in the case of proposed subdivision property. In a typical subdivision transaction one might find the sale conditioned upon such contingencies as:

☐ The purchaser obtaining rezoning from the present classification of A-1 to R-1

☐ Approval of a final subdivision map authorizing 75 lots

☐ Satisfactory soil tests

☐ Engineer's report that the cost of offsite improvements will not be in excess of $250,000.

Seller Precautions. In some cases, sellers may impose contingencies to protect their position. Often this is the result of their desire to limit the amount of time that the property is off the market if the buyers fail to qualify.

☐ The balance of the downpayment may be required in escrow within a specified number of days after escrow is opened to prove "good faith" on the part of the buyer, or the transaction may be terminated.

☐ The seller may require buyer credit approval on a new loan within a short time after opening escrow, otherwise escrow may be cancelled.

Cancellations   It is generally established that an escrow may be cancelled with the voluntary consent of all the principals. The cancellation process must address mutuality of all parties involved in the transaction, as well as the rights of third parties who may be affected by such action. Revocation of agency is what is really being done regarding the escrow agency. Principals and their agents need to use caution to clearly state if their intention is to "cancel" the escrow or to cancel the purchase contract between the buyer and seller.

Unfinished Business Creates Risk. When escrows are cancelled by the principals, and they involve payment of a commission, bills of third parties to be paid, assignments of proceeds, and irrevocable orders, some complicated rights can develop, and an element of risk and exposure may result to the escrowholder.

Whose Rights Recognized. Escrowholders approach such problems from different perspectives, depending on the agency that oversees their operation and on company policy. In the case of independent escrows, the California Division of Corporations recognizes only the principals to the transaction. Banks, on the other hand, may take a more liberal view as to parties in interest.

Disposal of Funds. If mutuality is never achieved in a cancellation, there are two possible fates for the funds on deposit.

☐ They may remain on deposit for a period of seven years, at which time they are reported to the state controller who publishes for claims. If no claim is received, the funds escheat to the state.

☐ If the deposit involves a substantial sum, the escrowholder may take the initiative under the general escrow instructions and have a court determine the rightful owner. An indirect method of accomplishing the same object is the initiation of an action by the buyer for return of the deposit, naming the seller and escrowholder as parties defendant.

Avoiding Cancellations. Cancellations are, in many instances, the direct result of the parties failing to inform each other or their agents of the true terms and conditions of the transaction as they perceive them.

RELATED TRANSACTIONS

Variants on the sale escrow may result from trustee situations created by certain financing devices. The following are among the various loan related documents that result from the sale or refinancing of real property and are commonly involved in escrow.

Land Contract Escrows   In recent years the land contract has emerged from relative obscurity as a security device to a significant financing instrument.

Definition. The land contract has some similarity to a sale escrow instruction since it is an agreement by the seller (vendor) to convey to the buyer (vendee) upon performance by the buyer. Usually this performance relates to payment of the balance of the purchase price over and above the down payment at a specified rate of interest and stipulated monthly payment to the maturity date as stated in the contract.

Cal-Vet Financing. Individuals who financed their property under the farm and home purchase program sponsored by the Department of Veterans Affairs of the State of California (Cal-Vet) are familiar with this instrument because it serves as the financing document for that program.

Application. With high interest rates in the early '80s, seller financing via a land contract which takes advantage of the lower rates on existing institutional financing became increasingly popular. Under certain conditions state courts limited the ability of institutional lenders to exercise their due-on-sale (acceleration) clause where a land contract was used.

Legal Questions. A new element of land contracts has entered the legal arena through the introduction of a trustee, usually a title company, as a party to the contract instrument, with powers in some cases exceeding those of a trustee in a deed of trust. Legal questions have been raised about the ability of the trustee to act, and for this reason most title insurers insist upon proper conveyances from the respective parties or initiation of appropriate legal action at the time of consummation or in case of default.

Form. To overcome the questionable nature of the trustee appointment, a land contract form has been introduced which is two distinct instruments. The first instrument is a land contract between vendor and vendee (one might view this device as a long-term sale escrow), the second a trust deed executed by vendee to vendor obligating the vendee to perform under the terms of contract.

Payment Procedure. Exhibit 36 outlines a typical land contract escrow. Paragraph 2(c) is typical of many land contract situations where an independent collection agency is to handle the remittance of payments plus impounds and the distribution of the vendee's moneys to the vendor after making the payment required to the holder of the underlying lien, in this case the $70,000 lien described in paragraph 3.

Two Types. In processing transactions of this nature two types of contracts are generally encountered.

☐ *All-Inclusive.* The first is referred to as "all-inclusive" and is represented by Exhibit 36. Here the entire balance of payment due ($85,000) has an overall rate of $9\frac{1}{2}\%$.

☐ *Equity Contract.* If the contract showed that $9\frac{1}{2}\%$ was to be paid on the vendor's equity portion of $15,000 (the difference between the $85,000 contract amount and the $70,000 loan of record) and the balance paid on the terms of the existing lien, this would represent the second type, an equity contract.

The equity contract usually results in lower payments for the vendee unless the underlying trust deed interest rate meets or exceeds the rate shown in the contract. In the illustrated escrow it would change the $714.73 monthly payment as follows:

$9\frac{1}{2}\%$ on $15,000 with 30 year amortization:	$126.13
$8\frac{1}{2}\%$ on $70,000 with 30 year amortization:	$538.24
	$664.37

Title with Vendor. In the land contract transaction, title remains with the vendor and, as a result, problems about the names on the fire insurance policy, communication with the existing lender, etc., can arise for the vendee. This is the reason for the indemnification clause in paragraph 3 of Exhibit 36.

Legal Advice. Because this transaction affects the legal position of each of the parties, obtaining independent counsel is essential to protect their respective interests. Note the language above the signatures in Exhibit 36.

All-Inclusive Deeds of Trust

The all-inclusive trust deed is similar in nature to the all-inclusive land contract except that title has passed to the buyer who executes the document as owner of the land.

Theory. California is a trust deed lien theory state, which means that California land owners take title subject to the lien, rather than the trustee holding title during the life of the trust deed. A majority of real estate is secured by a three party instrument, the deed of trust.

Parties. The parties to a trust deed are:

☐ *Trustor*: Borrower

☐ *Trustee*: Independent third party, holder of the trust during the life of the instrument, and

☐ *Beneficiary*: Owner of the indebtedness or successor in interest.

Foreclosure. Trust deeds allow for nonjudicial foreclosures conducted by the trustee.

Use in Sales. In a typical AITD transaction the seller is aiding in the buyer's financing by taking back a portion of the equity conveyed in the form of an all inclusive deed of trust.

Advantages. In times of expensive loan money this device becomes prevalent for it offers advantages to each of the parties. For example, if trust deed interest rates are higher than current financing on the property, the buyer can save by taking over the seller's original financing, while the seller receives return on his equity.

Example

To satisfy the needs of both, where prevailing rates are 11% and the existing loan is at $8\frac{1}{2}$%, an all-inclusive trust deed at $9\frac{1}{2}$% could be structured as follows:

Sale price	$100,000
All-inclusive trust deed	$85,000
Downpayment	$15,000

There are two advantages to this transaction:

☐ The buyer has an improved rate on financing at $9\frac{1}{2}$% instead of the current prevailing rate of 11%.

☐ The seller has a yield on his security instrument that exceeds 10%.

Legal Cautions. Preparation of this security device was the exclusive province of the legal profession when it first became popular in the early 1970s. The instrument has achieved fairly wide acceptance since, and trustees in some cases now provide standard forms for these documents. Escrowholders should be assured by the parties that counsel has been sought, however, just as in the land contract transaction.

As Loan Device. If an all-inclusive trust deed is contracted as a separate transaction, it would be handled as a loan escrow.

Deed in Lieu of Foreclosure

Rationale. Foreclosure by a corporate trustee conveys title to a beneficiary or successors in interest under a deed of trust as a result of a properly conducted trustee's sale. In some instances, the trustor is willing to voluntarily deed the property back to the beneficiary who may be the former owner in exchange for removing the lien of record and cancelling the unpaid dept. This is commonly called a "deed in lieu of foreclosure."

In Escrow. The deed in lieu becomes the principal instrument in an escrow transaction where the parties agree to this arrangement. In this sale escrow the consideration is the satisfaction of the debt to the beneficiary (lender) in return for a deed from the trustor (owner/borrower).

Protective Language. To assure the insurability of the deed, a recital must be added to the deed or a separate estoppel affidavit must be received from the trustor.

☐ **Standard Form.** The recital or estoppel normally incorporates language similar to the following:

> "This deed is an absolute conveyance, the grantor having sold land to the grantee for a fair and adequate consideration, in addition to that above recited, being full satisfaction of all obligations secured by the Deed of Trust executed by _____ to _____ as trustee recorded as document No. _____ Book _____ Page _____, Official Records of _____ County. Grantor declares that this conveyance is freely and fairly made, and that there are no agreements, oral or written, other than this deed between grantor and grantee with respect to said land."

☐ **Alternate Form.** The above recital is used in instances where the trustor/grantor remains personally liable. If no personal liability of the grantor is involved, the recital is:

> "Grantor(s) declares that this conveyance is freely and fairly made, grantor(s) having sold said land to grantee for a consideration equal to the fair value of grantor's interest in said land, and grantor(s) further declares that there are no agreements, oral or written, between grantor(s) and grantee with respect to said land."

Risk Involving Liens. Transactions of this nature involve considerable risk on the part of the holder of the indebtedness who is willing to accept a deed in lieu of foreclosure.

☐ **Foreclosure.** In a normal foreclosure, all junior liens contracted or imposed by operation of law upon the trustor or successors in interest are normally eliminated by foreclosure sale.

☐ **Deed in Lieu.** In the deed in lieu of foreclosure transaction all such liens remain against the property. There is a definite possibility that the total amount of liens against a property would make the assumption of ownership through this device too burdensome.

☐ **Alternatives.** This poses a strong argument for the parties to enter into a formal sale escrow arrangement to assure the deed-in-lieu purchaser the title bargained for in consideration of relinquishing his lien rights, or to consider some other trust arrangement.

Legal Restrictions. Several laws passed by a consumer-conscious California legislature in 1979 and later have inhibited the use of this device. Any deed issued in contemplation of foreclosure now faces serious questions by the title insurer, and prior to bargaining for such a conveyance the advice of competent counsel should be sought by the parties.

Trustee Situations   A long-term situation that has all of the earmarks of an escrow transaction is the trust relationship. Trustee relationships regularly result from trust deeds and land contracts. In addition, title to real and personal property can be held in trust for the benefit of named or unnamed parties.

Definition. Ogden's *California Real Property Law* provides the following guidelines:

> "In a broad sense, the term trust refers to 'a relation of personal confidence' between persons (California Civil Code § 2219). Examples of such trust relationship are guardian and ward, principal and agent, and the administrator of an estate and heirs or creditors.
>
> "In a strict sense, however, a trust is a fiduciary relationship with respect to property, subjecting the person by whom the property is held to equitable duties to deal with the property for benefit of another person.
>
> "The code divides trusts into (1) voluntary trusts, or those that arise from a personal confidence reposed in, and voluntarily accepted by one person for the benefit of another; and (2) involuntary trusts, or those that are created by operation of law (California Civil Code §§ 2216, 2217).
>
> "Another classification of strict trusts regards them as (a) express trusts, which arise as a result of a stated declaration of trust or some other external expression of intent to create the trust; (b) resulting trusts, where the intention to create a trust is implied by law from certain acts of the parties, and (c) constructive trusts, where a trust is imposed by law, not to effectuate intention, but to redress wrong or unjust enrichment."

In Escrow. The escrowholder is most familiar with express trusts, since the escrow relationship confers specific duties upon the trustee who must act within the scope of the authority granted. A trust relationship exists where the escrowholder holds documents and moneys in trust to be administered in accordance with conditions outlined in the escrow instructions. This conferring of fiduciary responsibility is the rock upon which the escrow process is constructed—trust and confidence.

In Deed of Trust. Under § 2924 of the California Civil Code, certain obligations are imposed upon trustees in a deed of trust relative to their exercise of the power of sale provisions in that instrument. The trustee also has the power to extinguish the debt by issuing a deed of reconveyance upon proper instructions from the beneficiary.

Other Situations. Other trust situations that one encounters regularly in real estate are:

- *Power of Attorney*. Powers conferred by a principal on an agent to act on behalf of the principal.

- *Declaration of Trust*. Specific powers conferred upon a trustee by court order or by direction of beneficiaries or by their legal representative.

- *Administrator or Executor of Estate of Decedent*. The representative of the estate, established by court appointment or by designation in a will.

- *Guardian or Conservator*. Representative of the estate of a minor or incompetent person.

The "Subject to" Escrow

The pressure of high interest rates has motivated buyers and sellers to take advantage of existing financing containing favorable terms. This situation may put a strain on the confidentiality of the escrow relationship as well as the neutrality enjoyed by the escrowholder.

Definition. In order to avoid lender notification upon sale, which might initiate acceleration of a trust deed of record, the "subject to" escrow has been created as a vehicle to effect transfer of the property and avoid acceleration by the existing lender.

Legality. An alienation clause (due-on-sale clause) is a special kind of acceleration clause permitting the lender to call the loan if the borrower alienates (conveys or transfers) title. The clause must be stated specifically in the note as well as the trust deed to be enforceable. Benefits the lender.

- *Federal Statute*. The Garn-St. Germain Depository Institutions Act of 1982 preempted state prohibitions on the exercise of due-on-sale clauses by all lenders.

- *Due-on-Sale Now Enforceable*. On October 15, 1985, all grace periods terminated, and due-on-sale clauses generally became enforceable except in very limited prescribed circumstances.

- *Exemptions*. On loans secured by liens on residential property of less than 5 units, a lender may not exercise a due-on-sale clause upon:

  - Creation of a junior lien

  - Creation of a purchase money security interest for household appliances

  - The death of a joint tenant

  - A lease of 3 years or less not containing an option to purchase

  - Transfer to a relative upon death of the borrower

□ A transfer to the spouse or children of the borrower

□ Dissolution of marriage

□ Transfer into an inter vivos trust with no transfer of occupancy.

Procedure and Risks. The usual posture taken by the escrowholder in dealing with an existing institutional lender is for a beneficiary statement to be obtained by an outside agency, usually an attorney. Instructions are then given to the escrowholder with appropriate exculpatory (hold harmless) language relative to handling the property transfer without complying with normal lender requirements (paying loan fee, increasing interest rate, credit approval of purchaser, etc.).

□ *Exculpatory Statement.* Some escrowholders have sought to protect their potential exposure to lender claims by obtaining an indemnification from the buyer. A sample exculpatory recital might be:

> "Buyer herein is satisfied that the obligation of payor (seller) on the loan of record (describe in detail) can be transferred, as per these instructions. Escrowholder is relieved of all liability (exculpated) as to the transferability of payor's obligation and as to whether lender actually changes records accordingly. Escrowholder is not liable or responsible for any changes in the law or lender's policy at some future date after the close of escrow whereby lender may impose charges on payor, including, but not limited to, loan fees, interest increases, and prepayment penalties, as may be reflected in original loan documents."

□ *Effectiveness.* The mere inclusion of exculpatory language by escrowholders may not relieve them of liability. Since they are considered by the courts to be more knowledgeable in these areas than their clients, the court may find them liable even though such language has been used.

□ *Collections.* The whole transaction depends on the new owner's ability to make payments. Sometimes a collection agent may be appointed to cover this problem.

□ *Insurance.* If the lender receives an endorsement indicating transfer of the fire insurance policy, the lender may attempt to accelerate the loan. If the insurance remains in the name of the seller, the buyer risks potential losses because of inappropriate coverage.

□ *Agent's Position.* The situation is further complicated by the escrow agent's attempt to avoid potential exposure in the transaction.

Legal Advice. In any event, parties involved in a "subject-to" sale should seek legal advice, and the escrow instruction should contain language similar to the bold print preceding the signatures in Exhibit 36.

REAL ESTATE PURCHASE CONTRACT AND RECEIPT FOR DEPOSIT
THIS IS MORE THAN A RECEIPT FOR MONEY. IT IS INTENDED TO BE A LEGALLY BINDING CONTRACT. READ IT CAREFULLY.
CALIFORNIA ASSOCIATION OF REALTORS® (CAR) STANDARD FORM

_____, California, _____, 19_____

Received from _____

herein called Buyer, the sum of _____ Dollars $_____

evidenced by ☐ cash, ☐ cashier's check, ☐ personal check or ☐ _____, payable to _____

_____, to be held uncashed until acceptance of this offer as deposit on account of purchase price of

_____ Dollars $_____

for the purchase of property, situated in _____, County of _____ California,

described as follows: _____

1. **FINANCING:** The obtaining of Buyer's financing is a contingency of this agreement.

   A. DEPOSIT upon acceptance, to be deposited into _____ $ _____

   B. INCREASED DEPOSIT within _____ days of acceptance to be deposited into _____ $ _____

   C. BALANCE OF DOWN PAYMENT to be deposited into _____ on or before _____ $ _____

   D. Buyer to apply, qualify for and obtain a NEW FIRST LOAN in the amount of . . . . $ _____

     payable monthly at approximately $_____ including interest at origination not to exceed _____%,

     ☐ fixed rate, ☐ other _____ all due _____ years from date of origination. Loan fee not to

     exceed _____. Seller agrees to pay a maximum of _____ FHA/VA discount points.

     Additional terms _____

   E. Buyer ☐ to assume, ☐ to take title subject to an EXISTING FIRST LOAN with an approximate balance of . . . . $ _____

     in favor of _____ payable monthly at $_____ including interest at _____% ☐ fixed rate,

     ☐ other _____. Fees not to exceed _____ .

     Disposition of impound account _____

     Additional terms _____

   F. Buyer to execute a NOTE SECURED BY a ☐ first, ☐ second, ☐ third DEED OF TRUST in the amount of . . . . $ _____

     IN FAVOR OF SELLER payable monthly at $_____ or more, including interest at _____% all due

     _____ years from date of origination, ☐ or upon sale or transfer of subject property. A late charge of _____

     _____ shall be due on any installment not paid within _____ days of the due date.

     ☐ Deed of Trust to contain a request for notice of default or sale for the benefit of Seller. Buyer ☐ will, ☐ will not execute a request

     for notice of delinquency. Additional terms _____

   G. Buyer ☐ to assume, ☐ to take title subject to an EXISTING SECOND LOAN with an approximate balance of . . . . $ _____

     in favor of _____ payable monthly at $_____ including interest at _____%

     ☐ fixed rate, ☐ other _____. Buyer fees not to exceed _____

     Additional terms _____

   H. Buyer to apply, qualify for and obtain a NEW SECOND LOAN in the amount of . . . . $ _____

     payable monthly at approximately $_____ including interest at origination not to exceed _____% ☐ fixed rate,

     ☐ other _____, all due _____ years from date of origination.

     Buyer's loan fee not to exceed _____. Additional terms _____

   I. In the event Buyer assumes or takes title subject to an existing loan, Seller shall provide Buyer with copies of applicable notes and Deeds

     of Trust. A loan may contain a number of features which affect the loan, such as interest rate changes, monthly payment changes, balloon

     payments, etc. Buyer shall be allowed _____ calendar days after receipt of such copies to notify Seller in writing of disapproval.

     FAILURE TO NOTIFY SELLER IN WRITING SHALL CONCLUSIVELY BE CONSIDERED APPROVAL. Buyer's approval shall not be

     unreasonably withheld. Difference in existing loan balances shall be adjusted in ☐ Cash, ☐ Other _____

   J. Buyer agrees to act diligently and in good faith to obtain all applicable financing. _____

   K. ADDITIONAL FINANCING TERMS: _____

     _____

     _____

     _____

   L. TOTAL PURCHASE PRICE . . . . $ _____

2. **OCCUPANCY:** Buyer ☐ does, ☐ does not intend to occupy subject property as Buyer's primary residence.

3. **SUPPLEMENTS:** The ATTACHED supplements are incorporated herein:

    ☐ Interim Occupancy Agreement (CAR FORM I0A-11)   ☐ _____

    ☐ Residential Lease Agreement after Sale (CAR FORM RLAS-11)   ☐ _____

    ☐ VA and FHA Amendments (CAR FORM VA/FHA-11)   ☐ _____

4. **ESCROW:** Buyer and Seller shall deliver signed instructions to _____ the escrow holder, within _____ calendar days

   of acceptance of the offer which shall provide for closing within _____ calendar days of acceptance. Escrow fees to be paid as follows: _____

   _____

Buyer and Seller acknowledge receipt of copy of this page, which constitutes Page 1 of _____ Pages.

Buyer's Initials (_____) (_____)   Seller's Initials (_____) (_____)

THIS STANDARDIZED DOCUMENT FOR USE IN SIMPLE TRANSACTIONS HAS BEEN APPROVED BY THE CALIFORNIA ASSOCIATION OF REALTORS® IN FORM ONLY. NO REPRESENTATION
IS MADE AS TO THE APPROVAL OF THE FORM OF ANY SUPPLEMENTS NOT CURRENTLY PUBLISHED BY THE CALIFORNIA ASSOCIATION OF REALTORS® OR THE LEGAL VALIDITY OR
ADEQUACY OF ANY PROVISION IN ANY SPECIFIC TRANSACTION. IT SHOULD NOT BE USED IN COMPLEX TRANSACTIONS OR WITH EXTENSIVE RIDERS OR ADDITIONS.

A REAL ESTATE BROKER IS THE PERSON QUALIFIED TO ADVISE ON REAL ESTATE TRANSACTIONS. IF YOU DESIRE LEGAL OR TAX ADVICE, CONSULT AN APPROPRIATE PROFESSIONAL

REAL ESTATE PURCHASE CONTRACT AND RECEIPT FOR DEPOSIT (DLF-14 PAGE 1 OF 4)

Exhibit 35.1

Subject Property Address: _____

5. **TITLE:** Title is to be free of liens, encumbrances, easements, restrictions, rights and conditions of record or known to Seller, other than the following: (a) Current property taxes, (b) covenants, conditions, restrictions, and public utility easements of record, if any, provided the same do not adversely affect the continued use of the property for the purposes for which it is presently being used, unless reasonably disapproved by Buyer in writing within _____ calendar days of receipt of a current preliminary report furnished at _____ expense, and (c) _____

_____

Seller shall furnish Buyer at _____ expense a California Land Title Association policy issued by _____ _____ Company, showing title vested in Buyer subject only to the above. If Seller is unwilling or unable to eliminate any title matter disapproved by Buyer as above, Buyer may terminate this agreement. If Seller fails to deliver title as above, Buyer may terminate this agreement; in either case, the deposit shall be returned to Buyer.

6. **VESTING:** Unless otherwise designated in the escrow instructions of Buyer, title shall vest as follows: _____ _____

(The manner of taking title may have significant legal and tax consequences. Therefore, give this matter serious consideration.)

7. **PRORATIONS:** Property taxes, payments on bonds and assessments assumed by Buyer, interest, rents, association dues, premiums on insurance acceptable to Buyer, and _____ shall be paid current and prorated as of ☐ the day of recordation of the deed; or ☐ _____ . Bonds or assessments now a lien shall be ☐ paid current by Seller, payments not yet due to be assumed by Buyer; or ☐ paid in full by Seller, including payments not yet due; or ☐ _____ . County Transfer tax shall be paid by _____ . The _____ transfer tax or transfer fee shall be paid by _____ . **PROPERTY WILL BE REASSESSED UPON CHANGE OF OWNERSHIP. THIS WILL AFFECT THE TAXES TO BE PAID.** A Supplemental tax bill will be issued, which shall be paid as follows: (a) for periods after close of escrow, by Buyer (or by final acquiring party if part of an exchange), and (b) for periods prior to close of escrow, by Seller. TAX BILLS ISSUED AFTER CLOSE OF ESCROW SHALL BE HANDLED DIRECTLY BETWEEN BUYER AND SELLER.

8. **POSSESSION:** Possession and occupancy shall be delivered to Buyer, ☐ on close of escrow, or ☐ not later than _____ days after close of escrow, or ☐ _____ .

9. **KEYS:** Seller shall, when possession is available to Buyer, provide keys and/or means to operate all property locks, and alarms, if any.

10. **PERSONAL PROPERTY:** The following items of personal property, free of liens and without warranty of condition, are included: _____ _____ _____

11. **FIXTURES:** All permanently installed fixtures and fittings that are attached to the property or for which special openings have been made are included in the purchase price, including electrical, light, plumbing and heating fixtures, built-in appliances, screens, awnings, shutters, all window coverings, attached floor coverings, TV antennas, air cooler or conditioner, garage door openers and controls, attached fireplace equipment, mailbox, trees and shrubs, and _____ except _____ .

12. **SMOKE DETECTOR(S):** State law requires that residences be equipped with an operable smoke detector(s). Local law may have additional requirements. Seller shall deliver to Buyer a written statement of compliance in accordance with applicable state and local law prior to close of escrow.

13. **TRANSFER DISCLOSURE:** Unless exempt, Transferor (Seller), shall comply with Civil Code §§1102 et seq., by providing Transferee (Buyer) with a Real Estate Transfer Disclosure Statement: (a) ☐ Buyer has received and read a Real Estate Transfer Disclosure Statement; or (b) ☐ Seller shall provide Buyer with a Real Estate Transfer Disclosure Statement within _____ calendar days of acceptance of the offer after which Buyer shall have three (3) days after delivery to Buyer, in person, or five (5) days after delivery by deposit in the mail, to terminate this agreement by delivery of a written notice of termination to Seller or Seller's Agent.

14. **TAX WITHHOLDING:** Under the Foreign Investment in Real Property Tax Act (FIRPTA), IRC §1445, *every* Buyer of U.S. real property *must*, unless an exemption applies, deduct and withhold from Seller's proceeds 10% of the gross sales price. Under California Revenue and Taxation Code §§18805 and 26131, the Buyer must deduct and withhold an additional one-third of the amount required to be withheld under federal law. The primary FIRPTA exemptions are: No withholding is required if (a) Seller provides Buyer with an affidavit under penalty of perjury, that Seller is not a "foreign person," or (b) Seller provides Buyer with a "qualifying statement" issued by the Internal Revenue Service, or (c) Buyer purchases real property for use as a residence and the purchase price is $300,000 or less and Buyer or a member of Buyer's family has definite plans to reside at the property for at least 50% of the number of days it is in use during each of the first two twelve-month periods after transfer. Seller and Buyer agree to execute and deliver as directed any instrument, affidavit, or statement reasonably necessary to carry out those statutes and regulations promulgated thereunder.

15. **MULTIPLE LISTING SERVICE:** If Broker is a Participant of an Association/Board multiple listing service ("MLS"), the Broker is authorized to report the sale, its price, terms, and financing for the publication, dissemination, information, and use of the authorized Board members, MLS Participants and Subscribers.

16. **ADDITIONAL TERMS AND CONDITIONS:**

ONLY THE FOLLOWING PARAGRAPHS 'A' THROUGH 'K' *WHEN INITIALLED BY BOTH BUYER AND SELLER* ARE INCORPORATED IN THIS AGREEMENT.

Buyer's Initials _____ Seller's Initials _____

A. PHYSICAL AND GEOLOGICAL INSPECTION: Buyer shall have the right, at Buyer's expense, to select a licensed contractor and/or other qualified professional(s), to make "Inspections" (including tests, surveys, other studies, inspections, and investigations) of the subject property, including but not limited to structural, plumbing, sewer/septic system, well, heating, electrical, built-in appliances, roof, soils, foundation, mechanical systems, pool, pool heater, pool filter, air conditioner, if any, possible environmental hazards such as asbestos, formaldehyde, radon gas and other substances/products, and geologic conditions. Buyer shall keep the subject property free and clear of any liens, indemnify and hold Seller harmless from all liability, claims, demands, damages, or costs, and repair all damages to the property arising from the "Inspections." All claimed defects concerning the condition of the property that adversely affect the continued use of the property for the purposes for which it is presently being used (☐ or as _____) shall be in writing, supported by written reports, if any, and delivered to Seller within _____ calendar days FOR "INSPECTIONS" OTHER THAN GEOLOGICAL, and/or within _____ calendar days FOR GEOLOGICAL "INSPECTIONS," of acceptance of the offer. Buyer shall furnish Seller copies, at no cost, of all reports concerning the property obtained by Buyer. When such reports disclose conditions or information unsatisfactory to the Buyer, which the Seller is unwilling or unable to correct, Buyer may cancel this agreement. Seller shall make the premises available for all Inspections. BUYER'S FAILURE TO NOTIFY SELLER IN WRITING SHALL CONCLUSIVELY BE CONSIDERED APPROVAL.

Buyer's Initials _____ Seller's Initials _____

B. CONDITION OF PROPERTY: Seller warrants, through the date possession is made available to Buyer: (1) property and improvements, including landscaping, grounds and pool/spa, if any, shall be maintained in the same condition as upon the date of acceptance of the offer, and (2) the roof is free of all known leaks, and (3) built-in appliances, and water, sewer/septic, plumbing, heating, electrical, air conditioning, pool/spa systems, if any, are operative, and (4) Seller shall replace all broken and/or cracked glass; (5) _____ .

Buyer's Initials _____ Seller's Initials _____

C. SELLER REPRESENTATION: Seller warrants that Seller has no knowledge of any notice of violations of City, County, State, Federal, Building, Zoning, Fire, Health Codes or ordinances, or other governmental regulation filed or issued against the property. This warranty shall be effective until the date of close of escrow.

Buyer and Seller acknowledge receipt of copy of this page, which constitutes Page 2 of _____ Pages.

Buyer's Initials (_____) (_____)   Seller's Initials (_____) (_____)

OFFICE USE ONLY

Reviewed by Broker or Designee _____

Date _____

REPRINTED BY PERMISSION CALIFORNIA ASSOCIATION OF REALTORS®. ENDORSEMENT NOT IMPLIED

REAL ESTATE PURCHASE CONTRACT AND RECEIPT FOR DEPOSIT (DLF-14 PAGE 2 OF 4)

Exhibit 35.2

Subject Property Address _____

Buyer's Initials   Seller's Initials

_____/_____ _____/_____ **D. PEST CONTROL:** (1) Within _____ calendar days of acceptance of the offer, Seller shall furnish Buyer at the expense of ☐ Buyer, ☐ Seller, a current written report of an inspection by _____ , a licensed Structural Pest Control Operator, of the main building, ☐ detached garage(s) or carport(s), if any, and ☐ the following other structures on the property: _____

(2) If requested by either Buyer or Seller, the report shall separately identify each recommendation for corrective measures as follows:

"Section 1": Infestation or infection which is evident.

"Section 2": Conditions that are present which are deemed likely to lead to infestation or infection.

(3) If no infestation or infection by wood destroying pests or organisms is found, the report shall include a written Certification as provided in Business and Professions Code § 8519(a) that on the date of inspection "no evidence of active infestation or infection was found."

(4) All work recommended to correct conditions described in "Section 1" shall be at the expense of ☐ Buyer, ☐ Seller.

(5) All work recommended to correct conditions described in "Section 2," if requested by Buyer, shall be at the expense of ☐ Buyer, ☐ Seller.

(6) The repairs shall be performed with good workmanship and materials of comparable quality and shall include repairs of leaking showers, replacement of tiles and other materials removed for repairs. It is understood that exact restoration of appearance or cosmetic items following all such repairs is not included.

(7) Funds for work agreed to be performed after close of escrow, shall be held in escrow and disbursed upon receipt of a written Certification as provided in Business and Professions Code § 8519(b) that the inspected property "is now free of evidence of active infestation or infection."

(8) Work to be performed at Seller's expense may be performed by Seller or through others, provided that (a) all required permits and final inspections are obtained, and (b) upon completion of repairs a written Certification is issued by a licensed Structural Pest Control Operator showing that the inspected property "is now free of evidence of active infestation or infection."

(9) If inspection of inaccessible areas is recommended by the report, Buyer has the option to accept and approve the report, or within _____ calendar days from receipt of the report to request in writing further inspection be made. BUYER'S FAILURE TO NOTIFY SELLER IN WRITING OF SUCH REQUEST SHALL CONCLUSIVELY BE CONSIDERED APPROVAL OF THE REPORT. If further inspection recommends "Section 1" and/or "Section 2" corrective measures, such work shall be at the expense of the party designated in subparagraph (4) and/or (5), respectively. If no infestation or infection is found, the cost of inspection, entry and closing of the inaccessible areas shall be at the expense of the Buyer.

(10) Other _____
_____ .

Buyer's Initials   Seller's Initials

_____/_____ _____/_____ **E. FLOOD HAZARD AREA DISCLOSURE:** Buyer is informed that subject property is situated in a "Special Flood Hazard Area" as set forth on a Federal Emergency Management Agency (FEMA) "Flood Insurance Rate Map" (FIRM), or "Flood Hazard Boundary Map" (FHBM). The law provides that, as a condition of obtaining financing on most structures located in a "Special Flood Hazard Area," lenders require flood insurance where the property or its attachments are security for a loan.

The extent of coverage and the cost may vary. For further information consult the lender or insurance carrier. No representation or recommendation is made by the Seller and the Broker(s) in this transaction as to the legal effect or economic consequences of the National Flood Insurance Program and related legislation.

Buyer's Initials   Seller's Initials

_____/_____ _____/_____ **F. SPECIAL STUDIES ZONE DISCLOSURE:** Buyer is informed that subject property is situated in a Special Studies Zone as designated under §§ 2621-2625, inclusive, of the California Public Resources Code; and, as such, the construction or development on this property of any structure for human occupancy may be subject to the findings of a geologic report prepared by a geologist registered in the State of California, unless such a report is waived by the City or County under the terms of that act.

Buyer is allowed _____ calendar days from acceptance of the offer to make further inquiries at appropriate governmental agencies concerning the use of the subject property under the terms of the Special Studies Zone Act and local building, zoning, fire, health, and safety codes. When such inquiries disclose conditions or information unsatisfactory to the Buyer, which the Seller is unwilling or unable to correct, Buyer may cancel this agreement. BUYER'S FAILURE TO NOTIFY SELLER IN WRITING SHALL CONCLUSIVELY BE CONSIDERED APPROVAL.

Buyer's Initials   Seller's Initials

_____/_____ _____/_____ **G. ENERGY CONSERVATION RETROFIT:** If local ordinance requires that the property be brought in compliance with minimum energy Conservation Standards as a condition of sale or transfer, ☐ Buyer, ☐ Seller shall comply with and pay for these requirements. Where permitted by law, Seller may, if obligated hereunder, satisfy the obligation by authorizing escrow to credit Buyer with sufficient funds to cover the cost of such retrofit.

Buyer's Initials   Seller's Initials

_____/_____ _____/_____ **H. HOME PROTECTION PLAN:** Buyer and Seller have been informed that Home Protection Plans are available. Such plans may provide additional protection and benefit to a Seller or Buyer. The CALIFORNIA ASSOCIATION OF REALTORS® and the Broker(s) in this transaction do not endorse or approve any particular company or program:

a) ☐ A Buyer's coverage Home Protection Plan to be issued by _____
Company, at a cost not to exceed $_____ , to be paid by ☐ Buyer, ☐ Seller; or

b) ☐ Buyer and Seller elect not to purchase a Home Protection Plan.

Buyer's Initials   Seller's Initials

_____/_____ _____/_____ **I. CONDOMINIUM/P.U.D.:** The subject of this transaction is a condominium/planned unit development (P.U.D.) designated as unit _____ and _____ parking space(s) and an undivided interest in community areas, and _____ . The current monthly assessment charge by the homeowner's association or other governing body(s) is $_____ . As soon as practicable, Seller shall provide Buyer with copies of covenants, conditions and restrictions, articles of incorporation, by-laws, current rules and regulations, most current financial statements, and any other documents as required by law. Seller shall disclose in writing any known pending special assessment, claims, or litigation to Buyer. Buyer shall be allowed _____ calendar days from receipt to review these documents. If such documents disclose conditions or information unsatisfactory to Buyer, Buyer may cancel this agreement. BUYER'S FAILURE TO NOTIFY SELLER IN WRITING SHALL CONCLUSIVELY BE CONSIDERED APPROVAL.

Buyer's Initials   Seller's Initials

_____/_____ _____/_____ **J. LIQUIDATED DAMAGES: If Buyer fails to complete said purchase as herein provided by reason of any default of Buyer, Seller shall be released from obligation to sell the property to Buyer and may proceed against Buyer upon any claim or remedy which he/she may have in law or equity; provided, however, that by initialling this paragraph Buyer and Seller agree that Seller shall retain the deposit as liquidated damages. If the described property is a dwelling with no more than four units, one of which the Buyer intends to occupy as his/her residence, Seller shall retain as liquidated damages the deposit actually paid, or an amount therefrom, not more than 3% of the purchase price and promptly return any excess to Buyer. Buyer and Seller agree to execute a similar liquidated damages provision, such as CALIFORNIA ASSOCIATION OF REALTORS® Receipt for Increased Deposit (RID-11), for any increased deposits. (Funds deposited in trust accounts or in escrow are not released automatically in the event of a dispute. Release of funds requires written agreement of the parties, judicial decision or arbitration.)**

Buyer and Seller acknowledge receipt of copy of this page, which constitutes Page 3 of _____ Pages.

Buyer's Initials (_____) (_____)   Seller's Initials (_____) (_____)

OFFICE USE ONLY

Reviewed by Broker or Designee _____

Date _____

REAL ESTATE PURCHASE CONTRACT AND RECEIPT FOR DEPOSIT (DLF-14 PAGE 3 OF 4)

Exhibit 35.3

Subject Property Address _____

K. ARBITRATION OF DISPUTES: Any dispute or claim in law or equity arising out of this contract or any resulting transaction shall be decided by neutral binding arbitration in accordance with the rules of the American Arbitration Association, and not by court action except as provided by California law for judicial review of arbitration proceedings. Judgment upon the award rendered by the arbitrator(s) may be entered in any court having jurisdiction thereof. The parties shall have the right to discovery in accordance with Code of Civil Procedure § 1283.05. The following matters are excluded from arbitration hereunder: (a) a judicial or non-judicial foreclosure or other action or proceeding to enforce a deed of trust, mortgage, or real property sales contract as defined in Civil Code § 2985, (b) an unlawful detainer action, (c) the filing or enforcement of a mechanic's lien, (d) any matter which is within the jurisdiction of a probate court, or (e) an action for bodily injury or wrongful death, or for latent or patent defects to which Code of Civil Procedure § 337.1 or § 337.15 applies. The filing of a judicial action to enable the recording of a notice of pending action, for order of attachment, receivership, injunction, or other provisional remedies, shall not constitute a waiver of the right to arbitrate under this provision.

Any dispute or claim by or against broker(s) and/or associate licensee(s) participating in this transaction shall be submitted to arbitration consistent with the provision above only if the broker(s) and/or associate licensee(s) making the claim or against whom the claim is made shall have agreed to submit it to arbitration consistent with this provision.

"NOTICE: BY INITIALLING IN THE SPACE BELOW YOU ARE AGREEING TO HAVE ANY DISPUTE ARISING OUT OF THE MATTERS INCLUDED IN THE 'ARBITRATION OF DISPUTES' PROVISION DECIDED BY NEUTRAL ARBITRATION AS PROVIDED BY CALIFORNIA LAW AND YOU ARE GIVING UP ANY RIGHTS YOU MIGHT POSSESS TO HAVE THE DISPUTE LITIGATED IN A COURT OR JURY TRIAL. BY INITIALLING IN THE SPACE BELOW YOU ARE GIVING UP YOUR JUDICIAL RIGHTS TO DISCOVERY AND APPEAL, UNLESS THOSE RIGHTS ARE SPECIFICALLY INCLUDED IN THE 'ARBITRATION OF DISPUTES' PROVISION. IF YOU REFUSE TO SUBMIT TO ARBITRATION AFTER AGREEING TO THIS PROVISION, YOU MAY BE COMPELLED TO ARBITRATE UNDER THE AUTHORITY OF THE CALIFORNIA CODE OF CIVIL PROCEDURE. YOUR AGREEMENT TO THIS ARBITRATION PROVISION IS VOLUNTARY."

"WE HAVE READ AND UNDERSTAND THE FOREGOING AND AGREE TO SUBMIT DISPUTES ARISING OUT OF THE MATTERS INCLUDED IN THE 'ARBITRATION OF DISPUTES' PROVISION TO NEUTRAL ARBITRATION."

Buyer's Initials   Seller's Initials
_____ / _____   _____ / _____

17. **OTHER TERMS AND CONDITIONS:** _____
_____
_____
_____
_____

18. **ATTORNEY'S FEES:** In any action, proceeding or arbitration arising out of this agreement, the prevailing party shall be entitled to reasonable attorney's fees and costs.

19. **ENTIRE CONTRACT:** Time is of the essence. All prior agreements between the parties are incorporated in this agreement which constitutes the entire contract. Its terms are intended by the parties as a final expression of their agreement with respect to such terms as are included herein and may not be contradicted by evidence of any prior agreement or contemporaneous oral agreement. The parties further intend that this agreement constitutes the complete and exclusive statement of its terms and that no extrinsic evidence whatsoever may be introduced in any judicial or arbitration proceeding, if any, involving this agreement.

20. **CAPTIONS:** The captions in this agreement are for convenience of reference only and are not intended as part of this agreement.

21. **AGENCY CONFIRMATION:** The following agency relationship(s) are hereby confirmed for this transaction:
LISTING AGENT: _____ is the agent of (check one):
(Print Firm Name)
☐ the Seller exclusively; or ☐ both the Buyer and Seller

SELLING AGENT: _____ (if not the same as Listing Agent) is the agent of (check one):
(Print Firm Name)
☐ the Buyer exclusively; or ☐ the Seller exclusively; or ☐ both the Buyer and Seller.

22. **AMENDMENTS:** This agreement may not be amended, modified, altered or changed in any respect whatsoever except by a further agreement in writing executed by Buyer and Seller.

23. **OFFER:** This constitutes an offer to purchase the described property. Unless acceptance is signed by Seller and a signed copy delivered in person, by mail, or facsimile, and received by Buyer at the address below, or by _____ who is authorized to receive it, on behalf of Buyer, within _____ calendar days of the date hereof, this offer shall be deemed revoked and the deposit shall be returned. Buyer has read and acknowledges receipt of a copy of this offer. This agreement and any supplement, addendum or modification relating hereto, including any photocopy or facsimile thereof, may be executed in two or more counterparts, all of which shall constitute one and the same writing.

REAL ESTATE BROKER _____   BUYER _____
By _____   BUYER _____
Address _____   Address _____
_____   _____
Telephone _____   Telephone _____

ACCEPTANCE

The undersigned Seller accepts and agrees to sell the property on the above terms and conditions and agrees to the above confirmation of agency relationships (☐ subject to attached counter offer).
Seller agrees to pay to Broker(s) _____
compensation for services as follows: _____.
Payable: (a) On recordation of the deed or other evidence of title, or (b) if completion of sale is prevented by default of Seller, upon Seller's default, or (c) if completion of sale is prevented by default of Buyer, only if and when Seller collects damages from Buyer, by suit or otherwise, and then in an amount not less than one-half of the damages recovered, but not to exceed the above fee, after first deducting title and escrow expenses and the expenses of collection, if any. Seller shall execute and deliver an escrow instruction irrevocably assigning the compensation for service in an amount equal to the compensation agreed to above. In any action, proceeding, or arbitration between Broker(s) and Seller arising out of this agreement, the prevailing party shall be entitled to reasonable attorney's fees and costs. The undersigned has read and acknowledges receipt of a copy of this agreement and authorizes Broker(s) to deliver a signed copy to Buyer.

Date _____ Telephone _____   SELLER _____
Address _____
                                                    SELLER _____
Real Estate Broker(s) agree to the foregoing.
Broker _____ By _____   Date _____
Broker _____ By _____   Date _____

┌─ OFFICE USE ONLY ─┐
Reviewed by Broker or Designee _____
Date _____

Page 4 of _____ Pages.

REAL ESTATE PURCHASE CONTRACT AND RECEIPT FOR DEPOSIT (DLF-14 PAGE 4 OF 4)

Exhibit 35.4

BILATERAL LAND CONTRACT ESCROW INSTRUCTIONS

ESCROW INSTRUCTIONS
(Agreement For Sale Of Real Property)

CONSIDERATION FOR SUBJECT PROPERTY

$ 1,000	Cash deposit on opening of escrow.
$ 14,000	Balance of cash deposit to be deposited prior to close of escrow
$ 85,000	Contract Balance
$	
$	
$ 100,000	Total Consideration

Escrow Company, a subsidiary of The _____ Company   Escrow No. __18765 ML__

Address: __1015 E. Chapman Ave.__   Escrow Officer __Mary Lee__

__Fullerton, California 92631__

Phone: __(714) 871-7050__   Date __6-1-88__

The undersigned Vendee and Vendor, to effect the transfer of that certain real property ("Subject Property") described as _____

_____Tract 2645 in the city of Orange, County of Orange, State of California, as per map_____

_____recorded in book 26, page 45 of Miscellaneous Maps, also known as 8769 Citrus Lane,_____ Orange, Ca.

hereby instruct   **Escrow Company** (a subsidiary of The _____ Company) ("Escrow Holder") as follows:

1. The total consideration for the Subject Property is $ __100,000 (one hundred thousand dollars)__ . Upon the opening of this Escrow, Vendee will hand to you the sum of $ __1,000 (one thousand and no/100)__ to be applied to the purchase price for the Subject Property, and on or before __8-31__ , 19 __88__ , ("Closing Date"), Vendee will hand to you the sum of $ __14,000 (fourteen thousand and no/100)__ , plus such additional funds as may be necessary to cover Vendee's portion of the closing costs and charges. The remaining portion of the purchase price in the amount of $ __85,000 (eighty five thousand & no/100)__ shall be paid in accordance with the terms of a Land Sale Contract With Power of Sale as furnished by __Your Favorite Title Company__

("Contract") which the parties shall execute in triplicate and cause to be delivered to you on or before the Closing Date. **Payments of $714.73 on the balance of that contract at the rate of 9-1/2% to mature 10 years from date thereof.**

2. Escrow Holder is hereby authorized and instructed to deliver to Vendee and Vendor one fully executed copy of the Contract (and to retain one copy of said Contract for your collection files) upon the deposit of the documents and funds required to be deposited hereunder and the satisfaction of each of the following conditions on or prior to the Closing Date or at such earlier time as may hereinafter be specified:

(a) The deposit into this Escrow on or before __ten days from receipt thereof__ of Vendee's written notification of Vendee's approval of the condition of title to the Subject Property, based upon a current Preliminary Title Report to be furnished to Vendee through this Escrow, and at Vendor's expense, on or before __twenty days from date__ . Such written approval shall satisfy all title requirements in this transaction.

(b) When Escrow Holder can obtain the usual form policy of title insurance issued by __Assurance Title Company__ . with total liability in the amount of the total purchase price, showing beneficial title in the Subject Property vested in Vendee, subject only to (i) the usual conditions and exceptions contained in said title insurer's standard form of title insurance policy, (ii) such matters shown as the preliminary title report as may be approved by Vendee in writing in accordance with paragraph 2(a), and (iii) the Contract.

(c) __Upon close of escrow, establish a collection account with XYZ Collection Company for the purpose of allocating payments as follows:__

Contract payment	714.73
Impounds	60.00
Collection fee	12.00
Total payment	$786.73

3. Vendee acknowledges that the Subject Property is covered and encumbered by a certain Deed of Trust securing a Promissory Note evidencing a loan to Vendor in the original principal amount of $ __70,000 (seventy thousand & no/100)__ made by a lender which is not involved in this transaction ("Lender"), that Vendee has been provided with a copy of said Deed of Trust and Promissory Note, and that Vendee approves the same. Vendee and Vendor hereby direct and instruct Escrow Holder not to contact said Lender in connection with, or inform said Lender of, this transaction. The parties hereto do hereby (a) waive the obtaining of a Beneficiary Statement as a condition to the consummation of this transaction, (b) relieve Escrow Holder of all responsibility, liability or concern due to the closing of this Escrow without the benefit of a Beneficiary Statement from said Lender, and (c) agree to defend, indemnify and hold Escrow Holder harmless from and against any and all claims, demands, judgments, liabilities, costs or expenses of any kind or nature whatsoever, including but not limited to reasonable attorneys' fees, based upon or arising out of the closing of this Escrow without the knowledge and/or consent of said Lender.

4. All Escrow, document preparation and other fees and charges relating to this Escrow shall be paid by __Vendor__

5. All real and personal property taxes, the premium cost for existing policies of fire insurance and __rents__ shall be prorated as of __close of escrow__ , and charge the account of Vendee, and credit the account of Vendor, with the existing balance of the impound account held by Lender in the amount of $ __329.50__ .

6. Your agency as Escrow Holder shall terminate six months following the Closing Date, and shall be subject to earlier termination by receipt by you prior to the close of escrow of written notice signed (1) in the case this escrow has not been placed in a condition to close by the Closing Date by any party hereto, or (2) if received prior to the Closing Date, but after there shall have been a failure of a condition of performance to be complied with or performed on or before a date, or within a period, stated herein, then by any party other than a party responsible for such compliance or performance. Any such termination shall be effective upon receipt of such notice, but you shall not return the documents or deposits by the revoking party prior to ten days after you have mailed a copy of such notice to each of the other parties. If the conditions of this escrow have not been complied with on or prior to the Closing Date, or any extension thereof, Escrow Holder shall nevertheless proceed to complete the escrow as soon as such conditions have been complied with, unless written notice shall have been delivered to Escrow Holder as herein provided. No notice, demand or change of instructions, except a demand for termination made in accordance

(1)

Exhibit 36.1

with this paragraph, shall be of any effect in this escrow unless given in writing by all parties affected thereby. In the event that this escrow shall terminate or shall fail to be consummated for any reason whatsoever, Escrow Holder is hereby authorized and instructed to remit all funds by Escrow Holder's check to the parties depositing the same, unless Escrow Holder is specifically instructed to the contrary. Escrow Holder may, in its sole discretion, condition the termination of the escrow upon the receipt of written mutual consent to such termination executed by the undersigned.

7. All prorations shall be made on the basis of a 30-day month and the close of escrow hereunder shall be the day the Contract is delivered to the parties hereto in accordance with paragraph 2 hereof. Prorate mortgage insurance premiums paid to the FHA during the last 12 months, based upon a statement to be furnished to you by the parties hereto. Prorate taxes on real property only based on last tax statements available and charge the Vendor and credit the Vendee with the amount of unpaid personal property tax which is a lien upon the property as shown on the latest tax statement. Prorate all rentals based upon a rental statement to be handed to Escrow Holder by Vendor. Escrow Holder shall assume that Vendor shall collect all rents which fall due prior to the close of this escrow, unless instructed to the contrary by Vendor in writing. There shall be no adjustment against Vendee for uncollected rentals prior to the close of escrow.

8. Escrow Holder shall not be held liable for the sufficiency or correctness as to form, manner of execution, or validity of any instrument deposited in this escrow, nor as to the identity, authority, or rights of any person executing the same, nor for failure to comply with any of the provisions of any agreement, contract, or other instrument filed herein or referred to herein and the duties of Escrow Holder hereunder shall be limited to the safekeeping of such money, instruments, or other documents received by Escrow Holder and for the disposition of the same in accordance with the written instructions accepted by Escrow Holder. The knowledge of Escrow Holder of matters affecting the Subject Property, provided such facts do not prevent compliance with these instructions, does not create any liability or duty in addition to the responsibility of Escrow Holder under these instructions. Escrow Holder shall not be obligated to make any physical examination of any real or personal property described in any document deposited into this escrow, the parties hereto agree that Escrow Holder is not making any representations whatsoever regarding said property, and the Vendee hereunder agrees to accept said property "as is" in its present condition.

9. Should Escrow Holder before or after the close of escrow receive or become aware of any conflicting demands or claims with respect to this escrow or the rights of any of the parties hereto, or of any money or property deposited herein or affected hereby, Escrow Holder shall have the right to discontinue any or all further acts on its part to be performed until such conflict is resolved to the satisfaction of Escrow Holder, and Escrow Holder shall have the further right to commence or defend any action or proceeding for the determination of such conflict. The parties hereto jointly and severally agree to pay all costs, damages, judgments and expenses, including reasonable attorneys' fees, suffered or incurred by Escrow Holder in connection with, or arising out of this escrow, including, but without limiting the generality of the foregoing, any suit in interpleader brought by Escrow Holder. In the event that Escrow Holder shall file any action in interpleader in connection with this escrow, Escrow Holder shall automatically be released and discharged from all further duties or obligations imposed upon Escrow Holder under these instructions.

10. The undersigned jointly and severally agree that, in the event of the cancellation or other termination of this escrow prior to the closing hereof, they shall pay to Escrow Holder any expenses which Escrow Holder has incurred or become obligated for pursuant to these instructions and also a reasonable escrow fee for the services contracted by the undersigned to be rendered by Escrow Holder and such expenses, if any, and fees shall be paid and put in escrow before any cancellation or other termination is effective. The undersigned agree that said charges for expenses and fees may be apportioned between the undersigned in a manner which, in the sole discretion of Escrow Holder, Escrow Holder may deem equitable, and that the decision of Escrow Holder in that respect will be binding and conclusive upon the undersigned. Any documents or funds deposited with Escrow Holder by the undersigned may be retained by Escrow Holder as a lien to secure to Escrow Holder the reimbursement and payment of expenses, if any, and fees as hereinabove provided.

11. Escrow Holder shall not be concerned with the giving of any disclosures required by Federal or State law including, but not limited to, any disclosures required under **Regulation Z** promulgated pursuant to the Federal Consumer Credit Protection Act, which may or should be given outside of this escrow, or the effect of any zoning laws, ordinances or regulations affecting any of the property transferred hereunder. The undersigned jointly and severally agree to indemnify and to save and hold Escrow Holder harmless by reason of any misrepresentations or omission by either party hereto or their respective agents or the failure of any of the parties hereto to comply with the rules and/or regulations of any governmental agency, state, federal, county, municipal or otherwise. Parties to this escrow have satisfied themselves outside of this escrow that the transaction covered hereby is not in violation of the Subdivision Map Act or any other law relating to land division, and Escrow Holder is relieved of all responsibility and/or liability in connection therewith, and is not to be concerned with the enforcement of said laws.

12. Escrow Holder is to make no provision for the assignment of any policies of hazard insurance covering the Subject Property; provided, however, that Escrow Holder shall obtain and deliver to Vendee upon the close of Escrow a "Vendee's Endorsement" on all such policies in favor of Vendee.

13. All deposits made by the parties hereto in connection with this transaction shall be deposited by Escrow Holder in an account designated as "Escrow Fund Account" with any local bank, without any liability for interest. All disbursements shall be made by check of Escrow Holder drawn on said account, provided that Escrow Holder shall not be obligated to identify or to guarantee the signature of any payee thereof. All documents and checks in favor of each of the parties hereto shall be mailed, unregistered, to the addresses of the respective parties set forth on the reverse side of these instructions.

14. Escrow Holder shall be under no obligation or liability for the failure to inform the parties hereto regarding any sale, loan, exchange, or other transaction, or facts within the knowledge of Escrow Holder, even though the same concern the property described herein, provided they do not prevent the compliance of Escrow Holder with these instructions.

15. Any policy of title insurance called for under these instructions will be subject to the exceptions and conditions contained in the standard from of the company issuing such insurance including, but not limited to, the exception that said company will not insure against loss by reason of the reservation or exception of any water rights, claims or title to water.

16. The parties hereto authorize the recordation of any instruments delivered through this escrow, if necessary or proper in the issuance of the policy of title insurance called for herein, and in connection therewith, funds and/or instruments received in this escrow may be delivered to, or deposited with, any title company situated in the county in which any o. the property covered hereby is situated for the purpose of complying with the terms and conditions of these escrow instructions. In addition, in the event that it may be necessary or proper for the consummation of this escrow, you are authorized to deposit or have deposited funds or documents, or both, with any bank, trust company, title insurance company, savings and loan association, building and loan association, industrial loan company, credit union, insurer or licensed escrow agent, or sub-escrow agent, subject to your order pursuant to closing this escrow, and such deposit shall be deemed a deposit in accordance with the meaning of these instructions.

17. Escrow Holder is hereby authorized to destroy or otherwise dispose of any and all documents, papers, instructions, correspondence and other material pertaining to this escrow at the expiration of five years from the date of these instructions, regardless of the date of any subsequent amendments hereto, additional or supplemental instructions or the date of the close of escrow, without liability and without further notice to the undersigned.

18. These instructions may be executed in counterparts, each of which so executed shall, irrespective of the date of its execution and delivery, be deemed an original and said counterparts together shall constitute one and the same instrument. Any amended and/or supplemental instructions hereto must be in writing, executed by all of the parties hereto, and deposited with Escrow Holder.

19. The signature of the undersigned on any documents and instructions pertaining to this escrow indicates their unconditional acceptance and approval of the same, and the undersigned hereby acknowledge the receipt of a copy of these instructions.

EACH OF THE UNDERSIGNED PARTIES HEREBY ACKNOWLEDGES THAT THEY HAVE BEEN GIVEN SUFFICIENT TIME TO SEEK AND CONSULT INDEPENDENT COUNSEL OF THEIR CHOICE PRIOR TO THE EXECUTION OF THE "CONTRACT" REFERRED TO HEREIN AND THESE INSTRUCTIONS.

VENDEE: VENDOR:

_____   _____
             Name   Name
                                    (2)

Exhibit 36.2

Chapter 10 Quiz

1. Reasons for using a land contract include:

   (A) To take advantage of existing financing at lower than market rate
   (B) To purchase with Cal-Vet financing
   (C) To make title more insurable
   (D) Both (A) and (B)

2. When an escrow is cancelled, all associated obligations such as commissions and bills of third parties are also automatically cancelled.

   (A) True
   (B) False

3. When the seller states that if the buyer's new loan is not approved by July 30 the escrow will be cancelled, this is referred to as:

   (A) A contingency
   (B) A cancellation
   (C) Liquidated damages
   (D) Automatic forfeiture

4. When an instruction states that if the transaction is not closed by July 30th the amount of $5,000 of the borrower's money will be forfeited to the seller, this is referred to as:

   (A) A contingency
   (B) A cancellation
   (C) Liquidated damages
   (D) Automatic forfeiture

5. Besides giving the sale details, a deposit receipt also:

   (A) Is the escrow instruction
   (B) Is incorporated in the escrow instruction
   (C) Serves as a consumer protection device
   (D) Is stapled to the escrow instruction

6. Cancellations of an existing escrow are most often the result of:

   (A) Failure to sign the instruction
   (B) Failure to properly inform the parties of the terms and conditions of the transaction
   (C) An "automatic" cancellation provision in the instruction
   (D) Forfeiture of the parties

7. In land contract escrows, fee title is held by:

   (A) The vendor
   (B) The trustor
   (C) The vendee
   (D) The grantee

8. In all-inclusive deed of trust escrows, title is held by:

   (A) The vendor
   (B) The trustor
   (C) The vendee
   (D) The trustee

9. A deed in lieu of foreclosure:

   (A) Wipes out all junior liens
   (B) Is a particularly safe investment
   (C) Involves risk through remaining liens
   (D) Can be prepared without legal advice

10. The "subject to" escrow represents an attempt to take advantage of:

    (A) The right to cancel an escrow
    (B) The right of redemption
    (C) Existing financing on favorable terms
    (D) Informal legal advice from the escrowholder

Chapter 11
Title Insurance—
A Partner in the Closing Process

PREVIEW

Nature of Title Insurance

Policy Coverages

Special Endorsements

Guarantees

Interim Title Binders

NATURE OF TITLE INSURANCE

As we note from the historical examination in Chapter 1, title insurance and escrow are concomitant outgrowths of increased real estate activity, combined with the need to process transfers in an expeditious and efficient manner. From the abstract or "chain of title" coupled with attorney's opinion, evolved the early guarantee of title. In order to establish a certain degree of liability for the conclusions of title to real property and the encumbrances that affect ownership, title insurance supplanted these earlier methods.

Implied Covenant of Clear Title Of particular importance in the transfer of title are the covenants implied in a grant deed. These are described in § 1113 of the Civil Code of the State of California as follows:

> "That previous to the time of the execution of such conveyance, the grantor has not conveyed the same estate, or any right, title or interest therein, to any person other than the grantee;
>
> "That such estate is at the time of the execution of such conveyance free from encumbrances done, made or suffered by the grantor, or any person claiming under him."

These implied covenants prevail in California unless they are restrained by express terms in the document of conveyance, and they encourage some form of protection to assure that there are no other conveyances or claims against the property. Thus the protective role of title insurance, to provide such assurance.

Insurers and Premiums

Risk Affects Rate. As in other forms of insurance there are varying degrees of title coverage, and the premium for each varies with the risk. In most title insurance markets, low liability policies are subsidized by larger liability policies. Premiums are set by competitive factors and geared to rate of return.

Underwritten Title Companies. In 1986, title companies underwritten by title insurance companies were issued guidelines by the Insurance Commissioner of the State of California. Net worth requirements, which are substantial, are based upon the actual or projected activity of the underwritten company.

POLICY COVERAGES

A thorough understanding of title insurance and the specific coverages that are available is essential in the escrow process. Title requirements vary with the degree of complexity of the transaction, the parties involved and their degree of sophistication.

Coverage Components

The type of title insurance must be matched to the specific needs of a particular situation.

Variables. The varieties and/or combinations of title insurance coverage reflect:

- *Type of Coverage*. Standard coverage, extended coverage, coverage modified by special endorsements.

- *Type of Estate*. For example, fee, leasehold, or equitable interest.

- *Parties Insured*. Owners, lenders, lessees, vendees, others.

Standard Conditions. Exhibit 37 presents the conditions and stipulations to the American Land Title Association (ALTA) owner's title insurance policy (1987 version). These provisions generally remain the same for all forms of title insurance. The 1987 ALTA policy was extensively revised and updated to reflect recent developments in financing and liability law, and to clarify language. The revised version became effective July 1, 1988.

- *Specialized Variants*. The conditions and stipulations for loan, leasehold, and construction policies contain additional provisions.

- *Residential Policy*. A much simplified and condensed text has been created for single-family homeowners.

Standard Coverage

Standard coverage owner's insurance, CLTA (California Land Title Association), is designed for, and usually adequate for the buyer of a home. The insuring clause in a CLTA standard form title insurance policy demonstrates the extent of standard title coverage:

"The company insures the insured, as of date of policy stated in schedule A, against loss or damage not exceeding the amount of insurance stated in schedule A and costs, attorneys' fees, and expenses which the company may be obligated to pay hereunder sustained or incurred by said insured by reason of:

☐ Title to the estate or interest described in schedule A being vested other than as stated therein;

☐ Any defect in or lien or encumbrance on such title;

☐ Unmarketability of such title; or

☐ Any lack of the ordinary right of any abutting owner for access to at least one physically open street or highway if the land, in fact, abuts upon one or more such streets or highways.

[In addition, the insuring clause provides further coverage to an insured lender for:]

☐ Invalidity of the lien of the insured mortgage (deed of trust) upon said estate or interest except to the extent that such invalidity, or claim thereof, arises out of the transaction evidenced by the insured mortgage and is based upon usury, or any consumer protection or truth in lending law;

☐ Priority of any lien or encumbrance over the lien of the insured mortgage, said mortgage being shown in schedule B in order of its priority; or

☐ Invalidity of any assignment as shown in schedule B."

Extended Coverages A standard title policy provides only limited coverage of *off-record matters*, the so-called insurance risks. Extended coverage goes beyond this, with exclusions outlined in Exhibit 38, Schedule B, Part I. Comprehensive extended coverage exists for these risks.

Modification of Standard Coverage. Standard coverage may be sufficient to meet title insurance requirements for transfer of title to a detached single-family residence. It may not be sufficient in all cases, however. In 1974 one major California title insurer amended its standard policy for homeowners to include several common encumbrances. (This parallels the implied covenants contained in a grant deed.) Since this amendment became effective other title insurers have introduced comparable coverage.

☐ Expanded encroachment coverage

☐ Expanded access to a public street coverage

☐ Unrecorded taxes or assessments—limited coverage

☐ Unrecorded mechanics' or materialmen's liens

- ☐ Violation of covenants, conditions, and restrictions

- ☐ Violation of zoning ordinances

- ☐ Damage from a holder of mineral rights exploring for or removing minerals from the property insured

- ☐ An inflation endorsement is available which can increase policy coverage up to 150% of the original policy amount.

ALTA The ALTA lender's policy resulted from discussions between the American Title Association (ATA), now the American Land Title Association (ALTA), and eastern lenders, principally insurance companies, in the late 1920s and early 1930s. This extended coverage, which is available at *considerably higher* premiums than standard coverage, protects against numerous risks that are *not a matter of record*. Institutional lenders usually require an ALTA extended coverage policy.

ALTA Coverage. Most of the exclusions listed in Exhibit 38 have been eliminated from today's ALTA policy with coverage now expanded to include:

- ☐ Those matters disclosed by a physical inspection of the premises not previously disclosed by public record.

- ☐ Those matters disclosed by inquiry of the occupants which might disclose other off-record matters.

- ☐ Matters disclosed by a current survey.

Definition of Encumbrances. Section 1114 of the Civil Code of the State of California defines this term as "taxes, assessments, and all liens upon real property." Later legal interpretations include building restrictions, encroachments, easements, and pending actions among "all liens." Off-record matters such as zoning ordinances, existing and obvious easements, and proposed assessments are not considered encumbrances. Any coverage would only be included in some form of expanded or extended coverage title insurance.

Interpretation of Title Needs **Proportionate to Investment**. Title requirements reflect the needs of the party obtaining the title insurance coverage. When a consortium of oil companies undertakes a multibillion dollar venture such as the Alaskan pipeline, there is a high degree of motivation to determine that the consortium's interest in the pipeline is irrefutable; ownership must be established with certainty. A developer who is purchasing a large parcel of acreage for a shopping center site would require extended coverage owner's insurance and order an extended coverage survey prepared. Major developments often involve complex forms of title.

- ☐ *Leaseholds*. Many landowners, such as the Irvine Company of Southern California, have been reluctant to sell real property because of tax considerations. In lieu of granting the property to a purchaser, a land lease is negotiated to give the "purchaser" the right to use the property up to the maximum of 99 years allowed by California law. Since such leaseholds involve considerable investment, especially in the case of commercial property, title insurance is required to assure the marketability of this leasehold title.

☐ *New Construction*. With millions of dollars invested in new construction, lenders are desirous of protecting their first lien position, and title insurance can offer this type of protection.

☐ *Mineral Rights*. The ownership of mineral rights can involve substantial cost, either through lease or outright purchase.

☐ *Ownership in Layers*. Title insurance can be obtained not only on vertical airspace, such as a condominium, but on horizontal layers below the ground as well.

Example

The bottom 50 feet of the top 200 feet, measured vertically from the surface as of July 15, 1990, of the following described land:

Lot 5 in block 2 of Norden's Townsite, in the city of Concord, county of Contra Costa, State of California, as per map recorded in book 12 page 15 of maps, in the office of the County Recorder of said county.

Extended Coverage Surveys. These reveal information which is disclosed by comprehensive investigation and onsite field work and checking with the local government agencies. A regular survey shows only matters of record, and indicates the positioning of improvements with respect to lot lines. Some items disclosed by the extended coverage survey and duly noted by the title insurer are:

☐ Shortages or overages in lot dimensions.

☐ Natural watercourses traversing the property.

☐ Unrecorded easements above or below the surface of the land. Title insurers take special care in the subsurface area.

☐ Encroachments of existing improvements from adjoining property onto the property in question and vice-versa.

☐ Any matters existing on the surface or subsurface of the land from which a claim may arise from other than the owner.

☐ Current owner's statement relative to the occupancy of the land, whether there has been work performed recently on the land, and if there are claims to the title that are not a matter of record.

☐ Inquiry of any occupants by field investigation, particularly if no owner's statement is available.

Owner's and Lender's Policies

Title needs vary based not only upon the type of property involved, but on whether the insured is an owner or lender. Common types of coverage are:

Standard Owner's or Joint Protection Policy. This is subject to the limitations outlined in Exhibit 37, and provides insurance to the lender and seller.

Standard Lender's Policy. This is the same coverage as above, providing insurance at the request of a lender. Many private lenders and a few institutional lenders request this coverage.

Extended Coverage Owner's Policy. This is a comprehensive policy whose coverage virtually eliminates exclusions shown in Exhibit 38, numbers 1 through 5.

ALTA Lender's Policy. This policy is available for coverage relative to the validity of title to a leasehold or subleasehold estate. It is available in standard coverage or extended coverage. (In the case of a standard coverage oil leasehold policy no general exception would be made for mining claims or patent reservations. They would be shown as encumbrances.)

Easement Ownership. This is available only in report form to cover the ownership rights of an easement holder.

Vendee's Policy. This standard coverage policy relates to insurance of the equitable title of the vendee created by a contract of sale (land contract), and the legal title of the vendor or successor in interest.

Lender's Concerns **Coverage Required.** A lender's title requirements include any problems that affect the value of the loan security. Some of the risks that would be covered by an ALTA extended coverage lender's policy, with CLTA endorsement #100, include:

☐ Violations of recorded covenants, conditions, and restrictions.

☐ Encroachments of improvements onto existing easements.

☐ Any unrecorded easement rights disclosed by inspection.

☐ The rights of other parties, possessory or otherwise, disclosed by inspection.

☐ Unrecorded leases of tenants occupying the land.

☐ Unrecorded assessments as disclosed by public works activity in the area and inspection of tax office records (if work of improvement is in progress).

☐ Unrecorded claims resulting from work performed or materials provided for recent improvement of the land.

Responsibility for Inspection. Although the prudent lender's representative makes a thorough investigation of the property as a potential security, the trained eye of a title inspector can discern problems that may evade the lender's scrutiny. Lenders should, however, not neglect their "due diligence" in property inspection because extended coverage inspections are not made in all instances by title companies. This is why a majority of institutional lenders require extended coverage title insurance.

Special Situations Other unique title problems arise in transactions involving Indian lands, public lands, tidelands, submerged lands, cemetery lands, dedications, spurious title claims, eminent domain proceedings (condemnation), bankruptcy, foreclosure proceedings, homesteads, partitions, dissolution proceedings, quiet title proceedings, probate proceedings, and guardianships.

Indian Lands. These require special attention due to the unique legal status assigned to Native Americans by the United States Government, under the Department of Interior's Bureau of Indian Affairs. Many legal requirements are involved in the hypothecation and leasing of such lands. Escrow instructions must also provide for Bureau of Indian Affairs fees in conjunction with such transfer.

Tidelands. Tidelands are lands situated between the ordinary high-water and ordinary low-water lines of tidal waters. Establishing the line of mean (average) high tide can dramatically affect the title to valuable beach land. This constantly changing line is established by agreement between the sovereign agency and the private property owner. Rights to tideland property involve a complex study of court decisions, treaties, and other matters that may not be a part of a normal search of the record and should be left to title experts. There may be unusual exceptions relative to rights of others (including the public); any prudent purchaser would want to be aware of these rights and of their effect on value.

Submerged Lands. This refers to lands whose shoreward boundaries coincide with the seaward boundaries of tidelands. Knowledge of ownership in this area is extremely important for oil companies desiring to do offshore drilling, but title insurance is not normally available for that purpose. Establishment of offshore ownership rights was the subject of controversy for many years due to the valuable royalty income derived from this area in California. At present it appears that the rights of the United States to these lands is paramount over the state or local jurisdiction outside of the three-mile limit.

Cemetery Lands. Properties of this type involve such complexities as to vex the most adventurous of title insurers. It is doubtful that one could obtain any satisfactory form of title insurance to a cemetery plot because of the rights of other lot owners, and other rights.

Dedications. In dedications of interest in real property it is important to know that title cannot be automatically transferred to a public agency, such as a city or county, without a corresponding acceptance by the agency.

Spurious Title. Many times the buying public is confronted with spurious title claims, such as adverse possession. In order to establish such a claim, certain facts have to be ascertained, such as open and uninterrupted occupation of the land for a 5-year period, payment of taxes, and a claim or color of title. A title insurer may be required to define the rights of the insured in such a case through issuance of a quiet title guaranty.

Eminent Domain. The right to take land for a public purpose (eminent domain) with just compensation is well established. Governments, utilities, and like parties exercising this power utilize title insurers to obtain the names of the parties necessary to name as parties defendant (owners, lenders, easement holders, and so on) in the proceedings for eminent domain and to perfect the title.

Bankruptcy. In the past, title passed to the trustee of a bankrupt estate. Under the Bankruptcy Reform Act of 1978, title may or may not pass. Title can be transferred pursuant to proper court notice and hearing of confrontation. Title insurers examine the bankruptcy file to determine that proper procedure has been followed for notification and protection of creditors prior to the disposition of property by the bankrupt estate and prior to issuing a conclusion of ownership status in the form of a title report or title policy.

Foreclosure. Trust deeds have reduced the time required in foreclosure of a property. Because of possible multiple liens, reinstatement rights, etc., there may be complications in the title to a property that has been through foreclosure.

Homestead. By filing a valid declaration of homestead (a method to protect the owner-occupied single family residence from seizure by judgment creditors), an owner may cause potential problems. When equity is reduced by refinance after a homestead is declared, the increased amount is not subtracted from the money subject to execution. Title insurers need to be aware of this and make their conclusions as to title accordingly.

Example

If the homestead exemption were $45,000 with the following conditions:

Property value	$150,000
First deed of trust	80,000
Second trust deed refinance	40,000

the portion subject to execution would be $25,000—the $150,000 value less $125,000 representing the balance of the first trust deed plus the amount of the exemption, but not deducting the refinance.

Partition. When co-owners hold title to property, one or more may bring partition proceedings to divide the ownership of the land. For example, if Green, Smith, and Jones own 1/3 each of parcels A, B, and C, the court may award parcel A to Green, parcel B to Smith, and parcel C to Jones. The Subdivided Lands Act and the Subdivision Map Act may impose further obligations on the parties.

Dissolution. Divorce may dispose of property and create certain reciprocal rights among the parties. A thorough understanding of the title implications can be of extreme importance in the resale of such property.

Probate and Guardianship Proceedings. Both involve representation of the ownership entity by the court. Any disposition of properties of the deceased or incompetent requires court action. Affidavits from the principals may suffice in a transfer of joint tenancy or community property following the death of one of the spouses.

Quiet Title Proceedings. Many times matters such as unexercised easement rights, color or claims to title, or other matters of record can be perfected or cleared only by initiating a quiet title proceeding naming the parties in question as parties defendant.

SPECIAL ENDORSEMENTS

A wide variety of endorsements can expand, modify, or delete coverage of the basic policy. Modification of coverage requirements arises from five key sources:

☐ The needs of the parties

☐ The amount of consideration

☐ The type of property

☐ The complexity of the transaction

☐ The title exceptions and encumbrances affecting the property.

Major available types of endorsements are listed by number in Exhibit 39. They fall into several general categories.

Construction Related Policies Standard or extended coverage policies may be modified by endorsement relative to the priority of the mortgage lien over mechanics' liens relating from the commencement of work on a project.

During Construction. During the course of construction other endorsements may be requested for the issuance of construction payments in accordance with the building loan agreement, as well as for such things as indicating that the foundation erected conforms to the setback requirements of recorded restrictions and does not encroach on adjoining property.

After Completion. Upon completion of the construction, the construction policy may be reissued as a standard or extended coverage policy. Extended coverage insurance will also insure against any violation of existing restrictions by endorsement.

Assignee's Insurance Under an existing loan policy, a lender may sell the indebtedness to a purchaser and provide the purchaser with coverage by endorsement of the original policy. This endorsement indicates that the lien is valid, not reconveyed or modified other than as indicated.

Lender's Extended Coverage Endorsement

This is a specific endorsement which states:

"The Company hereby insures against loss which said Insured shall sustain by reason of any of the following matters:

Any incorrectness in the assurance which the Company hereby gives:

☐ That there are no covenants, conditions, or restrictions under which the lien of the mortgage referred to in Schedule A can be cut off, subordinated, or otherwise impaired.

☐ That there are no present violations on said land of any enforceable covenants, conditions, or restrictions.

☐ That, except as shown in Schedule B, there are no encroachments of buildings, structures, or improvements located on said land onto adjoining lands, nor any encroachments onto said land of buildings, structures, or improvements located on adjoining lands.

Any *future violations* on said land of any covenants, conditions, or restrictions occurring prior to acquisition of title to said estate or interest by the Insured, provided such violations result in loss or impairment of the lien of the mortgage referred to in Schedule A, or result in impairment or loss of the title to said estate or interest if the Insured shall acquire such title in satisfaction of the indebtedness secured by such mortgage.

Unmarketability of the title to said estate or interest by reason of any violations on said land occurring prior to acquisition of title to said estate or interest by the Insured, or of any covenants, conditions, or restrictions.

Damage to existing improvements, including lawns, shrubbery, or trees:

☐ Which are located or encroached upon that portion of land subject to any easement shown in Schedule B, which damage results from the exercise of the right to use or maintain such easement for the purposes for which the same was granted or reserved.

☐ Resulting from the exercise of any right to use the surface of said land for the extraction or development of the minerals excepted from the description in Schedule B.

Any final court order or judgment requiring removal from any land adjoining said land of any encroachment shown in Schedule B.

Wherever in this endorsement any or all the words 'covenants, conditions, or restrictions' appear, they shall not be deemed to refer to or include the terms, covenants and conditions contained in any lease referred to in Schedule A."

Other Lender's Coverage **Designation of Improvements.** This endorsement states the street address of the property as well as the improvements located thereon. In addition it assures the lender that the map provided shows the proper location and lot dimensions in accordance with the record.

Modification of Trust Deed. This covers subsequent modifications and specifically outlines the provisions of each such modification. An additional endorsement may be required to assure the lender that the modification retains priority over any subsequent or intervening liens to the lien being modified.

Additional Advances. This type of insurance is provided to the holder of an "open end" deed of trust, or a trust deed modified to provide for additional advance, for subsequent advances of funds by a lender. This endorsement will also cover priority of the advance over any intervening liens.

Partial Reconveyance. Endorsement for either standard or extended coverage is available. The endorsement indicates that the issuance of the partial reconveyance does not impair the validity of the lender's lien.

Usability of Property **Zoning Coverage.** Governmental regulations, including zoning ordinances, are a normal exclusion on all forms of title insurance. Many recent local ordinances require special zoning reports to be rendered in connection with the transfer of title to real property. Limited coverage in the form of an endorsement has been provided to indicate type of zoning, the use permitted, and the conformance of existing improvements.

Access. If access to a public thoroughfare is in question, an access endorsement is used to guarantee access to a public street for the insured property (in standard policies only).

Contiguity. When more than one parcel is included in the policy, it may be helpful that they are determined to be contiguous if they are used in conjunction with each other. There is a special endorsement to provide such assurance of contiguity.

Liability Coverage Endorsements are available not only to increase the amount of policy coverage (Title Insurance Plus is one example) but to allocate coverage to individual lots or parcels described in the title policy.

Other Coverages Many unique situations occur in the transfer and finance of real property which dictate some specific coverage. As these situations arise, the title insurer should be contacted to determine whether special coverage is available. Exhibit 39 provides some further details.

GUARANTEES

In contrast to policies and endorsements, guarantees are specific limited-use coverages for special situations. Examples include:

Subdivision Guarantee This is a title coverage preceded by a preliminary subdivision report that satisfies the real estate commissioner's requirements relative to filing a public report. The public report is a consumer-based document issued to potential purchasers in a subdivision, and no sales can be consummated until a final public report has been issued. In addition, the parties required to sign the subdivision map prior to recordation are outlined in the preliminary guarantee.

Litigation Guarantee Many times customers require information as to parties defendant in the case of eminent domain proceedings (condemnation), quiet title proceedings, partition proceedings, dissolution proceedings (divorce), or any other form of legal proceedings requiring a proper listing of such parties.

Trustee's Sale Guarantee The Civil Code of the State of California provides for a nonjudicial proceeding for beneficiaries under deeds of trust to foreclose a property held as security in the event of default. This guarantee is issued for the benefit of the trustee and beneficiary to enable the trustee to act as the agent for the beneficiary to serve notice on the required parties as outlined in the code.

Applicability to Land Contracts. This principle of nonjudicial foreclosure has been extended to land contracts. The validity of this theory is still subject to question. Title insurance available on this type of contract and resultant action by the trustee is somewhat limited. Some title insurance companies have devised a deed of trust which is supported by the mutual promises of the vendor and vendee under contract, which appears to be enforceable on a non-judicial basis.

Chain of Title and Search Guarantees Certain circumstances involving either real or personal property might require a chain of title guarantee or property search guarantee.

Role of the Preliminary Title Report. The preliminary title report outlines the legal description of the property in question, title vesting, and list of the encumbrances. These encumbrances show what exceptions will be in the title insurance policy and allow the insured to select what exceptions he or she will allow to exist on their title policy and which ones will have to be "removed" in escrow before the close of escrow. It is called a "preliminary" title report because it is issued prior to rendering a title policy. Parties must be able to rely on its accuracy in regard to:

☐ *Parcel Dimensions.* In addition to showing the condition of title, a property sketch (plat mat) with a basic disclaimer normally accompanies the report. It is rendered to escrow as a matter of convenience to indicate approximate dimensions of the parcel. The disclaimer indicates that the title insurance does not guarantee lot dimensions, unless extended coverage insurance is provided.

□ *Parties' Identity and Capacity*. In connection with the issuance of a preliminary title report, a statement of identity is obtained in order to search the general index (personal names) to determine if there are any matters affecting the parties' financial status or capacity, such as divorce, bankruptcy, guardianship, tax liens, etc.

Insurer's and Abstractor's Liability. Not only can there be claims against title insurers for inaccurate data provided in title policies, but a second type of liability, which emanates from its predecessor, the abstract of title, may be incurred from a faulty preliminary title report. This is called abstractor's liability. It has been diluted considerably, reducing damages available.

INTERIM TITLE BINDERS

In certain instances parties require a commitment to issue a title insurance policy in the future under certain terms and conditions. This coverage is widely used by relocators who move parties throughout the country reselling their previous residences. The binder commits to issuance of a policy within a certain period of time upon performance of the conditions outlined in the binder.

"DRE WARNS LICENSEES: DON'T TAKE ILLEGAL COMPENSATION FROM TITLE INSURERS!"

The Department of Real Estate will pursue, vigorously, allegations against its licensees involving illegal acceptance of compensation from title insurers for business referrals, according to Real Estate Commissioner James A. Edmonds, Jr.

"The department will coordinate its investigations in such cases with the California Departments of Insurance and Corporations, when it's appropriate for us to do so," the Commissioner said.

The strong warning to licensees follows consumer complaints and title insurance industry concerns that some real estate licensees "are shaking-down" title insurance firms, the Commissioner explained.

"We have complaints that some real estate licensees have demanded compensation from title companies for business referrals ranging from outright fee payments to vacations to expensive office machines.

In two instances currently under investigation by the department, it's alleged that real estate licensees demanded fax machines in return for the referral of clientele.

"I have met with the Departments of Insurance and Corporations on this issue," Commissioner Edmonds said.

"Their resolve to stop or preclude such illegal activity is equally determined. We will work in close association with these departments whenever possible to stop what may be a growing practice among some real estate licensees and title insurance companies."

Commissioner Edmonds noted that § 10177.4 of the Business and Professions Code clearly prohibits such activity and says, in part:

"The commissioner may . . . suspend or revoke the license of a real estate licensee who claims, demands, or receives a commission, fee or other consideration, as compensation or inducement, for referral of customers to any escrow agent, structural pest control firm, home protection company, title insurer, controlled escrow company, or underwritten title company."

"The law is clear on this matter," Commissioner Edmonds noted. "Violations will not be tolerated."

Reprinted from the *"Real Estate Bulletin"* (California Department of Real Estate), Fall, 1989, p. 8.

CONDITIONS AND STIPULATIONS

1. The following terms when used in this policy mean:

(a) "insured": The insured named in Schedule A, and, subject to any rights or defenses the Company would have had against the named insured, those who succeed to the interest of the named insured by operation of law as distinguished from purchase including, but not limited to, heirs, distributees, devisees, survivors, personal representatives, next of kin, or corporate or fiduciary successors.

(b) "insured claimant": an insured claiming loss or damage.

(c) "knowledge" or "known": actual knowledge, not constructive knowledge or notice which may be imputed to an insured by reason of the public records as defined in this policy or any other records which impart constructive notive of matters affecting the land.

(d) "land": the land described or referred to in the Schedule [A][C], and improvements affixed thereto which by law constitute real property. The term "land" does not include any property beyond the lines of the area described or referred to in Schedule [A][C], nor any right, title, interest, estate or easement in abutting streets, roads, avenues, alleys, lanes, ways or waterways, but nothing herein shall modify or limit the extent to which a right of access to and from the land is insured by this policy.

(e) "Mortgage": mortgage, deed of trust, trust deed, or other security instrument.

(f) "public records": records established under state statutes at Date of Policy for the purpose of imparting constructive notice of matters relating to real property to purchasers for value and without knowledge. With respect to Section 1(a)(iv) of the Exclusions From Coverage, "public records" shall also include environmental protection liens filed in the records of the clerk of the United States district court for the district in which the land is located.

(g) "unmarketability of the title": an alleged or apparent matter affecting the title to the land, not excluded or excepted from coverage, which would entitle a purchaser of the estate or interest described in Schedule A to be released from the obligation to purchase by virtue of a contractual condition requiring the delivery of marketable title.

2. Continuation of Insurance after Conveyance of Title.

The coverage of this policy shall continue in force as of Date of Policy in favor of an insured only so long as the insured retains an estate or interest in the land, or holds an indebtedness secured by a purchase money mortgage given by a purchaser from the insured, or only so long as the insured shall have liability by reason of covenants of warranty made by the insured in any transfer or conveyance of the estate or interest. This policy shall not continue in force in favor of any purchaser from the insured of either (i) an estate or interest in the land, or (ii) an indebtedness secured by a purchase money mortgage given to the insured.

3. Notice of Claim to be Given by Insured Claimant.

The insured shall notify the Company promptly in writing (i) in case of any litigation as set forth in Section 4(a) below, (ii) in case knowledge shall come to an insured hereunder of any claim of title or interest which is adverse to the title to the estate or interest, as insured, and which might cause loss or damage for which the Company may be liable by virtue of this policy, or (iii) if title to the estate or interest, as insured, is rejected as unmarketable title. If prompt notice shall not be given to the Company, then as to the insured all liability of the Company shall terminate with regard to the matter or matters for which prompt notice is required; provided, however, that failure to notify the Company shall in no case prejudice the rights of any insured under this policy unless the Company shall be prejudiced by the failure and then only to the extent of the prejudice.

4. Defense and Prosecution of Actions; Duty of Insured Claimant to Cooperate.

(a) Upon written request by the insured and subject to the options contained in Section 6 of these Conditions and Stipulations, the Company, at its own cost and without unreasonable delay, shall provide for the defense of an insured in litigation in which any third party asserts a claim adverse to the title or interest as insured, but only as to those stated causes of action alleging a defect, lien or encumbrance or other matter insured against by this policy. The Company shall have the right to select counsel of its choice (subject to the right of the insured to object for reasonable cause) to represent the insured as to those stated causes of action and shall not be liable for and will not pay the fees of any other counsel. The Company will not pay any fees, costs or expenses incurred by the insured in the defense of those causes of action which allege matters not insured against by this policy.

(b) The Company shall have the right, at its own cost, to institute and prosecute any action or proceeding or to do any other act which in its opinion may be necessary or desirable to establish the title to the estate or interest, as insured, or to prevent or reduce loss or damage to the insured. The Company may take any appropriate action under the terms of this policy, whether or not it shall be liable hereunder, and shall not thereby concede liability or waive any provision of this policy. If the Company shall exercise its rights under this paragraph, it shall do so diligently.

(c) Whenever the Company shall have brought an action or interposed a defense as required or permitted by the provisions of this policy, the Company may pursue any litigation to final determination by a court of competent jurisdiction and expressly reserves the right, in its sole discretion, to appeal from any adverse judgment or order.

(d) In all cases where this policy permits or requires the Company to prosecute or provide for the defense of any action or proceeding, the insured shall secure to the Company the right to so prosecute or provide defense in the action or proceeding, and all appeals therein, and permit the Company to use, at its option, the name of the insured for this purpose. Whenever requested by the Company, the insured, at the Company's expense, shall give the Company all reasonable aid (i) in any action or proceeding, securing evidence, obtaining witnesses, prosecuting or defending the action or proceding, or effecting settlement and (ii) in any other lawful act which in the opinion of the Company may be necessary or desirable to establish the title to the estate or interest as insured. If the Company is prejudiced by the failure of the insured to furnish the required cooperation, the Company's obligations to the insured under the policy shall terminate, including any liability or obligation to defend, prosecute, or continue any litigation, with regard to the matter or matters requiring such cooperation.

5. Proof of Loss or Damage.

In addition to and after the notices required under Section 3 of these Conditions and Stipulations have been provided the Company, a proof of loss or damage signed and sworn to by the insured claimant shall be furnished to the Company within 90 days after the insured claimant shall ascertain the facts giving rise to the loss or damage. The proof of loss or damage shall describe the defect in, or lien or encumbrance on the title, or other matter insured against by this policy which constitutes the basis of loss or damage and shall state, to the extent possible, the basis of calculating the amount of the loss or damage. If the Company is prejudiced by the failure of the insured claimant to provide the required proof of loss or damage, the Company's obligations to the insured under the policy shall terminate, including any liability or obligation to defend, prosecute, or continue any litigation, with regard to the matter or matters requiring such proof of loss or damage.

In addition, the insured claimant may reasonably be required to submit to examination under oath by any authorized representative of the Company and shall produce for examinaiton, inspection and copying, at such reasonable times and places as may be designated by any authorized representative of the Company, all records, books, ledgers, checks, correspondence and memoranda, whether bearing a date before or after Date of Policy, which reasonably pertain to the loss or damage. Further, if requested by any authorized representative of the Company, the insured claimant shall grant its permission, in writing, for any authorized representative of the Company to examine, inspect and copy all records, books, ledgers, checks, correspondence and memoranda in the custody or control of a third party, which reasonably pertain to the loss or damage. All information designated as confidential by the insured claimant provided to the Company pursuant to this Section shall not be disclosed to others unless, in the reasonable judgment of the Company, it is necessary in the administration of the claim. Failure of the insured claimant to submit for examination under oath, produce other reasonably requested information or grant permission to secure reasonably necessary information from third parties as required in this paragraph, unless prohibited by law or governmental regulation, shall terminate any liability of the Company under this policy as to that claim.

6. Options to Pay or Otherwise Settle Claims; Termination of Liability.

(a) To Pay or Tender Payment of the Amount of Insurance.

Exhibit 37.1

To pay or tender payment of the amount of insurance under this policy together with any costs, attorneys' fees and expenses incurred by the insured claimant, which were authorized by the Company, up to the time of payment or tender of payment and which the Company is obligated to pay.

Upon the exercise by the Company of this option, all liability and obligations to the insured under this policy, other than to make the payment required, shall terminate, including any liability or obligation to defend, prosecute, or continue any litigation, and the policy shall be surrendered to the Company for cancellation.

(b) To Pay or Otherwise Settle With Parties Other than the Insured or With the Insured Claimant.

(i) to pay or otherwise settle with other parties for or in the name of an insured claimant any claim insured against under this policy, together with any costs, attorneys' fees and expenses incurred by the insured claimant which were authorized by the Company up to the time of payment and which the Company is obligated to pay; or

(ii) to pay or otherwise settle with the insured claimant the loss or damage provided for under this policy, together with any costs, attorneys' fees and expenses incurred by the insured claimant which were authorized by the Company up to the time of payment and which the Company is obligated to pay.

Upon the exercise by the Company of either of the options provided for in paragraphs (b)(i) or (ii), the Company's obligations to the insured under this policy for the claimed loss or damage, other than the payments required to be made, shall terminate, including any liability or obligation to defend, prosecute or continue any litigation.

7. Determination, Extent of Liability and Coinsurance.

This policy is a contract of indemnity against actual monetary loss or damage sustained or incurred by the insured claimant who has suffered loss or damage by reason of matters insured against by this policy and only to the extent herein described.

(a) The liability of the Company under this policy shall not exceed the least of:

(i) the amount of Insurance stated in Schedule A; or

(ii) the difference between the value of the insured estate or interest as insured subject to the defect, lien or encumbrance insured against by this policy.

(b) In the event the Amount of Insurance stated in Schedule A at the Date of Policy is less than 80 percent of the value of the insured estate or interest or the full consideration paid for the land, whichever is less, or if subsequent to the Date of Policy an improvement is erected on the land which increases the value of the insured estate or interest by at least 20 percent over the Amount of Insurance stated in Schedule A, then this Policy is subject to the following:

(i) where no subsequent improvement has been made, as to any partial loss, the Company shall only pay the loss pro rata in the proportion that the amount of insurance at Date of Policy bears to the total value of the insured estate or interest at Date of Policy; or

(ii) where a subsequent improvement has been made, as to any partial loss, the Company shall only pay the loss pro rata in the proportion that 120 percent of the Amount of Insurance stated in Schedule A bears to the sum of the Amount of Insurance stated in Schedule A and the amount expended for the improvement.

The provisions of this paragraph shall not apply to costs, attorneys' fees and expenses for which the Company is liable under this policy, and shall only apply to that portion of any loss which exceeds, in the aggregate, 10 percent of the Amount of Insurance stated in Schedule A.

(c) The Company will pay only those costs, attorneys' fees and expenses incurred in accordance with Section 4 of these Conditions and Stipulations.

8. Apportionment.

If the land described in Schedule [A][C] consists of two or more parcels which are not used as a single site, and a loss is established affecting one or more of the parcels but not all, the loss shall be computed and settled on a pro rata basis as if the amount of insurance under this policy was divided pro rata as to the value on Date of Policy of each separate parcel to the whole, exclusive of any improvements made subsequent to Date of Policy, unless a liability or value has otherwise been agreed upon as to each parcel by the Company and the insured at the time of the issuance of this policy and shown by an express statement or by an endorsement attached to this policy.

9. Limitation of Liability

(a) If the Company establishes the title, or removes the alleged defect, lien or encumbrance, or cures the lack of a right of access to or from the land, or cures the claim of unmarketability of title, all as insured, in a reasonably diligent manner by any method, including litigation and the completion of any appeals therefrom, it shall have fully performed its obligations with respect to that matter and shall not be liable for any loss or damage caused thereby.

(b) In the event of any litigation, including litigation by the Company or with the Company's consent, the Company shall have no liability for loss or damage until there has been a final determination by a court of competent jurisdiction, and disposition of all appeals therefrom, adverse to the title as insured.

(c) The Company shall not be liable for loss or damage to any insured for liability voluntarily assumed by the insured in settling any claim or suit without the prior written consent of the Company.

10. Reduction of Insurance; Reduction or Termination of Liability.

All payments under this policy, except payments made for costs, attorneys' fees and expenses, shall reduce the amount of the insurance pro tanto.

11. Liability Noncumulative.

It is expressly understood that the amount of insurance under this policy shall be reduced by any amount the Company may pay under any policy insuring a mortgage hereafter executed by the insured or assumed or agreed to by the insured and which is a charge or lien on the estate or interest described or referred to in Schedule A, and the amount so paid shall be deemed a payment under this policy to the insured owner.

12. Payment of Loss.

(a) No payment shall be made without producing this policy for endorsement of the payment unless the policy has been lost or destroyed, in which case proof of loss or destruction shall be furnished to the satisfaction of the Company.

(b) When liability and the extent of loss or damage has been definitely fixed in accordance with these Conditions and Stipulations, the loss or damage shall be payable within 30 days thereafter.

13. Subrogation Upon Payment or Settlement.

(a) The Company's Right of Subrogation.

Whenever the Company shall have settled and paid a claim under this policy, all right of subrogation shall vest in the Company unaffected by any act of the insured claimant.

The Company shall be subrogated to and entitled to all rights and remedies which the insured claimant would have had against any person or property in respect to the claim had this policy not been issued. If requested by the Company, the insured claimant shall transfer to the Company all rights and remedies against any person or property necessary in order to perfect this right of subrogation. The insured claimant shall permit the Company to sue, compromise or settle in the name of the insured claimant and to use the name of the insured claimant in any transaction or litigation involving these rights or remedies.

If a payment on account of a claim does not fully cover the loss of the insured claimant, the Company shall be subrogated to these rights and remedies in the proportion which the Company's payment bears to the whole amount of the loss.

If loss should result from any act of the insured claimant, as stated above, that act shall not void this policy, but the Company, in that event, shall be required to pay only that part of any losses insured against by this policy which shall exceed the amount, if any, lost to the Company by reason of the impairment by the insured claimant of the Company's right of subrogation.

(b) The Company's Rights Against Non-insured Obligors.

The Company's right of subrogation against non-insured obligors shall exist and shall include, without limitation, the rights of the insured to indemnities, guaranties, other policies of insurance or bonds, notwithstanding any terms or conditions contained in those instruments which provide for subrogation rights by reason of this policy.

14. Arbitration.

Unless prohibited by applicable law, either the Company or the insured may demand arbitration pursuant to the Title Insurance Arbitration Rules of the American Arbitration Association. Arbitrable matters may include, but are not limited to, any controversy or claim between the Company

Exhibit 37.2

182 *Title Insurance—A Partner in the Closing Process*

and the insured arising out of or relating to this policy, any service of the Company in connection with its issuance or the breach of a policy provision or other obligation. All arbitrable matters when the Amount of Insurance is $1,000,000 or less shall be arbitrated at the option of either the Company or the insured. All arbitrable matters when the Amount of Insurance is in excess of $1,000,000 shall be arbitrable only when agreed to by both the Company and the insured. Arbitration pursuant to this policy and under the Rules in effect on the date the demand for arbitration is made or, at the option of the insured, the Rules in effect at Date of Policy shall be binding upon the parties. The award may include attorneys' fees only if the laws of the state in which the land is located permit a court to award attorneys' fees to a prevailing party. Judgment upon the award rendered by the Arbitrator(s) may be entered in any court having jurisdiction thereof.

The law of the situs of the land shall apply to an arbitration under the Title Insurance Arbitration Rules.

A copy of the Rules may be obtained from the Company upon request.

15. Liability Limited to this Policy; Policy Entire Contract.

(a) This policy together with all endorsements, if any, attached hereto by the Company is the entire policy and contract between the insured and the Company. In interpreting any provision of this policy, this policy shall be construed as a whole.

(b) Any claim of loss or damage, whether or not based on negligence, and which arises out of the status of the title to the estate or interest covered hereby or by any action asserting such claim, shall be restricted to this policy.

(c) No amendment of or endorsement to this policy can be made except by a writing endorsed hereon or attached hereto signed by either the President, a Vice President, the Secretary, an Assistant Secretary, or validating officer or authorized signatory of the Company.

16. Severability.

In the event any provision of the policy is held invalid or unenforceable under applicable law, the policy shall be deemed not to include that provision and all other provisions shall remain in full force and effect.

17. Notices, Where Sent.

All notices required to be given the Company and any statement in writing required to be furnished the Company shall include the number of this policy and shall be addressed to the Company at (fill in).

NOTE: Bracketed [ ] material optional.

Exhibit 37.3

SCHEDULE B

This policy does not insure against loss or damage (and the Company will not pay costs, attorneys' fees or expenses) which arise by reason of:

PART I

1. Taxes or assessments which are not shown as existing liens by the records of any taxing authority that levies taxes or assessments on real property or by the public records.
   Proceedings by a public agency which may result in taxes or assessments, or notices of such proceedings, whether or not shown by the records of such agency or by the public records.
2. Any facts, rights, interests or claims which are not shown by the public records but which could be ascertained by an inspection of the land or by making inquiry of persons in possession thereof.
3. Easements, liens or encumbrances, or claims thereof, which are not shown by the public records.
4. Discrepancies, conflicts in boundary lines, shortage in area, encroachments, or any other facts which a correct survey would disclose, and which are not shown by the public records.
5. (a) Unpatented mining claims; (b) reservations or exceptions in patents or in Acts authorizing the issuance thereof; (c) water rights, claims or title to water.
6. Any right, title, interest, estate or easement in land beyond the lines of the area specifically described or referred to in Schedule A, or in abutting streets, roads, avenues, alleys, lanes, ways or waterways, but nothing in this paragraph shall modify or limit the extent to which the ordinary right of an abutting owner for access to a physically open street or highway is insured by this policy.
7. Any law, ordinance or governmental regulation (including but not limited to building and zoning ordinances) restricting or regulating or prohibiting the occupancy, use or enjoyment of the land, or regulating the character, dimensions or location of any improvement now or hereafter erected on the land, or prohibiting a separation in ownership or a reduction in the dimensions or area of the land, or the effect of any violation of any such law, ordinance or governmental regulation.
8. Rights of eminent domain or governmental rights of police power unless notice of the exercise of such rights appears in the public records.
9. Defects, liens, encumbrances, adverse claims, or other matters (a) created, suffered, assumed or agreed to by the insured claimant; (b) not shown by the public records and not otherwise excluded from coverage but known to the insured claimant either at Date of Policy or at the date such claimant acquired an estate or interest insured by this policy or acquired the insured mortgage and not disclosed in writing by the insured claimant to the Company prior to the date such insured claimant became an insured hereunder; (c) resulting in no loss or damage to the insured claimant; (d) attaching or created subsequent to Date of Policy; or (e) resulting in loss or damage which would not have been sustained if the insured claimant had been a purchaser or encumbrancer for value without knowledge.

Exhibit 38

SUMMARY OF PRINCIPAL TITLE ENDORSEMENTS AND THEIR USES

Endorsement No.	Brief Description of Coverage
100 - ALTA, lender	Multiple extended coverage for lenders
100.6 - ALTA or Standard Coverage, owner or lender	Restrictions not legally enforceable
100.12 - ALTA or Standard Coverage, owner or lender	Coverage against right of re-entry under existing restrictions
100.23 - ALTA, lender	Improvements damage caused by severed oil rights
100.28 - ALTA or Standard Coverage, owner or lender	Violation of existing CC&R by contemplated improvements
100.29 - ALTA or Standard Coverage, owner or lender	Damage to improvements by exercise of oil rights
101 - Standard coverage, lender	Mechanics' liens—loss of priority
101.3 - ALTA or Standard Coverage, owner or lender	Expanded mechanics' lien coverage after work commenced
101.6 - ALTA or Standard Coverage, owner or lender	Mechanics' lien coverage after filing of notice of completion
102.4 & 102.5 ALTA or Standard Coverage, owner or lender	Foundation endorsements
103.1 - ALTA or Standard Coverage, owner or lender	Blanket easement damage to improvements
103.7 - ALTA or Standard Coverage, owner or lender	Land abuts on a physically open street
104 - ALTA, lender	Insurance of trust deed assignment
104.1 - ALTA or Standard Coverage, lender	Limited coverage of assignment of beneficial interest
104.6 - ALTA, lender	Insurance of valid assignment of rents
107.2 - ALTA or Standard Coverage owner or lender	Increased title coverage endorsement
107.9 - ALTA or Standard Coverage owner or lender	Covers transfer of ownership between related parties
108.8 - ALTA, lender	Insures additional advances under a loan

Exhibit 39.1

110.5 - ALTA, lender	Insures trust deed modifications
110.7 - ALTA or Standard Coverage owner or lender	Elimination of an item in a previously issued policy
111 - ALTA or Standard Coverage lender	Coverage protecting issuance of a partial reconveyance
111.5 - ALTA or Standard Coverage lender	Variable payment mortgage coverage
111.8 - ALTA or Standard Coverage lender	Graduated payment or negative amortization mortgage coverage
115 - ALTA or Standard Coverage lender	Condominium coverage
116 - ALTA or Standard Coverage lender	Location of improvements
116.1 - ALTA or Standard Coverage owner or lender	Incorporation of survey in title policy
116.4 - ALTA or Standard Coverage owner or lender	Contiguity endorsement for multiple parcels
119.2 - ALTA, lender	Covers validity of lease in chain of title
122 - ALTA, lender	Date down for mechanic's lien coverage
123.2 - ALTA or Standard Coverage owner or lender	Limited zoning coverage
124.1, 124.1, 124.3 - ALTA or Standard Coverage owner or lender	Special shopping center covenant coverage
126 - ALTA or Standard Coverage	Coverage of option validity options
40C - Standard Coverage, condominium owner	Augments standard coverage for owner occupied condominium unit
40H - Standard Coverage, owner	Similar to above for one to four unit residences
43 - ALTA or Standard Coverage lender	Special coverage for lines of credit secured by real estate: priority of lien under a revolving credit agreement
46 - ALTA or Standard Coverage owner or lender	Partnership and joint venture coverage in co-venture projects
8,8.1 - ALTA, lender or owner	Limited coverage for environmental protection liens

Exhibit 39.2

Chapter 11 Quiz

1. Standard title insurance coverage involves inspection of the premises and inquiry of the occupants.

   (A) True
   (B) False

2. A standard title insurance policy includes coverage against all but:

   (A) Forgery
   √(B) Zoning matters
   (C) Marketability of title
   (D) Title being in a name other than the insured

3. Extended coverage insurance includes:

   (A) Matters disclosed by physical inspection not a matter of record
   (B) Matters disclosed by inquiring of the occupants
   (C) Matters disclosed by a current survey
   √(D) All of the above

4. Extended coverage surveys reveal:

   (A) Dimensions of adjoining property
   (B) Dimensions of the entire block
   √(C) Encroachments of improvements on neighboring property
   (D) Any encroachments in the entire block

5. Institutional lenders usually require:

   (A) A standard coverage loan policy
   (B) An ALTA lender's policy
   (C) A CLTA insurance policy
   (D) A lot book report

6. A leasehold can extend on other than oil and agricultural leases to ____ years.

   (A) 51
   (B) 15
   (C) 99
   (D) 75

7. The buyer of a home would normally purchase:

   √(A) Standard coverage owner's insurance
   (B) Optionee's insurance
   (C) Vendee insurance
   (D) Extended coverage insurance

8. Extended coverage owner's insurance:

   (A) Is used on all house sales
   (B) Is used on a sale of a mobilehome
   (C) Is used in all cases
   (D) Would possibly be used by a purchaser of valuable property to be developed commercially

9. Special title problems may arise in transactions involving:

   (A) Indian lands
   (B) Tidelands
   (C) Probate and guardianship
   √(D) All of the above

10. Endorsements:

   (A) Represent a separate title policy
   √(B) Modify or expand title coverage
   (C) Have no connection with the title policy
   (D) Are issued for lender's coverage only

Chapter 12
Automation and
the Closing Process

PREVIEW

Automated Functions

Title Insurance

Escrow

AUTOMATED FUNCTIONS

In the past decade both closing and title insurance have become heavily reliant upon computer systems as a means of assimilation and reproduction of data as well as for word processing. This has been particularly evident in the title insurance business. The types of software systems required are dependent upon the tasks at hand. These functions can be classified as:

- ☐ Word and text processing
- ☐ Storage and retrieval of data
- ☐ Communications
- ☐ Decision support
- ☐ Graphics
- ☐ End-user application development.*

*(Davis, Gordon B., and Olson, Margrethe H., *Management Information Systems, Conceptual Foundations, Structure, and Development*, 2nd edition, McGraw Hill, New York, 1985, page 416.)

TITLE INSURANCE

The potential for automation in title insurance is revealed by breaking down the steps involved in rendering this service.

Title Searching Title searching consists primarily of information retrieval.

> **Chain of Title.** Various systems are available classifying real property by legal description or assessor's parcel number to locate data affecting the property since the previous title search. This is basically a storage and retrieval process as a method of decision support.

> **Compilation of Documents.** Upon completion of the search the documents listed in the chain are duplicated for title examination. This may involve the use of computer communications and graphics.

General Index Run. A search of items not identified by legal description such as dissolution proceedings (divorce), insanity, parole proceedings, guardianship, probates, bankruptcy filings, judgments, tax liens, powers of attorney and the like is generated based upon the names of the parties involved. This is computerized in most jurisdictions.

Other Search Related Activities. Other functions required to complete the compilation of information for title examination and for the customer are less susceptible to automation:

☐ *Legal Opinions*. The title examiner must often obtain legal opinions on matters in the chain of title such as partition and quiet title actions, orders confirming sale, attachments and executions, dissolution proceedings, and probates.

☐ *Copies*. It is often necessary to procure of copies of prior recorded documents. The most common item is covenants, conditions and restrictions (CC&Rs), required for extended coverage insurance and particularly for new construction. Under certain circumstances full copies or certified copies of other documents such as trust deeds may be required for the customer.

Title Examination   The data assimilated in the title search is interpreted and rendered in the form of a title report. Once the human examiner has performed this interpretation process, the information can be placed on a hard or floppy disk for future retrieval in print for the title report and later the title policy. At the title policy stage, the data is modified to reflect new documents recorded (reconveyances, deed of trust, etc.) in rendering the final version to the insured parties.

Peripheral   Other functions which support the principal activity of title policy issuance
Activities   may also involve data processing:

Sub-Escrows. Institutional lenders often involve the title insurer as a sub-escrow by sending demands for payoff to the title company rather than to the escrow agent for payment. In addition, if new financing is involved, the net proceeds are often remitted to the title company instead of the escrow agent. A sophisticated accounting program is required to compute lender demands for the appropriate payoff amounts, process the checks for payment, keep track of sub-escrows, and refund the excess to the escrowholder.

Complex Financing. In the case of new financing, loan proceeds may be used to pay off an existing lender's loan or, in the case of the same lender, net proceeds (less the existing loan) may be sent to the title company. Variable interest rate financing, graduated payments and negative amortization, prepayment fees, late charges, and lender fees for rendering the demand all complicate the calculation of a proper figure for payment of a demand. A custom sub-escrow program may need to be developed.

Accounting. Processing of financial data for the rendering of financial statements, investments of excess cash, maintenance and reconciliation of bank accounts, and customer billing and follow-up are important elements in a total data processing system.

Marketing. Maintenance of customer profiles, tracking customer activity, analysis of customer volume, and other customer related functions comprise a marketing support system.

ESCROW

One of the important functions of escrow is to protect the integrity of the moneys that flow through the transaction. Appropriate allocation of charges to the responsible parties, supported by appropriate instructions, is one of the principal functions of escrow. Automated systems for the escrow office must be capable of an exacting range of accounting and document processing.

Choice of Accounting Systems

To assure proper accounting of deposited funds, an accounting system must be appropriate to the size of the escrow operation, the number and type of transactions, and the basic management and information requirements of the firm.

Manual or Automated. Two basic methods are used for the accounting of the trust funds under escrow control: manual and automated. Each meets some needs of some firms.

☐ *Method*. In manual bookkeeping all receipts and disbursements are posted to individual ledger cards by escrow number and then posted and balanced to the office escrow account. The principal source of information in this process is the ledger card, which requires individual scrutiny to prepare further reports. Though an automated system takes over the subsequent balancing and reporting, it is still essential that individual posting be done daily to avoid overdrafts and errors.

☐ *Choice*. Manual procedure can be satisfactory in a single escrow office that maintains a steady but limited volume of business. A multi-branch escrow operation involving a diversity of transactions will almost certainly need an automated method. Even in smaller offices automated systems are being adopted as essential to tracking deposited funds.

Outside Accounting Services. Escrowholders may utilize data processing services provided by banks or private firms. The earnings from the bank trust balances usually offset, either directly or indirectly, the cost to the depository bank for providing such service. Under such an arrangement, each report has a cost that is charged against the earnings of the compensating balances, which may reduce the amount of other commercial services from the bank that can be utilized such as account reconcilement, etc.

Types of Information Available. An online source of business information may be vital to one firm, but not significant to a small broker-owned escrow. An accounting code for the type of escrow handled (sale, loan, and so on) may be meaningful to an independent or bank escrow, but of little value to a firm that specializes in only one type of transaction. Trends in average liabilities can be of great importance to all escrowholders. Accounting systems are available that can provide this and more information as a management tool and means of funds control.

Automated Accounting

Accounting may be done on a small office's desktop microcomputer, or a bank or title corporation's mainframe. Type, amount, and complexity of data put in will determine the types of information and documents available as output (reports). Because the field is changing so rapidly, inquiry should be made of other escrowholders presently using such systems to determine which best suits your particular business and market.

Example

Some of the reports and input forms now available are illustrated by Exhibits 40 through 45, supplied through the courtesy of Computer Data Control, Inc., Calabasas, California. These forms and reports are representative of types generated in an escrow accounting system operated by a bank or data processing service.

Input

The basic input documents for a typical accounting system include the following. Note that if accounting is done in-house, some of these steps (e.g., adjustment slips) may not exist on paper.

Start Card. This instrument provides the initial data for entering the transaction into the system, such basic information as company number, names of buyer and seller, amount of consideration, date escrow opened, legal description or street address of property, type of escrow, escrow officer assigned, title company assigned, and any other special information required in connection with the file (Exhibit 40).

Escrow Receipt. As funds are deposited in the escrow account it is the function of the receipt to serve as an audit trail for money being processed through the system.

Adjustment Slips. These forms are used to rectify input errors made by the escrowholder or data processor.

Escrow Checks. These are drawn against receipted funds in the escrow account, and data processing accounts for each individual check debit.

Fee Slips. To receive payment for its work on the individual account, the escrowholder draws a fee slip for services, and this money is transferred to the bank's fee account. These funds are then drawn down periodically by check as required by the escrowholder for transfer to its operating account.

Reports Using this basic input, a variety of reports are available for management information. These reports cover three basic areas, account control, peripheral data, and marketing analysis.

Account Control. This includes following the progress of each escrow handled.

☐ Report of new escrow—derived from start cards (Exhibit 41)

☐ Receipt listing and adjustments

☐ Disbursement activity and adjustments (Exhibit 42)

☐ Overdraft report

☐ Fee report—cumulative

☐ Status reports—indicate active files and files to be purged (removed) (Exhibits 43 and 44)

☐ Master control and summary of activity

☐ Closed escrow report—held open pending purge at specified period (60-90-120 days)

☐ List of missing start cards—receipts processed with no start cards found

☐ Unprocessed and voids—list of voided checks and items rejected during the processing stage. It should be examined daily to ascertain any unusual activity.

Peripheral Data. This refers to various kinds of data supporting the basic transactions.

☐ *Indices*. Cross-references by escrow number, buyer, seller, broker, legal description, property address, type of escrow, or other meaningful index for the office.

☐ *Trial Balance*. Used for auditing purposes, internal or external, to monitor escrows open for a prolonged period.

☐ *Ledger Card*. Produced usually at the end of the month after final file disbursements (Exhibit 45). This serves as the permanent file record. Between statements the master control and summary of activity report serves as the temporary ledger card.

☐ *Reconciliation*. This report reconciles the balance in the trust bank account to the balance shown in the trust accounting system.

☐ *Checks Outstanding*. A list of checks issued and as yet unpaid by the bank. If an inordinate time is involved, letters should be sent to the payees to determine if checks are lost. The program can be set up to identify such overdue checks.

☐ *Purged Escrow Listing*. A list of escrows removed from the system, either through cancellation or through closing, i.e., final disbursement of all deposited funds.

☐ *Roster of Escrow Officers*. List of parties assigned to escrows with numerical designation for system input.

☐ *Roster of Business Sources*. A client list with numerical designation.

☐ *Roster of Title Companies*. A list of title insurance sources most frequently used by the escrowholder, with numerical code.

☐ *Audit Confirmation Letters*. Many data processors provide upon request preprinted and addressed audit letters to the parties depositing moneys in escrow to confirm the balances in the trust account. This service is usually performed during an annual audit.

☐ *Customer Reports*. Preparation of the final file accounting (the closing statement) and issuance of supporting disbursements.

Marketing Analysis. Basic data can be sorted and analyzed to reveal significant patterns in the business.

☐ *Escrow Activity*. A list of open, closed and cancelled escrows by month and location, with totals for the organization. Comparisons are available for previous time periods.

☐ *Income Analysis by Officer*. This report indicates the productivity of escrow officers within the organization. It can also serve as a basis for evaluating the fee structure and type of escrow business generated.

☐ *Income Analysis by Source*. This list not only shows where strengths exist in the marketplace, it also points out areas that require further marketing activity.

☐ *Title Business Placement*. This report lists total consideration (purchase price or loan amount) placed with each rostered title company by month and year to date.

Management Tool. A fully utilized escrow accounting system can serve as a valuable management tool. Trends can be developed, personnel requirements noted, and weaknesses in operation can be perceived.

Word Processing Word processing has become an increasingly important aspect of the closing process. "Laundry lists" for loan documentation have become the order of the day, from which many word processors can prepare all the closing documents. Available systems range from memory typewriters to sophisticated software for personal computers, such as WordPerfect and Microsoft Word.

Role of Word Processing in Escrow. Many aspects of escrow closing are repetitive in nature and are adaptable to programmable steps. First efforts in this direction were in tract escrow processing and loan escrow documentation, followed by other escrows that contain more variable elements.

☐ *Evolution of Word Processing.* Prior to electronic automation, tract escrow instructions were simply preprinted with the standard provisions applicable to a particular type of project. A logical and economical extension of preprinting was the IBM memory and magnetic card machine, which could store an entire page for retrieval later. The operator entered a basic escrow instruction with all the uniform items, and manually inserted the variables, such as parties, consideration, and lot number for each new escrow.

☐ *Programmed Applications.* Computer manufacturers and users soon recognized the advantages of combining the computer's calculation and reporting capabilities with its word processing potential to produce loan documentation from escrow instructions, notes and trust deeds, and disclosure statements and RESPA forms for delivery to escrow. From a list of the variables for a particular loan ("laundry list"), programs can be set up to compute and print an entire loan documentation package.

☐ *Packaged Software.* Many computer software firms now offer escrow documentation packages that are adaptations of word processing formats designed originally for the legal profession. Standard escrow phraseology and forms are available for retrieval and use. Using data from the accounting system, laundry list, etc., the machine prints out a customized instruction for each particular transaction.

☐ *Growing Prevalence.* With the increasing uniformity of institutional lending geared to the secondary market, word processing is the rule, not the exception. All escrow operations of any appreciable size utilize word processing equipment to a greater or lesser degree.

Choice of Word Processing System. As with accounting, the choice of systems will vary with the applications desired. For example, the firm may decide to utilize this equipment for subdivision escrow instructions and closing statements only, or it might want a system capable of preparing all documentation.

The Decision to Automate

In-House Equipment. Most computer systems are expensive and require considerable training and development. When selecting a word processing or accounting system the following should be considered:

- ☐ What percentage of word processing is repetitive in this office?

- ☐ Will the office be more effective if a system is installed?

- ☐ How can personnel be used more effectively once a processing system is installed?

- ☐ What amount of training will be required for each system under consideration?

- ☐ Who is presently using these systems? What is their experience?

- ☐ How reliable is the equipment? What about the availability of service?

- ☐ Would all work cease if the electronic equipment became inoperable? What would be used as a back-up system?

Service Bureaus. It is not wise to purchase computer equipment just because it is "the thing to do" and is advertised as a great time saver. For some firms an alternative to a hasty decision implementing internal word processing or accounting may be to employ a service bureau to take care of the data processing storage, retrieval, and printing, and leave escrow personnel to devote productive time to decision making and execution.

Results of Automation

New Careers. The advent of automation in the escrow industry has opened new career paths for those people who have escrow and computer training as specialists in system analysis, installation and training, maintenance of existing systems, or system enhancement. Employment opportunities are available nationwide within the escrow industry or directly in the computer software industry.

Vanishing Skills? Reliance on automated documentation and closing systems is thought by some to have produced a new generation of escrow employees who have not learned the mechanics of escrow such as prorations, file balancing, and payoff computations. In fact it is still necessary to understand fully the principles behind the automated process, to be sure the right data goes in the right place at the right time. The computer only obeys the user's instructions.

ESCROW START CARDS

A four part snap-out card. This card, when completed by your office, is a set of cross reference cards. It also supplies the computer with all information necessary to open an escrow on the system.

COMPUTER DATA CONTROL, INC.

Escrow #	Office #
Buyer	Title Co.
Seller	Officer #
Address	Officer Name
Estimated Fees	Opened
Primary Business Source	Est. Close Date
Secondary Business Source	Consideration

Exhibit 40

NEW ESCROW REPORT (Daily and month end)

A report showing new escrows opened on a daily basis and a report showing activity for the month. This report also flags escrows being reopened.

```
JOHN DOE ESCROW INC          DAILY ESCROW TRANSACTION ACTIVITY              04-30-88
ESCROW TRUST ACCOUNT                   ESCROWS OPENED                       PAGE   1
OFFICE # : 97

FIELD TITLE          DETAILS                 FIELD TITLE          DETAILS
********************************************************************************************

                     NEW                                          REOPEN
ESCROW NUMBER        00000517-0              ESCROW NUMBER        00000518-0
DATE OPENED          04-30-88                DATE OPENED          04-30-88
BUYER                R MORGAN                BUYER                BARTLETT, DAVID
SELLER               D WAINWRIGHT            SELLER               REMINGTON, R
ADDRESS              8240 COMPTON AVE        ADDRESS              11410 ANGELENO DRIVE
CITY                 LOS ANGELES             CITY                 LOS ANGELES
STATE                CA                      STATE                CA
ESTIM FEES                      691.00       ESTIM FEES                      846.00
PRIMARY SOURCE       CENTURY 21              PRIMARY SOURCE       ACE REALTY
SECONDARY SOURCE                             SECONDARY SOURCE
TITLE COMPANY        AMERICAN TITLE CO       TITLE COMPANY        SECURITY TITLE
CONSIDERATION               106,000.00       CONSIDERATION               149,000.00
ESCROW OFFICER       200 JANE SMITH          ESCROW OFFICER       300 GLORIA JONES
ESTIMATED CLOSING    06-30-88                ESTIMATED CLOSING    06-30-88

    TOTAL NEW ESCROWS OPENED FOR COMPANY NO. 97 IS ... 2
```

Exhibit 41

DISBURSEMENT JOURNAL AND DEBIT ADJUSTMENT
(Daily and Monthly)

A journal of all checks and adjustments in numerical order. Any missing check numbers are flagged with the term "GAP".

```
JOHN DOE ESCROW INC              DAILY ESCROW TRANSACTION ACTIVITY           04-30-88
ESCROW TRUST ACCOUNT             POSTED DISBURSEMENTS & ADJUSTMENTS          PAGE   1
OFFICE  # : 97


        CHECK            TRANSACTION     ESCROW       PAID TO/                     CHECK
        NUMBER           DATE            NUMBER       DESCRIPTION                  AMOUNT
******************************************************************************************
    DISBURSEMENTS
        002253           04-30-88        00000500-0   J BROWN                      1,500.00
        002254           04-30-88        00000504-0   JOHN DOE ESCROW FEES           404.00
        002255           04-30-88        00000506-0   TERMITE INC                     86.00
        002256           04-30-88        00000506-0   GORSKY, R                   20,000.00
        002257           04-30-88        00000508-0   LANDRY DEVELOPMENT CO        6,000.00
        002258           04-30-88        00000518-0   JOHN DOE ESCROW CO             322.00
        002259           04-30-88        00000511-0   PRUDENTIAL INS                 461.00
        002260           04-30-88        00000518-0   REMINGTON R                 32,000.00
        002261           04-30-88        00000518-0   ACE REALTY                   5,000.00
        002262           04-30-88        00000517-0   BRIGHT INS                     600.00
        002263           04-30-88        00000506-0   HOME MORTGAGE                8,000.00
        002264           04-30-88        00000516-0   ACE TITLE CO                16,000.00
        002265           04-30-88        00000000-0   VOID                             0.00
        002266           04-30-88        00000517-0   ROYALTY CONSTRUCTION        20,000.00

                         TOTAL DISBURSEMENTS                                     110,373.00


                         TOTAL ADJUSTMENTS                                             0.00

                                        SUMMARY
******************************************************************************************
              ----TODAY----            MONTH-TO-DATE              YEAR-TO-DATE
         NUMBER    AMOUNT           NUMBER    AMOUNT           NUMBER    AMOUNT
DISBURSEMENTS  14  110,373.00         40    409,135.80          66    537,101.38
ADJUSTMENTS     0        0.00          0          0.00           0          0.00
NET TOTALS     14  110,373.00         40    409,135.80          66    537,101.38
```

Exhibit 42

ACTIVE ESCROW REPORT

A report of each escrow in numerical order with current balances on a daily basis.

```
JOHN DOE ESCROW INC          DAILY ESCROW TRANSACTION ACTIVITY      04-30-88
ESCROW TRUST ACCOUNT             DAILY ACTIVE ESCROW REPORT         FAGE   1
OFFICE # : 97
```

ESCROW NUMBER	DATE	OFFICER NUMBER	BUYER	SELLER	BALANCE
00000000-0	- -	200	MISC ACCT		0.00
00000500-0	03-01-88	200	JAMES, FREDRICK	BROWN, JACK AND MILDRED	1,016.00
00000501-0	03-01-88	200	SMITH, HARRY AND ANN	GREEN, ROBERT AND ELLEN	0.00
00000502-0	03-05-88	200	BUTLER, JOSEPH & DIANNE	CANON, JAKE & BEVERLY	0.00
00000503-0	03-05-88	200	O'CONNOR, WILLIAM	DEVELOPMENT CORP	188.16
00000504-0	03-05-88	300	YU, SHINN AND TERRY	BRACKEN, DARREL ANU SUE	4,556.00
00000505-0	03-06-99	300	JOHNSON, THOMAS	BROWN, BETTY	0.00
00000506-0	03-08-88	200	JACOBS, HARVEY & ROSE	GORSKY, RICHARD AND DALE	92,914.00
00000507-0	03-10-88	300	JACKSON, RALPH & CARRIE	SMITH, BRENT & FREDA	40.59
00000508-0	03-20-88	200	JOHNSON, GRANT	HAYWARD, FRANKLIN	5,500.00
00000509-0	03-25-88	300	HANSEN, CHRISTIAN	GRAMZA, THEODORE	5,494.00
00000510-0	03-29-88	300	KAUFFMAN, MICHAEL E	SCHAFFER, THOMAS AND JANE	11,414.00
00000511-0	04-04-88	200	BROWN, N N	WILLIAMS, G L	61,539.00
00000512-0	04-06-88	300	KRAFT, H A	ALSINA, F	9,636.00
00000513-0	04-10-88	200	JANSEN, L	BAKER, R	13,682.00
00000514-0	04-18-88	300	THOMPSON, D	ATKENS, M	13,585.00
00000515-0	04-19-88	200	EASTWOOD, N	COOPER, S	7,000.00
00000516-0	04-26-88	300	LANDERS, R	STEVENS, O	122,319.00
00000517-0	04-30-88	200	R MORGAN	D WAINWRIGHT	85,400.00
00000518-0	04-30-88	300	BARTLETT, DAVID	REMINGTON, R	112,000.00
				SUB-TOTAL	546,283.75
99999999-9	- -		FEE ACCOUNT		3,035.60
				TOTAL	549,319.35

Exhibit 43

ESCROW STATUS REPORT
(Daily or weekly and month end)

A daily or weekly list of all escrows showing all transactions processed. You can see at a glance the complete audit trail of any escrow. A full and complete printout is sent at each month end.

```
ESCROW ACCOUNTING              DAILY ESCROW TRANSACTION ACTIVITY              04-30-88
ESCROW TRUST ACCOUNT                 ESCROW STATUS REPORT                     PAGE   6
OFFICE  # : 97                       FOR JOHN DOE ESCROW INC
```

ESCROW NUMBER	TRANSACTION DATE	TRAN TYPE	RECEIPT OR CHECK NO	IDENTIFICATION	DEBITS	CREDITS	RUNNING BALANCE
00000517-0	BUYER: R MORGAN			CONSIDER : 106,000.00		ADDRESS: 8240 COMPTON AVE	
	SELLER: D WAINWRIGHT			OFFICER: 200 JANE SMITH		SOURCE: CENTURY 21	
	04-30-88 DATE OPENED						
	04-30-88	R	001139	MORGAN, R		47,000.00	47,000.00
	04-30-88	R	001142	TITLE CO		59,000.00	106,000.00
	04-30-88	C	002262	BRIGHT INS	600.00		105,400.00
	04-30-88	C	002266	ROYALTY CONSTRUCTION	20,000.00		85,400.00
00000518-0	BUYER: BARTLETT, DAVID			CONSIDER : 149,000.00		ADDRESS: 11410 ANGELENO DRIVE	
	SELLER: REMINGTON, R			OFFICER: 300 GLORIA JONES		SOURCE: ACE REALTY	
	04-30-88 DATE OPENED						
	04-30-88	R	001140	BARTLETT		29,800.00	29,800.00
	04-30-88	R	001141	TITLE CO		119,200.00	149,000.00
	04-30-88	C	002260	REMINGTON R	32,000.00		117,000.00
	04-30-88	C	002261	ACE REALTY	5,000.00		112,000.00
				SUB-TOTAL OF BALANCES 546,283.75			
99999999-9	BUYER: FEE ACCT			CONSIDER : 0.00		ADDRESS:	
	SELLER:			OFFICER: 200 JANE SMITH		SOURCE:	
	DATE OPENED						
	- -	FT		*** B A L F W D *		1,128.80	1,128.80
	04-30-88	FT		CLOSED 000005020		510.80	1,639.60
	04-30-88	FT		CLOSED 000005090		306.00	1,945.60
	04-30-88	FT		CLOSED 000005120		364.00	2,309.60
	04-30-88	FT		CLOSED 000005040		404.00	2,713.60
	04-30-88	FT		CLOSED 000005100		322.00	3,035.60
				TOTAL ESCROW BALANCES 549,319.35			

Exhibit 44

PERMANENT ESCROW LEDGER
(Monthly)

This escrow ledger is provided so that the escrow company will have a permanent file as a history of each transaction from escrow opening to closing. This card must be retained in your permanent files.

ESCROW LEDGER

COMPANY NO.		ESCROW NUMBER	DATE	PAGE NO.
97		00000500-0	4/30/88	1

BUYER	ESCROW OFFICER	DATE OPENED
James, Frederick	Jane Smith	3/1/88

SELLER	PRIMARY BUSINESS SOURCE	ESTIMATED CLOSING
Brown, Jack and Mildred	Main Realty	4/30/88

PROPERTY - LEGAL ADDRESS - 1	SECONDARY BUSINESS SOURCE	TYPE OF ESCROW
12876 Washington St.		

PROPERTY - LEGAL ADDRESS - 2	TITLE COMPANY	CONSIDERATION
12876 Washington St.	Title Co.	125,000.00

POSTING DATE	RECEIPT/ CHECK NO.	DESCRIPTION	DEBIT	CREDIT	BALANCE
3/1/88	001001	Fred James		1,000.00	1,000.00
4/4/88	001119	T. Harper		3,000.00	4,000.00
4/1/88	002226	State Farm Ins. Co.	256.00		3,744.00
4/1/88	002227	Termite Co.	80.00		3,664.00
4/2/88	002228	Title Co.	248.00		3,416.00
4/4/88	002231	A. J. Smith	900.00		2,516.00
4/30/88	002254	J. Brown	1,500.00		1,016.00
4/30/88	002254	J. Brown	816,00		200.00
4/30/88	999999	Fee Transfer	200.00		.00

Exhibit 45

Chapter 12 Quiz

1. Data processing in the closing process:

   (A) Is used for title searching only
   (B) Is used to prepare loan documents only
   √ (C) Is used extensively by title and escrow personnel
   (D) None of the above

2. Software systems are used for:

   (A) Word and text processing
   (B) Decision support
   (C) Graphics
   (D) All of the above

3. Which of the following is *not* involved in the modern title insurance process:

   (A) Title searching
   (B) Handwritten title reports for notarization
   (C) Data retrieval and storage
   (D) Title examination

4. Title search is performed:

   (A) By property identification based on tax assessor's parcel number only
   (B) By property description only
   (C) By a combination of description and names of involved parties
   (D) Only by a search of the grantor-grantee index of the recorder's office

5. Choice of an accounting system for an escrow office will depend on:

   (A) Size of the firm
   (B) Number and type of transactions
   (C) Management and information requirements
   (D) All of the above

6. Title examination is most likely to benefit from computerization in:

   (A) Performing the general index search
   (B) Obtaining copies of documents
   (C) Interpreting the title chain and reporting results
   (D) Getting legal opinions

7. Sub-escrows are likely to require:

   (A) Only simple calculations
   (B) Word processing only
   (C) Sophisticated accounting programs
   (D) None of the above

8. Common elements of automated escrow and title insurance systems are:

   (A) Word processing only
   (B) Accounting only
   (C) Marketing only
   (D) All of the above

9. Word processing for loans is commonly performed by a service bureau from:

   (A) A "laundry list" completed by the lender
   (B) Sample handwritten documents provided by the lender
   (C) Magnetic tape input by lender
   (D) Telephone instructions from the lender

10. Word processing systems:

    (A) Are always necessary in the closing process
    (B) Should be considered on the basis of the individual office's needs
    (C) Are not needed unless the process is repetitive
    (D) Do not require backup

Chapter 13
Consumer Protection
in the Closing Process

PREVIEW

Trends in Consumerism

Lending Disclosures

Disclosure by the Parties

Disclosure by Licensees and Escrowholders

Government Regulation

Professional Ethics

TRENDS IN CONSUMERISM

When dealing with the public, a commercial enterprise has a certain implied liability to the customers served. If the service is performed in a negligent or irresponsible manner, the customer may be entitled to restitution for any harm that results. Many times disputes between the business and the customer require independent evaluation. For this reason our court system has developed consumer-related procedures, in tandem with consumer legislation and the quasijudicial arbitration process.

Disclosure The real estate industry is not unlike other businesses in that any sale involves certain unpleasantries, such as costs. Whether it be points in a loan transaction, structural pest control reports, or closing costs, there is a certain natural reluctance to disclose total costs fully. However, the end product of this less than candid approach is an ongoing wave of consumerism with heavy emphasis on disclosure. In some cases, as in Truth in Lending legislation, the consumer may have the option of negating the entire transaction.

Early Legislation— Regulation Z In the 1960s many consumers were victimized by hucksters purveying various types of home improvements. While the consumer was still spellbound by the sales pitch, the salesperson would perform some work, like removing siding or digging up a driveway, that would establish mechanics' lien rights. This practice was regulated in the first significant piece of consumer legislation, Title I of the Consumer Credit Protection Act, commonly referred to as Regulation Z, or Truth in Lending.

RESPA The Real Estate Settlement Procedures Act seeks to regulate closing costs. Since the inception of this act in 1974, the U.S. Department of Housing and Urban Development has gathered massive amounts of data about comparative closing costs throughout the country. The Federal Trade Commission has also investigated real estate boards and escrow groups to ascertain if any conspiracy exists to fix prices on commission rates and service charges.

Regulation. In 1979 an experimental program by FHA (based upon HUD-1 statement closing data) provided a list of "suggested" maximum closing costs through selected offices. These "suggested" costs are now mandatory, with geographic variation. Unfortunately, in some cases (FHA and VA transactions) the basic data may have been biased due to limitations on closing costs allowed to the borrower.

Equal Opportunity Laws Other consumer-oriented legislation is evident in the Fair Credit Reporting Act, which relates to the handling of credit inquiries; the Equal Credit Opportunity Act, which deals with discrimination in lending; and the Fair Housing Act, which offers equal opportunity in housing choice. These laws, together with anti-redlining legislation, recognize the rights of individuals in a real estate transaction.

Alienation Clauses Serious challenges have been raised to the fairness of the "due on sale" clause prevalent in institutional deeds of trust, which accelerates the debt upon the sale or further indebtedness incurred in the security. With the passage of the Garn St. Germain Depository Institutions Act of 1982, this challenge was abated as to institutional lenders, by declaring that "due on sale" clauses are enforceable except under very special circumstances.

LENDING DISCLOSURES

Several laws afford consumer protection in real estate lending and other credit situations, by requiring disclosure of loan terms.

Truth in Lending On July 1, 1969, Title I of the Consumer Credit Protection Act became law. Its purpose was to allow a consumer to understand and compare the cost of credit for a contemplated purchase. This is implemented through a disclosure statement such as Exhibit 46.

Applicability. The parties regulated by this act are all those who in the course of their business dealings normally provide, extend, or offer to extend consumer credit. In real estate this law is most generally applicable to lenders and/or their agents or representatives.

Enforcement. Nine regulatory agencies enforce the provisions of this act. Agencies are assigned by lender category, such as the Comptroller of Currency for national banks. The Federal Trade Commission serves as the principal agency implementing the enforcement of the act.

Annual Percentage Rate (APR). This is the key term in Truth in Lending. In an extension of credit the device used for comparison shopping is the "annual percentage rate," expressed to the nearest $\frac{1}{4}$ of 1%. This is prominently displayed in the bold box at the top of Exhibit 46.

Definition. This rate represents the nominal rate shown on the note discounted over the life of the debt by the amount of prepaid finance charges. For purpose of computing the annual percentage rates, the prepaid insurance charge is considered as a deduction from the gross loan amount.

Calculation. Exhibit 47 outlines the steps involved in computing the annual rate. The Federal Reserve Board provides charts that convert the ratio of finance charge to amount financed into an annual percentage rate. On the chart, our ratio of 141.83044 is interpolated in the 300 payment column as lying between 141.57 and 146.64, which means that the actual annual percentage rate exceeds 8.50% but is less than 8.75%. Since our factor is very close to the 8.5% figure, the annual percentage rate disclosed to the buyer is the nearest $\frac{1}{4}$ of 1%, or 8.50%

Financial Calculators. Modern real estate practice makes extensive use of pocket financial calculators, which perform not only the four basic arithmetic functions of adding, subtracting, multiplying and dividing, but also do the mathematics of amortization, discounting, tax depreciation schedules, annual percentage rates, compounding, balloon payments, effective yield rates, etc. The major problem that confronts the user of any calculator is that one cannot use the calculator to do arithmetic problems without first deciding what arithmetic to do (GIGO: garbage in; garbage out).

Rescission. One unique feature of Regulation Z is that any credit extension on a personal residence, other than a purchase money first lien or for purposes of new construction, is rescindable. (See Exhibit 48, Notice of Right to Cancel.) This means that any refinance or new junior mortgage credit may be rescinded by the borrower within three working days after midnight of the day the contract was executed.

Purpose. This three-day "cooling off" period was designed to allow a borrower sufficient time to assess the consequences of the contract after being provided with a total cost disclosure statement, together with the right of rescission at the inception of the transaction.

Risk to Lenders. To protect themselves, lenders need to obtain reaffirmation of a borrower's desire to consummate the transaction. This is necessary because the transaction may be rescinded by the mere act of a borrower mailing a notice of rescission to the lender, whether or not the lender receives that notice.

Risk to Mechanics. If the transaction involves work that improves the property, laborers or materialmen who perform work or deliver materials to the job during this three-day "cooling off" period do so at their peril, because the credit transaction can possibly be negated.

Role in Escrows. Escrow practitioners are constantly exposed to Truth in Lending disclosures, through involvement with lenders in a sale, or when closing the loan for a lending institution. The regulations affect nearly all one to four unit residential real estate irrespective of the sale amount, and the disclosure statement has become an integral part of residential real estate transfers because most transactions involve an extension of credit from a "creditor" under Regulation Z.

Non-Real Estate Transactions. Credit transactions that involve amounts of $25,000 or more, except real estate, are exempt from the Consumer Credit Protection Act. Covered transactions that involve less than $25,000 include personal, family and household credit extended by "creditors," charge card sales, department store and retailer accounts, and credit extended by professional people. There are also stringent rules relating to advertisements involving the mention of credit sales.

Usury Law The California usury law provides a 10% ceiling for some loans. Certain lenders and broker arranged transactions are exempt, with certain other lenders subject to regulated ceilings in other than purchase money transactions.

Loan Brokerage: Article 7 If an extension of credit on real estate involves loan brokerage as outlined in Article 7, Chapter 3 of the California Real Estate Law, further disclosures to the client are required.

The Mortgage Loan Disclosure Statement. A real estate licensee who arranges a loan that is subject to the provisions of Article 7 is required to provide a mortgage loan disclosure statement. The contents of this statement are outlined in Section 102411 of the California Real Estate Law. A sample disclosure statement is shown as Exhibit 49. Escrowholders are not involved in preparing this statement unless they process loans for mortgage loan brokers.

Prerequisite to Transaction. The mortgage loan disclosure statement, like the Truth in Lending disclosure, must be presented to the borrower for signature prior to the time that the borrower becomes committed to the transaction.

Purpose. This disclosure requirement precedes the Real Estate Settlement Procedures Act statement in the process, but the objective is similar. The disclosure form indicates to the borrower an estimate of the loan funds available after all closing costs are deducted.

☐ Section I summarizes the loan amount, less all deductions outlined in Section III, and summarizes the estimated loan proceeds available to the borrower.

☐ Section II describes the loan terms including any balloon payment, the location of the security, existing liens, occupancy status, and any credit life or disability insurance that is required.

   ☐ Trust deed holders are now required to provide notice to payors of the due date of the balloon no sooner than 150 days nor later than 90 days prior to maturity.

□ Section III details the costs and expenses, broker's commission, and borrower-authorized fees.

    □ The costs and expenses outlined in sub-section A may not exceed 5% of the principal amount of the loan, with a minimum of $195.00 to a maximum of $350.00 for loans exceeding $7,000.

    □ In sub-section B, the maximum commission on a junior trust deed where the amount is less than $10,000 and maturity is three years or more is 15%.

    □ Sub-section C concerns the use to be made of loan funds, for example the payment of a mechanics' lien or future improvement work.

□ By signing, the broker certifies that the loan transaction is made in compliance with the California Real Estate Law.

Applicability. The mortgage loan broker law which mandates this statement applies to first deeds of trust less than $20,000 and second deeds of trust less than $10,000. For loans above those amounts, there are no legal limits on commissions, costs, and expenses, but the mortgage loan disclosure requirement applies.

Real Estate Settlement Procedures Act Early consumer disclosure was intended to permit comparison shopping for credit by the prospective buyer. In the Real Estate Settlement Procedures Act of 1974, a much more ambitious disclosure that involved the total spectrum of costs incurred by buyer and seller was mandated. The required disclosure has given escrowholders a considerable responsibility for providing full and complete accounting to the parties in the closing.

Applicability. The Real Estate Settlement Procedures Act of 1974 became effective on June 20, 1975. The objective of the act was to extend the Truth in Lending disclosures to include all of the closing costs in residential loan transactions.

□ *Properties.* One to four family properties including homes, condominiums, cooperative apartments, mobilehome lots, and lots acquired for the purpose of erecting a house or placement of a mobilehome are covered. Thus most institutional lenders involved in first mortgage lending on residential property come within the purview of the act as amended.

□ *Lenders.* Any lending agency that makes more than $100,000 per year in real estate loans, or any lender that is affiliated with any part of the federal government, such as the Federal Reserve Bank, the Comptroller of Currency, the Federal Deposit Insurance Corporation, the Federal Savings and Loan Insurance Corporation, the Veterans Administration, or the agencies of the Department of Housing and Urban Development is affected by the disclosure requirements of the act. This effectively includes all institutional lenders of any significance.

Estimate of Costs. As amended in 1976, RESPA requires a good-faith estimate of all costs at the time of the loan application or within 3 business days. (The original act provided for 12-day advance disclosure, which was both cumbersome and impractical, required prior to the examination of any loan documents. Another impractical requirement was that a closing statement showing actual costs be delivered within 3 days after closing.)

Information Booklet. The lender must provide a settlement costs booklet to the borrower which details two specific areas:

☐ *Part One* consists of consumer information on how to deal with parties involved in the closing process, the nature of the charges involved, and remedies available to the borrower if certain aspects of the transaction seem illegal or unethical.

☐ *Part Two* describes each item in the settlement statement, and how the consumer can comparison shop the costs of these items.

Preparation. The revision also shifted responsibility for preparation of the settlement statement from the lender to the closing agent or escrowholder. Each item in the settlement statement has a numerical designation. Exhibit 50 represents a closing statement designed to comply with the disclosure requirements of RESPA. This statement, together with the appropriate certification, eliminates the need for preparing a separate disclosure statement.

Certification. Administrative changes in 1986 expanded the certification requirement for escrowholders and the parties to the following forms:

I have carefully reviewed the HUD-1 Settlement Statement and to the best of my knowledge and belief, it is a true and accurate statement of all receipts and disbursements made on my account or by me in this transaction. I further certify that I have received a copy of the HUD-1 Settlement Statement.

_____   _____
Borrowers   Sellers

The HUD-1 Settlement Statement which I have prepared is a true and accurate account of this transaction. I have caused the funds to be disbursed in accordance with this statement.

_____   _____
Settlement Agent   Date

In addition, when lenders submit loan packages to FHA for insurance endorsement, a closing package certification is to be included as follows:

We (name of company), Mortgagee at the time of closing of this mortgage loan, certify that we have reviewed the outstanding commitments, legal instruments, closing statements and other documents of mortgage loan closing. Our review indicates that the mortgage loan has been closed in accordance with the statutory and regulatory requirements of the National Housing Act and HUD and that the terms of the outstanding commitments have been satisfied to the best of our knowledge and belief.

DISCLOSURE BY THE PARTIES

In the transfer of either real or personal property, the constraints placed upon exercise of ownership can be of considerable importance. Reasonable assurance must be had that the property can be used for the intended purpose, with respect to both legal restrictions and physical condition. A number of laws encourage disclosure of this information.

Zoning Statements

Many municipalities require that upon sale of residential property the seller obtain and provide the borrower/buyer with a zoning statement.

Definition. This statement describes the present zoning of the property, the use allowed (single family residence, number of living units, etc.), the permit(s) issued for original improvements, and any additional permits allowed for modifications and/or additions.

Rationale. Many properties that do not conform to zoning codes have been sold to unsuspecting buyers, and the planning or building department may then require the new owner to correct the nonconforming use. Zoning is one of the exclusions from title insurance coverage, and only limited coverage is available by special endorsement to cover such matters.

> ### Example
>
> A permit had been issued for an 8-unit apartment building. The owner, contrary to zoning regulations, converted the eight units to ten units and sold the property as a 10-unit building. A purchaser could have discovered this if a zoning report had been required as a condition of transfer.

Role in Escrow. Obtaining and delivering the zoning statement may or may not be the obligation of the escrowholder, depending upon the municipality.

Restrictions and Association By-Laws

Zoning is an example of police power, but there are also private rights governing the use of property to be considered. With the community planning that has increased in sophistication and scale since World War II, uniformity and conformance of property improvements have been of considerable concern to private owners and developers.

CC&Rs. Covenants, conditions, and restrictions provide the privately imposed blueprints for land use to which purchasers must conform.

☐ *Restrictions* are any limitations as to the use of the land; they are manifested in the form of *covenants* and *conditions*.

☐ A *covenant* is an agreement to abide by certain rules, enforceable by action for damages or injunction.

□ A *condition* is a powerful device. It can only be created by conveyance, and the remedy for its breach is reversion of title to the former owner. Courts tend to interpret restrictions regarding real property to be covenants rather than conditions with reversion unless the wording of the condition is unequivocal.

□ A "good faith" clause in most restrictions insulates lenders from the remedies that the owners of the rights of reversion have, by stating:

> "Provided also that a breach of any of the foregoing conditions, or any re-entry by reason of such breach, shall not defeat or render invalid the lien of any mortgage or deed of trust made in good faith and for value as to said property or any part thereof; but said conditions shall be binding upon and effective against any owner of said property whose title is acquired by foreclosure, trustee's sale, or otherwise."

□ Some conditions have become unenforceable as a matter of law or custom. The principal example of this type is a condition that restricts the sale or use of property on the basis of race, color, marital status, sex, or creed. (See Exhibit 14.2, Exception 4)

Association By-Laws. Where homeowners' associations are involved, their by-laws determine how prospective purchasers' activities as owners will be affected. Some items controlled by these documents are:

□ Duties and powers of the homeowners' association

□ Whether homeowners' association has right of first refusal when an owner offers a residence for sale

□ Officers of the association, and their term of office

□ How maintenance fees are determined and assessed

□ Procedure for monitoring costs and future increases of maintenance fees

□ Handling of delinquent maintenance fees.

Disclosure Situations. Prospective purchasers are entitled to know in advance the ground rules of ownership under which they will be conducting themselves.

□ *Building Lots.* Purchasers of lots who intend to build need copies of the CC&Rs of record in order to determine that the contemplated improvement to the property conforms. This is in addition to the zoning investigation noted above.

□ *Subdivisions.* Under the Subdivided Lands Act (see following), upon the initial sale of subdivided property, the developer is required to provide a copy of the general plan of restrictions for the tract.

□ *Planned Communities*. If the development involves a homeowners' association, the developer is also required to provide copies of its by-laws, budget, and any protective restrictions that apply to original and subsequent buyers in these planned communities.

Subdivision Disclosures

The division and subsequent resale of real property has received considerable legislative attention, which can affect escrow procedures.

Origins. Prior to 1929 there was no meaningful control over the division of property and the filing of subdivision maps. During the 1920s there were many "paper" subdivisions where developers sold lots from maps indicating street access, when the streets were mere lines on paper and the land had little or no value. In some cases, municipal lighting was funded through improvement bonds but the bonded indebtedness exceeded the value of the lot, and many of these lots were foreclosed. The Map Filing Act of 1929, which evolved into the Subdivision Map Act, was the first step toward protecting the interests of the buying public.

The Subdivision Map Act

This act authorizes implementation of subdivision ordinances by city and county governments within the parameters outlined in the act. The act applies to all subdivisions of land into two or more parcels. The basic objectives of this act are twofold:

□ To coordinate subdivision plans and planning, including lot design, street patterns, easements for public utilities, and the like, with the master plan conceived by local planners for the community.

□ To provide public assurance that dedicated public areas (streets, alleys, and the like) are improved properly, leaving only future maintenance as a taxpayer responsibility.

Effect on Escrow. Escrowholders who handle subdivision escrows must be aware of state and local requirements for processing of subdivision maps as they work with the title insurance companies which serve as the focal point for map processing and recording.

□ *Partial Release Clause*. Any lien of record on a subdivision must contain a partial release clause enabling the individual lots to be released subsequent to map filing.

□ *Parties in Interest*. All parties in interest (owners, etc.) are required to sign the map, indicating their interest in the project.

□ *Applicability*. If an escrow is being processed where a parcel of land is being divided, the Subdivision Map Act, as amended in 1974, probably applies, since this division minimally requires the filing of a parcel map.

Approval Process. The route of a subdivision begins at the preliminary feasibility stage, progressing through satisfaction of state, local, title company, and lender requirements:

□ Environmental impact reports

□ Coastal commission approval, if required

□ Preparation of a tentative map leading to local planning approval

□ Preparation of final map with required signatures

□ Submission for final approval by local government

□ Recording of the approved map

DRE Filing. If the Subdivided Lands Act applies, a copy of the recorded map is sent by the developer to the Department of Real Estate preliminary to issuance of a public report.

Time Frame. If a map filing is involved, the escrowholder must be realistic when estimating the closing time. The filing of a parcel map or Record of Survey can take six to nine months, and a formal tract map filing process involves twelve to eighteen months.

Subdivided Lands Act The Subdivided Lands Act (Sections 11000-11201, Business and Professions Code) directly affects the activities of escrowholders throughout the state and involves particular disclosure problems.

Public Report. This act was intended to protect the consumer from fraudulent marketing practices in the sale of subdivided parcels (including condominiums). The device used to inform the public is a subdivision public report. This may be preliminary (pink) where reservations can be taken, or final (white) where sales can be initiated.

Applicability. Any residential tracts marketed in California, whether physically located in the state or not, require the public report issued prior to sale. Subsequent to the initial subdivision, if a resale purchaser owns five or more lots or parcels within the same subdivision, a new public report is required prior to offering these parcels for subsequent resale. Tracts entirely within a city limit consisting of improved property, homes, are exempt from this regulation, as are commercial or industrial lots.

Disclosure. It is often difficult for an escrowholder to ascertain whether the seller of a condominium unit owns five or more units in a particular project. With the speculative nature of this type of real estate, it is not uncommon. Escrowholders must rely on information from the seller or title insurer as to potential violations of the Act. Many escrowholders include exculpatory language in the general provisions of their escrow instructions to cover this risk.

Homeowner Protection Warranty Limited insurance is available against latent physical defects in a property. Real estate groups or franchises are the main purveyors of these policies, which protect the home buyer from any extraordinary expense entailed in the replacement of faulty mechanical systems during the first year.

Development. The industry is presently in its early development. The first major company was formed in 1971. The reasons for promoting this insurance are threefold.

□ *Broker Liability*. Real estate agents have faced exploding costs in their errors and omissions insurance, as claims have been filed for defects in properties.

□ *Purchaser Protection*. Insurance against difficulties with systems or appliances in newly purchased residences during the first year of ownership is consistent with trends in consumer protection.

□ *Marketing*. The homeowner warranty program provides a means of making the purchase more attractive to the buyer.

Content. A typical warranty contract provides assurance to the homeowner that the protection company will provide services, parts, or materials to repair or replace items within four basic areas:

□ *Plumbing Systems*. Water lines and main water valves inside the home are covered, including risers, limited water closet protection, and electrical or gas water heater protection.

□ *Electrical Systems*. These are warranted within the confines of the structure.

□ *Heating Systems*. Insurance principally covers furnace and forced air systems and their accessible components.

□ *Built-In Appliances*. Garbage disposals, dishwashers, gas and electric surface ranges, gas and electric ovens, and bathroom and kitchen exhaust fans are covered.

Role in Escrow. Escrowholders may be directed to pay the premiums for these warranty contracts. Several points must be considered.

□ *Cancellation Charges*. A warranty company may impose charges to the seller if the contract is cancelled prior to closing. The escrow must have sufficient funds on deposit to defray the cost of cancelling a transaction. An escrowholder who undertakes a transaction without money on deposit assumes the risk of no payment for services rendered, plus out-of-pocket costs for the services of others.

□ *Coverage During Escrow*. Some companies require inspection prior to policy issuance, but practically all warranty companies provide seller protection prior to closing.

□ *Impartiality*. It is not the duty of the escrowholder to recommend a specific program to clients.

Limited Scope. Recent court cases have greatly expanded sellers' and brokers' responsibility to discover and disclose physical defects in a property. Potential liability extends far beyond these simple mechanical systems policies, and is addressed by a combination of full disclosure and hold-harmless language.

DISCLOSURE BY LICENSEES AND ESCROWHOLDERS

The escrow profession walks an extremely precarious tightrope in its quest to retain its neutrality as a stakeholder. Disclosure problems evolve as a result of ownership interest in one's company, customer pressure, increasingly complicated transactions, and temptations for personal gain.

Resale (Double Escrow) In *Blackburn vs. McCoy*, 1 Cal. App. (2d) 648, the unique limited agency aspect of escrow was held to mean that the escrow agent has no duty to disclose to a seller a concurrent resale transaction. This doctrine is succumbing to the pressure of consumerism. In the so-called "double escrow," disclosure of a resale may be required.

Situation. If a sale escrow is being processed from A to B with subsequent resale from B to C, disclosure of the second sale to the lender for B in the initial sale is required. Additionally, if seller A took back a purchase money loan from B in the first transaction, the resale to C should be disclosed.

Policy. The problem of disclosure by the escrow officer is a difficult one, and sometimes the safest rule is: when in doubt, disclose. Ruffled feathers may be preferable to a future lawsuit.

Real Estate Agent Acting as Principal Although there is no specific requirement that a licensee disclose that he or she is acting as a principal in a real estate transaction, certain aspects of real estate law strongly suggest that it is prudent to do so. The duties of a licensee acting as a principal are more stringent than those of a nonlicensed person.

Legal Basis. This implication of a higher standard of performance can be found in sections of the California Real Estate Law.

☐ Section 10176(a) deals with misrepresentation. A licensee may be vulnerable to violation of this section when the licensee's acting as a principal is not disclosed.

☐ Section 10176(b) deals with statements a licensee may make about future acts. For example, a licensee as seller promises to fix a roof. If the roof is not repaired the licensee could be liable and thus place his or her license in jeopardy even though the promise was oral.

☐ Section 10176(c) covers flagrant violations through continuing misrepresentation.

☐ Section 10176(d) requires that a licensee disclose when she or he is representing more than one party to a transaction (the common case is representative of both buyer and seller). This also applies when the licensee is acting as a principal.

Disclosure Statement. The language used in cases of this nature is a matter of choice. A typical recital in an instruction could be: "As a matter of record with which escrow is not to be concerned, buyer is aware of the fact that seller is a real estate licensee acting as a principal in this transaction."

Financial Interest in the Transaction An escrowholder sometimes has a financial interest in an escrow transaction, and this situation provides the ultimate test for a fiduciary.

Definition. Our entire concept of financial interest is being reassessed in light of the consumer movement. The following situations might be considered "financial interest" and worthy of disclosure:

☐ Escrow agencies controlled through company ownership by real estate agents entitled to a commission in the transaction.

☐ Escrow agencies employed by financial institutions that are providing real estate loans for the transaction.

☐ Other agencies where principals of these firms derive financial gain other than normal fees from the transaction.

Regulation. Of principal concern is the possibility of kickbacks to those who direct escrow business to escrow agents. Through various bills in recent years the California legislature has addressed this problem, singling out real estate licensees, contractors, and independent escrow companies with regulations relating to the direction of escrow business.

GOVERNMENT REGULATION

Government on the city, county, state, and federal levels is becoming increasingly involved in the closing process, through use of the "police power" (e.g., zoning) and the power to levy ad valorem taxes and income taxes. Some examples of this trend are examined below.

Retrofit Ordinances and Public Safety Various municipal and county agencies are imposing energy conservation and safety requirements on properties sold within their jurisdiction. These include:

Energy. Insulation, solar panels, energy conserving appliances, etc.

Safety. Smoke detectors, adequate wiring and mechanical systems, removal of life threatening components like asbestos.

Example

The Los Angeles city requirement (effective October 21, 1986) that exterior glass sliding doors be installed with shatterproof glass is a typical ordinance of this nature.

Zoning Compliance Many municipalities now require reports in escrow to determine that the improvements on the property transferred are authorized by permit. Such a requirement is designed to regulate non-conforming properties, and to protect purchasers from finding themselves unable to use the premises.

Change of Ownership Report A change of ownership report is required whenever an interest in real property is transferred. This form varies by county. The basic objective is to expedite the tax collection process and determine whether or not the property is subject to reassessment under the provisions of Proposition 13.

Supplemental Tax Roll Supplemental tax rolls are prepared by the tax collector from recorded property transfers, the change of ownership form, building permit records, and other sources. This is part of a continuing effort on the part of government to prevent escaped assessments.

Upward Adjustment for Sale or Improvement. These rolls represent a prorated allocation of the adjusted taxes upon sale or improvement of real property. Under normal circumstances the level of taxes will increase to approximately 1% of the sales price plus local indebtedness, or 1% of the value with the new improvement (addition or new construction).

Possible Reduction. In certain instances of natural disaster or disinflation of the housing market there may be, in fact, a reduction in property taxes resulting in a credit for taxes already paid.

Foreign Investment in Real Property Tax Act (FIRPTA) Unless specifically exempted by the filing of an appropriate affidavit, alien sellers will find that 10% of sale proceeds will be withheld from escrow for the Internal Revenue Service. This applies to commercial property sales of $50,000 or more and residential sales of $300,000 or more, pursuant to the 1984 tax act.

The 1986 Tax Reform Act Escrow is affected mainly from a reporting standpoint. IRS Form 1099-S (Exhibit 12, Chapter 5) is prepared by escrowholders to indicate the consideration received by the seller. Additionally, a move is under way to require escrows to report commissions paid to real estate agents.

PROFESSIONAL ETHICS

The real estate professions in California are governed from a consumer and ethical point of view by both state directive and industry self-regulation.

National Association of Realtors® As the largest of many professional organizations which promote ethical standards among their members, NAR's code is widely known and followed. Its basic documents are:

Code of Ethics. This was first adopted in 1913 and has been frequently revised to reflect changing conditions.

Standards of Practice. This document supplements the Code of Ethics with guidelines for professional conduct in specific situations.

Commissioner's Regulation 2785, formerly known as "Code of Ethics and Professional Conduct," was first adopted in 1979, to enhance professionalism and maximize protection for the public. The Code was rewritten and became effective June 9, 1990, and is now known as "Code of Professional Conduct." It is followed by a statement of "Suggestions for Professional Conduct," which is intended to "encourage real estate licensees to maintain a high level of ethics and professionalism in their business practices." The Code of Professional Conduct follows:

COMMISSIONER'S REGULATION 2785. PROFESSIONAL CONDUCT

In order to enhance the professionalism of the California real estate industry, and maximize protection for members of the public dealing with real estate licensees, whatever their area of practice, the following standards of professional conduct and business practices are adopted:

(a) Unlawful Conduct in Sale, Lease and Exchange Transactions. Licensees when performing acts within the meaning of Section 10131 (a) of the Business and Professions Code shall not engage in conduct which would subject the licensee to adverse action, penalty or discipline under Sections 10176 and 10177 of the Business and Professions Code including, but not limited to, the following acts and omissions:

Comm. Reg. 2785. (a)(1). Knowingly making a substantial misrepresentation of the likely value of real property to:

(a) Its owner either for the purpose of securing a listing or for the purpose of acquiring an interest in the property for the licensee's own account.

(b) A prospective buyer for the purpose of inducing the buyer to make an offer to purchase the real property.

Comm. Reg. 2785. (a)(2). Representing to an owner of real property when seeking a listing that the licensee has obtained a bona fide written offer to purchase the property, unless at the time of the representation the licensee has possession of a bona fide written offer to purchase.

Comm. Reg. 2785. (a)(3). Stating or implying to an owner of real property during listing negotiations that the licensee is precluded by law, by regulation, or by the rules of any organization, other than the broker firm seeking the listing, from charging less than the commission or fee quoted to the owner by the licensee.

Comm. Reg. 2785. (a)(4). Knowingly making substantial misrepresentations regarding the licensee's relationship with an individual broker, corporate broker, or franchised brokerage company or that entity's/person's responsibility for the licensee's activities.

Comm. Reg. 2785. (a)(5). Knowingly underestimating the probable closing costs in a communication to the prospective buyer or seller of real property in order to induce that person to make or to accept an offer to purchase the property.

Comm. Reg. 2785. (a)(6). Knowingly making a false or misleading representation to the seller of real property as to the form, amount and/or treatment of a deposit toward the purchase of the property made by an offeror.

Comm. Reg. 2785. (a)(7). Knowingly making a false or misleading representation to a seller of real property, who has agreed to finance all or part of a purchase price by carrying back a loan, about a buyer's ability to repay the loan in accordance with its terms and conditions.

Comm. Reg. 2785. (a)(8). Making an addition to or modification of the terms of an instrument previously signed or initialed by a party to a transaction without the knowledge and consent of the party.

Comm. Reg. 2785. (a)(9). A representation made as a principal or agent to a prospective purchaser of a promissory note secured by real property about the market value of the securing property without a reasonable basis for believing the truth and accuracy of the representation.

Comm. Reg. 2785. (a)(10). Knowingly making a false or misleading representation or representing, without a reasonable basis for believing its truth, the nature and/or condition of the interior or exterior features of a property when soliciting an offer.

Comm. Reg. 2785. (a)(11). Knowingly making a false or misleading representation or representing, without a reasonable basis for believing its truth, the size of a parcel, square footage of improvements or the location of the boundary lines of real property being offered for sale, lease or exchange.

Comm. Reg. 2785. (a)(12). Knowingly making a false or misleading representation or representing to a prospective buyer or lessee of real property, without a reasonable basis to believe its truth, that the property can be used for certain purposes with the intent of inducing the prospective buyer or lessee to acquire an interest in the real property.

Comm. Reg. 2785. (a)(13). When acting in the capacity of an agent in a transaction for the sale, lease or exchange of real property, failing to disclose to a prospective purchaser or lessee facts known to the licensee materially affecting the value or desirability of the property, when the licensee has reason to believe that such facts are not known to nor readily observable by a prospective purchaser or lessee.

Comm. Reg. 2785. (a)(14). Willfully failing, when acting as a listing agent, to present or cause to be presented to the owner of the property any written offer to purchase received prior to the closing of a sale, unless expressly instructed by the owner not to present such an offer, or unless the offer is patently frivolous.

Comm. Reg. 2785. (a)(15). When acting as the listing agent, presenting competing written offers to purchase real property to the owner in such a manner as to induce the owner to accept the offer which will provide the greatest compensation to the listing broker without regard to the benefits, advantages and/or disadvantages to the owner.

Comm. Reg. 2785. (a)(16). Failing to explain to the parties or prospective parties to a real estate transaction for whom the licensee is acting as an agent the meaning and probable significance of a contingency in an offer or contract that the licensee knows or reasonably believes may affect the closing date of the transaction, or the timing of the vacating of the property by the seller or its occupancy by the buyer.

Comm. Reg. 2785. (a)(17). Failing to disclose to the seller of real property in a transaction in which the licensee is an agent for the seller the nature and extent of any direct or indirect interest that the licensee expects to acquire as a result of the sale. The prospective purchase of the property by a person related to the licensee by blood or marriage, purchase by an entity in which the licensee has an ownership interest, or purchase by any other person with whom the licensee occupies a special relationship where there is a reasonable probability that the licensee could be indirectly acquiring an interest in the property shall be disclosed to the seller.

Comm. Reg. 2785. (a)(18). Failing to disclose to the buyer of real property in a transaction in which the licensee is an agent for the buyer the nature and extent of a licensee's direct or indirect ownership interest in such real property. The direct or indirect ownership interest in the property by a person related to the licensee by blood or marriage, by an entity in which the licensee has an ownership interest, or by any other person with whom the licensee occupies a special relationship shall be disclosed to the buyer.

Comm. Reg. 2785. (a)(19). Failing to disclose to a principal for whom the licensee is acting as an agent any significant interest the licensee has in a particular entity when the licensee recommends the use of the services or products of such entity.

Comm. Reg. 2785. (a)(20). The refunding by a licensee, when acting as an agent for seller, all or part of an offeror's purchase money deposit in a real estate sales transaction after the seller has accepted the offer to purchase, unless the licensee has the express permission of the seller to make the refund.

(b) Unlawful Conduct When Soliciting, Negotiating or Arranging a Loan Secured by Real Property or the Sale of a Promissory Note Secured by Real Property.

Licensees when performing acts within the meaning of subdivision (d) or (e) of Section 10131 of the Business and Professions Code shall not violate any of the applicable provisions of subdivision (a), or act in a manner which would subject the licensee to adverse action, penalty or discipline under Sections 10176 and 10177 of the Business and Professions Code including, but not limited to, the following acts and omissions:

Comm. Reg. 2785. (b)(1). Knowingly misrepresenting to a prospective borrower of a loan to be secured by real property or to an assignor/endorser of a promissory note secured by real property that there is an existing lender willing to make the loan or that there is a purchaser for the note, for the purpose of inducing the borrower or assignor/endorser to utilize the services of the licensee.

Comm. Reg. 2785. (b)(2). (a) Knowingly making a false or misleading representation to a prospective lender or purchaser of a loan secured directly or collaterally by real property about a borrower's ability to repay the loan in accordance with its terms and conditions;

(b) Failing to disclose to a prospective lender or note purchaser information about the prospective borrower's identity, occupation, employment, income and credit data as represented to the broker by the prospective borrower.

(c) Failing to disclose information known to the broker relative to the ability of the borrower to meet his or her potential or existing contractual obligations under the note or contract including information known about the borrower's payment history on an existing note, whether the note is in default or the borrower in bankruptcy.

Comm. Reg. 2785. (b)(3). Knowingly underestimating the probable closing costs in a communication to a prospective borrower or lender of a loan to be secured by a lien on real property for the purpose of inducing the borrower or lender to enter into the loan transaction.

Comm. Reg. 2785. (b)(4). When soliciting a prospective lender to make a loan to be secured by real property, falsely representing or representing without a reasonable basis to believe its truth, the priority of the security, as a lien against the real property securing the loan, i.e. a first, second or third deed of trust.

Comm. Reg. 2785. (b)(5). Knowingly misrepresenting in any transaction that a specific service is free when the licensee knows or has a reasonable basis to know that it is covered by a fee to be charged as part of the transaction.

Comm. Reg. 2785. (b)(6). Knowingly making a false or misleading representation to a lender or assignee/endorsee of a lender of a loan secured directly or collaterally by a lien on real property about the amount and treatment of loan payments, including loan payoffs, and the failure to account to the lender or assignee/endorsee of a lender as to the disposition of such payments.

Comm. Reg. 2785. (b)(7). When acting as a licensee in a transaction for the purpose of obtaining a loan, and in receipt of an "advance fee" from the borrower for this purpose, the failure to account to the borrower for the disposition of the "advance fee."

Comm. Reg. 2785. (b)(8). Knowingly making a false or misleading representation or representing, without a reasonable basis for believing its truth, when soliciting a lender or negotiating a loan to be secured by a lien on real property about the market value of the securing real property, the nature and/or condition of the interior or exterior features of the securing real property, its size or the square footage of any improvements on the securing real property.

Authority: Business and Professions Code Section 10080. Reference: Business and Professions Code Sections 10176 and 10177.

SUGGESTIONS FOR PROFESSIONAL CONDUCT

Note: The Real Estate Commissioner has issued Suggestions for Professional Conduct in Sale, Lease and Exchange Transactions and Suggestions for Professional Conduct When Negotiating or Arranging Loans Secured by Real Property or Sale of a Promissory Note Secured by Real Property.

The Purpose of the Suggestions is to encourage real estate licensees to maintain a high level of ethics and professionalism in their business practices when performing acts for which a real estate license is required.

The Suggestions are not intended as statements of duties imposed by law nor as grounds for disciplinary action by the Department of Real Estate, but as suggestions for elevating the professionalism of real estate licensees.

Copies of the suggestions may be obtained from the Department.

As a part of the effort to promote ethical business practices of real estate licensees, the Real Estate commissioner has issued the following **Suggestions for Professional Conduct** as a companion to the **Code of Professional Conduct** (Section 2785, Title 10, California Code of Regulation):

(a) **Suggestions for Professional Conduct in Sale, Lease and Exchange Transactions.** In order to maintain a high level of ethics and professionalism in their business practices, real estate licensees are encouraged to adhere to the following suggestions in conducting their business activities:

(1) Aspire to give a high level of competent, ethical and quality service to buyers and sellers in real estate transactions.

(2) Stay in close communication with clients or customers to ensure that questions are promptly answered and all significant events or problems in a transaction are conveyed in a timely manner.

(3) Cooperate with the California Department of Real Estate's enforcement of, and report to that Department evident violations of, Real Estate Law.

(4) Use care in the preparation of any advertisement to present an accurate picture or message to the reader, viewer or listener.

(5) Submit all written offers in a prompt and timely manner.

(6) Keep oneself informed and current on factors affecting the real estate market in which the licensee operates as an agent.

(7) Make a full, open and sincere effort to cooperate with other licensees, unless the principal has instructed the licensee to the contrary.

(8) Attempt to settle disputes with other licensees through mediation or arbitration.

(9) Advertise or claim to be an expert in an area of specialization in real estate brokerage activity, e.g., appraisal, property management, industrial siting, mortgage loan, etc., only if the licensee has had special training, preparation or experience.

(10) Strive to provide equal opportunity for quality housing and a high level of service to all persons regardless of race, color, sex, religion, ancestry, physical handicap, marital status or national origin.

(11) Base opinions of value, whether for the purpose of advertising or promoting real estate brokerage business, upon documented objective data.

(12) Make every attempt to comply with these Suggestions for Professional Conduct and the Code of Professional Conduct and the Code of Ethics of any organized real estate industry group of which the licensee is a member.

(b) **Suggestions for Professional conduct When Negotiating or Arranging Loans Secured by Real Property or Sale of a Promissory Note Secured by Real Property.** In order to maintain a high level of ethics and professionalism in their business practices when performing acts within the meaning of subdivisions (d) and (e) of Section 10131 and Sections 10131.1 and 10131.2 of the Business and Professions Code, real estate licensees are encouraged to adhere to the following suggestions, in addition to any applicable provisions of subdivision (a), in conducting their business activities:

(1) Aspire to give a high level of competent, ethical and quality service to borrowers and lenders in loan transactions secured by real estate.

(2) Stay in close communication with borrowers and lenders to ensure that reasonable questions are promptly answered and all significant events or problems in a loan transaction are conveyed in a timely manner.

(3) Keep oneself informed and current on factors affecting the real estate loan market in which the licensee acts as an agent.

(4) Advertise or claim to be an expert in an area of specialization in real estate mortgage loan transactions only if the licensee has had special training, preparation or experience in such area.

(5) Strive to provide equal opportunity for quality mortgage loan services and a high level of service to all

borrowers or lenders regardless of race, color, sex, religion, ancestry, physical handicap, marital status or national origin.

(6) Base opinions of value in a loan transaction, whether for the purpose of advertising or promoting real estate mortgage loan brokerage business, on documented objective data.

(7) Respond to reasonable inquiries of a principal as to the status or extent of efforts to negotiate the sale of an existing loan.

(8) Respond to reasonable inquiries of a borrower regarding the net proceeds available from a loan arranged by the licensee.

(9) Make every attempt to comply with the standards of professional conduct and the code of ethics of any organized mortgage loan industry group of which the licensee is a member.

The conduct suggestions set forth in subsections (a) and (b) are not intended as statements of duties imposed by law nor as grounds for disciplinary action by the Department of Real Estate, but as guidelines for elevating the professionalism of real estate licensees.

FEDERAL REAL ESTATE LOAN DISCLOSURE STATEMENT

CALIFORNIA ASSOCIATION OF REALTORS® STANDARD FORM

Broker: _____   Creditor: _____

_____   _____
(name)   (name)

_____   _____
(address)   (address)

YOUR LOAN IN THE AMOUNT OF $ 22,500.00 IS TO BE SECURED BY A DEED OF TRUST IN FAVOR OF CREDITOR ON REAL PROPERTY LOCATED AT _____

_____,

ANNUAL PERCENTAGE RATE The cost of your credit as a yearly rate.	FINANCE CHARGE The dollar amount the credit will cost you.	AMOUNT FINANCED The amount of credit provided to you or on your behalf.	TOTAL OF PAYMENTS The amount you will have paid after you have made all payments as scheduled.
8.5 %	$ 30,216.99	$ 21,305.01	$ 51,522.00

YOUR PAYMENT SCHEDULE WILL BE:

Number of Payments	Amount of Payments	When Payments Are Due
300	$171.74	monthly commencing 11/1/88

ITEMIZATION OF THE AMOUNT FINANCED OF $_____

Amount given to you .... $_____

Amount paid on your account .... $_____

Amount paid to others on your behalf:

1. Appraisal .... $ 25.00
2. Credit report .... $ 5.00
3. Notary .... $ 2.00
4. Recording .... $ 4.80
5. Title insurance .... $ 288.19
6. Document preparation Loan fee $ 225.00
7. Property insurance .... $_____
8. Other Finder's fee .... $ 600.00
9. Other Escrow/tax service $ 45.00
   (DESCRIBE)

Insurance:
Property insurance may be obtained by Borrower through any person of his choice. If it is to be purchased through Broker or Creditor, you will pay $_____
Credit life and disability insurance are not required to obtain this loan.

Late Charge: If any payment is not made within _____ days after it is due, a late charge must be paid by Borrower as follows: _____

Prepayment: If you pay off early, you ☐ MAY ☐ WILL NOT have to pay a penalty.

Acceleration: If the property securing this loan is sold or otherwise transferred, the Creditor ☐ HAS ☐ DOES NOT have the option to require immediate payment of the entire loan amount.

SEE YOUR CONTRACT DOCUMENTS FOR ANY ADDITIONAL INFORMATION ABOUT NONPAYMENT, DEFAULT, ANY REQUIRED REPAYMENT IN FULL BEFORE THE SCHEDULED DATE, AND PREPAYMENT REFUNDS AND PENALTIES.

I HAVE READ AND RECEIVED A COMPLETED COPY OF THIS STATEMENT.

Date _____, 19_____ .   Borrower_____

Borrower_____

*IMPORTANT NOTE:

Asterisk denotes an estimate.
To order, contact—California Association of Realtors®
525 South Virgil Avenue, Los Angeles, California 90020
Copyright ©1970, 1978, by California Association of Realtors®
(Revised, 1983)   FORM LD-11

TT-L5-FG

REPRINTED BY PERMISSION CALIFORNIA ASSOCIATION OF REALTORS®. ENDORSEMENT NOT IMPLIED

Exhibit 46

ANNUAL PERCENTAGE RATE COMPUTATION
(Compare disclosure form, Exhibit 46)

Single advance (except FHA) loans with equal monthly payments.

	Amount of loan	22,500.00
−	Prepaid finance charge	− 1,194.99
	Amount financed	21,305.01
	Monthly payment	171.74
x	Number of months	x 300
	Total payments	51,522.00
−	Amount of loan	− 22,500.00
	Total interest	29,022.00
+	Prepaid finance charge	+ 1,194.99
	Finance charge	30,216.99

Ratio of Finance Charge to Amount Financed:

$$\frac{\text{Finance Charge} \times 100}{\text{Amount Financed}} = \frac{302}{213} = 141.8$$

Refer to table to determine APR.

ANNUAL PERCENTAGE RATE TABLE FOR MONTHLY PAYMENT PLANS
SEE INSTRUCTIONS FOR USE OF TABLES

FRB-309-M

Number of Payments	6.00%	6.25%	6.50%	6.75%	7.00%	7.25%	7.50%	7.75%	8.00%	8.25%	8.50%	8.75%	9.00%	9.25%	9.50%	9.75%
	(FINANCE CHARGE PER $100 OF AMOUNT FINANCED)															
241	72.29	75.79	79.32	82.89	86.49	90.13	93.80	97.50	101.24	105.01	108.81	112.65	116.51	120.41	124.33	128.28
242	72.63	76.15	79.70	83.29	86.91	90.57	94.26	97.98	101.74	105.53	109.35	113.21	117.09	121.01	124.95	128.93
243	72.98	76.51	80.08	83.69	87.33	91.01	94.72	98.46	102.24	106.05	109.89	113.76	117.67	121.61	125.57	129.57
244	73.33	76.88	80.47	84.09	87.75	91.45	95.18	98.94	102.74	106.57	110.43	114.32	118.25	122.21	126.19	130.21
245	73.67	77.24	80.85	84.49	88.17	91.89	95.64	99.42	103.24	107.09	110.97	114.88	118.83	122.81	126.82	130.85
246	74.02	77.61	81.24	84.90	88.59	92.33	96.10	99.90	103.74	107.61	111.51	115.44	119.41	123.41	127.44	131.50
247	74.37	77.98	81.62	85.30	89.02	92.77	96.56	100.38	104.24	108.13	112.05	116.01	119.99	124.01	128.06	132.14
248	74.72	78.34	82.00	85.70	89.44	93.21	97.02	100.86	104.74	108.65	112.59	116.57	120.58	124.62	128.69	132.79
249	75.06	78.71	82.39	86.11	89.86	93.65	97.48	101.34	105.24	109.17	113.13	117.13	121.16	125.22	129.31	133.44
250	75.41	79.08	82.77	86.51	90.29	94.10	97.94	101.83	105.74	109.69	113.68	117.69	121.74	125.83	129.94	134.08
286	88.20	92.54	96.92	101.36	105.83	110.36	114.92	119.53	124.19	128.88	133.61	138.39	143.20	148.05	152.94	157.86
287	88.56	92.92	97.32	101.78	106.27	110.82	115.40	120.04	124.71	129.42	134.18	138.97	143.81	148.68	153.59	158.53
288	88.92	93.30	97.72	102.20	106.71	111.28	115.89	120.54	125.23	129.97	134.74	139.56	144.42	149.31	154.24	159.21
289	89.28	93.68	98.13	102.62	107.16	111.74	116.37	121.04	125.75	130.51	135.31	140.15	145.02	149.94	154.89	159.88
290	89.65	94.06	98.53	103.04	107.60	112.20	116.85	121.54	126.28	131.06	135.88	140.73	145.63	150.57	155.54	160.56
291	90.01	94.44	98.93	103.46	108.04	112.66	117.33	122.05	126.80	131.60	136.44	141.32	146.24	151.20	156.20	161.23
292	90.37	94.83	99.33	103.88	108.48	113.13	117.82	122.55	127.33	132.15	137.01	141.91	146.85	151.83	156.85	161.91
293	90.74	95.21	99.73	104.30	108.92	113.59	118.30	123.05	127.85	132.69	137.58	142.50	147.46	152.47	157.51	162.58
294	91.10	95.59	100.14	104.73	109.37	114.05	118.78	123.56	128.38	133.24	138.15	143.09	148.08	153.10	158.16	163.26
295	91.46	95.98	100.54	105.15	109.81	114.52	119.27	124.06	128.91	133.79	138.71	143.68	148.69	153.73	158.82	163.94
296	91.83	96.36	100.94	105.57	110.25	114.98	119.75	124.57	129.43	134.34	139.28	144.27	149.30	154.37	159.48	164.62
297	92.19	96.75	101.35	106.00	110.70	115.44	120.24	125.08	129.96	134.89	139.85	144.86	149.91	155.00	160.13	165.30
298	92.56	97.13	101.75	106.42	111.14	115.91	120.72	125.58	130.49	135.43	140.43	145.46	150.53	155.64	160.79	165.98
299	92.92	97.52	102.16	106.85	111.59	116.38	121.21	126.09	131.02	135.98	141.00	146.05	151.14	156.28	161.45	166.66
300	93.29	97.90	102.56	107.27	112.03	116.84	121.70	126.60	131.54	136.53	141.57	146.64	151.76	156.91	162.11	167.34

Exhibit 47

NOTICE OF RIGHT TO CANCEL

CALIFORNIA ASSOCIATION OF REALTORS® STANDARD FORM

_____
(Creditor)

_____
(Office)

_____
(City)

Name(s) of Customer(s) _____

Type of Loan _____

Amount of Loan _____ $ _____

Notice to Customer Required By Federal Law:

You have entered into a transaction on _____ , 19_____ which may result in a lien, mortgage, or other security interest on your home. You have a legal right under federal law to cancel this transaction, if you desire to do so, without any penalty or obligation within three business days from the above date or any later date on which all material disclosures required under the Truth in Lending Act have been given to you. If you so cancel the transaction, any lien, mortgage, or other security interest on your home arising from this transaction is automatically void. You are also entitled to receive a refund of any downpayment or other consideration if you cancel.

If you decide to cancel this transaction you may do so by notifying:

_____
(Name of Creditor)

at _____
(Address of Creditor's Place of Business)

by mail or telegram sent not later than midnight of _____ , 19_____ .

(Date 3 business days after date
of receipt of this notice.)

You may also use any other form of written notice identifying the transaction if it is delivered to the above address not later than that time. This notice may be used for that purpose by dating and signing below.

I hereby cancel this transaction.

_____ , 19_____   _____
(Date)   (Customer's Signature)

                                               _____

ACKNOWLEDGEMENT OF RECEIPT

I hereby acknowledge receipt of TWO copies of the foregoing **Notice of Right to Cancel.**

_____ , 19_____   _____
(Date)   (Customer's Signature)

                                               _____
                                               (All joint owners must sign)

See reverse side for important information about your right of rescission.

Exhibit 48.1

EFFECT OF RESCISSION

When a customer exercises his right to rescind, he is not liable for any finance or other charge, and any security interest becomes void upon such a rescission. Within 10 days after receipt of a notice of rescission, the creditor shall return to the customer any money or property given as earnest money, downpayment, or otherwise, and shall take any action necessary or appropriate to reflect the termination of any security interest created under the transaction. If the creditor has delivered any property to the customer, the customer may retain possession of it. Upon the performance of the creditor's obligations under this section, the customer shall tender the property to the creditor, except that if return of the property in kind would be impracticable or inequitable, the customer shall tender its reasonable value. Tender shall be made at the location of the property or at the residence of the customer, at the option of the customer. If the creditor does not take possession of the property within 10 days after tender by the customer, ownership of the property vests in the customer without obligation on his part to pay for it.

NOTICE OF INTENT TO PROCEED

I hereby certify that I have elected not to cancel or rescind the transaction referred to on the reverse side and that I have not delivered, mailed or filed for transmission by telegram to the Creditor any notice of cancellation or rescission of that transaction.

_____ , 19 _____   _____
(Date and mail or deliver no sooner than   (Customer's Signature)
3 business days after date of receipt)

                                              _____
                                                   (All joint owners must sign)

(2)

Exhibit 48.2

MORTGAGE LOAN DISCLOSURE STATEMENT (BORROWER)

CALIFORNIA ASSOCIATION OF REALTORS® STANDARD FORM

_____

(Name of Broker/Arranger of Credit)

_____

(Business Address of Broker)

I. SUMMARY OF LOAN TERMS

    A. PRINCIPAL AMOUNT OF LOAN . . . . $ _____

    B. ESTIMATED DEDUCTIONS FROM PRINCIPAL AMOUNT

        1. Costs and Expenses (See Paragraph III-A) . . . . $ _____

        2. Commission/Loan Origination Fee (See Paragraph III-B) . . . . $ _____

        3. Liens and Other Amounts to be Paid on Authorization of Borrower
          (See Paragraph III-C) . . . . $ _____

    C. ESTIMATED CASH PAYABLE TO BORROWER (A less B) . . . . $ _____

II. GENERAL INFORMATION ABOUT LOAN

    A. If this loan is made, you will be required to pay the principal and interest at _____ % per year, payable as

      follows: _____ _____ payments of $ _____
              (number of payments)   (monthly/quarterly/annually)

      and a FINAL/BALLOON payment of *$ _____ to pay off the loan in full.

          *CAUTION TO BORROWER: If you do not have the funds to pay the balloon payment
          when due, it may be necessary for you to obtain a new loan against your property
          for this purpose, in which case you may be required to again pay commissions,
          fees, and expenses for arranging a new loan. Keep this in mind in checking upon
          the amount and terms of the loan that you obtain at this time.

    B. This loan will be evidenced by a promissory note and secured by a deed of trust in favor of lender/creditor on
      property located at (street address or legal description):

      _____

      _____

    C. Liens against this property and the approximate amounts are:

      Nature of Lien   **Amount Owing**

      _____   _____

      _____   _____

      _____   _____

      CAUTION TO BORROWER: Be sure that the amount of all liens is stated as accurately as possible. If you
      contract with the broker for this loan, but it cannot be made or arranged because you did not state these lien
      amounts correctly, you may be liable to pay commissions, fees, and expenses even though you did not obtain
      the loan.

    D. If you wish to pay more than the scheduled payment at any time before it is due, you may have to pay a
      PREPAYMENT PENALTY computed as follows:

      _____

      _____

      _____

      _____

    E. The purchase of credit life or credit disability insurance is not required of the borrower as a condition of
      making this loan.

    F. The real property which will secure the requested loan is an "owner-occupied dwelling"*   YES ___ NO ___
                                                                   (Borrower initial opposite
                                                                    YES or NO)

      *An "owner-occupied dwelling" means a single dwelling unit in a condominium or cooperative or a residential
      building of less than three separate dwelling units, one of which will be owned and occupied by a signatory
      to the mortgage or deed of trust for this loan within 90 days of the signing of the mortgage or deed of trust.

To order, contact—California Association of Realtors®
525 S. Virgil Avenue, Los Angeles, California 90020
(Revised 1983)   FORM MS-14   EQUAL HOUSING OPPORTUNITY Continued on reverse side

Exhibit 49.1

III. DEDUCTIONS FROM LOAN PROCEEDS

A. ESTIMATED MAXIMUM COSTS AND EXPENSES to be paid by borrower out of the principal amount of the loan are:

PAYABLE TO

	Broker	Others
1. Appraisal fee	_____	_____
2. Escrow fee	_____	_____
3. Fees for policy of title insurance	_____	_____
4. Notary fees	_____	_____
5. Recording fees	_____	_____
6. Credit Investigation fees	_____	_____
7. Other Costs and Expenses:		
	_____	_____
	_____	_____

TOTAL COSTS AND EXPENSES . . . . $ _____

*B. LOAN BROKERAGE COMMISSION/LOAN ORIGINATION FEE . . . . $ _____

C. LIENS AND OTHER AMOUNTS to be paid out of the principal amount of the loan on authorization of the borrower are estimated to be as follows:

PAYABLE TO

	Broker	Others
1. Fire or other property insurance premiums	_____	_____
2. Credit life or disability insurance premium (see Paragraph II-E)	_____	_____
3. Beneficiary statement fees	_____	_____
4. Reconveyance and similar fees	_____	_____
5. Liens against property securing loan:		
	_____	_____
	_____	_____
6. Other:		
	_____	_____

TOTAL TO BE PAID ON AUTHORIZATION OF BORROWER $ _____

If the loan to which this disclosure statement applies is a loan secured by a first deed of trust in a principal amount of less than $20,000 or a loan secured by a junior lien in a principal amount of less than $10,000, the undersigned certifies that the loan will be made in compliance with Article 7 of Chapter 3 of the Real Estate Law.

*This loan ☐ may/☐ will/☐ will NOT (check one) be made wholly or in part from broker-controlled funds as defined in Section 10241(j) of the Business and Professions Code.

*NOTICE TO BORROWER: This disclosure statement may be used if the broker is acting as an agent in arranging the loan by a third person or if the loan will be made with funds owned or controlled by the broker. The broker must indicate in the above statement whether the loan "may" be made out of broker-controlled funds. If broker-controlled funds are then used to make this loan, the broker must notify the borrower of that fact before the close of escrow.

_____   _____
(Name of Broker)   (Name of Designated Representative)

_____   _____
(License Number)   (License Number)

                    OR

_____   _____
(Signature of Broker)   (Signature)

NOTICE TO BORROWER

DO NOT SIGN THIS STATEMENT UNTIL YOU HAVE READ AND UNDERSTOOD ALL OF THE INFORMATION IN IT. ALL PARTS OF THE FORM MUST BE COMPLETED BEFORE YOU SIGN.

Borrower hereby acknowledges the receipt of a copy of this statement.

DATED: _____   _____
                                        (Borrower)

                                        _____
                                        (Borrower)   Approved DRE 3/10/83

REPRINTED BY PERMISSION CALIFORNIA ASSOCIATION OF REALTORS®. ENDORSEMENT NOT IMPLIED

Exhibit 49.2

HUD-1 SETTLEMENT STATEMENT.

HUD-Rev. 7 80

Form Approved
OMB NO. 63-R-1501

	B. TYPE OF LOAN		
CLT Continental Lawyers Title Company	1. □ FHA	2. □ FmHA	3. □ CONV. UNINS.
	4. □ VA	5. □ CONV. INS.	
Subsidiary of Lawyers Title Insurance Corporation	6. File Number		7. Loan Number
	8. Mortgage Insurance Case Number		

C. NOTE: *This form is furnished to give you a statement of actual settlement costs. Amounts paid to and by the settlement agent are shown. Items marked "(p.o.c.)" were paid outside the closing; they are shown here for informational purposes and are not included in the totals.*

D. NAME OF BORROWER:	E. NAME OF SELLER:	F. NAME OF LENDER:
G. PROPERTY LOCATION:	H. SETTLEMENT AGENT:	I. SETTLEMENT DATE:
	PLACE OF SETTLEMENT:	

J. SUMMARY OF BORROWER'S TRANSACTION		K. SUMMARY OF SELLER'S TRANSACTION	
100. GROSS AMOUNT DUE FROM BORROWER:		**400. GROSS AMOUNT DUE TO SELLER:**	
101. Contract sales price		401. Contract sales price	
102. Personal property		402. Personal property	
103. Settlement charges to borrower *(line 1400)*		403.	
104.		404.	
105.		405.	
Adjustments for items paid by seller in advance.		*Adjustments for items paid by seller in advance.*	
106. City/town taxes to		406. City/town taxes to	
107. County taxes to		407. County taxes to	
108. Assessments to		408. Assessments to	
109.		409.	
110.		410.	
111.		411.	
112.		412.	
120. GROSS AMOUNT DUE FROM BORROWER:		**420. GROSS AMOUNT DUE TO SELLER:**	
200. AMOUNTS PAID BY OR IN BEHALF OF BORROWER:		**500. REDUCTIONS IN AMOUNT DUE TO SELLER:**	
201. Deposit or earnest money		501. Excess deposit *(see instructions)*	
202. Principal amount of new loan(s)		502. Settlement charges to seller *(line 1400)*	
203. Existing loan(s) taken subject to		503. Existing loan(s) taken subject to	
204.		504. Payoff of first mortgage loan	
205.		505. Payoff of second mortgage loan	
206.		506.	
207.		507.	
208.		508.	
209.		509.	
Adjustments for items unpaid by seller.		*Adjustments for items unpaid by seller.*	
210. City/town taxes to		510. City/town taxes to	
211. County taxes to		511. County taxes to	
212. Assessments to		512. Assessments to	
213.		513.	
214.		514.	
215.		515.	
216.		516.	
217.		517.	
218.		518.	
219.		519.	
220. TOTAL PAID BY/FOR BORROWER:		**520. TOTAL REDUCTION AMOUNT DUE SELLER:**	
300. CASH AT SETTLEMENT FROM/TO BORROWER:		**600. CASH AT SETTLEMENT TO/FROM SELLER:**	
301. Gross amount due from borrower *(line 120)*		601. Gross amount due to seller *(line 420)*	
302. Less amounts paid by/for borrowers *(line 220)*		602. Less reductions in amount due seller *(line 520)*	
303. CASH (□FROM) (□TO) BORROWER:		**603. CASH (□ TO) (□ FROM) SELLER:**	

Page 1

Exhibit 50.1

HUD-1 SETTLEMENT STATEMENT

L. SETTLEMENT CHARGES			PAID FROM BORROWER'S FUNDS AT SETTLEMENT	PAID FROM SELLER'S FUNDS AT SETTLEMENT
700. TOTAL SALES / BROKER'S COMMISSION based on price $	@	%		
Division of Commission (line 700) as follows:				
701. $	to			
702. $	to			
703. Commission paid at Settlement				
704.				
800. ITEMS PAYABLE IN CONNECTION WITH LOAN				
801. Loan Origination Fee	%			
802. Loan Discount	%			
803. Appraisal Fee	to			
804. Credit Report	to			
805. Lender's Inspection Fee				
806. Mortgage Insurance Application Fee	to			
807. Assumption Fee				
808.				
809.				
810.				
811.				
900. ITEMS REQUIRED BY LENDER TO BE PAID IN ADVANCE				
901. Interest from	to	@ $ /day		
902. Mortgage Insurance Premium for	months to			
903. Hazard Insurance Premium for	years to			
904.	years to			
905.				
1000. RESERVES DEPOSITED WITH LENDER				
1001. Hazard Insurance	months @ $	per month		
1002. Mortgage Insurance	months @ $	per month		
1003. City property taxes	months @ $	per month		
1004. County property taxes	months @ $	per month		
1005. Annual assessments	months @ $	per month		
1006.	months @ $	per month		
1007.	months @ $	per month		
1008.	months @ $	per month		
1100. TITLE CHARGES				
1101. Settlement or closing fee	to			
1102. Abstract or title search	to			
1103. Title examination	to			
1104. Title insurance binder	to			
1105. Document preparation	to			
1106. Notary fees	to			
1107. Attorney's fees	to			
(includes above items numbers:				
1108. Title insurance	to			
(includes above items numbers:				
1109. Lender's coverage	$			
1110. Owner's coverage	$			
1111.				
1112.				
1113.				
1200. GOVERNMENT RECORDING AND TRANSFER CHARGES				
1201. Recording fees. Deed $	: Mortgage $	: Release $		
1202. City/county tax/stamps: Deed $	: Mortage $			
1203. State tax/stamps: Deed $	: Mortage $			
1204.				
1205.				
1300. ADDITIONAL SETTLEMENT CHARGES				
1301. Survey	to			
1302. Pest inspection	to			
1303.				
1304.				
1305.				
1400. TOTAL SETTLEMENT CHARGES (enter on lines 103, Section J and 502, Section K)				

FORM 5000-LT (5/83)

Exhibit 50.2

Chapter 13 Quiz

1. Title I of the Consumer Credit Protection Act is known as the:

   (A) Rumford Act
   (B) Better Business Law
   (C) Truth in Lending Law
   (D) Equal Credit Opportunity Act

2. A first trust deed loan in excess of _____ is exempted from the commission and loan cost requirements of the Mortgage Loan Disclosure Act.

   (A) $20,000
   (B) $10,000
   (C) $15,000
   (D) $17,500

3. The Real Estate Settlement Procedures Act requires the rendering of a HUD-1 statement involving institutional first trust deed financing in the following instances:

   (A) Sale of a 12-unit apartment
   (B) Home refinancing
   (C) Sale of a one to four family residential property
   (D) Financing a 12-unit apartment

4. Maximum closing costs involving FHA insured loans are:

   (A) Uniform throughout the country
   (B) Merely suggested with no maximums
   (C) Published maximum costs by geographic areas
   (D) None of the above

5. The Subdivision Map Act applies for division into _____ or more parcels:

   (A) 2
   (B) 4
   (C) 5
   (D) 10

6. Purchasers in subdivisions involving homeowners' associations must be provided with copies of:

   (A) By-laws
   (B) Covenants, conditions, and restrictions
   (C) Budget
   (D) All of the above

7. The act requiring retention of 10% of the sale proceeds from aliens is:

   (A) 1986 Tax Reform Act
   (B) Title I of the Consumer Credit Protection Act
   (C) RESPA
   (D) FIRPTA

8. Disclosure on the part of escrowholders may be required when:

   (A) They are entitled to a fee
   (B) They are employed by real estate brokers having a financial interest in the transaction
   (C) There is a concurrent resale with no financing involved
   (D) They personally hold a real estate license

9. The Real Estate Commissioner's Code of Professional Conduct applies to real estate licensees engaged in:

   (A) Residential sales only
   (B) Residential sales and lending only
   (C) Escrow processing only
   (D) All areas of practice

10. The Real Estate Commissioner's Code of Professional Conduct discourages all of the following practices except:

    (A) Stating that commissions are fixed by law
    (B) Misrepresenting the form, amount, or treatment of a deposit
    (C) A brokerage processing its own escrows
    (D) Playing down closing costs to entice prospective buyers or sellers

Chapter 14
The Loan Escrow and Related Transactions

LOAN INSTRUMENTS

Mortgage lending, with the advent of deregulation and the Garn-St. Germain Depository Institutions Act of 1982, has become a veritable supermarket of loan terms. The principal loser in this battle for profit margin is the fixed rate 30-year mortgage which is originated by approved lenders such as banks and savings and loan associations and sold to the secondary market, basically FNMA and FHLMC.

New Mortgage Instruments A wide variety of alternative mortgage instruments have taken a commanding position in the marketplace. The principal types of alternative instruments are described below. Each of these instruments manipulates one or more of the different variables that exist in a mortgage:

- ☐ Amount of the principal

- ☐ Interest rate

- ☐ Payments, varied by time and amount

- ☐ Amortization

- ☐ Repayment term.

Graduated Payment Mortgage (GPM). This instrument is used primarily for qualifying first time borrowers by providing an initial payment considerably below that of a 30-year fixed mortgage. There is a period of negative amortization during the first three years. Each year the monthly payment is adjusted upward for a period of five years. At the end of the five years the level monthly payment for the remaining 25 years is usually considerably above where a 30-year fixed rate loan negotiated five years earlier would have been. The FHA 245 loan is an example of this type of mortgage instrument.

Adjustable-Rate Mortgage (ARM). Payment is geared to some form of index (prime rate, 11th District cost of funds, one year treasury bills, etc.). There may be "caps" (ceilings) on increases in monthly payments as well as in the rate of the loan. A common "cap" is $7\frac{1}{2}\%$ on payments and 5% on interest rate. Payment adjustment can be immediate, quarterly, semi-annual, or annual, up to as much as three years. In some cases, the GPM is combined with the ARM as one instrument.

Renegotiable Rate Mortgage (RRM). Sometimes referred to as the "Canadian Rollover" mortgage. This instrument offers fixed rate terms up to five years, at the end of which the borrower may renegotiate with the lender for the following five years, refinance, or pay off without penalty.

Growing Equity Mortgage (GEM). The growing equity mortgage is a variation on the GPM with no negative amortization. Its initial payment is based upon a 30-year fixed rate loan at the prevailing rate, with programmed increases in principal payments over a specified time period. Annual increases are made in monthly payments. As a result, loan balance is reduced more quickly. This is designed for a buyer who wants to accelerate maturity. A mortgage designed for payments every two weeks could also offer both accelerated maturity and reduced interest costs.

Role in Escrow **Documentation.** Since many lenders farm out documentation to outside agencies, forms similar to the "laundry list" (Exhibit 51) are used to provide instructions concerning documents required and loan conditions. Once the documents are prepared they are usually transmitted with lender instructions to an escrow processing the sale or loan.

Disclosure. The variety of loan terms complicates disclosure to the point that in many cases only representative examples of the annual percentage rate, monthly payment, and total of payments can be shown.

Separate Loan Escrow. An escrow may be set up solely to process the loan. From a procedural standpoint, it is usually best to separate the loan from the sale transaction, since the seller is not normally involved in the loan unless it is an FHA-insured or VA-guaranteed transaction or the seller is personally taking back a portion of the equity conveyed in the form of a deed of trust.

LENDER REQUIREMENTS

Lender requirements for processing a loan vary according to the type of loan, type of lender, and the underwriting policies of the lender involved. To reflect the relative positions of both borrower and lender properly in a loan escrow, a basic instruction form (Exhibit 52) is prepared, outlining the responsibilities of both parties in the loan transaction. This will be amended or amplified according to the requirements of the particular lender.

Type of Lender Loan escrows have another type of variable—the lender. Requirements vary between individual and corporate lenders since the objectives of credit extension are usually dissimilar.

Corporate. Corporate lenders (normally institutional) have stringent credit requirements because they are responsible to depositors, shareholders, or policyholders for a proper return on invested dollars with due regard for prudence.

Individuals. Individuals may take greater risk with their capital, especially on purchase money credit obligations that involve a considerable appreciation of the seller's equity which did not involve actual invested capital.

Underwriting. Underwriting involves the basic business risk undertaken by granting real estate credit. These decisions are based partly upon fulfilling the requirements of regulatory agencies, and partly upon the lender's internal credit requirements. For example, a property qualifies for a $70,000 VA loan, but the lender is willing to lend only $60,000 after reviewing the borrower's credit application in the belief that the applicant can only afford a $60,000 loan.

FHA Loans **Purpose.** Since its inception in 1934, the Federal Housing Administration (now an agency under the supervision of the Department of Housing and Urban Development—HUD) has promoted uniform building standards, wider home ownership, and establishment of realistic criteria for the creation of mortgage credit. Since then this agency's interest has extended from residential property to a larger commercial spectrum. FHA project financing is a unique area which offers special loan terms and requires specialized processing.

Loan Amounts. FHA lending programs combine an appraisal of the property for loan purposes with an analysis of the borrower's credit. The purpose of the appraisal is to set the upper loan limit, not to establish the sales price.

□ *Regulated Maximum.* On a single family (one to four unit) residential loan, the maximum FHA loan amount may vary, according to geographical location and regulatory changes.

□ *Downpayment.* The downpayment is based on the sales price and on Section 203(b) of the National Housing Act.

□ *Mortgage Calculation.* Loan program mortgage amounts are computed as follows:

> Owner-occupant mortgagors
>
> 97% of value for the first $25,000
>
> 95% of the remaining value to maximum loan amount (subject to regulatory change)
>
> Non-occupant mortgagors
>
> 85% of the maximum loan to occupant mortgagors (subject to regulatory change)

Term. Loan terms are limited to 30 years or three quarters of the remaining economic life of the property, whichever is less, with certain exceptions.

Prepayment. No prepayment bonus is required, but 30 days' interest in lieu of notice is allowed to lenders. Therefore, escrowholders who intend to pay off FHA-insured loans should prepare a 30-day notice of intent to pay off to avoid this charge to the seller.

Interest Rates. Interest rates are based on rates for competing obligations in the marketplace. Any disparity is adjusted by charging "points" (1 point is 1% of the loan amount) to adjust the yield, over and above the 1% loan origination fee chargeable to the borrower. In addition, FHA loans are now negotiated on the basis of market or prevailing rate and interest rate "buy down" programs for borrowers.

Escrow Documents

Commitment to Insure. When handling an escrow with FHA financing, the escrowholder should be careful to obtain all documentation required by the lender and to make provisions for the fees as outlined in the escrow instructions provided by the lender. Careful examination of the FHA commitment to insure is of extreme importance, especially the structural pest control requirements or other work required for closing.

> Sometimes an innocent item can be very costly to the lender. There is a case of a commitment to insure being issued on a modest dwelling in a semi-rural area in Northern California that required the property to be connected to a sewer. The loan processor overlooked this item and closed the loan. The nearest sewer hookup was nine miles away!

FHA-Amended Instructions. An additional instruction similar to the FHA-amended escrow instruction shown in Exhibit 53 is obtained by the selling broker in conjunction with the deposit receipt and is confirmed later by the parties in escrow. The purpose of this instruction is threefold:

☐ To establish FHA valuation and to acknowledge that the difference of any sales price exceeding this valuation is to be paid in cash

☐ To establish the loan fee and authorization of charges

☐ To provide for fire insurance coverage.

Sale Instructions and Allocation of Charges. Special sale instructions are designed for both FHA and VA loan transactions—the VA type is shown in Exhibit 54. Certain financing requirements are spelled out and a clear picture is provided to the contracting parties regarding allocation of charges and the responsibility for obtaining a structural pest control report. Exhibit 56 compares cost allocation under FHA and VA programs.

VA Loans

Purpose. Under Title III of the Servicemen's Readjustment Act of 1944, a program for real estate loans for World War II veterans was established. Since then the program has been expanded to include veterans of other conflicts or police actions. The program provides guarantees, not direct loans.

Eligibility. Eligibility requirements are determined by the U.S. Department of Veterans Affairs (formerly Veterans Administration), which is the governing agency. Upon submission of appropriate supporting data by the veteran (see Exhibit 55), a certificate of eligibility is issued that outlines the veteran's entitlement.

☐ *Automatic.* This certificate may be unconditional, if the veteran still has total eligibility and the loan can be processed as an automatic guaranteed loan.

☐ *Conditional.* Conditional certificates are issued in cases where a portion of the entitlement has been used by the veteran and where prior approval is required to assure VA coverage for the lender.

Loan Amounts. The present maximum guarantee on a VA loan is 60% of the loan or $46,000 (effective January 1, 1990), whichever is less. The lender's maximum loan amount is limitless. Underwriting considerations usually restrict the lender's investment to that amount beyond the guarantee that could be advanced on a conventional basis.

Example

If a life insurance company, which by state regulations is limited to conventional real estate loans, advances of 75% of the appraisal value, the maximum VA assisted loan would be $184,000. Of this loan, $138,000 represents the conventional loan (75%) and the balance, $46,000, the amount of the maximum VA guarantee.

Veterans Administration guaranteed loans in some cases exceed $184,000, because not all lenders have the same underwriting restrictions. For example, if a lender could advance 80% on a conventional basis, the maximum allowable VA loan would be $230,000.

Downpayment. Normally downpayment is not required unless:

☐ The sales price exceeds VA appraisal, or

☐ To reduce the loan amount to a level where the veteran's income can satisfactorily cover the monthly payment for principal, interest, taxes, and insurance.

Term. A VA loan is usually for 30 years, but the term is established by the lender. Maximum term may not exceed:

☐ Thirty years and 32 days. (The 32 days allows adjustment from the date of note to the date of first payment.) Loan processors should be extremely cautious when dating VA loan documents to avoid having a maturity date or terms that exceed VA requirements.

☐ The remaining economic life of the property as outlined in the VA appraisal.

Prepayment. The loan may be prepaid at any time with no prepayment charges.

Allocation of Charges. Specific requirements apply, as outlined in Exhibit 56. For example, in Southern California the seller pays the total escrow fees.

Cal-Vet Loans   **Purpose**. The California Home and Farm Purchase Program, one of the oldest such programs in the nation, was created in 1921 to assist veterans of World War I. Upon voter approval, bonds are issued by the State of California to provide a revolving loan fund which is replenished periodically by veterans' monthly payments on existing contracts.

Market Share. Although this form of credit does not represent a significant share of the state mortgage market, brokers and escrowholders are constantly deluged with customer inquiries about this program because interest rates are less than those of competing mortgage instruments.

Program Features. Eligibility and participation are similar to the USDVA program, but with two differences:

☐ *Eligibility*. Veterans are eligible only if they are California natives or were bona fide residents of the state at the time of entry into service, in addition to fulfilling specific active duty requirements. As in the VA loan, an application for certificate of eligibility (Form DVA) serves to determine eligibility. As part of this application, evidence of service must be provided.

☐ *Direct Loan*. The Department of Veterans Affairs lends the money directly to the veteran, rather than just guaranteeing a loan from a conventional lender.

Eligible Property. Existing or new construction on single family dwellings, condominium, mobilehome, or townhouse units are eligible for Cal-Vet loans. Funds are also available for existing farm properties that have a past income record which would assure loan repayment. The veteran must intend to occupy the premises.

Security Instrument. Whereas loans insured by the FHA or guaranteed by the VA are represented by a note secured by a deed of trust (see Exhibits 20 and 21, 30 and 31), a Cal-Vet loan is secured by a land contract (Exhibit 36). Instead of the borrower holding fee title, the interest conveyed is an equitable one with legal title being retained by the Department of Veterans Affairs, State of California.

Loan Term and Interest. Twenty-five years is normally the maximum, determined by loan amount, age of property, condition of the property, and the borrower's financial ability. The interest rate is variable, depending upon market conditions. Maturity may be extended due to changes in rate and advances for taxes and insurance.

Loan Amount. As in all these government-assisted programs, amounts are subject to change, being frequently revised to reflect changing market conditions. As of mid-1990, the following rules apply:

☐ *Sales under $35,000*. Where the purchase price is $35,000 or less, the Department may lend 97% of the appraised value of the property.

☐ *Maximum $125,000*. Where the purchase price is greater than $35,000, the Department may lend 95% of the appraised value of the property, but in no event may the loan be more than the purchase price or $125,000, whichever is less.

☐ *Farms*. On farm properties, the loan amount cannot exceed 95% of the Department's appraised value which is based upon net income from agricultural production.

Secondary Financing. Secondary lenders have difficulty perfecting their interest in properties financed with a land contract, since the borrower has only an equity interest in the property. The DVA now allows secondary financing under the following conditions:

☐ The junior loan cannot exceed 50% of the Cal-Vet loan amount.

☐ The combined amount of the Cal-Vet and junior loans cannot exceed 90% of the Department's valuation of the property.

☐ The combined average interest rate may not exceed by 2% the current Cal-Vet rate.

☐ The veteran and lender must execute a subordination agreement prepared by the Department. This is a method of lien acknowledgment to provide enforceability in the event of default.

Example of Loan Calculations

Purchase price and DVA valuation—	$60,000
Cal-Vet eligibility—	$43,000
Secondary financing—	$10,000 Rate: 10% per annum.
Total loan exposure allowed:	$60,000 x 90% = $54,000
Cal-Vet Loan amount	$43,000 x 50% = $21,500
Secondary loan	$10,000
Combined total loans	$53,000

Total eligible loan amount is $54,000; therefore the combined total is within acceptable limits.

```
            Example of Interest Calculations
Cal-Vet                $43,000 x 6.25%   =   $2,687.50
2nd Loan               $10,000 x 10.00%  =   $1,000.00
                                              $3,687.50

$3,687.50 /$53,000 = 6.958% overall interest rate.

Using the Department's 2% rule, the overall average interest rate is
acceptable because it is less than 8.25%, the maximum average rate
allowed.
```

Cost. There are no loan processing fees or appraisal fees required for this type of financing. A loan origination fee of $530 is presently required.

Insurance. Cal-Vet requires the buyer to carry two types of insurance to protect the lender's interest.

☐ *Life Insurance*. Mortgage redemption under age 65 is required. The insurance plan for a Cal-Vet loan provides disability benefits toward contract payments after 90 days of illness.

☐ *Fire Insurance*. This is available through a group of fire insurance companies under an agreement with the Department of Veterans Affairs.

Restrictions. Since title is retained by the lender, veteran borrowers are restricted in the use of such property; restricted activities include remodeling or alteration, using the property as a rental, or transferring contract interest to other than an eligible Cal-Vet.

Documentation. Title requirements and instructions to the escrowholder are coordinated by the Department of Veterans Affairs in Sacramento. Payoff of a Cal-Vet loan is similar to obtaining a demand for payment in full on trust deed financing, except that a deed from the Department of Veterans Affairs is provided together with the payoff figures to the escrow agent. To process loans initiated by California Department of Veterans Affairs, the escrowholder must be approved by that agency.

Federal Home Loan Mortgage Corporation

The FHLMC ("Freddie Mac") was established in 1970 as a secondary financing source for savings and loan associations that originate FHA, VA and conventional loans. This corporation issues commitments to associations that apply for the purchase of these loans funded on allocations made by Congress to the Federal Home Loan Bank Board.

Uniform Instruments. The formation of this federal agency was the first step toward the creation of national uniform security instruments.

☐ *Underwriting*. Most institutional real estate financing has a loan underwriting approach similar to VA and FHA loan applications. The applicant's employment and deposit verifications are used in a manner similar to the FHA/VA loan programs.

□ *Terminology.* The note and trust deed forms have omnibus terms that assure uniform acceptability throughout the country. The FHLMC note and deed of trust come the closest to being uniform instruments nationwide.

□ *Local Variation.* Modifications of these forms are still required in states where mortgages are the primary credit instrument and where the "lien theory" rather than "title theory" defines the lender's interest in the security.

Marketability. These forms are now the most prevalent loan documents, combined as FHLMC/FNMA approved documents, since savings and loan associations are the leading residential real estate lenders. To preserve liquidity these instruments and supporting documentation are used to create a marketable loan package to FHLMC.

Escrow Compliance. The escrowholder should examine the lender instructions relative to execution of each of these documents. Documentation required from the escrowholder (including certified escrow instructions, amendments, special borrower certifications, special title requirements, etc.) should be examined very carefully for complete compliance.

FNMA and GNMA

The Federal National Mortgage Association (FNMA or "Fannie Mae") and the Government National Mortgage Association (GNMA or Ginnie Mae") occupy an important place in real estate finance.

Purpose and Development. Established in 1938 to provide a secondary market for FHA insured mortgages, the FNMA had its genesis in 1935 when the Reconstruction Finance Mortgage Corporation was organized as a subsidiary of the Reconstruction Finance Corporation. Each of these agencies was the result of massive efforts to resuscitate the collapsed economy of the early 1930s, when many properties went into foreclosure.

Evolution of FNMA. FNMA has since evolved into an agency purchasing FHA, VA, and conventional loans. In 1968 FNMA attained private stockholder-owned corporation status when the Government National Mortgage Association (GNMA or "Ginnie Mae") was formed.

GNMA. GNMA was created by the Housing and Urban Development Act of 1968 as a wholly government-owned corporate entity, under the auspices of the Department of Housing and Urban Development.

□ *Public Housing Function.* The principal function of GNMA is to support special assistance programs such as subsidized housing projects, low to moderate income housing, public housing, and similar programs in the public interest.

□ *Money Market Function.* Another significant function of GNMA is to convert mortgage-backed notes issued by lenders into liquid money market instruments, by guaranteeing payment of these notes to institutional or individual lenders.

Role in Escrow. As secondary lenders the same ground rules apply to FNMA and GNMA as to FHLMC, as far as the escrowholder is concerned.

☐ *Procedure*. Accuracy in assembling the loan package and supporting credit and loan documentation is necessary to the successful consummation of FNMA purchase of eligible home loans. The escrowholder should meticulously follow the lender's documentation requirements in order to provide a marketable loan package.

☐ *Limited Use in California*. In single family conventional loan activity, secondary market operations are somewhat limited in California, due to loan ceilings not in concert with the high average sales price for residential real estate.

Residential Funding Corporation This is a new player in the secondary residential real estate lending market, a creation of Wall Street, in particular Salomon Brothers brokerage concern. Loans are specifically originated to create mortgage pool backed securities which are marketed by the brokerage community. They use standard FNMA/FHLMC documentation in their origination, and have similar underwriting requirements.

Conventional Loans In years past a conventional loan was any loan that was not FHA insured, VA guaranteed, or Cal-Vet supported, and such a loan was comparatively unregulated. Today, with private mortgage insurance and the secondary market operations of FHLMC and FNMA, conventional loan closing requirements assume new dimensions and greater uniformity.

Loan Escrow Instructions **Separate Document.** Depending upon the structure of the sale escrow instructions (if a sale is involved), separate loan escrow instructions may be prepared (Exhibit 52).

Execution Requirements. The instructions are prepared for execution by the borrowers. In some cases merely execution of the lender's escrow instructions by the borrower will suffice. Due to recent court rulings, certain instances may require the seller's concurrence if a seller is involved. This is especially true if the seller is taking back a purchase money second.

Amendments. If terms deviate from those described in the original instructions, the escrowholder must prepare instructions to amend and supersede the original instructions stating the new loan terms and the borrower's concurrence with these revised terms.

Supporting Documents. With the introduction of automation, much supportive loan documentation can be produced by computer. Some of the documents necessary in a loan escrow include:

JUNIOR LENDERS

When handling secondary financing, an escrowholder who remains aware of the laws and forces that affect the transaction will be able to provide adequate protection to all parties as well as to the escrow itself. Three major areas concern escrowholders when processing junior loans:

☐ The Real Property Loan Brokerage Law

☐ Possible usury problems

☐ Due-on-sale (acceleration) clauses on superior liens.

The Real Property Loan Brokerage Law This section of the California Real Estate Law regulates broker-arranged loans of less than $20,000 on junior loans and less than $30,000 on first loans.

Statutory Fee Limits. The Real Property Loan Brokerage Law of 1955, together with amendments through 1990, sets the processing fees allowed (including escrow), loan fees, and allowance for balloon payments, based upon loan maturity. Also, it is a violation of this law for a broker to charge a loan fee in a transaction where the broker is named beneficiary.

Effect on Escrow. Due to the statutory fee limits, most of these loans are processed by the originating loan brokers. Escrowholders in California should be aware that broker-arranged financing is subject to these limitations. Transactions that are in violation of the Real Property Loan Brokerage Law should not be accepted.

Possible Usury Problems In recent years, rapidly escalating mortgage rates have focused attention on California's 10% usury law.

Purchase Money Exception. Purchase money instruments taken back by sellers have been exempted from this law under a leading case dating back to the 1920s, and a recent court decision in *Boemer vs. Colwell Company* has substantiated the ruling. The justification for this exception is that selling under credit terms is an adjustment of the purchase price by the seller.

Broker Loan Exception. In California, with the passage of Proposition 2 in 1979, loans secured by real property made or arranged by licensed real estate brokers are exempt from usury law.

Discount Rate Basis. Other real estate lenders regulated by the usury law may now charge 10% or a rate that is 5% above the rate charged by the Federal Reserve Bank in San Francisco to its member banks (the discount rate).

Personal Use Loans. Loans for personal, family, or household purposes are still subject to the prior law. Purchase money real estate loans are not considered to be for a personal, family, or household purpose.

Financial Institutions. The usury law does not apply to loans made by any building and loan association, industrial loan company, credit union, pawnbroker or personal property broker, or any bank.

Legal Advice. Competent counsel should be obtained if there is any question concerning usury.

Due-on-Sale (Acceleration) Clauses on Superior Liens

Again due to escalating interest rates, the preservation of favorable interest rates on existing loans has become an issue. Controversy revolves around the due-on-sale clause in most conventional loans, which provides that upon sale (and, in some cases, further borrowing) the old loan becomes due and payable immediately.

Creative Devices. To avoid this costly requirement new buyers have used devices such as the land sale contract and the all-inclusive or "wraparound" deed of trust, to avoid the exercise of due-on-sale clauses. Lenders have been just as aggressive in attempting to enforce these clauses.

Case Law. As a result, a myriad of court cases at all levels were generated in the 1970s as alternative financing developed.

☐ *Tucker vs. Lassen Savings* was the first case to modify the effectiveness of the due-on-sale clause. It was determined that if the vendor (original borrower) had significant equity interest at the inception of a land contract, the existing lender could not require payment based on the due-on-sale clause.

☐ In *Wellenkamp vs. Bank of America*, the court ruled that the clause could not be enforced unless the security was impaired or the property was in imminent default. No ruling was made relative to individual beneficiaries in this case.

☐ Federally chartered savings and loan associations were exempted from the *Wellenkamp* ruling for loans that originated after 1976 when the Federal Home Loan Bank Board established its underwriting rule regarding due-on-sale. Subsequent case law extended federally chartered associations' ability to enforce the clause on loans that originated prior to 1976.

- ☐ In the *Pas vs. Hill* case in 1978, enforced payment was denied because the party acquired ownership by deed in lieu of foreclosure. Due to the circumstances of that case, it did not provide a clear-cut rule for situations involving individual trust deed holders.

- ☐ A 1979 ruling, *Medovoi vs. American Savings*, allowed American Savings to enforce a due-on-sale clause on a six unit building. In this ruling, however, the California District Court of Appeals limited its interpretation of the scope of the *Wellenkamp* ruling to single (one to four) family owner-occupied dwellings.

Garn-St. Germain Act. All of this litigation was made somewhat moot by the Garn-St. Germain Depository Institutions Act of 1982, which reaffirmed the right of acceleration for institutional lenders for transactions after October 15, 1985.

LOAN PROCESSING

With the proliferation of disclosure requirements, sensitivity to the borrower's right to privacy, and the need to provide a fully documented loan credit package, the loan processor has an exacting job.

Trend Toward Lender Processing Due to recent policy decisions of the agencies, VA and FHA loans can only be processed by employees or agents of the lenders. This means that the principal loan processing or "packaging" performed by escrowholders is incidental to their handling of subdivisions, and on conventional loans. Even in this area considerable pressure by FHLMC has been imposed upon lenders to handle this matter internally. In this case the loan application must be completely taken by the lender's employee or agent.

Documentation Loan processors, whether as lender employees or agents, or as independent escrowholders, complete the loan application for signature by the borrower, obtain credit and employment verifications, obtain confirmatory credit reports, and generally supervise the flow of the credit file. In certain instances they are requested by the lender to prepare all supporting loan documentation upon completion of credit approval. The loan processor must be given the appropriate forms by the lender.

Qualifying Credit approval is often the most time-consuming phase in a loan. Experienced loan processors can be of great assistance by prequalifying borrowers; this can shorten the time that a property is withheld from the market because of an unqualified purchaser.

COMPLIANCE WITH INSTRUCTIONS

Once approval has been secured and all pertinent legal and title requirements outlined by the lender's loan committee, the escrowholder turns to complying with lender instructions. Use of loan funds without proper compliance may cause liability on the part of the escrowholder.

Lender Instructions Letter A typical loan escrow document package is organized around the lender instructions (transmittal) letter (Exhibit 57). This letter provides the escrowholder with a wealth of information and orchestrates the timing of the balance of the closing process.

General Compliance. Each element of the lender instruction must be analyzed to assure that the escrowholder can comply. The enclosures should be signed and directed as indicated in the letter. If there is any deviation of the loan terms from the original escrow instructions, additional borrower approval is required.

Pre-Recording Checklist. The "prior to recording section" indicates whether the essential documents have been received: note and trust deed, disclosures, a preliminary title report and a certified copy of escrow instructions, as well as the structural pest control report and fire insurance to meet the lender's requirement. If the property falls within a flood-impacted area administered by the Department of Housing and Urban Development, the appropriate box would be checked or statement added to require flood insurance.

Time Limit. Following the "prior to recording section" the lender indicates a time limit for having all necessary documents prior to funding. The funding check and transmittal letter are often generated by computer, and the lender must complete a "laundry list" to enable the data processor to generate these documents.

Conditional Delivery. The lender's instruction letter conditionally delivers the lender's deed of trust for recording, predicated upon certain specified conditions of title being evident such as:

☐ *Taxes*. If the first installment of current taxes is still due or taxes of prior years are due, they must be paid.

☐ *Title Report*. Any items not yet approved on the preliminary title report must be capable of elimination before recording and use of the funds.

☐ *Private Utilities*. If the property is supplied with water by a private water company, assignment of the stock certificate of this water company is required.

☐ *Closing Statement*. Closing statements that verify the passing of consideration and its allocation between buyer and seller are required.

Distribution of Funds. The lender's instructions detail information relative to the transmittal of proceeds to the title company and deductions of authorized fees. The fees outlined, as well as the impounds allocated and the interest charges imposed, should be double-checked for correctness. For example, the daily interest rate factor should be checked with the stated rate on the note to determine that the factor is the proper one for that rate.

Cautions. It is important to read and understand the pitfalls indicated in any preprinted general provisions, for example:

- □ *Cancellation.* The right to cancel can be invoked within 30 days and cancellation fees will be imposed.

- □ *Double Escrow.* Disclosure requirements should be carefully observed.

- □ *Due-on-Sale Provisions.* Paragraph 17 of the trust deed (Exhibit 21, Chapter 7) also warns against evasion of this provision.

Additional Documents Loan escrows that involve income-producing properties require additional documentation, especially in FHA financing. Some of these documents include assignments of rents and leases, ALTA surveys, security agreements, financing statements, inventories, rental certifications, etc.

Closing When the escrowholder is finally assured that all loan conditions are in compliance and that all other terms of the collateral sale are in order, then the loan funding can be initiated and recording ordered from the title company to close the transaction.

LOAN INFORMATION FORM ("LAUNDRY LIST")

PREPARED BY:_____ PHONE NO. (___) _____ PROGRAM # _____
3: LOAN REP BRANCH_____ 4: LOAN REP_____
5: REFI____ PUD____ CONDO____ 7: LOAN #_____ 8: DOCUMENT DATE(___/___/ 19___)
11: DOC EXPIRATION DATE(___/___/ 19___)

12: BUYER #1 NAME_____ 13: VESTING_____
14: BUYER #2 NAME_____ 15: VESTING_____
16: BUYER #3 NAME_____ 17: VESTING_____
18: BUYER #4 NAME_____ 19: VESTING_____

24: SELLER #1 NAME_____ 25: SELLER #2 NAME_____
26: SELLER #3 NAME_____ 27: SELLER #4 NAME_____

28: ESCROW CO._____ 29: ESCROW OFFICER_____
30: ADDRESS_____ CITY_____ STATE_____ ZIP_____
31: ESCROW #_____

32: TITLE CO._____ 33: TITLE OFFICER_____
34: ADDRESS_____ CITY_____ STATE_____ ZIP_____
35: ORDER #_____ 36: PRELIM DATE(___/___/19___) 37: ADDT. END._____
38: APPROVED ITEMS_____ 39: FISCAL YEAR_____ 40: INSTALLMENT (1=1ST 2=2ND 3=BOTH) ___
41: TAX MESSAGE_____
42: PROPERTY ADDRESS_____ CITY_____ STATE_____ ZIP_____
43: PROPERTY CITY AREA_____ 44: PROPERTY COUNTY_____
45: PUD/CONDO NAME_____
46: LEGAL LINE #1_____
47:        #2_____
48:        #3_____
49:        #4_____
50:        #5_____

51: AMORT. TERM____ 52: LOAN AMT._____ 53: SALES PRICE_____ 54: APPRAISED VALUE_____
55: 2ND T.D. AMT._____ 56: LOAN TERM_____ 57: INT. RATE_____ 58: 1ST PMT. DATE(___/___/ 19___)
59: # DAYS PREPAID INT._____

60: DISC. POINTS____ + $____ 61: ORIG. FEE____ + $____ 62: CREDIT REPORT(DUE)_____ (PAID)_____
63: APPRAISAL FEE(DUE)_____ (PAID)_____ 64: PHOTO INSPECTION_____ 65: INITIAL PMI_____
66: DOC. FEE_____ 67: EXTRA FEE #1_____ DESCP._____
68: EXTRA FEE #2_____ DESCP._____ 69: EXTRA (PREP) FEE #3_____ DESCP._____
70: EXTRA (PREP) FEE #4_____ DESCP._____ 71: NOTARY FEE_____ 72: TITLE POLICY (ALTA)_____
73: RECORDING FEE_____ 74: TERMITE FEE_____ 75: TAX SERVICE FEE_____ 76: PROCESSING_____
78: WAREHOUSE FEE_____ 79: ESCROW FEE_____ 80: (PRPD) PROCESSING FEE_____
81: (PRPD) DOCUMENT FEE_____

82: PREPAID PENALTY (YES=1 NO=0)_____ 83: LOAN ASSUMABLE (YES=1;MAYBE,SUBJECT TO CONDITIONS=2;NO=3)_____
84: DEMAND FEATURE (YES=1 NO=0)___ 85: BUYER ENTITLED TO REFUND (YES=1 NO=0)___

86: ANNUAL TAXES_____ 87: # MONTHS_____ 88: ANNUAL HAZARD INSURANCE_____ 89: # MONTHS_____
90: ANNUAL FLOOD INSURANCE_____ 91: # MONTHS FLOOD INSURANCE IMPOUND___ 92: ANNUAL PMI/MMI INSURANCE_____
93: # MONTHS_____ 94: PMI CO. NAME_____
95: PMI CO. ADDRESS_____ CITY_____ STATE_____ ZIP_____
96: PMI FACTOR_____ 97: PMI FACTOR (ANNUAL=1, MONTHLY=2)___ 98: PMI FOR FULL TERM (YES=1 NO=0)___

99: ATTACHMENT 'A' APPRAISAL (YES=1 NO=0)_____ 100: TERMITE REPORT (YES=1 NO=0)_____
101: FINAL COMPL. INS. (YES=1 NO=0)___ 102: AMEND. ESCROW INS. RE:_____
103: ESCROW (SHORT) REQUIREMENT #1_____
104: ESCROW (SHORT) REQUIREMENT #2_____
105:        REQ. #3_____
106:        REQ. #4_____
107:        REQ. #5_____
108:        REQ. #6_____
109:        REQ. #7_____
110:        REQ. #8_____
111:        REQ. #9_____

113: MAILING ADDRESS_____ CITY_____ STATE_____ ZIP_____
114: LIEN #1 AMOUNT_____ DESCRP._____
115: LIEN #2 AMOUNT_____ DESCRP._____
117-C: IS THERE TAX AND HAZARD IMPOUND ACCTS (YES=1 NO=0)_____ 118-C: IS THERE PMI IMPOUND ACCT (YES=1 NO=0)___
119: MULTI UNITS (YES=1 NO=0)___ 120: BASIS POINTS_____ 121: CURRENT INDEX_____
124: LIFETIME RATE CAP %_____ 125: ANNUAL RATE CAP %_____ 126-B: INTEREST CHANGE DATE(___/___/ 19___)

Exhibit 51

LOAN ESCROW INSTRUCTIONS

LENDER

ESCROW NO. _____

The Bilateral Escrow Company

_____ California _____ 19____

A I will hand you the sum of $

B and will deliver to you any instrument which this escrow requires shall be executed or delivered by me, all of which you are instructed to use, pursuant to obtaining on or before _____ a (   ) CLTA   (   ) ALTA standard coverage policy of title insurance with the usual Title Company's exceptions with a liability of not less than $ _____ , covering the property in the City of _____ County of _____ , State of California, described as follows:

Showing title vested in

C SUBJECT TO: _____ installment(s) of General and Special County, and City (if any) Taxes, including any special district levies, payments for which are included therewith, for current fiscal year, not delinquent, including taxes for the ensuing year, if any, a lien but not yet payable.

(   ) Conditions, restrictions, including reservations, covenants, rights, rights of way, easements and the exception of minerals, oil, gas, water, carbon and hydro-carbons on or under said land, now of record, and in deed to file, if any, affecting the use and occupancy of said property.

(   ) Trust Deed on your form, or form handed you, executed by vestees, to secure _____ Note for $ _____ dated _____ 19____ with interest at _____ % per annum; principal and interest payable in installments of $ _____ , or more, on the _____ day of each _____ commencing _____ , and continuing

Said Note and Trust Deed to be drawn in favor of

_____ and the Trust Deed shall be designated as a _____ Trust Deed.

Endorse above note on back thereof showing interest to accrue from

D The foregoing terms, conditions and instructions, as well as the "GENERAL INSTRUCTIONS" as set forth on the reverse hereof, have been read and are understood and agreed to by each of the undersigned, and are hereby concurred in, approved and accepted in their entirety, as if fully set forth in this paragraph.

Lender _____

BORROWER

E The foregoing terms, conditions and instructions, as well as the "GENERAL INSTRUCTIONS" as set forth on the reverse hereof, have been read and are understood and agreed to by each of the undersigned, and are hereby concurred in, approved and accepted in their entirety, as if fully set forth in this paragraph.

All conditions and demands above are hereby approved and I will hand you the necessary documents called for on my part to cause title to be shown as above, which you are authorized to deliver upon payment to you for my account the sum of $ _____

within the time as above provided. Pay your escrow charges and my proper recording fee, also charges for evidence of title called for above (whether or not this escrow is consummated), and you are authorized to pay off any bonds, assessments and/or taxes, also any encumbrances of record, plus accrued interest and bonus, if any, to show title as called for above and/or necessary to comply with same. Instruct the title company to begin search of title at once.

I have received a copy of these instructions as evidenced by my signature below.

Borrower _____

| | Present Address | City | Zip | Phone |

Borrower _____

| | Present Address | City | Zip | Phone |

Notes:
A. This represents lender's commitment to fund, predicated upon the conditions outlined in the instruction.
B. This section covers the extent of the commitment period and the condition of title acceptable to the lender, as well as the form of title policy desired.
C. This section describes the form and substance of the encumbrances and debt documentations.
D. This section binds the lender to the general provisions that govern the escrow relative to the handling of documentation and the deposits, and provides space for execution of the instructions by the lender.
E. The remaining portion of the instructions covers the borrower's assent to the terms and conditions of the loan escrow.

Exhibit 52

FHA-AMENDED
ESCROW INSTRUCTIONS

ESCROW NO. _____

DATE: _____

ESCROW COMPANY

Amending my/our previous instructions dated _____ in regards only to the following:

____ It is expressly agreed that, notwithstanding any other provisions of this contract, the purchaser shall not be obligated to complete the purchase of the property described herein or to incur any penalty by forfeiture of earnest money deposits or otherwise unless the seller has delivered to the purchaser a written statement issued by the Federal Housing Administration, setting forth the appraised value of the property for mortgage insurance purposes of not less than $_____, which statement the seller hereby agrees to deliver to the purchaser promptly after such appraised value statement is made available to the seller.

The purchaser shall, however, have the privilege and option of proceeding with the consummation of this contract without regard to the amount of the appraised valuation made by the Federal Housing Administration.

____ Buyers agree to pay 1% loan fee plus usual charges in connection with obtaining a loan.

____ You are hereby authorized and instructed to deduct the _____% new loan fee from the net proceeds due the sellers herein through this escrow.

____ Buyer reserves the option of obtaining new fire insurance coverage, or prorating existing policy, if satisfactory to the Lender. In the event the Buyer does obtain new coverage escrow holder is authorized and instructed to pay the premium covering same, upon presentation of a bill and from Buyer's funds at close of escrow, and is further authorized to return existing fire policy to Seller at close of escrow, for cancellation at his discretion.

All other instructions remain the same.

SIGNATURE_____   SIGNATURE_____

SIGNATURE_____   SIGNATURE_____

These instructions may be executed in counterparts, all of which when taken together shall be deemed to be the instrument. I have received a copy of these instructions as evidenced by my signature above.

Exhibit 53

SALE ESCROW INSTRUCTIONS
BUYER

Escrow No.   California   , 19

The undersigned Buyer and Seller, hereby mutually understand and agree, that the statements set forth herein shall be construed, by all those concerned, as unconditionally incorporated in these Buyer's and Seller's escrow instructions, to-wit:

(A) 1. Buyer will hand you . . . . $

    2. . . . . $

    3. Broker will hand you, for account of Buyer . . . . $

    4. . . . . $

    5. Proceeds from a VA Guaranteed loan to be procured by Buyer . . . . $

    6. . . . . $

    7. TOTAL CONSIDERATION. . . . . $

(B) and Buyer will deliver to you any instruments and/or funds required from Buyer to enable you to comply with these instructions, all of which you are authorized to use and/or deliver pursuant to obtaining on or before   a standard Policy of Title Insurance, with the Title Company's exceptions, provided that said policy has a liability of at least the amount of the above total consideration, (new title policy to be delivered to lien holder) covering the property in the City of   and County of   , State of California, described as follows:

insuring title vested in:

(C) SUBJECT TO: installment(s) of General and Special County, and City (if any), Taxes, including any special district levies, payments for which are included therein and collected therewith, for current fiscal year, not delinquent, including taxes for the ensuing year, if any, a lien not yet payable.

(YES) Conditions, restrictions, reservations, covenants, rights, rights of way, easements and the exception of minerals, oil, gas, water, carbons and hydro-carbons on or under said land, now of record, and in deed to file, if any, affecting the use and occupancy of said property.

(YES) Deed of Trust, (loan) to file, and note secured thereby for $ as per their terms. You are authorized and instructed to comply with lender's requirements, further approval of which is hereby waived through this escrow by Buyer and Seller, the proceeds of which shall be used to apply on purchase price, to be payable in monthly installments   including interest at   % per annum.

(D) Charge Seller's account with Lender's loan discount fee not to exceed   % of the amount of the new loan obtained herein and related costs which may include but are not limited to fees for documents, photos, inspections, recording assignment of Trust Deed, other than those to be paid by the Buyer as set forth below.

Charge buyer's account with costs of obtaining new loan, including but not limited to credit report, prepaid interest as required by lender, appraisal fees if ordered in the Buyer's name, impounds for taxes and hazard insurance, lender's title policy, tax service, recording fees, and 1% of loan amount representing the lender's loan processing fee. If necessary, you are authorized to immediately release funds from the Buyer's account to cover cost of credit report and for VA appraisal fee charges, said costs not reimbursable.

(E) This escrow is to be contingent upon Buyer and Property qualifying for a VA Guaranteed loan under the terms called for above.

(F) Except for costs of any VA appraisal and credit report to be paid for by the Buyer: "It is expressly agreed that, notwithstanding any other provisions of this contract, the purchaser shall not incur any penalty for forfeiture of earnest money or otherwise or be obligated to complete the purchase of the property described herein, if the contract purchase price or cost exceeds the reasonable value of the property established by the Veterans Administration. The purchaser shall, however, have the privilege and option of proceeding with the consummation of this contract without regard to the amount of the reasonable value established by the Veterans Administration."

(G) Seller is to furnish Buyer through escrow with a current report in writing from a licensed structural pest control operator covering an inspection of visible and accessible areas of house and garage. If the report should disclose any debris under the house, termites, dry rot, or other infestation, the Seller is to eliminate it and all work recommended in said report to repair damage caused by infestation or infection of wood-destroying pests or organisms found and all work to correct conditions that caused such infestation or infection, as well as other work required by VA, shall be done at the expense of Seller. Funds for work to be done at the expense of Seller shall be held in escrow and disbursed upon receipt in escrow of certificate of completion by the structural pest control operator or upon close of escrow, whichever occurs later.

(H) In accordance with the manner specified under "GENERAL INSTRUCTIONS", the following are to be adjusted or prorated to . . . .

    (   ) Taxes   (   ) Fire Insurance on Property   (   ) Rents

(I) In addition to the aforementioned sum Buyer will hand you, before the date of recording, sufficient funds to cover charges and prorations as hereinbefore set out, also for your Buyer's service charge, if any, and premium on any new fire insurance policy.

(J) As a matter of record only between Buyer and Seller, property address is known as:

The foregoing terms, conditions and instructions, as well as the "GENERAL INSTRUCTIONS" as set forth on the reverse hereof, have been read and are understood and agreed to by each of the undersigned, and are hereby concurred in, approved and accepted in their entirety, as if fully set forth in this paragraph.

Exhibit 54.1

Buyer		Present Address		City	Zone	Phone

Buyer		Mailing Address After Close of Escrow		City	Zone	Phone

SELLER

(K) The foregoing terms, conditions and instructions, as well as the "GENERAL INSTRUCTIONS" as set forth on the reverse hereof, have been read and are understood and agreed to by each of the undersigned, and are hereby concurred in, approved and accepted in their entirety, as if fully set forth in this paragraph. The undersigned Seller will hand you all instruments and/or funds necessary to enable you to comply therewith, including deed(s) to the herein described property, all of which you are authorized to use and/or deliver, pursuant to your obtaining in this escrow for the account of the undersigned party(ies) within the time limit as above provided for, the monies, being the total on line 7, page 1 hereof plus or minus above prorations and charges, and instruments called for under these instructions. From said monies, together with any necessary funds I hand you, you shall deduct and pay my costs in connection with new loan as set forth above, all escrow fees, seller's drawing and recording fees, also for evidence of title called for above, Documentary Transfer Tax stamp as required on Deed to property I am conveying; and you are authorized to pay off any bonds, assessments, and/or taxes, also any encumbrances of record, plus accrued interest, charges, and bonus if any, to show title as called for above and/or necessary to comply with same. Instruct the title company to begin search of title at once.

Seller		Present Address		City	Zone	Phone

Seller		Mailing Address After Close of Escrow		City	Zone	Phone

Form 11 VA

SUMMARY OF VA SALE ESCROW INSTRUCTIONS

A. Memo box area outlines the elements of the total consideration which includes loan proceeds and down payment, if any.

B. This area describes the buyers obligation to provide money and documents when the escrow is in a position to vest title in the manner prescribed by the instruction on the property described. (A complete legal description of the property is required).

C. Acceptable conditions of title are described together with the terms of the new VA loan being created.

D. Fees and charges are allocated between buyer and seller in accordance with VA regulations. Buyer is limited as to the type of fees that are chargeable and is not allowed to pay escrow fees.

E. This is the standard contingency in a VA transaction. Escrowholders should be cautioned relative to retaining any of the veteran's monies in a cancellation situation, as they can only be retained for specific cost incurred.

F. This describes the conditions under which a portion of the buyers deposit can be retained as well as authority to continue even though the certificate of reasonable value does not equate the sales price. If this does occur, however, further instructions should be obtained from the parties to the effect that buyer will deposit the cash difference between the amount of the Certificate of Reasonable Value and the sales price.

G. This instruction is in conformance with VA requirements relating to the provision of a structural pest control report to meet the specifications of the agency.

H. This summary paragraph outlines more specific provisions outlined in paragraphs 1 to 8 of the general instructions which more specifically outlines the conditions of pro-ration.

I. This paragraph provides specific authorization by the buyer to be responsible for any charges allowable by the Veterans Administration.

J. This paragraph is a "clean up" item to verify street address and incorporate all the conditions on the reverse thereof. The execution following indicates buyers assent to escrow conditions.

K. The language of this paragraph secures the seller's concurrence with the stipulated instructions together with specific obligations to pay costs incurred over and above those not authorized by the Veteran's Administration to be incurred by the buyer-borrower.

Exhibit 54.2

VA Veterans Administration

VETERANS ADMINISTRATION
ATTN: LOAN GUARANTY DIVISION

REQUEST FOR DETERMINATION OF ELIGIBILITY AND AVAILABLE LOAN GUARANTY ENTITLEMENT

TO

NOTE: Please read instructions on reverse before completing this form. If additional space is required attach separate sheet.

1. FIRST - MIDDLE - LAST NAME OF VETERAN	2A. ADDRESS OF VETERAN (No., Street or rural route, City or P.O., State and ZIP Code)

2B. VETERAN'S DAYTIME TELEPHONE NO. (Include Area Code)	3. DATE OF BIRTH	

4. MILITARY SERVICE DATA (ATTACH PROOF OF SERVICE -- SEE INSTRUCTIONS ON REVERSE (Paragraphs F and G.1))

PERIOD OF ACTIVE SERVICE		NAME (Show your name exactly as it appears on your separation papers (DD214) or Statement of Service)	SERVICE NUMBER (Enter Social Security No., if appropriate)	BRANCH OF SERVICE
DATE FROM	DATE TO			
A.				
B.				
C.				
D.				

5A. WERE YOU DISCHARGED, RETIRED OR SEPARATED FROM SERVICE BECAUSE OF DISABILITY OR DO YOU NOW HAVE ANY SERVICE-CONNECTED DISABILITIES? ☐ YES ☐ NO (If "Yes," Complete Item 5B)	5B. VA CLAIM FILE NUMBER C-	6. IS A CERTIFICATE OF ELIGIBILITY FOR LOAN GUARANTY PURPOSES ENCLOSED? (If "No," Complete Items 7A and 7B) ☐ YES ☐ NO

7A. HAVE YOU PREVIOUSLY APPLIED FOR A CERTIFICATE OF ELIGIBILITY FOR VA LOAN PURPOSES? ☐ YES ☐ NO (If "Yes," give location of VA office(s))	7B. HAVE YOU PREVIOUSLY RECEIVED SUCH A CERTIFICATE? ☐ YES ☐ NO (If "Yes," give location of VA office(s))	7C. COMPLETE THE FOLLOWING CERTIFICATION IF YOU HAVE PREVIOUSLY RECEIVED A CERTIFICATE OF ELIGIBILITY WHICH IS NOT ENCLOSED AND THIS IS A REQUEST FOR A DUPLICATE CERTIFICATE. ☐ THE CERTIFICATE OF ELIGIBILITY PREVIOUSLY ISSUED TO ME HAS BEEN LOST OR STOLEN. IF RECOVERED, IT WILL BE RETURNED TO THE VA.

8. HAVE YOU PREVIOUSLY ACQUIRED PROPERTY WITH THE ASSISTANCE OF A GI LOAN? ☐ YES ☐ NO (If "Yes," complete Items 9 through 18. Please attach a separate sheet if more than one loan is involved. If "No," skip to Items 19 through 22.)	9. ADDRESS OF REGIONAL OFFICE(S) WHERE LOAN WAS OBTAINED (City and State)

10. STATE TYPE(S) AND NUMBER OF LOAN(S) (Home, Manufactured Home, Condominium, Direct, Farm, Business, etc.)	11. ADDRESS(ES) OF PROPERTY PREVIOUSLY PURCHASED WITH GUARANTY ENTITLEMENT	12. DATE YOU PURCHASED THE PROPERTY(IES)

13. DO YOU NOW OWN THE PROPERTY DESCRIBED IN ITEM 11? ☐ YES ☐ NO (If "Yes," do not complete Items 14 and 15)	14. DATE(S) THE PROPERTY WAS SOLD	15. IS THERE ANY UNDERSTANDING OR AGREEMENT WRITTEN OR ORAL, BETWEEN YOU AND THE PURCHASERS THAT THEY WILL RECONVEY THE PROPERTY TO YOU? ☐ YES ☐ NO

NOTE: It will speed processing if you can complete Items 16, 17, and 18.

16. NAME AND ADDRESS OF LENDER(S) TO WHOM LOAN PAYMENTS WERE MADE	17. LENDER'S LOAN OR ACCOUNT NUMBER
	18. VA LOAN NUMBER(S)

I certify that the statements herein are true to the best of my knowledge and belief.

19. SIGNATURE OF VETERAN	20. DATE SIGNED

FEDERAL STATUTES PROVIDE SEVERE PENALTIES FOR FRAUD, INTENTIONAL MISREPRESENTATION, CRIMINAL CONNIVANCE OR CONSPIRACY PURPOSED TO INFLUENCE THE ISSUANCE OF ANY GUARANTY OR INSURANCE BY THE ADMINISTRATOR.

21. THIS SECTION FOR VA USE ONLY

21A. DATE CERTIFICATE ISSUED AND DISCHARGE OR SEPARATION PAPERS AND VA PAMPHLETS GIVEN TO VETERAN OR MAILED TO ADDRESS SHOWN BELOW	21B. TYPE OF DISCHARGE OR SEPARATION PAPERS RETURNED	21C. INITIALS OF VA AGENT	21D. NAME AND ADDRESS TO WHOM CERTIFICATE MAILED

VA FORM 26-1880, MAR 1984   DO NOT DETACH

IMPORTANT - You must complete Item 22 since the Certificate of Eligibility along with all discharge and separation papers will be mailed to the address shown in Item 22 below. If they are to be sent to you, your current mailing address should be indicated, or if they are to be sent elsewhere, the name and address of such person or firm should be shown in Item 22.

The amount of loan guaranty entitlement available for use is endorsed on the reverse of the enclosed Certificate of Eligibility. This certificate must be returned to the VA at the time a loan application or loan report is submitted.

NOTE - PLEASE DELIVER THE ENCLOSED PAMPHLETS AND DISCHARGE OR SEPARATION PAPERS TO THE VETERAN PROMPTLY

NOTE - PLEASE DELIVER THE ENCLOSED PAMPHLETS AND DISCHARGE OR SEPARATION PAPERS TO THE VETERAN PROMPTLY

26-1880   EXISTING STOCKS OF VA FORM 26-1880, JUN 1982, WILL BE USED.

DO NOT DETACH

22. PLEASE BE SURE THAT NAME AND ADDRESS ARE ENTERED IN THE SPACE INDICATED TO INSURE PROMPT DELIVERY OF DOCUMENTS

Exhibit 55

ALLOCATION OF CHARGES

Buyer's and Seller's Cost Allocation (FHA Loans)

Buyer's Responsibility

1. Downpayment (must be in funds verified on deposit and cannot be borrowed)

2. 1/2 of escrow fee (not to exceed a sliding scale based upon total consideration, from $65-120)*

3. 1% loan fee (maximum)

4. Recording deed of trust and grant deed*

5. Lender's title policy*

6. Credit report report and any FHA requirements relative thereto.

7. Appraisal fee

8. Initial impounds: two months fire insurance and appropriate tax impounds

9. Tax prorations

10. Adjusted interest on new loans.

Seller's Responsibility

1. Escrow fee—balance not assumed by the seller under agency limitations**

2. Payoff of existing liens/loans

3. Documentary transfer tax**

4. Owner's title policy

5. Sales commission

6. Structural pest control

7. Proration of taxes

---

* As the result of studying average costs throughout the country, the Federal Housing Administration has established, on a regional basis, guidelines on maximum escrow fees, title fees, and recording charges.

** Applicable in California. Note: The buyer's costs outlined in items 2-7 may be assumed by the seller, which could adjust the loan amount since it is based on buyer's "acquisition cost."

Exhibit 56.1

BUYER'S AND SELLER'S COST ALLOCATION (VA LOANS)

Buyer's Responsibility	Seller's Responsibility
1. 1% loan fee—max.	1. Discount
2. No escrow fee*	2. Total escrow fee, including veteran's share*
3. Recording deed of trust and grant deed	3. Documentary transfer tax**
4. Lender's title policy	4. Owner's title policy
5. Credit report	5. Payoff of existing liens/loans
6. Tax proration	6. Proration of taxes
7. Initial impounds: two months fire insurance and appropriate tax impounds	7. Structural pest control report and repairs required by VA
8. Adjusted interest on new loans	8. Sales commissions
9. Appraisal fee—only if veteran's name appears on VA appraisal	9. The seller may pay any or all of the veteran's costs, though it is referred to as a "VA no no"

---

* In areas supervised by the L.A. regional office. The San Francisco regional office allows allocation of escrow fees.

** Applicable in California.

Exhibit 56.2

	MONTHLY PAYMENT:	
TO: • NORTHERN TITLE CO.	P & I	471.79
•	TAX	
• OAKLAND, CA 94612	INS.	
	PMI/MMI	} IMPOUNDS SUB-TOTAL
	TOTAL	471.79

ATTN: ATTN:

We enclose the following documents necessary to complete the above-captioned loan. Return all documents completed as shown at the time funds are requested.

  1 Copy of note and deed of trust to borrower.

(X) Note: Execute original and conform two copies.   ( ) Amendment to Note

(X) Deed of Trust: Conform and certify two copies.   ( ) Impound Authorization

(X) Disclosure Statement   (X) Recission Notice   ( ) Occupancy Statement

( ) VA Form 1876 in Quadruplicate.   ( ) Premium Payment Auth.

( ) Affidavit: Purchaser and Vendor   ( ).

(X) Addendum to Instructions: Escrow Officer to acknowledge   ( )

( ) RESPA Settlement Statement — complete & return after recordation

( ) Borrowers Instructions

( ) FHA Firm Commitment in Duplicate: Buyer to execute and return both copies.

( ) Insurance Requirements

IN ADDITION TO THE ABOVE, FURNISH US THE FOLLOWING WHEN REQUESTING FUNDS:

( ) Termite Report and Clearance: In duplicate. Required FHA/VA statement must be typed on the report/clearance and signed by borrowers.

(X) Amendment to Escrow Instructions Re: LOAN AMOUNT FROM 60,000 to 53,200.00

(X) COMPLETE AGREEMENT SECTION ON 1003/STATEMENT RE: FULL USE OF

(X) PROCEEDS/SATISFACTORY EXPLA FOR LATE MORTGAGE PMT AT HARVEST

(X) SAVINGS & LOAN/AMENDMENT FROM ESCROW & QUITCLAIM DEED FOR VESTING

(X) HAZ INS PREPAID 1 YR IN ADV FROM CLOSE IN AN AMT EQUAL TO OR

(X) GREATER THAN ALL LIENS NAMING BENEFIT SAVINGS CORPORATION

(X) AND/OR ITS ASSIGNS AS FIRST MORTGAGEE.

( )

PRIOR TO FUNDING WE WILL OBTAIN: THIS LOAN MUST RECORD PRIOR TO: SEPTEMBER 16, 1988

( ) Final Compliance Inspection Report. Notify this office when work has been completed

( ) Waivers from FHA/VA Re:

    ALTA POLICY must contain indorsements 100, 116 and   with liability in the amount of our

    loan on property described herein. LIABILITY SUBJECT ONLY TO: (Gen. & Spec. taxes) Fiscal Year 19 87-88 BOTH HALVES**

    Funds may be used for account of the vestees, and you will record all instruments when you comply with the following:

      1. Issue said form of Policy showing title vested as shown below. **PLUS PENALTY AND ANY TAXES DUE

      2. Issue said form of Policy free from encumbrances except items   of preliminary Title Report

        dated 8/06/1988   Secondary financing in the amount of $ has been approved.

                FHA OR VA BUYER CANNOT BE CHARGED FOR ANY INDORSEMENTS TO ALTA POLICY

Vesting: JACQUES AND MARIE BORREAU HUSBAND AND WIFE AS JOINT TENANTS	Case No.	County: ALAMEDA
Address 12345 CONCORDE PLACE HAYWARD, CA 94545	First Payment Date: 11/01/1988	Int. Rate: 10.125
	Last Payment Date 10/01/2018	Term 360 mos.

				SALES PRICE	
				DEBIT AMOUNT	
LOAN REP. N. NGUYEN		BRANCH OAKLAND		53,200.00	
	CREDIT AMOUNT			CREDIT AMOUNT	
LOAN FEE	1,314.00	% DISCOUNT			
CREDIT REPORT		$ 14.96 PER DIEM INTEREST			
APPRAISAL		FROM TO 10/01/1988			
ENDORSEMENT & SETUP	75.00	MOS TAX @			
PHOTOS & INSPECTION		MOS INS @			
TAX SERVICE CONTRACT	54.00	MOS MMI/PPI @			
DOCUMENT FEE	150.00	TOTAL IMPOUNDS			
ALTA BRING DOWN IND.		INSURANCE PREMIUM			
			CHECK NO.		
MISC. _____					
DEDUCTIONS SUBTOTAL ►►				1,593.00	
CHECK TO THE TITLE COMPANY		CHECK NO.		$	
		DRAFT NO.		$	

**CHARGE TO SELLER   By _____   Date _____

                               Authorized Signature

Exhibit 57.1

Loan No. __010021__

ITEMIZATION OF AMOUNT FINANCED OF: $ __51,443.04__

AMOUNT GIVEN TO YOU DIRECTLY:

_____ $ __51,218.04__

AMOUNT PAID ON YOUR ACCOUNT:

    Tax and Insurance Reserves $ _____

    _____ $ _____

    _____ $ _____

AMOUNT PAID TO OTHERS ON YOUR BEHALF:

    Loan Proceeds to _____

    _____ $ _____

    Recording/Filing Fees to _____

    _____ $ _____

    Credit Report Fees to Credit Bureau $ _____

    Appraisal Fees to Appraiser $ _____

    Document Preparation Fee to _____ $ __150.00__

    Loan Escrow/Closing Fee to _____

    _____ $ _____

    Property Insurance Premiums to Insurance Agency

    _____ $ _____

    ENDORSEMENT & SETUP $ __75.00__

    _____ $ _____

    _____ $ _____

XXXXXXXXXXXXXXXXXXXXXXXXXXXXXXXXXXXXXXXXXXXXXXXXXXXXXXXXXXXXXXXXXXXXXXXXXX

Prepaid Finance Charge:

Loan Fee 2.00 + 250.00 $ __1,314.00__

Prepaid Int. (26 days) $ __388.86__

Processing Fee $ _____

Tax Service Contract $ __54.00__

Mortgage Ins. Premium $ _____

Termite Inspection $ _____

_____ $ _____

                            Total Prepaid $ __1,756.96__

Neither you nor the lender previously has become obligated to make or accept this loan, nor is any such obligation made by the delivery or signing of this disclosure.

_____   _____
Borrower   Date

_____   _____
Borrower   Date

Exhibit 57.2

Chapter 14 Quiz

1. The strictest loan requirements are likely to be imposed by:

   (A) Individual lenders
   (B) Corporate lenders
   (C) Sellers extending credit
   (D) None of the above, because lenders' requirements are uniform and fixed by law

2. FHA loans are:

   (A) Insured
   (B) Guaranteed
   (C) Conventional
   (D) Junior

3. VA loans are:

   (A) Insured
   (B) Guaranteed
   (C) Conventional
   (D) Junior

4. The maximum VA guarantee on a VA assisted loan of $110,000 is:

   (A) $110,000
   (B) 60% of $110,000
   (C) $46,000
   (D) 80% of $110,000

5. The maximum interest rate permitted by California's usury law on real property loans negotiated by real estate brokers is:

   (A) 10%
   (B) The Federal Reserve Bank's discount rate
   (C) The Federal Reserve Bank's discount rate plus 5%
   (D) Not limited by the usury law

6. For a lender who could make a 75% conventional loan, the maximum VA guaranteed loan amount would be:

   (A) $46,000
   (B) $75,000
   (C) $108,000
   (D) $184,000

7. Cal-Vet loans secure the debt with:

   (A) A mortgage
   (B) A land contract
   (C) A deed
   (D) A deed of trust

8. Cal-Vet loans allow no secondary financing.

   (A) True
   (B) False

9. With the creation of FHLMC:

   (A) An additional secondary loan market was created
   (B) A step was made toward loan document uniformity
   (C) Loan processing was created similar to VA/FHA standards
   (D) All of above

10. FNMA:

    (A) Is a stockholder owned corporation
    (B) Is normally a direct lender
    (C) Guarantees mortgage-backed notes
    (D) Is not interested in the secondary market

Chapter 15
Other Transactions
Encountered in Escrow

HOLDING ESCROWS

The "holding escrow" is the classic example of escrow's role as a stakeholder. A typical situation involves the escrowholder holding stakes (usually money or documents) that are released upon performance of a condition. Title insurance is not involved here and, therefore, the instructions can be tailor-made to fit the needs of the transaction. Some situations that might involve the holding escrow are:

Contests Prizes for an athletic or other contest are often deposited with an impartial holder for future distribution in accordance with the terms of the contest.

Subdivision Reservations Escrow may be used for taking reservations on a subdivision project that is being sold using the Preliminary Public Report ("pink report") issued by the Department of Real Estate prior to receipt of the Final Public Report.

Construction Funds Distribution of construction loan proceeds under the terms of a building loan agreement may be handled through an escrow.

Stock Distribution — Transfer of stock that represents majority interest in a corporation often involves an escrow. This is an extremely specialized transaction, with regulatory agency involvement, so only personnel who are totally familiar with the needs of the parties and the intricacies of this process should handle such transactions. It parallels the real estate escrow process, with different subject matter. Some basic requirements are:

Offer to Purchase. An offer to purchase is made to the stockholders, executed by the buyer in clear and distinct language. Depending upon the nature of the enterprise, approvals may be required by appropriate regulatory agencies.

Compliance. The basic escrow instruction between buyer and seller must be in compliance with the purchase offer.

Funds. Costs of acquisition, availability of purchase money, price per share, and the minimum number of shares required to complete the purchase must be spelled out in detail in the instruction of the parties.

Delivery. If the purchaser's terms are not complied with, instructions should state how the shares deposited are to be returned, preferably registered or certified mail.

Processing Cost. The cost to the escrowholder in a transaction of this complexity should not be underestimated, and the service should be priced accordingly.

Advice. Legal counsel should be secured.

Commodities Escrows — Many escrow agents have been asked to handle the transfer of warehoused or sequestered merchandise (e.g., in a safe deposit box) such as gold, silver, platinum, precious gems, and so on. Because the escrowholder has little or no control over such merchandise and no way of realistically establishing its true value, escrows of this nature are usually avoided unless suitable controls have been established.

Other Holding Situations — The subject matter of an escrow is almost endless. The key to the successful conclusion of each transaction is the reduction of the intent of the parties to a meaningful instruction capable of legal compliance by the escrowholder.

SALE OF A TRUST DEED

Many of the institutional loans originated today change hands during the life of the loan. They are bought and sold in the secondary mortgage market, and like other sales, these transactions may go through escrow.

Mortgage Banking   **Origins.** The mortgage banking industry emerged from its infancy in the 1930s to a powerful force in the marketplace following World War II. The original objective of mortgage banking was to import real estate investment capital from the East Coast to the capital-deprived West. A mortgage banker would originate the loan and sell it to an eastern investor.

Desirable Investments. The most popular loans for this type of transaction were those insured by the Federal Housing Administration and guaranteed by the Veterans Administration. With the advent of more uniform conventional lending documents under the influence of the Federal National Mortgage Association and the Federal Home Loan Mortgage Corporation, the conventional loan has increased in attractiveness as an investment.

Procedure. Upon discovery of a suitable investor for the mortgages, the mortgage banker sells the mortgages but continues to act as agent of the investor for purposes of payment collection, administration of impound accounts, and general stewardship of the terms between borrower and lender. As payment for these services, the mortgage banker receives a loan administration or "servicing" fee.

Widening Market. Today the traditional mortgage banker has been joined by other institutional lenders, formerly considered primary lenders. Banks, savings and loans, insurance companies, savings banks, credit unions and others now make, sell, and service loans for the secondary market as a very profitable ancillary activity.

Processing   **Focal Instrument.** Each escrow transaction has a primary instrument as its focal point. In a sale escrow this is the deed; in a real estate loan escrow it is the trust deed. The actual evidence of the debt is a note or promise of the borrower to pay the lender under the terms of the indebtedness.

Assignment. If the holder of the note secured by the deed of trust desires to sell the ownership interest, the instrument of transfer is the *assignment of trust deed*. The purchaser may require an escrow and title insurance coverage to assure his receipt of satisfactory evidence of title to the indebtedness.

Escrow   The purpose of the sale of trust deed escrow is to assure that the **Instructions** conditions of transfer are met prior to consummation of the transaction. The basic escrow instruction (Exhibit 58) is designed with this purpose in mind. Accordingly, it addresses the following:

Consideration. The opening sentence describes the consideration passing in the transaction.

Description of Debt. Paragraph 1 describes the details of the indebtedness (trust deed and note) being transferred, including the payment dates, interest rate, monthly payment amount, current balance, and date of maturity. Often the debt is sold at a discount. This simply means that the purchase price is less than the current balance. In the example the discount is almost 20%, which is not uncommon in the case of relatively new loans (less than a year and a half) with an extended period (more than 10 years) remaining until maturity.

Description of Property. In paragraph 2 the real estate secured by the indebtedness is described both formally by use of a legal description and informally by street address. The recording reference of the trust deed is included to identify with absolute certainty the indebtedness involved in this transfer.

Title Insurance. In Paragraph 3 the assignor is asked to provide the title policy insuring his trust deed, to be forwarded to the title company together with the assignment of trust deed. The escrowholder would then provide instructions to record the assignment upon further instructions if the title company is in a position to insure the title.

☐ *Transfer Endorsement*. Such insurance would normally take the form of an endorsement to the original title policy covering the validity of the transfer. The transfer should also be recorded on the reverse of the note in language matching that of the instructions, such as:

> Fresno, California, April 15, 1990
>
> For value received, the undersigned hereby assigns to John Assignee and Mary Assignee, husband and wife, as community property the within note together with all rights accrued or to accrue under the deed of trust securing same as far as the same relates to this note without recourse.
>
> s/ A.B. Lender

☐ *Other Endorsements*. Various endorsements are available to existing lenders, including insurance of an additional loan advance, priority over mechanics' liens after completion of construction, and so on. Your title insurer is an excellent source of information in determining the endorsement that fits the need of a particular loan transaction.

Assignment of Trust Deed. In this transaction the basic document of transfer is the assignment of trust deed, referred to in paragraph 4. The principal elements of this document are:

☐ Identification of the indebtedness by parties and recording data.

☐ Operative language ". . . hereby transfers and assigns to . . ." In this case it would be A.B. Lender transferring to Mr. and Mrs. Assignee.

☐ Execution (affixing of a signature) by the assignor, A.B. Lender.

☐ To make the document acceptable for recordation, acknowledgment of the assignor's signature by a notary is required.

□ The escrowholder may provide the legal description of the property on the document, although recording reference of the original indebtedness is sufficient to accomplish this purpose.

Request for Notice. Even though holders of senior indebtedness (in this case Anytown Savings and Loan) are required to provide a copy of any notice of default of their loan to all junior encumbrance holders, the period allowed for rendering this notice is 30 days. By filing a specific request for notice for the benefit of the assignee (Paragraph 5), this notice period is reduced to 10 days and the assignee is assured that it will be mailed to the proper address.

Fire Insurance. Loan purchasers want to be sure that their interest is reflected properly in the fire insurance policy that covers the property so that they are able to assert their position in case of fire loss. Paragraph 6 covers this by requesting the escrowholder to assign the current holder's interest on the fire policy.

Special Instructions. The special instructions in this case involve the protection of the assignee (purchaser).

□ As verification of the assignor's representation that the loan balance is $18,525, the assignee has requested that this balance be verified by the payors (trustors or successors).

□ Because the trust deed is relatively new, the purchasers have required, in addition, that a credit report be rendered on the payors in order that the purchasers can determine if their investment is a prudent credit risk.

□ The balance of the instruction concerns binding the parties to the terms of this transaction and the allocation of charges. Here the assignor is paying all costs.

SUBDIVISION ESCROWS

Holding the funds for a subdivision escrow is only part of a much more involved story. Subdividing has become a complex and costly process. As a result, the time involved from the inception of the project to sale and closing of the finished project has doubled and tripled. In handling escrows of this nature, the cost of holding open escrow inventory over time must be considered in establishing fees. This is an area of specialization that is the exclusive province of certain escrowholders providing service to builders.

The Subdivision Process The conversion of raw land to a completed project is a journey that involves planning and execution by the combined team of subdivision engineer, builder, lender, and escrowholder.

Land Acquisition. After completion of a feasibility study to determine the suitability of a project, the builder must make financial arrangements to consummate the purchase and enter into escrow for its acquisition.

Review and Permit Process. Preparation of topographical maps, test borings for soil study, review by governmental agencies, and so on, culminate in approval and recordation of a subdivision map, and the issuance of a final public report by the Real Estate Commissioner's office. Environmental impact reports must often be prepared and submitted. If the property falls within the purview of the Coastal Commission, an additional permit to construct must be obtained over and above the one required from the city or county planning department.

Escrow Processing A subdivision escrow involves the basic sale escrow instruction with adaptations to meet specific requirements of the subdivision process.

Repetitive Documentation. Escrowholders who handle subdivisions take advantage of multiple transactions with similar requirements. Instructions can be preprinted or stored in a computer. Today this type of transaction is highly automated to reduce the cost of processing.

Reservations under Preliminary Report. A typical subdivision escrow evolves as follows: If the sales program is established under the Preliminary Report (pink), a reservation form is prepared by the subdivider and the escrowholder and an escrow depository established. Individual deposits are then taken from potential buyers to reserve their lots (Exhibit 59) until sales are authorized under the white Public Report.

Public Report. Upon receipt of the Public Report by the subdivider, it is forwarded to the escrowholder. In this report any required bonding (either cash or fidelity) is spelled out as it relates to offsites, payment of taxes, required community facilities, or other provisions. The white form also outlines any special requirements for the escrow instructions. For example, if the subdivision is within an area designated by the Department of Housing and Urban Development as a "Flood Hazard," special flood insurance will be required.

Review of Escrow Instructions. All of the appropriate provisions for escrow instructions would be included by the escrowholder in a sample sale escrow instruction submitted in writing for the subdivider's approval and provided to the Department of Real Estate for approval as to form. This is usually done through the title company that is processing the tract map for the subdivider and his engineer. Any omissions or corrections in the instructions would be communicated from that source.

Master File. Timing is extremely important to the builder customer, so a complete status report of the project, provided periodically, is essential. One method used to keep centralized control of the paperwork in a subdivision project is to establish a master file for pertinent documents. Some of the items that would be included in this file are:

☐ A copy of the Department of Real Estate Public Report.

☐ A copy of the general plan declaration of restrictions previously recorded by the builder.

□ The homeowners' association by-laws and articles of incorporation, for planned unit developments or condominium projects.

□ The original agreement with the builder relating to fees for services provided.

□ The original instructions concerning payment of real estate commission.

□ A complete address list for the tract by lot number.

□ Name(s) and address(es) of any construction or other lender, for purposes of obtaining a master demand covering the entire indebtedness and appropriate release requirements. Any loan of record is required to establish a partial release price per lot.

□ Proration instructions relative to taxes (normally unsegregated on the roll) and homeowners' association dues, if applicable.

□ For a homeowners' association, the name and address of the management company.

□ Name, address, and telephone number of the insurance agent holding the master policy, as well as information regarding the premium payment as part of the association dues and appropriate builder/seller instructions if prorations are required.

Preliminary Title Report Upon completion of the master file with the supporting instructions, the title insurer of the tract is asked to provide a master preliminary title report. Each individual lot escrow should also contain a copy of a preliminary report covering that lot.

Condo and PUD Rights. If a planned unit development or condominium is involved, all appurtenant rights, such as common areas, storage units, and garages should be considered before a sample deed is prepared by the escrowholder or title insurer, to be reprinted for use in the subdivision escrow transaction after review and appraisal by the builder/seller and the title company.

Required Minimum Sales. In some cases (usually condominiums) a certain percentage of sales is required before any escrows can close. This is controlled by state Department of Real Estate regulations and can sometimes be changed by the builder/seller's posting of a bond.

Differences from Other Sale Escrows From this point on the subdivision escrow is similar to any sale escrow described in earlier chapters. The basic differences are that the subject of the escrow is property under construction and that certain economies of volume exist.

New Construction. In new construction, special requirements for certifications and personal property are needed, as well as appropriate provisions in the escrow instructions concerning warranties.

Options and Extras. Although a basic sales price has been set for each lot, the purchase agreement and/or deposit receipt must be scrutinized before drawing instructions because of extras or options available. For example, purchasers may take a carpet allowance or accept the carpet that the builder furnishes; this is an option. Extras might include central air conditioning, a lawn sprinkler system, landscaping, and upgraded wall or floor covering and/or appliances.

Completion Notice. To obtain title insurance on the individual lot, a notice of completion is required. To retain control of the transaction, this instrument should be recorded through escrow because it must be recorded within 10 days of completion to be valid. Normally, a buyer does not have to wait 30 or 60 days following recording of the notice of completion because the builder usually has an indemnity agreement with the title company.

Economies of Volume. Escrow instructions may be adaptable to preprinting or the use of computer-generated forms. Instruments such as deeds, trust deeds, etc., may also be preprinted and require only lot/parcel numbers and the names of the purchaser/trustors.

Future Resales. Subdivision escrows have proved to be a very profitable source of business for escrowholders since they can lead to the more profitable resale escrows from original lot purchasers.

LEASEHOLD ESCROWS

There are certain instances where the title to property transferred is not in fee. These transfers can also involve escrow.

Nature of Lease Ogden describes a lease on real property as "a grant or conveyance by the owner of an estate to another of a portion of his interest therein for a term less than his own." The basic parties to this document are the lessor or maker (landlord) and the lessee (tenant) upon whom the grant is conferred. The operative language in a document of this nature is: "A hereby leases, lets, and demises to B the following described property." The interest conveyed by this document is referred to as a leasehold estate. Under certain conditions, lessees may, in turn, convey all or a portion of their interest to other parties and this new interest becomes a subleasehold estate.

Types of Leases. There are two basic forms of lease that can be involved in escrows:

☐ *Land Lease.* Such a contract conveys the right to use the land, and subsequent improvements, for a specified number of years under the terms and conditions provided (the subject matter of most leasehold escrows).

□ *Space Lease*. A space lease involves a particular suite or unit located on the land. Examples are apartment leases, industrial and office space, and commercial uses.

Effect on Title. Since a lease is a contract between parties and its contents are subject to interpretation, title insurance is particularly important where a sizable monetary investment is involved. There are so many items to consider in determining the validity of a lease that title insurance is a modest investment to protect the transfer of this estate, and assure that the condition of title is in accordance with the wishes of the parties to the transfer.

Investment Advantages. The lease, as a form of security device (since it is indirectly a form of installment financing), has become extremely popular for lessors to avoid the capital gains aspect of a sale, and for lessees who do not want to tie up investment capital in real estate.

□ *Tax Effects*. A dynamic example of the use of a leasehold estate was the development of the first residential subdivisions in the Irvine Ranch in the Orange County area of California during the mid-1960s. The developers' acquisition cost of this vast area was minimal and the use of a lease tended to minimize the tax effects.

□ *Construction Financing*. Many large industrial and commercial buildings have been constructed by lessees who obtained leasehold financing to erect multimillion dollar structures. The leasehold transaction has become a significant factor in industry, commerce, and residential development.

Escrow Processing Other than the instruments of creation and transfer, the handling of a leasehold escrow is not dissimilar to a loan escrow, if the leasehold is to be encumbered.

Depository Function. When handling the transfer of this estate an escrowholder would normally be involved with the depository of an assignment of the leasehold interest to a new recipient (transferee).

Special Instruments. Special instruments dealing with leasehold, such as rent rolls, offset statements, estoppel certificates, declarations of merger, and other documents may serve as an integral part of the escrow.

Legal Counsel. In a majority of leasehold escrows, both parties are represented by legal counsel. Note that the escrow officer would not prepare the basic lease document, as that would be tantamount to the practice of law.

MOBILEHOME ESCROWS

In an area where the economy is geared to recreation and/or retirement living, sale or transfer of mobilehomes (manufactured homes) can be big business. The dealer who sells the mobilehome, the trucker who transports it, and the contractor who sets up the unit and installs accessories all participate in the economic fruits reaped by this industry. Sale of mobilehomes and the resulting escrows may involve either leased or fee land, but the principal ingredient of this transfer is personal property. Mobilehome escrows are complex because of the number of regulatory laws and agencies involved.

Health and Safety Code   The primary law governing the transfer of a mobilehome unit in the state of California is the Mobilehomes-Manufactured Housing Act of 1980, Health and Safety Code Sections 18000 et seq., enforced by the Department of Housing and Community Development (HCD).

Escrow Required. Section 18035 of the Health and Safety Code establishes that most mobilehome transfers require an escrow as a matter of law. Provisions include:

☐ *Basic Requirement.* "For every sale by a dealer of a new or used manufactured home or mobilehome subject to registration under this part, the dealer shall execute in writing and obtain the buyer's signature on a purchase order, conditional sale contract, or other document evidencing the purchase . . ., shall establish an escrow account with an escrow agent, and shall cause to be deposited into that escrow account any cash or cash equivalent received at any time prior to the close of escrow . . . .

The parties shall provide for escrow instructions that identify the fixed amounts of the deposit, downpayment, and balance due prior to the closing consistent with the amounts set forth in the purchase documents and receipt for deposit . . . .

If an item of cash equivalent is, due to its size, incapable of physical delivery to the escrow holder, the property may be held by the dealer . . . and, if available, its certificate of title shall be delivered to the escrow holder."

☐ *State Notification.* A notice of escrow opening (and cancellation, if it occurs) must be filed with the Housing and Community Development Department.

☐ *Lien Status Reports.* Demands for statements of lien release or assumption are to be sent to the legal owner and junior lienholders, and a demand for tax clearance certificate to the county tax collector.

☐ *Accessories.* "If a portion of the amount in escrow is for accessories, . . . that portion shall not be released until the accessories are actually installed."

□ *Independent Escrow.* The escrowholder may not be an agency subject to the Department of Corporations in which the mobilehome dealer or seller holds more than 5% ownership interest.

□ *Other Provisions.* In addition the code includes a definition of a mobilehome unit, further escrow and dealer duties and responsibilities, the role of the deposit receipt and Truth in Lending disclosures, and penalties for non-compliance.

□ *Installation on Foundation System.* Permanent installation (Section 18551) converts the unit to a real property improvement, which modifies the escrow and registration requirements. A document for recordation indicating delivery and placement on a foundation system is to be presented to the escrowholder.

Real Estate Law Real estate brokers who are under the supervision of the Real Estate Commissioner may handle the sale of a used mobilehome unit that has been registered for more than one year.

Real Estate Transfers. Most mobilehome transactions which include the transfer of real estate (mobilehome lot) are handled by real estate licensees.

Dealer's License. If this activity is more than just an occasional sale, the broker may be required to be licensed as a mobilehome dealer.

Vehicle Code Up to 1980, mobilehome sales were governed by Section 11950 of the Motor Vehicle Code.

Grandfather Provision. Mobilehomes which were registered with the DMV prior to 1980, and have been continuously registered since, may remain registered as vehicles as long as registration is kept current.

Tax Effect. Taxes on a mobilehome registered as a vehicle will almost certainly be lower than local property taxes would be for the same home.

Escrow Processing If mobilehome transactions are handled frequently, escrowholders should develop specialized memorandum or take sheets and instruction forms. The sample take sheet in Exhibit 60 outlines the necessary information and procedures. This form is for sales of used homes by non-dealers, the type of transaction most likely to be encountered in the real estate field.

Memo Box. Sources of funds are summarized as in any other sale escrow.

Closing Date. This is also standard information for any escrow.

Property Description. This section completely describes the mobilehome unit, including serial number, Department of Housing and Community Development identifying number, size of unit, manufacturer, model, and location.

Parties' Names. Again, this is standard information. Note, however, that in section 8 below, the buyer and lender are identified using personal property terminology, as "registered owner" and "legal owner."

Personal Property Documents. Since personal property is involved,

☐ The documents transferred are the *certificate of title* and the *registration card*.

☐ As with other personal property, a *bill of sale* (Exhibit 61) may be used to transfer interest in the coach.

☐ Financing documents are a *security agreement* which secures the debt, and the *financing statement* which is filed with the Secretary of State evidencing the debt.

☐ If real estate is involved, a *blanket trust deed* incorporating the real and personal property aspects may be used.

Fees and Charges. In addition to allocating commission and escrow fees, this section covers the special HCD requirements of *license fee*, *use tax* (sales tax: used homes subject to local property tax are exempt), and *transfer fee*.

Agent's Duties. Items in this section specific to mobilehomes are:

☐ Title search obtained from Department of Housing and Community Development

☐ Notice of escrow opening

☐ Park rental agreement and approval of buyer

☐ County tax clearance certificate.

Many Variables. Escrow processing and documentation requirements vary extensively depending on the mobilehome's age, siting, registration category, etc. The full code should be consulted, and advice sought from experienced processors.

BULK SALES

Another personal property escrow transaction is the "bulk sale" or "bulk transfer," the sale of a business as described in Division 6 of the Uniform Commercial Code:

"Any transfer not in the ordinary course of business by a retail or wholesale merchant or by a baker, cafe or restaurant owner, garage owner, or cleaner and dyer of a substantial part of his inventory, is subject to this Division as is a transfer of a substantial part of his equipment. The term 'transfer' includes the creation of a security interest."

Specialized Fields Many firms handle this type of business exclusively as their only form of escrow processing. This also holds true for brokers who deal in business opportunities. This field is somewhat contra-cyclical to real estate sales. The business opportunity field flourishes during periods of lagging home sales.

Purpose The basic purpose of the bulk sale process when a business is being sold is to afford protection to creditors of the business, so they can submit unpaid bills for payment. For this reason, the sale is advertised in legal publications as a notice to creditors and closing cannot be effected until 12 business days after posting date (as defined in section G107a of the Business and Professions Code).

Procedure The basic procedure is similar to other escrows, but a number of additional documents are involved.

Take Sheet and Instruction. The basic information for the sale is outlined in the take sheet (Exhibit 62) and converted to an instruction (Exhibit 63). In addition, a check sheet, Bulk Sale Register (Exhibit 64), is used to assure the escrowholder that the flow of paperwork appropriate to each transaction is secured.

U.C.C. Requirements. "Sale" here includes a security interest (chattel mortgage). Division 9 of the Uniform Commercial Code outlines the requirements in perfecting a security interest.

Real Estate. There can be an additional factor, the transfer of the real estate which houses the business, calling for a sale escrow in conjunction with this personal property transaction.

Liquor License Transfers These involve further processing requirements with appropriate questions on a specialized take sheet being used for the additional information.

Notice. The notice and publication form is different and the premises are posted by the department of Alcoholic Beverage Control (ABC) for a period of 30 days prior to license transfer.

Additional Instructions. Two additional forms, liquor license supplemental instruction (Exhibit 65) and creditor priority liquor license transfers (Exhibit 66) are added to the basic bulk escrow instruction for sale of the business.

EXCHANGES

One of the more creative areas of real estate involves the exchange of property, popularized by Section 1031 of the Internal Revenue Code. An exchange may be perceived as a multiple sale and will be presented accordingly.

Equity-Based Transaction Real estate practitioners are generally attuned to sales price or loan amount as the basis of the transaction. In the case of exchanges, equity becomes the basis of the transaction. Section 1031 of the Internal Revenue Code states:

"No gain or loss shall be recognized if property held for productive use in a trade or business or for investment (not including stock in trade or other property held primarily for sale, nor stocks, bonds, notes, choses in action, certificates of trust or beneficial interest, or other securities or evidences of indebtedness or interest) is exchanged for property of a like kind to be held either for productive use in trade or business or investment . . ."

Legal Aspects
Escrow processing cannot deal with the legal or tax aspects of this transaction. This is a job for legal professionals. Some general observations can guide the escrow processing.

Tax Aspects. The transaction may be fully tax deferred, partially tax deferred, or offering no tax deferment whatsoever depending on circumstances and the ever-changing tax laws. This has traditionally been a popular device for tax deferment.

Structure. The device should be structured by the exchange specialist or legal counsel, not the escrowholder. The escrow is a repository for instructions, not the inventor. In taking the basic data, exchanges should be viewed as a series of sales which may, for simplicity's sake, be diagrammed to derive the net result.

Escrow Processing
Exhibits 67 and 68 show how data for a simple exchange of parcels A and B would be taken down for escrow purposes. This intent is then converted to an instruction as shown in Exhibit 69.

Treated as Sale. Whether or not this is technically considered a sale, sale related items such as funds clearance, retrofit matters, local ordinance requirements, and FIRPTA are issues that must be incorporated in the instructions, as applicable.

Settlement Statement. The complexity of this transaction is reflected in the settlement statement shown in Exhibit 70.

Analysis. Visualization can be helpful. Exhibit 71 illustrates diagramming of a typical "accommodator" transaction, where one of the exchanging parties does not desire to retain ownership.

OTHER ESCROWS

Government Acquisition
Another expansive area is the acquisition of property by government agencies through negotiation and purchase or by means of eminent domain proceedings. Special legal and title requirements, such as acceptance by the governmental body, condemnation guaranties, and so forth, represent another complex field of specialization in the closing process.

Unlimited Applications
Whether it be the transfer of stock, an undivided interest in a cooperative apartment, the ownership of an ocean vessel, sale of an aircraft, a herd of cattle and feed, timber rights, mineral rights, or copyrights—whatever the ownership of real or personal property may be, escrow or the presence of an escrow relationship may be involved.

ESCROW INSTRUCTIONS
FOR PURCHASE OF TRUST DEED

DATE ___4/15/88___
ESCROW NO. ___12345___

ESCROW COMPANY

I/We will hand you the sum of $15,000, which you are authorized and instructed to use when you can hold for my/our account the following:

1. Deed of Trust Note for $19,500, dated __12/6/1987__ executed by __Jane B. Trustor__ in favor of __A. B. Lender__, with interest from _____ on unpaid principal at the rate of __10__ per cent per annum; principal and interest payable in installments of $__195.00__ or more on the __1st__ day of each and every month, next payment due on __5/1/88__ and continuing until __11/30/99__, at which time the then remaining unpaid principal and interest shall become due and payable. Said note __does not__ contain an acceleration clause in the event of the sale or transfer of subject property. Present unpaid balance of note is $__18,525.00__

2. Deed of Trust securing said note covering property in the County of __Mendocino__, State of California, described as Lot __23__, Tract __2468__, as per Map recorded in Book __222__ Pages __19__ of Maps O.R.. Property is known as __1357 Home Ct., Anytown, California__.

3. Copy of Title Policy __#98765__ showing above trust deed subject to:
   a. Taxes for the fiscal year __2nd half of 1988-89__.
   b. Covenants, conditions, restrictions, reservations, rights, rights of way and easements of record.
   c. First Deed of Trust in favor of __Anytown Savings and Loan, in the original__.
   amount of $156,000.

4. Prepare and record Assignment of the above Deed of Trust and Note in favor of _____ John Assignee and Mary Assignee, h/w as community property, __without__ recourse.

5. Request for Notice of Default to be recorded in favor of assignee.

6. Memo of Fire Insurance Policy showing mortgagee clause in favor of assignee.

SPECIAL INSTRUCTIONS:
Assignor to provide offset statement from trustor or successors in interest to verify loan balance set forth in paragraph 1.

Escrow to obtain credit report on trustor or successors in interest satisfactory to assignee. Assignees' approval or disapproval of credit report will not be unreasonably withheld and will be given within five days from receipt thereof.

The undersigned reserves the right to demand return of funds and cancellations of these instructions at any time after 30 (thirty) days from date, if you are unable to comply with these instructions. We hereby approve the above instructions in their entirety and hereby acknowledge receipt of a copy of same.

__John Assignee__
Signature

__Mary Assignee__
Signature

Address

Phone

We hereby approve the above instructions in their entirety and hereby acknowledge receipt of a copy of same and will hand you assignment and documents as called for above, when you can hold for our account in this escrow the sum of $15,000, less all expenses incurred herein.

__A.B. Lender__
Signature

__Fresno, CA__
Address

Exhibit 58

RESERVATION OF LOT, PARCEL OR UNIT
THIS IS A *TENTATIVE RESERVATION* AGREEMENT
AND IS *NOT* A CONTRACT TO PURCHASE

Wilson Development Company
_____, hereinafter called

"Owner", acknowledges receipt from ___Gladys Burden_____

hereinafter called "Prospective Buyer", of the sum of $ _/000 —_____ ,

for the reservation of Lot, Parcel or Unit Number _32_____

of Tract Number _7649_____

(If no Tract number, give name of Project)

City of _Irvine_____ County of _Orange_____

State of _California_____ .

$104,900 —

Owner hereby reserves said Lot, Parcel or Unit for _____

Gladys Burden

(Name of Prospective Buyer)

of _18369 Van Oppen Place, Atwater, CA 93687_____

(Address)

Owner agrees that the aforesaid deposit and a signed copy of this Reservation Agreement shall be placed in the following neutral escrow depository:

_____ Commonwealth Escrow Co.

(Name)

_4500 Campus Drive_____ Newport Beach, Ca. 92660

(Address)

Execution (signing) of this Reservation Agreement does not create a contractual obligation to buy or sell on the part of either Owner or Prospective Buyer. Either party may cancel this Reservation without incurring liability to the other at any time until Prospective Buyer has read the Real Estate Commissioner's Final Public Report for this subdivision and has executed a contract to purchase the subdivision interest described above. In the event of cancellation by either party, the aforesaid deposit shall be immediately returned to Prospective Buyer without interest or charge.

The price and other terms of purchase will be those set forth in the Contract to Purchase.

This reservation to be voided, if not converted to Purchase agreement within 14 days

OWNER: Wilson Development Co. _____

BY: _____

(Authorized Agent)

PROSPECTIVE BUYER: _____

from this date August 13, 1988

(Date)

/s/ Gladys Burden

Exhibit 59

270 Other Transactions Encountered in Escrow

USED MOBILEHOME SALE ORDER/TAKE FORM
(NON-DEALER)

To: Wells Fargo Escrow Services   Escrow No.: _____

_____   Date: _____

1). Terms of Sale:

     ____ Cash Deposit (Initial deposit) $ _____
     ____ Cash Deposit $ _____
     ____ New Loan (Name and address of lender (legal owner) $ _____
     _____

     ____ Existing loan balance (Name, address and loan no. of lender) $ _____
     _____

     ____ Paid outside of escrow $ _____

     TOTAL CONSIDERATION - (PURCHASE PRICE) $ _____

2). Close of escrow date: _____

3). Mobile Home manufacturer's name _____, Model _____, Year _____,

Serial No.(s) _____, Size (length x width) _____ (excluding hitch),

HCD Insignia No.(s) or Federal Label No.(s) _____, License No.(s) _____,

Presently located at: _____ Park Name: _____

4). **BUYER**   **SELLER**

Name(s): _____   Name(s): _____

Address: _____   Address: _____

_____   _____

Phone Number: (Home) _____   Phone Number: (Home) _____

Phone Number: (Business) _____   Phone Number: (Business) _____

5). Documentation delivered through escrow:

     ____ Registration Card(s)   ____ Certificate(s) of Title
     ____ Application for Registration   ____ Certification of Retail Value and Purchase Price
     ____ Power of Attorney from Seller naming   ____ Power of Attorney from Buyer naming
          as attorney infact   as attorney infact
     ____ Broker(s)' Commission Instructions   ____ Other Dept. of Housing (HCD) Transfer/Registration

Documentation: _____

6). Fees, Charges and Payments:

Paid by Buyer: **Paid by Seller:**

     ____ Commission of $ _____ to: ____ Commission of $ _____ to:
     Name/Address: _____   Name/Address: _____

     ____ Charge for: ☐ Full ☐ One-half Escrow Fee   ____ Charge for: ☐ Full ☐ One-half Escrow Fee

     ____ Other: _____   ____ Other: _____

License fee of $ _____ Use Tax $ _____

Transfer fee of $ _____

7). Duties of Escrow Agent:

     ____ Obtain payoff demand from existing lender for payment at close of escrow.
     ____ Order assumption papers on current loan from existing lender.
     ____ Notify new lender of escrow.
     ____ Obtain (☐ Formal   ☐ Informal) Title Search from HCD ☐ file a Notice of Escrow Opening.
     ____ Obtain Park Rental Agreement Statement.
     ____ Approval of Buyer by Park Manager.
     ____ Obtain Tax Clearance Certificate from County Tax Collector.
     ____ Other: _____

8). Title of new Registered Owner _____ AND/OR _____

Title of new Legal Owner, if any _____

Title of Junior Lienholder, if any _____

9). Adjustments, prorations and other charges upon date of disbursement of all funds and documents: _____

_____

10). ____ Holdback $ _____ from ☐ Seller ☐ Buyer for HCD verification of acceptance of title/registration documents and fees.

     ____ Other: _____

ESC 508(T) (06/84)   COPYRIGHT 1984, WELLS FARGO BANK, N.A.

Exhibit 60

BILL OF SALE

By delivery of this Bill of Sale, Seller,   John Q. Citizen and Jane A. Citizen

ratifies the fact of transfer of title to Buyer,   Fred A. Buyer and Mary Ann Buyer

of that personal property and goods identified as: 1980 Sweethome Mobilehome, Serial Nos. S3449X &
S3449U, License No. AAY4354, DOH Nos. 234567 & 234568

And warrants that title so conveyed is good, and its transfer rightful, and that the goods are free of any security
interest, lien or encumbrance of which Buyer, at the time of contracting had no knowledge.

Signed: ___September 6_____, 19_88___

_____   _____
                                         John Q. Citizen

_____   _____
                                         Jane A. Citizen

Exhibit 61

**BULK SALE PRELIMINARY
ESCROW INSTRUCTIONS
(Liquor and Non-Liquor)**

ESCROW NO. _____
DATE: _____

SELLER/TRANSFEROR

ADDRESS: SOCIAL SECURITY NO.
Zip Code: FEDERAL TAX NO.
                                                           TELEPHONE:

BUYER/TRANSFEREE:

ADDRESS: SOCIAL SECURITY NO.
Zip Code: .   FEDERAL TAX NO.
                                                           TELEPHONE:

NAME OF BUSINESS:
ADDRESS OF BUSINESS: BUSINESS PHONE:

If Liquor License is being transferred, type of license: _____ LICENSE NO. _____
Previous Business Name(s) and Addresses for past 3 years:

SALE DATE:
POSSESSION DATE: BREAKDOWN OF SALES PRICE

                                                           Stock in Trade $_____
If Liquor Transfer & proceeds are insufficient to satisfy creditors, will Seller   Goodwill $_____
   deposit additional cash? _____   Fixtures & Equip. $_____
                                                           License (Liquor) $_____
CONSIDERATION: $_____, payable as follows: Leasehold $_____
   Cash through escrow: $_____   Covenant $_____
   Note to Seller $_____   Secured/Unsecured Other $_____
   Other $_____

Secured/Unsecured Note in favor of _____ For $_____ dated _____
Interest at _____ from _____ payable _____
Principal and interest payable in _____ installments of $_____ each, or more, on the _____ day of each and
every _____ beginning _____ and continuing until _____

SECURITY AGREEMENT:
Financing Statement to be filed with Secretary of State:
BILL OF SALE to cover: Materials/Supplies/Merchandise/Inventory/Fixtures/Equipment/Covenant/Leasehold/Other:
      *If itemized list of fixtures and equipment, who will provide *typewritten* list? _____

PUBLICATION:

PRORATIONS AND/OR ADJUSTMENTS:
   LEASE OR RENTS: Monthly @_____ paid to _____
                    Deposit and/or Advance Rental of $_____ .
   TAXES: Personal Property
              Sales and/or Use—Reimbursement
              Real Estate
              Other
   INSURANCE:

RELEASE CERTIFICATES
   State Board of Equalization: Through Escrow/Outside: If through escrow, prior to close? _____
   Dept. Benefit Payments: Through Escrow/Outside: If through escrow, prior to close? _____
   If delayed releases, amount of Seller's funds to be impounded pending receipt $_____

UCC-3 Request for Financing Search with Secretary of State? _____ .
   If so, on: Individual(s)—Business name

ESCROW CHARGES:
INVENTORY SERVICE COSTS:

PAY NET PROCEEDS TO:
   Corporate Resolution? _____   Copy of Partnership Agreement? _____

MISCELLANEOUS: CONTINGENCIES:

Exhibit 62

ESCROW NO. __123-B.S.__

Escrow Officer: __Susan Holder__

TO:

ESCROW COMPANY

__Main__ OFFICE __April 10__ , 19 __88__

ESCROW	SUMMARY
Cash through escrow $	__18,000__
Existing obligations $	
New encumbrance $	__5,000__
TOTAL $	__23,000__

1. PRIOR TO __May 15__ 19 __88__ each party will hand you all funds and
2. instructions necessary to enable you to comply with these instructions.
3. The SELLER, __Jose Seller and Marta Seller__
4.
5. whose business address is __Deluxe Coffee Shop__
6. _____ and all of whose other business names and
7. addresses used within three years last past are __None other than subject__
8. __business__
9.
10.
11. will hand you a Bill of Sale executed by Seller to __Chun C. Buy and Ying Li Buy__
12. __husband and wife__ BUYER,
13. whose business address is __321 Via Alegre, Fresno CA__ , for all
14. stock in trade, fixtures, equipment, and good will of a certain __Restaurant__ business
15. known as __Deluxe Coffee Shop__
16. and located at __173 Main Street, Fresno__ , __Fresno__ County, California,
17. and said Buyer will hand you $ __23,000 and any additional funds and documents required to enable you__
18. __to comply with these instructions.__
19. __Seller to provide a covenant not to compete within a 15-mile radius of subject__
20. __business. As a matter of record with which the escrow is not to be concerned, the__
21. __parties acknowledge the following:__
22. __1) Possession to be transferred as of the close of escrow__
23. __2) Sellers will remain for two weeks following close of escrow to provide__
24. __training to the buyers.__
25.
26. __Irrespective of the provisions in Paragraph 13 of page 2 of this instruction, if insuf-__
27. __ficient funds are available to settle all claims filed in this Escrow and Escrowholder__
28. __has not elected to withdraw or file appropriate interpleader proceedings, the note and__
29. __security agreement will be retained by the escrowholder. Escrowholder is directed to__
30. __apply all payments received to creditors in appropriate priorities until all creditors'__
31. __claims be satisfied, at which time the note and security agreement will be released to__
32. __the seller. Such distribution will be at the discretion of the Escrowholder, and seller__
33. __will be responsible for collection costs to be deducted from such payments.__
34.
35. __On or before close of escrow, seller will deposit in this escrow full and complete re-__
36. __leases from State Board of Equalization and the Department of Employment, State of Calif.__
37. Buyer will hand you Note for $ __5,000__ , dated during escrow, due (if straight note) _____ n
38. in favor of __Jose Seller and Marta Seller__
39. or order
40. payable at your Office __as holders designate__
41. interest from __close of escrow__ at rate of __8.0__ per cent per annum, payable __monthly__
42. principal and interest payable $ __50.00__ or more on the __15th__ day of each _____ month,
43. beginning on the __15th__ day of __May__ , 19 __88__
44.
45. _____ and continuing until ~~April~~ __April 15, 1992~~ executed by
46. above Buyer _____ and Security Agreement securing same, covering Fixtures and Equipment,
47. referred to above, together with a Financing Statement executed by Seller and Buyer.
48. Seller and/or Buyer herein will hand you a duly executed "Notice of Bulk Transfer" and/or a "Notice of Intention to Create a Security Interest", affect-
49. ing the above business, which Notice(s), you are hereby authorized and instructed to mail to a local newspaper service with your instructions, to the
50. effect that they shall cause to be RECORDED, in the office of the County Recorder of the County shown in said Notice(s), the original of said Notice(s),
51. at least twelve (12) business days before the Sale Date specified therein AND cause to be PUBLISHED a copy of said Notice(s) one time in a newspaper
52. of general circulation in the appropriate Judicial District or County, at least twelve (12) business days before the Sale date specified therein AND cause
53. to be MAILED, by registered or certified mail, a copy of the Notice at least twelve (12) business days before the Sale date. The Notice(s) provide in part
54. as follows: "The Bulk Transfer will be consummated on or after the __15th__ day of __May__ , 19 __88__
55. at __One__ P.M. at __Trust__ ESCROW COMPANY, __842 Main St.__ ,
56. County of _____ , State of California." You are relieved of all responsibility as to said
57. Notice(s) being published in the correct Judicial District and of any loss or damage suffered in connection therewith.
58. (X) Pro-rate personal property taxes, based on tax bill, as handed escrow, as of __close of escrow__
59. (X) Pro-rate rents to __close of escrow__ based on a monthly rental of $ __500.00__ , paid in advance to: __6-1-88__
60. (X) Debit Buyer and credit Seller with the sum of $ __5,000__ , representing __Goodwill and covenant__
61. (X) Hold for Buyer fire and other insurance, as handed you, and pro-rate to __close of escrow__ __/not to compete__
62. (X) Escrow fees are to be apportioned by Seller agreeing to pay __one-half__ of escrow fees and charges and Buyer agrees to pay __one-half__
63. of the escrow fees and charges.
64. (X) Seller agrees to pay commission of $ __1,500__ to __Shop R.E. Sales__ Broker's license No. __0-5826149__
65. address __322 Main Street, Fresno CA__
66. (X) Hold for Buyer __5-yr. lease__ Lease as handed escrow. Obtain consent to assignment as provided for in said Lease, together
with the necessary assignment thereof in favor of Buyer.
67. (X) At the close of escrow, credit Seller and debit Buyer with the sum of $ __960.00__
based upon fixture and equipment valuation of $ __16,000__ representing a rebate of the
68. California Use Tax previously paid by Seller.
69. (X) Provide a data search (UCC-3) to determine the existence of any outstanding financing statements affecting the property being transferred.

Exhibit 63.1

GENERAL PROVISIONS

1.   If the conditions of this escrow have not been complied with at the time provided on Page 1, or any extension thereof, you are nevertheless to complete the escrow as soon as the conditions, except as to time, have been complied with, unless written demand shall have been made upon you not to complete it.

2.   You will hold the money and documents, other than Notice of Bulk Transfer, in escrow until the closing day specified in said notice, at which time PROVIDED you hold said money and documents and sufficient money is in escrow available to pay all approved bills and claims, together with prorations, your costs and charges and the agent's commission if payable through the escrow, and to enable you to hold the amount of all unapproved bills and claims plus 50% thereof; you will then deliver to the Buyer said Bill of Sale unrecorded, file for record the Financing Statement, if any, and deliver to the Seller, the Security Agreement and Note, if any, described on Page 1, deduct the charges and costs of the escrow which the Seller has agreed to pay, pay all bills and other items which have been approved in writing by Seller, withhold the amount of all unapproved bills and claims plus 50% thereof and pay the balance to the Seller or order.

3.   In the event the funds deposited in escrow are insufficient to pay in full all claims filed and all other cash requirements of the escrow, then delay closing escrow for a period of not less than ten (10) nor more than twenty (20) days from scheduled date of closing, and send a written notice to each creditor, who has filed a claim within two (2) business days after the scheduled date of closing stating the amount of cash deposited in escrow and the percentage which it represents of the aggregate of all claims filed and stating that escrow will be closed at the place, date and time specified by you which shall be not less than ten (10) nor more than twenty (20) days from scheduled date of closing.

4.   You are not to be concerned as to any unpaid beverage, unemployment, old age, social security, personal property or retail sales tax or sales tax on fixtures, equipment, etc., being sold, or any other tax or contribution, or any unpaid salaries or wages, even though Buyer may be personally liable for payment thereof, unless otherwise specifically instructed in this escrow.

5.   No examination of the property described in the Bill of Sale, Financing Statement or any other document deposited in this escrow, or of the title thereto held by Seller or as taken by Buyer, is to be made or procured by you, nor is protection given with regard to the previous matters or as to property purchased on contract or under conditional sale agreement. You are not to be concerned with any transfer of title of any motor vehicles on the records of the Department of Motor Vehicles, laws governing such transfers nor any sales tax in connection therewith.

6.   Seller will file forthwith in escrow a signed copy of Seller's letter notifying any secured party under an existing security agreement or other security instrument of the Seller's intended sale, transfer or further encumbrance, and stating the name and place of residence of the intended Buyer and/or new secured party.

7.   You are to pay on demand, whether or not this escrow closes, any charges incurred by you on our behalf. Regardless of the consummation of the transactions contemplated hereby, and without limiting the joint and several liability of Buyer and Seller for all compensation, fees, costs and expenses herein, the Buyer and Seller, jointly and severally, agree to pay to you any expenses which you have incurred or become obligated for in this escrow and a reasonable escrow fee for the services contracted by the undersigned to be rendered by you and such expenses, if any, and fees shall be paid and put into Escrow before any cancellation, consummation or other termination of this Escrow is effective. Buyer and Seller agree that said charges for expenses and fees may be apportioned between the Buyer and Seller in a manner which, in your sole discretion you shall deem equitable, and that your decision in that respect shall be binding and conclusive upon Buyer and Seller. Any documents or funds deposited with you by the Buyer and/or Seller may be retained by you as a lien to secure to you the reimbursement and payment of expenses, if any, and fees as herein provided.

8.   Use your usual instrument forms and insert dates and terms on instruments if executed incomplete in such particulars, provided the insertions comply with our written instructions.

9.   Make each proration on the basis of a 30-day month. The singular word shall mean the plural or vice versa. Obtain Beneficiary's Statement to verify the encumbrance principal balance; make adjustments and prorations required based on the figures therein set forth. All funds and monies deposited in this escrow shall be deposited by you in an account designated "Escrow Fund Account" with any bank, trust company, title insurance company, savings and loan association, building and loan association, industrial loan company, credit union, insurer or licensed escrow agent, or subescrow agent, and such deposits shall be deemed deposited in accordance with the meaning of these instructions.

10.   You will, on behalf of the parties hereto, assign any fire and other insurance policies handed you by Seller. You are not to be concerned with the coverage in said policies, and you may assume that the premiums have been paid and that the policies have not been hypothecated.

11.   If the property being transferred is held in joint tenancy any cash derived therefrom in this escrow shall be joint tenancy funds.

12.   You shall have no obligation to inform Buyer and/or Seller regarding any transaction or facts within your knowledge concerning the property described herein. You shall have no liability for the sufficiency or correctness as to form, manner of execution, or validity of any instruments deposited, nor as to identity, authority, or liability of any person executing the instruments. Your liability shall be confined to the matters specifically stated in our instructions accepted by you.

13.   Buyer and Seller understand that, upon the expiration of 180 days after scheduled closing date and any time thereafter, you reserve the right to discontinue the escrow and return all documents and monies to the depositors thereof less your costs and fees. You shall have the right, not limited by the provisions of the preceding sentence and of paragraph 7 above, to discontinue and withdraw from this escrow at any time.

14.   Should you, before or after close of escrow, receive or become aware of any conflicting demands or claims with respect to this escrow or the rights of any of the parties hereto, or any money or property deposited herein or affected hereby, you shall have the right to discontinue any or all further acts on your part until such conflict is resolved to your satisfaction, and you shall have the further right to commence or defend any court proceedings for the determination of such conflict. Buyer and Seller jointly and severally agree to pay all costs, damages, judgments and expenses, including reasonable attorney's fees, with regard to any such proceedings or otherwise suffered or incurred by you in connection with or arising out of this escrow.

15.   You are hereby authorized to destroy or otherwise dispose of any and all documents, papers, instructions, correspondence and other material pertaining to this Escrow at the expiration of five (5) years from the date hereof.

16.   These Instructions may be executed in counterparts, each of which so executed shall, irrespective of the date of its execution and delivery, be deemed an original and said counterparts together shall constitute one and the same instrument. Any amended and/or supplemental instructions hereto must be in writing, executed by all of the parties hereto, and deposited with you.

17.   The signature of Buyer and Seller on any documents and instructions pertaining to this escrow indicates their unconditional acceptance and approval of the same. Buyer and Seller, and each of them, hereby acknowledge receipt of a copy of these Instructions and their agreement to each and all of the terms and provisions hereof.

```
BUYER AND SELLER HAVE READ AND AGREE TO ALL THE INSTRUCTIONS
ON THE REVERSE HEREOF AND THE ABOVE GENERAL PROVISIONS
```

Seller's Signature ___(s) Jose Seller___	Buyer's Signature ___(s) Chun C. Buy___	
___(s) Marta Seller___	___(s) Ying Li Buy___	
Street Address ___321 Via Alegre___	Street Address ___328 Third Street___	
City and Zip Code ___Fresno , CA 90831 (298) 753-8101___ (Telephone)	City and Zip Code ___Fresno , CA 90831 (298) 754-3271___ (Telephone)	

Exhibit 63.2

"BULK SALE REGISTER"

ESCROW NO. _____

SELLER (Secured Party—Transferor—Licensee)		BUYER (Debtor-Transferee)	
Escrow Instructions		Escrow Instructions	
Notice of Intent to Create Security Int.		Notice of Bulk Transfer	
Notice of Intent to Transfer Liquor License		Notice of Intent to Transfer Liquor License	
Security Agreement		Security Agreement	
Tax Bill on Unsecured Property Taxes		Note	
Insurance Policies		Approval of Inventory	
Bill of Sale		Amount to use for tax rebate	
Inventory		Certificate of Bus. Fictitious Name	
Financing Statement		Financing Statement	
Rent Statement		Approval of Rent Statement	
Lease		New Insurance and Bill	
Assignment of Lease		Money	
Consent to Assignment of Lease			
Claims Approved:			
1. _____			
2. _____			
3. _____			
4. _____			
5. _____			
6. _____			
7. _____			

Escrow

Send Notices to L.A. Daily Journal		Affidavit of Publication & Bill—Notice (of Bulk Transfer—1 time	
Notices Recorded on _____		Affidavit of Publication & Bill—Notice (to Create Security Interest—1 time	
Notices Published on _____		Affidavit of Publication of Certification of (Business Fictitious Name—4 times	
Send Financing Statement to Sacramento		Department of Employment Release	
Acknowledgement of Filing by Sacramento		State Board of Equalization Release	
		Liquor License Transferred	
		New License issued by A.B.C. to Buyer	
		Hold SALE on or after _____	

DATE SALE HELD _____ TIME: _____ BY _____ WITNESSED BY _____

Exhibit 64

TRANSFER OF LIQUOR LICENSE
SUPPLEMENT TO BULK SALE ESCROW INSTRUCTIONS

The Bulk Sale Escrow Instructions dated _____ given to you by the undersigned are hereby supplemented as follows:

Items to be transferred to Buyer include the transfer of an alcoholic beverage license for the premises and business located at the address stated in the said Bulk Sale Escrow Instructions.

The undersigned will hand you a copy of a Notice of Intended Sale described in said Bulk Sale Instructions, together with a Notice of Intended Transfer of Liquor License(s), which will contain the information required by law, and particularly by Section 24073 of the Business and Professions Code, and Section 3440.1 of the Civil Code, which you will record and publish in a newspaper of general circulation in the appropriate judicial district (if no judicial district, then in the appropriate County) wherein the personal property therein referred to is located, in the manner required by law, and obtain for Seller a certified copy of said Notice.

Undersigned Buyer will hand you or cause to be handed you the full amount of the purchase price or consideration of said license(s) and of said business described in said Notice and in said Bulk Sale Escrow Instructions.

Seller and Buyer agree that they shall comply with Section 24074 of the Business and Professions Code and that no payment shall be made and that the escrow shall not close until AFTER the transfer to said license(s) has been approved by the Alcoholic Beverage Control Department, and that you as escrow holder shall pay out of said cash portion of said purchase price or consideration for the transfer of the license(s) and the business conducted thereunder the claims of the bona fide creditors of the Seller who file their claims with you before you are notified by the Alcoholic Beverage Control Department of its approval of the transfer of the subject license, and such payment or distribution shall be made only within a reasonable time after the completion of the transfer of said license(s). Seller's written approval of any claim shall be conclusive evidence that such claim is bona fide.

If the cash portion of the said purchase price is not sufficient to pay all such creditors in full, distribute the cash consideration pro rata among such creditors in accordance with their instructions AND THOSE OF THE SELLER.

Any part of the purchase price remaining after such payment of distribution shall be paid or distributed by you in accordance with the Seller's instructions.

Seller shall obtain before the date of closing, all consents and releases and instruments of any kind and nature, whether from public authorities, creditors, or otherwise, which may be required herein to consummate this escrow.

All fees and costs of recording, publishing, filing, including your escrow fees, shall be paid by Seller and Buyer equally unless otherwise provided herein.

Should any provision of this supplement be inconsistent with any provision of the aforesaid Bulk Sale Instructions, the provision of this supplement shall control. For the purposes of prorating, "close of escrow" shall mean the date you are notified the license has been transferred or the closing date set forth in the Notice of Intended Transfer of Liquor License, whichever is the later date.

EACH PARTY HERETO ACKNOWLEDGES THAT HE HAS READ AND UNDERSTANDS THE FOREGOING TERMS AND CONDITIONS.

BUYER	SELLER

Exhibit 65

CREDITOR PRIORITY--LIQUOR LICENSE TRANSFERS

THE FOLLOWING IS HEREBY MADE A PART OF THE ORIGINAL ESCROW INSTRUCTIONS OF EVEN DATE, AS THOUGH ACTUALLY CONTAINED THEREIN:

ESCROWHOLDER: After the requirements for transfer, as provided in Section 24049 as revised November 10, 1969, are satisfied; is directed to pay out of the purchase price or consideration, the claims of the Bona Fide Creditors of the licensee who file their claims with the escrowholder before the escrowholder is notified by the Department of its approval of the transfer of the license, or, if the purchase price or consideration is not sufficient to pay the claims in full, to distribute the consideration as follows:

FIRST: To the payment of claims for wages, salaries, or fringe benefits of employees of seller or transferor earned or accruing within ninety (90) days prior to to the sale, transfer, or opening of an escrow for the sale thereof;

SECOND: To the payment of claims of secured creditors to the extent of the proceeds which arise from the sale of the security;

THIRD: To the United States for claims based on income or withholding taxes; and thereafter for claims based on any tax other than taxes specified in Section 24049;

FOURTH: To the payment of mechanics' liens;

FIFTH: To the payment of escrow fees, and claims for prevailing brokerage fees for services rendered, and claims for reasonable attorney's fees for services rendered;

SIXTH: To the payment of claims for goods sold and delivered to the transferor for resale at his license premises;

SEVENTH: To the payment of all other claims. The last category of creditors for whom there are not sufficient assets available for the payment of claims in full shall be paid pro-rata.

IF THE TRANSFEROR LICENSEE DISPUTES ANY CLAIM, THE ESCROWHOLDER SHALL NOTIFY THE CLAIMANT, AND THE AMOUNT OF PRO-RATA AMOUNT THEREOF SHALL BE RETAINED BY THE ESCROWHOLDER FOR A PERIOD OF 25 DAYS, AND, IF NOT ATTACHED, SHALL BE PAID TO THE TRANSFEROR LICENSEE. ESCROWHOLDER SHALL MAKE THE PAYMENT OR DISTRIBUTION WITHIN A REASONABLE TIME AFTER THE COMPLETION OF THE TRANSFER OF THE LICENSE.

BUYERS: SELLERS:

_____   _____

_____   _____

_____   _____

_____   _____

Exhibit 66

MEMORANDUM SHEET--TRANSFER OF PARCEL A

PROPERTY ADDRESS __3135-37 Lipton, Walnut Creek, CA 94595__	ESCROW NO. __12345__

PARCEL A
TRANSACTION MEMO DATA
TITLE CO. _____

SELLER __Juan Gomez and Maria Gomez__
Borrower
__h/w as joint tenants__

Address: __3215 Birch St.,__

__Anytown, CA__ _____Phone:_____

Legal: __Lot #3, Block B, Tract 3549 of__

__38/45-46 Maps, 3135 Lipton,__

__Walnut Creek CA 94595__

BUYER __Rewards Limited, a limited__
Lender
__partnership__

Address: __145 Main Street,__

__Anytown, CA 92632__ _____Phone:_____

Deliver through Escrow:

Leases_____ Water Stock_____

Bill of Sale_____ Termite Report__X__

Adjustments and date of prorations as of_____
(pay 2nd installment taxes)

Taxes __X__ Bonds_____ Impounds_____

Rents __X__ Interest_____ Insurance __obtained__   New policy to be
Roof certification __X__

Adjust principal of T.D. of record in_____

(Cash)_____ (T.D. to file)_____ (Purchase Price)_____

Pay_____% Commission

To_____ Board Listing No._____ $_____

Address _____

To __Broker's Realty Co.__ $ __4,560__

Address __123 Main Street, Anytown CA 92632__
__0-468329-9__

To_____ $_____

Address _____

Time Limit __3-30-88__
Charges_____ Documentary stamps
of deed: $75.90

Paid Outside Escrow to_____	$_____
Deposit _____	1,000
Cash through Escrow by Broker	67,700
Cash through Escrow by Buyer	7,300
Trust Deed of Record (balance)	_____
Trust Deed of Record (balance)	_____
Trust Deed to file	_____
Trust Deed to file	_____
Total Consideration	$ 76,000
Subject to:_____taxes current fiscal year	
Bonds of Record, unpaid balance	$_____

Trust Deed of record unpaid balance $ __7,300__
monthly prin. and interest installments of
$ __75.00__ _____ including interest
at __6½__ % (inc.) (plus) Impounds buyer
to make payment due__5-1-88__
Loan No. __Gomez__

Beneficiary: __A.B. Lender__

Trust Deed of record unpaid balance $_____
monthly prin. and interest installments of
$_____ including interest
at_____% buyer to make payment
due _____
Loan No. _____

Beneficiary:

LOAN Trust Deed to file in amount of $_____
monthly prin. and interest installments of
$_____ including interest
at_____% beginning _____

Beneficiary:

PMTD Trust Deed to file in amount of $_____
monthly prin. and interest installments of
$_____ including interest
at_____% beginning _____
all due_____Accel. Clause_____
Request-Notice_____
Beneficiary:

Pay off of Existing Trust Deed of Record: Amt. $_____
Name of Holder: _____

Address: _____

Loan No. _____

Pest control report required--not to exceed $400.
Adjustments upward or downward on trust deed of record to balance equities in exchange for Parcel A.
Title report deemed approved within 3 days after receipt by parties.
Concurrent closing with Escrow #303614 at Your Title Insurance Co.--funds to be transferred to this escrow.

Exhibit 67

MEMORANDUM SHEET--TRANSFER OF PARCEL B

PROPERTY ADDRESS ____ 2217 E. Poplar, Oakland CA 94606 ____ ESCROW NO. __12345__

PARCEL B

TRANSACTION MEMO DATA

TITLE CO. _____

SELLER __Rewards Limited, a limited__
Borrower

__partnership__

Address: __145 Main Street,__

__Anytown CA__ ____ Phone: ____

Legal: __Lot 3, Tract 1015 of 52/7-8__

__Miscellaneous Maps__

__2217 E. Poplar, Oakland CA 94606__

BUYER __Juan Gomez and Maria Gomez__
Lender

__h/w as joint tenants__

Address: __3215 Birch St.__

__Anytown, CA__ ____ Phone: ____

Deliver through Escrow:

Leases ____ Water Stock ____

Bill of Sale ____ Termite Report ____ X

Adjustments and date of prorations as of ____ C/E

Taxes __X__ Bonds ____ Impounds __X__

Rents __X__ Interest ____ Insurance __obtained__
New policy to be

Adjust principal of T.D. of record in ____

(Cash) ____ (T.D. to file) ____ (Purchase Price) __X__

Pay __6__ % Commission

To ____ Board Listing No. ____ $ ____

Address ____

To __Investment Realty Co.__ $ __$16,200__

Address __456 Main Street, Anytown CA 92635__
0-567327-8

To ____ $ ____

Address ____

Time Limit __3-30-88__

Charges ____
Documentary tax stamps
of Deed: $139.15

Paid Outside Escrow to ____ $ ____

Deposit ____ 2,000 *

Proceeds of 3rd T. D. 25,500
~~Cash through Escrow by Broker~~

Cash through Escrow by Buyer 63,000

Trust Deed of Record (balance) 144,500

Trust Deed of Record (balance) ____

Trust Deed to file - 2nd 35,000

Trust Deed to file ____

Total Consideration $ 270,000
* Add'l $2,000 to be deposited
by 3-9-89
Subject to: ____ taxes current fiscal year

Bonds of Record, unpaid balance $ 144,500

Trust Deed of record unpaid balance $ ____
monthly prin. and interest installments of
$ __1250.00__ including interest
at __9½__ % (%%.) (plus) Impounds buyer
to make payment due __5-1-88__
Loan No. __82924__

Beneficiary: __Allright Savings and Loan Assn.__

Trust Deed of record unpaid balance $ ____
monthly prin. and interest installments of
$ ____ including interest
at ____ % buyer to make payment
due ____
Loan No. ____

Beneficiary:

LOAN Trust Deed to file in amount of $ 35,000
monthly prin. and interest installments of
$ __298.33__ including interest
at __10__ % beginning __30 days after__
C/E--maturity on or before 4 yrs
Beneficiary: after C/E
__Rewards Ltd__

~~3rd Acceleration Clause~~ 30,000
PMTD Trust Deed to file in amount of $ ____
monthly prin. and interest installments of
$ __300.00__ including interest (net 22,500)
at __10__ % beginning __6-1-88__
all due __5-31-89__ Accel. Clause __X__
Request-Notice ____
Beneficiary:
__Anytown Loan Co.__

Pay off of Existing Trust Deed of Record: Amt. $ 6,300
Name of Holder: __James Smith__

Address: __452 Main Street, Anytown CA__

Loan No. __Rewards, Ltd.__

Pest control report required. Adjustments upward or downward on trust deed of record
to balance equities in exchange for Parcel A. Walk through required prior to closing.
Personal property transferred--no B/S or security interest search. $25,500 approximate
proceeds from sale of 3rd Trust Deed with adjustments to be made at close of escrow
for approximate amount.

Exhibit 68

EXCHANGE ESCROW INSTRUCTIONS

Address: _____

Phone: _____

ESCROW NO. __12345__

Escrow Officer __John L. Escrow__

Date: __March 6, 1988__

	Parcel A	Parcel B
Grantor's Valuation	$ 76,000.00	$ 270,000.00
Less Encumbrance'(s) of Record	7,300.00	144,500.00
Equity Conveyed	68,700.00	125,500.00

		First Party	Second Party
To Balance Equities: Cash through Escrow: (If Required) Initial Deposit	↑	$ 2,000.00	$ 1,000.00
To Be Deposited	A	63,000.00	67,700.00
Cash outside of Escrow	D D	144,500.00	7,300.00
New Trust Deed		35,000.00	-0-
Other	↓	25,500.00	-0-
TOTALS		$ 270,000.00	$ 76,000.00

The undersigned, __Juan Gomez and Maria Gomez, husband and wife, as joint tenants__

(hereinafter referred to as "First Party"), and __Rewards, Ltd., a limited partnership__

(hereinafter referred to as "Second Party") to effect the exchange of certain parcels of real property as hereinbelow described hereby instructs Escrow Company, a subsidiary of The   Company (hereinafter referred to as "Escrow Holder") as follows:

INSTRUCTIONS

1. Term of Escrow and Termination

Your agency as Escrow Holder shall terminate six months following the date set forth next below, and shall be subject to earlier termination by receipt by you prior to the close of escrow of written notice signed (1) in case this escrow has not been placed in a condition to close by __March 30, 1988__ by any party hereto, or (2) if received prior to said date, but after there shall have been a failure of a condition or performance to be complied with or performed on or before a date, or within a period, stated herein, then by any party other than a party responsible for such compliance or performance. Any such termination shall be effective upon receipt of such notice, but you shall not return the documents or deposits by the revoking party prior to ten days after you have mailed a copy of such notice to each of the other parties. If the conditions of this escrow have not been complied with prior to the date set forth in this Section 1, or any extension thereof, Escrow Holder shall nevertheless proceed to complete the escrow as soon as such conditions have been complied with, unless written notice shall have been delivered to Escrow Holder, as herein provided. No notice, demand or change of instructions, except a demand for termination made in accordance with the foregoing paragraph, shall be of any effect in this escrow unless given in writing by all parties affected thereby. Escrow Holder is hereby further authorized and instructed to remit all funds by the check of Escrow Holder to the party or parties depositing the same in this escrow if this escrow is not consumated, unless specifically instructed to the contrary.

2. Deposit of First Party.

On or before __March 30,__ 19 __88__, First Party will cause to be handed to you the sum of $ __68,700__ and a Grant Deed naming Second Party (or his or her nominee) as grantee therein, executed and acknowledged by First Party and in all other respects in form sufficient for recording, covering that certain real property located in the City of __Walnut Creek__, County of __Contra Costa__, State of California hereinafter referred to as "Parcel A" and described in "Exhibit A", attached hereto and incorporated herein by this reference.
Lot 3, Block B of Tract 3549, as per map recorded in Book 38, pgs 45-46 of Miscellaneous Maps

3. Deposit of Second Party.

On or before __March 30__ 19 __88__, Second Party will cause to be handed to you the sum of $ __65,000__ and a Grant Deed naming First Party (or his or her nominee) as grantee therein, executed and acknowledged by Second Party and in all other respects in form sufficient for recording, covering that certain real property located in the City of __Oakland__, County of __Alameda__, State of California, hereinafter referred to as "Parcel B" and described in "Exhibit B", attached hereto and incorporated herein by this reference.
Lot 3 of Tract 1015 as per map recorded in Book 52, pgs 7-8 of Miscellaneous Maps, office of Record Recorder of said county.

4. Valuation.

For purposes of this exchange, the value of Parcel A is deemed to be $ __76,000.00__, and the value of Parcel B is deemed to be $ __270,000.00__; the total amount of encumbrances against Parcel A is $ __7,000__, and the total amount of encumbrances against Parcel B is $ __144,500.00__; and the difference in the values of the equities (the value of each parcel less encumbrances) of Parcel A and Parcel B is deemed to be $ __56,800.00__, which difference shall be compensated for, as follows:

First party has deposited $2,000 into escrow and will deposit an additional $2,000 not later than 3-9-81. The balance of $61,000 will be deposited prior to close of escrow. First party will execute a note and trust deed in favor of second party, on order dated during escrow for $35,000 with interest to accrue at 10% per annum, payable monthly, beginning 30 days after close of escrow, such note to mature 4 years after close of escrow. Escrowholder is instructed to insert said beginning and maturity dates as close of escrow in fulfillment of this instruction, even though the note has been previously signed. Said note is to be secured by a deed of trust describing parcel B. Said note and trust deed to contain usual acceleration clause and trust deed to contain the following recitals "This Deed of Trust is subordinate and junior to a trust deed of record in favor of Allright Savings and Loan Assn." First party will cause to be handed you loan funds for $25,500, together with appropriate instructions for their use secured by Parcel B. First party's signatures on said instructions and supportive documents will be deemed approval of loan terms and conditions.
See paragraph 11, page 2 for additional condition regarding deposit of funds.

Exhibit 69.1

5. Delivery of Deeds and Title Insurance.

Escrow Holder will close this escrow by delivering the grant deed to Parcel A to Second Party, or his or her nominee, and the grant deed to Parcel B to First Party, or his or her nominee, and by paying each party his respective amount, when Escrow Holder can obtain both (1) the usual form Policy of Title Insurance issued by ___Your Title Company___

with total liability of $ ___76,000.00___ , showing title to Parcel A vested in Second Party, or nominee, subject only to (a) non-delinquent general and special real and personal property taxes and assessments, if any; and (b) conditions, restrictions, reservations, covenants, rights, rights of way, easements and the exception of minerals, oil, gas, water, carbons and hydro-carbons on or under said land, now of record, and in deed to file, if any, affecting the use and occupancy of said property; and (c) the following Deeds of Trust to/of record in favor of _____

___Trust deed of record in favor of J.Thirdparty with an approximate balance of $7300.00___

and (2) the usual form Policy of Title Insurance issued by ___Their Title Company___

with total liability of $ ___270,000.00___ , showing title to Parcel B vested in First Party, or nominee, subject only to (a) non-delinquent general and special real and personal property taxes and assessments, if any; and (b) conditions, restrictions, reservations, covenants, rights, rights of way, easements and the exception of minerals, oil, gas, water, carbons and hydro-carbons on or under said land, now of record, and in deed to file, if any, affecting the use and occupancy of said property; and (c) the following Deeds of Trust to/of record in favor of ___Allright Savings and Loan___

___Association in approximate unpaid balance of $144,500.00 Second trust deed to record in favor of second party, per its terms in the amount of $35,000.00. Third trust deed for $30,000 in favor of One Low Loan Co., per its terms for $30,000.___

6. Terms of Exchange.

The terms of this exchange are as follows: ___Closing is contingent upon both parties approving preliminary title reports on their respective purchases within 3 days of receipt of same. Said reports are deemed approved at the expiration of said time limit unless you are in receipt of a statement from either party hereto to the contrary.___

___Each party will provide evidence of insurance on their respective purchases satisfactory to existing and/or new lenders. Each is to be charged for the premium relating to the respective purchase per insurance agent's statement and no further approval is required.___

7. Prorations as to Parcel A.

The following matters with respect to Parcel A shall be prorated to the close of escrow:

(a) Real property taxes and assessments, if any;

(b) Rents and insurance, if any, upon the basis of statements handed to Escrow Holder, as approved by both parties; and

(c) ___From second party deposit, you are to pay second instalment of 1987-88 Contra Costa County taxes.___

___Adjust prepaid rentals and/or deposits in favor of 2nd party at close of escrow.___

___Remaining value of roof certification to be adjusted. A rental statement will be provided by the first party for delivery to second party for approval prior to close of escrow.___

8. Prorations as to Parcel B.

The following matters with respect to Parcel B shall be prorated to the close of escrow:

(a) Real property taxes and assessments, if any;

(b) Rents and insurance, if any, upon the basis of statements handed to Escrow Holder, as approved by parties; and _____

(c) ___Adjust prepaid rentals and/or security deposits in favor of first party as of the close of escrow.___

___A rental statement will be provided by second party for delivery to first party for approval prior to close of escrow.___

9. Broker's Commissions.

If this escrow closes by title to Parcel A passing to Second Party, or his or her nominee, and title to Parcel B passing to First Party, or his or her nominee, First Party agrees to pay a broker's commission for the conveyance of Parcel A to Second Party of $ ___4560.00___ ,

to ___Broker's Real Estate Co.___

whose address is ___123 Main Street, Anytown, CA 92632___

(Real Estate Broker's License No. ___0-468327-9___), payable through escrow at the close of escrow, and second party agrees to pay a broker's commission for the conveyance of Parcel B to First Party, of $ ___16,200___ to ___Investment Realty Company___

_____ whose address is ___456 Main Street, Anytown, CA 92635___

(Real Estate Broker's License No. ___0-567327-8___) payable through escrow at the close of escrow.

10. Other Expenses.

All other costs and authorized expenses incurred by Escrow Holder pursuant to this escrow shall be borne by the parties in accordance with the customary practices of Escrow Holder. In the event of the cancellation or other termination of this escrow prior to the closing thereof, the parties hereto shall pay Escrow Holder equally for any expenses which it may have incurred or become obligated for pursuant to these instructions and also a reasonable escrow fee for the services contracted by the undersigned to be rendered by Escrow Holder, and such expenses, if any, and fees shall be paid and put into escrow by the parties hereto before any cancellation or other termination is effected. Any documents or funds deposited with Escrow Holder may be retained by Escrow Holder as a lien to secure the reimbursement and payment of expenses, if any, and fees above provided for.

11. Deposit of Funds.

On or before the close of escrow, each party will deposit into this escrow his respective share of the costs and expenses called for under these instructions.

In addition to first party's obligation shown in paragraph 4 herein, second party will deposit $1,000 upon execution of these instructions and will deposit $67,700.00 prior to close of escrow.

Both parties understand the escrowholder will proceed with the processing of this escrow and in the event of cancellation of same, escrowholder will retain $200.00 of the funds on deposit from each party as payment for services in connection with this escrow.

See Page 2-A for additional agreements.

(2)

Exhibit 69.2

First and second party understand, with respect to parcel B only, with which escrow holder is not to be concerned and entered as a matter of record only:

a) First party has inspected parcel B and accepts property subject to termite instruction incorporated herein.

b) First party reserves privilege of walking through parcel B and inspecting all plumbing, heating and electrical systems and verifying that property has been maintained in condition as shown. Placement of balance of funds at close of escrow by first party shall indicate her/his approval of condition of same.

c) These instructions are not intended to amend, cancel, or supersede that certain purchase agreement dated 2-23-88 as amended 2-24-88 and 2-25-88 and all warranties contained therein in favor of first party shall be assigned to first party and accrue to benefit of first party.

Second party will deposit inventory of furniture and furnishings contained in parcel B for approval of first party and for delivery to first party at close of escrow.

Close of this escrow shall be concurrent with and contingent upon close of Escrow No. 303614 at Your Title Insurance Company in which second party herein is a seller therein of parcel A.

The parties hereto acknowledge that the properties herein are located in two counties and the confirmation of concurrent recordings may not be possible. You are nonetheless to proceed with the closing of this transaction by recording the deed from first party to second party on parcel A first, and upon verification of said recording, you shall proceed with the recording of the deed from second party to first party on parcel B as quickly thereafter as possible. Escrow holder is relieved of all liability and/or responsibility as to lapse of time incurred by location of properties described herein.

Personal property being conveyed with parcel B is included in total consideration, and no Bill of Sale or Security Interest search is required.

The parties hereto understand the second party is accomodating the first party for the purpose of creating an exchange and that the property described as parcel A has, or will be, sold to a third party. First party agrees to indemnify second party against any loss relating to any warranties, either written or implied, by virtue of the fact that a Grant Deed being delivered to said buyer has been executed by second party hereto.

First party will furnish said buyer a residential property report as required by City Ordinance at close of $15.00. You are to make necessary adjustment at close of escrow, if required, by Your Title Company Escrow No. 303614 for payment of said report.

The parties hereto acknowledge that all of the funds required to settle this escrow agreement may not be deposited until after close of Escrow No. 303614 at Your Title Company and said conditions are satisfactory to all parties hereto. In the event the unpaid balances of loans of record should be more or less than the amounts shown in these instructions, you are to adjust the amounts of cash required from both first and second parties.

SUPPLEMENTAL ESCROW INSTRUCTIONS
PERTAINING TO PEST CONTROL REPORTS

Seller is to furnish buyer through escrow with a current report in writing from a licensed pest control operator covering an inspection of visible and accessible areas of house and garage. If the report should disclose any debris under the house, termites, dry rot, or other infestation, the seller is to eliminate it, and all work recommended in said report to repair damage caused by infestation or infection of wood-destroying pest or organisms found and all work to correct conditions that caused such infestation or infection shall be done at the expense of seller. Funds for work to be done at the expense of seller shall be held in escrow and disbursed upon receipt in escrow of certificate of completion by the structural pest control operator, or upon close of escrow, whichever occurs later.

| /S/ Juan Gomez | /S/ Maria Gomez | /S/ Rewards, Limited, a Limited Partnership by: Henry Smith, General Partner |

Exhibit 69.3

12. General Instructions.

    (a) Escrow Holder shall not be held liable for the sufficiency or correctness as to form, manner of execution, or validity of any instrument deposited in this escrow, nor as to the identity, authority, or right of any person executing the same, nor for failure to comply with any of the provisions of any agreement, contract, or other instrument filed herein or referred to herein and the duties of Escrow Holder hereunder shall be limited to the safekeeping of such money, instruments or other documents received by Escrow Holder and for the disposition of the same in accordance with the written instructions accepted by Escrow Holder. Your knowledge of matters affecting the property, provided such facts do not prevent compliance with these instructions, does not create any liability or duty in addition to your responsibility under these instructions.

    (b) Should Escrow Holder before or after the close of escrow receive or become aware of any conflicting demands or claims with respect to this escrow or the rights of any of the parties hereto, or of any money or property deposited herein or affected hereby, Escrow Holder shall have the right to discontinue any or all further acts on its part to be performed until such conflict is resolved to the satisfaction of Escrow Holder, and Escrow Holder shall have the further right to commence or defend any action or proceedings for the determination of such conflict. The parties hereto jointly and severally agree to pay all costs, damages, judgments and expenses, including reasonable attorneys' fees, suffered or incurred by Escrow Holder in connection with, or arising out of this escrow, including, but without limiting the generality of the foregoing, any suit and interpleader brought by Escrow Holder. In the event that Escrow Holder shall file any action and interpleader in connection with this escrow, Escrow Holder shall automatically be released and discharged from all obligations further to perform any and all duties or obligations imposed upon Escrow Holder by the terms hereof.

    (c) Escrow Holder shall not be concerned with the giving of any disclosures required by federal or state law including, but not limited to, any disclosures required under Regulation Z promulgated pursuant to the Federal Consumer Credit Protection Act, which may or should be given outside of this escrow, or the effect of any zoning laws, ordinances or regulations affecting any of the property transferred hereunder. The undersigned jointly and severally agree to save and hold Escrow Holder harmless by reason of any misrepresentation or omission by either party hereto or their respective agents or the failure of any of the parties hereto to comply with the rules and/or regulations of any governmental agency, state, federal, county, municipal or otherwise.

    (d) The parties to this escrow have satisfied themselves outside of this escrow that the transaction covered hereby is not in violation of the Subdivision Map Act or any other law relating to land division, and Escrow Holder is relieved of all responsibility and/or liability in connection therewith, and is not to be concerned with the enforcement of said laws.

    (e) Escrow Holder shall, as agent for the parties hereto, assign any fire and other insurance of the parties hereto handed you or policies of insurance that the beneficiaries thereof inform Escrow Holder that they hold.

    (f) All proration shall be made on the basis of a 30-day month. All deposits made by the parties hereto in connection with this transaction shall be deposited by Escrow Holder in an account designated as "Escrow Fund Account" with any local bank, without any liability for interest. All disbursements shall be made by check of Escrow Holder drawn on said account.

    (g) Escrow Holder shall mail all fire and other insurance policies to the respective holders of first encumbrances, if any. All policies of title insurance shall be mailed to the holders of existing encumbrances provided there is to be a substitution of liability thereon; otherwise, to the respective holders of the prior encumbrances recorded concurrently with the documents herein or, if there is no such encumbrance, then to the respective grantees. Other documents and checks in favor of each of the parties hereto shall be mailed, unregistered, to the addresses of the respective parties hereinbelow set forth.

    (h) Escrow Holder shall be under no obligation or liability for the failure to inform the parties hereto regarding any sale, loan, exchange, or other transaction, or facts within the knowledge of Escrow Holder, even though the same concern the property described herein, provided they do not prevent the compliance of Escrow Holder with these instructions.

    (i) These instructions may be executed in counterparts, each of which so executed shall, irrespective of the date of its execution and delivery, be deemed an original and said counterparts together shall constitute one and the same instrument. Any amended and/or supplemental instructions hereto must be in writing, executed by all of the parties hereto, and deposited with Escrow Holder.

    (j) Any policy of title insurance called for under these instructions will be subject to the exceptions and conditions contained in the standard form of the company issuing such insurance including, but not limited to, the exception that said company will not insure against loss by reason of the reservation or exception of any water rights, claims or title to water.

    (k) Your company is authorized to destroy or otherwise dispose of any and all documents, papers, instructions, correspondence and other material pertaining to this escrow at the expiration of five (5) years from the date of these instructions, regardless of the date of any subsequent amendments hereto, additional or supplemental instructions or the date of the close of escrow, without liability and without further notice to the undersigned.

    (l) The parties hereto hereby authorize the recordation of any instruments delivered through this escrow, if necessary or proper in the issuance of the policy of title insurance called for, and in connection therewith, funds and/or instruments received in this escrow may be delivered to, or deposited with, any title company situated in the county in which any of the property covered hereby is situated for the purposes of complying with the terms and conditions of these escrow instructions.

    (m) In the event that it may be necessary or proper for the consumation of this escrow, you are authorized to deposit or have deposited funds or documents, or both, with any bank, trust company, title insurance company, savings and loan association, building and loan association, industrial loan company, credit union, insurer or licensed escrow agent, subject to your order pursuant to closing this escrow, and such deposit shall be deemed a deposit in accordance with the meaning of these instructions.

    (n) The signature of the undersigned on any documents and instructions pertaining to this escrow indicates their unconditional acceptance and approval of the same, and the undersigned hereby acknowledge the receipt of a copy of these instructions.

Rewards, Ltd. a limited partnership
by:

| Juan Gomez | First Party | Maria Gomez | J.B. Officer, | Second Party | General Partner |

Address: 2325 Easy Street
Anytown, CA

Address: Anytown, CA

Phone No.: Res. (213)628-1344
Off. (714) 991-0781

Phone No.: (714) 990-1520

These instructions may be executed in counterparts, all of which, when taken together, shall be deemed to be the instrument. I have received a copy of these instructions as evidenced by my signature above.

Exhibit 69.4

EXCHANGE ESCROW CLOSING STATEMENT

ESCROW STATEMENT

Parcel A -- 3135-37 Lipton, Walnut Creek CA 94595
Parcel B -- 2217 E. Poplar, Oakland CA 94606

(Sale of A, acquire B.   Sale of B, acquire A.)

LOT _____ TRACT _____   ESCROW NO. _____

SELLER-BORROWER 1st Party, Gomez

BUYER-LENDER 2nd Party, Rewards, Ltd.

SELLER DEBITS	SELLER CREDITS	PROPERTY:	BUYER DEBITS	BUYER CREDITS
	9,000 00			57,345 20
	25,469 60	DEPOSIT Third Loan Proceeds (Parcel A)		
	76,000 00	TOTAL CONSIDERATION (Parcel A)	76,000 00	
270,000 00		TOTAL CONSIDERATION (Parcel B)		270,000 00
7,245 25		FIRST TRUST DEED OF RECORD (Parcel A)		7,245 25
	143,739 53	FIRST TRUST DEED OF RECORD (Parcel B)	143,739 53	
	35,000 00	SECOND TRUST DEED OF RECORD (Parcel B)	35,000 00	
		ALL PRORATIONS TO 4-12-88		
	83 19	Taxes of $189.51 for 6 mo paid to 7-1-88 (Parcel A)	83 19	
262 51		Taxes of $598.14 for 6 mo paid to 7-1-88 (parcel B)		262 51
27 51		Interest $7245.25 @ 6.5% from 3-19-88 (Parcel A)		27 51
	1,024 14	Interest $143,739.53 @ 9.5% from 3-15-88 (Parcel B)	1,024 14	
245 17		Rental Prorations: SEE REVERSE (Parcel A)		245 17
166 00		Rental Adjustment: prepaid deposit (Parcel A)		166 00
	1,230 51	Rental Reparations: SEE REVERSE (Parcel B)	1,230 51	
	515 00	Rental Adjustment: prepaid (Parcel B)	515 00	
1,277 00		ALLRIGHT SAVINGS - April 15 payment (Parcel B)		
1,288 72		Adjustment for impounded funds		1,288 72
	15 00	Forward fee and adjustment	20 00	
179 60		ALL RISK INSURANCE COMPANY (Parcel B)		
		Demand of Smith -- Principal (Parcel B)	6,296 23	
		Interest @ 10% from 3-9-88 to 4-12-88	57 72	
255 00		Adjustment for roof certification (Parcel A)		255 00
5,000 00		Adjustment for assignment of note and TD (Parcel B)		5,000 00
			16,200 00	
4,560 00		Commission (Parcel A)	468 00	4,560 00
		Commission (Parcel B)		400 00
		Termite Report (Parcel A)		234 28
400 00		Termite Report (Parcel B)		301 70
234 28		County Tax Collector - 2nd half (Parcel A)	157 50	
301 70		Title Insurance Policy (Parcel A)		
		Title Insurance Policy - binder rate (Parcel B)		
75 90		Documentary transfer Tax - to Gomez (Parcel A)		75 90
83 60		Documentary Transfer Tax - to Resale (Parcel A)		83 60
		Documentary Transfer Tax (Parcel B)	139 15	
7 00		Recording Deed and Trust Deed (Parcel B)		
3 00		Recording Reconveyance (Parcel A)		3 00
3 00		Recording Deed to (Parcel A)		3 00
5 00		Recording Assignment Trust Deed (Parcel A)		5 00
25 00		Reconveyance Fee (Parcel A)		25 00
		Reconveyance Fee (Parcel B)	35 00	
200 00		Escrow Fee and Assignment (Parcel A)		
450 00		Escrow Fee (Parcel B)	465 00	
		Drawing 2 Deeds (Parcel A)		
10 00		Drawing Deed (Parcel B)	10 00	
		Securing Lender's Statements (Parcel B)	10 00	
97 58		Adjustment for Your Title Fee (Parcel A)		97 58
		Recording Reconveyance (Parcel B)	3 00	
		BALANCE DUE YOU (Parcel B)	66,170 40	
	625 85	BALANCE DUE THIS OFFICE (Parcel A)		
292,702 82	**292,702 82**	**TOTALS**	**347,624 42**	**347,624 42**

DATE__April 12, 1988_____   BY_____

ESCROW OFFICER

PLEASE RETAIN THIS STATEMENT FOR INCOME TAX PURPOSES

Exhibit 70

DIAGRAMMING AN EXCHANGE TRANSACTION

"ACCOMMODATOR" TRANSACTION WITH RESALE

Consider an owner of a three-unit building (first party) who desires to trade up to a six-unit building using a tax deferred exchange as a device. The owner of the six unit building (second party) is willing to cooperate, providing a purchaser can be found for the three-unit building (third party).

Property I		Property II
3-unit building		6-unit building
First Party deeds 3-unit to Second Party & adds consideration	*Exchange* – – – –*occurs*– – – – *here*	Second Party deeds 6-unit to First Party
• • •		
Second Party deeds 3-unit to Third Party on resale	*Resale or leg occurs here*	

This is a fairly simple exchange transaction. However, any exchange can be visualized as two sales. Multiple transactions where more than one party is to receive tax benefit should be broken down to verify that an actual exchange has taken place in each instance.

There are three primary items to remember in diagramming and planning an exchange:

1. Verify that an actual exchange occurs (i.e., property is transferred by a party in exchange for properties of another party).

2. Identify the party or parties seeking tax deferment.

3. See that the deeds prepared to consummate the escrow fulfill the needs of the parties.

Exhibit 71

Chapter 15 Quiz

1. The sale of an existing trust deed may require a separate escrow because many institutional loans today:

    (A) Remain with the original lender
    (B) Are prepared using the originating lending institution's tailor made documents
    √(C) Are sold in the secondary market
    (D) Are unmarketable

2. The operative language of an assignment is:

    (A) Transfer to trustee in trust
    (B) Sell and convey
    (C) Lease, let and demise
    (D) Transfers and assigns to

3. The following represents a holding escrow:

    (A) Lot reservations in a tract
    (B) Stock transfers of privately held companies
    (C) Construction loan proceeds allocation
    (D) All of the above

4. Subdivision escrows:

    (A) Are no different from any other sale
    √(B) Are adaptable to word processing
    (C) Require individualized preparation
    (D) Are not concerned with covenants, conditions, and restrictions

5. Leasehold escrows:

    (A) Involve transfer of the right to use the land of another
    (B) Involve transfer of the fee title
    (C) Are a perpetual estate transfer
    (D) Have the operative language "grant and convey"

6. Mobilehomes:

    (A) May be real or personal property
    (B) May be registered as a motor vehicle or assessed as real estate
    (C) May be transferred by bill of sale and ownership transfer or by deed
    (D) All of the above

7. Mobilehome escrows:

    (A) Involve only the sale of new units
    (B) Involve only the sale of units in a park
    √(C) Are usually processed by specialists
    (D) Are processed by all escrowholders

8. A bulk sale involves:

    (A) Transfer of a thousand cases of All Bran
    (B) Sale of a business defined in Commercial Code
    (C) Sale of anything in bulk
    (D) Sale of real and personal property

9. Special considerations and responsibilities in bulk sale escrows may include:

    (A) Publication of legal notices to creditors
    (B) Compliance with U.C.C. requirements on security interests
    (C) Alcoholic Beverage Control regulations
    (D) All of the above

10. An exchange escrow:

    √(A) Involves the sale of two or more parcels of real estate
    (B) Is primarily concerned with sales price and loan amounts
    (C) Has no tax ramifications
    (D) Is handled by a majority of escrowholders

Appendix

"Analysis of California's Escrow Industry as it Affects Real Estate Licensees"[1]

The California Department of Real estate (DRE) issued a Request for Proposals (RFP) to Conduct an Analysis of California's Escrow Industry as it Affects Real Estate Licensees. Arthur Young's response to the RFP was presented in its proposal dated January 15, 1988. A contract with Arthur Young to perform the study was approved on May 5, 1988. Quoted below are the following sections from the report: Introduction, Study Background, Problem Statement, and Recommendations

---

INTRODUCTION

California escrow activities are presently regulated by various government agencies at both the federal and State level. As a result of the number of agencies involved, the diversity of their authority, and regional differences in escrow practices, the laws, customs, and regulations that affect the escrow industry often vary, depending on the nature and location of the escrow business and the license or authority under which it operates. This report presents the results of our analysis and evaluation of California's escrow industry as it affects real estate licensees, as well as of the possible need for changes to government regulation of that industry.

The remainder of this introduction is organized under the following headings: Study Background, Problem Statement, Study Goals and Objectives, Study Approach.

Subsequent sections of the report are organized as follows:

☐ Section II — Profile of California's Escrow Industry

☐ Section III — Summary of Federal and State Legislation and Regulations Governing California's Escrow Industry

☐ Section IV — Summary of Escrow Service Provider Survey Responses

☐ Section V — Analysis of Statutes and Regulations Governing California's Escrow Service Providers

☐ Section VI — Recommendations.

Following Section VI is Appendix A which contains a copy of the survey instrument mailed as part of this study to independent escrow companies, title companies, real estate brokers,and banks and savings and loan associations.

---

[1] A study conducted by Arthur Young under a grant from the Department of Real Estate, December 31, 1988.

STUDY BACKGROUND

Under early English common law, ownership of real property was transferred by delivery of possession. This transfer was effected by a delivery of the land itself or something symbolic of the land, such as a twig, stone, or handful of dirt. This mode transferring property was sufficient to meet the needs of those times because ownership was widely known and transfer was seldom made except in descent from father to son. However, due to the increased complexity of real estate transactions, the large sums of money involved, and the varying parties involved, transfer of real property today cannot be accomplished by simple delivery of possession. Instead, transfer or conveyance of ownership to real property is most often by a written instrument called a deed, and consummation of the transaction is usually handled through the agency of an escrowholder, with the preparation, execution, and delivery of the deed handled through escrow.

The most common use and purpose of an escrow is to enable the buyer and seller to deal with each other without risk. Upon entering into a purchase contract, the buyer and seller have established a binding agreement between themselves as to the exchange of assets. However, this agreement typically is subject to the fulfillment of specific terms and conditions. For the buyer, it is important to assure that the title to the property is clear of any outstanding encumbrances. The buyer does not want to relinquish control over the purchase funds until assurances have been received that the title conveys certain ownership. Likewise, the seller does not want to relinquish title to the property until assured of the complete payment of the negotiated purchase price.

To facilitate the exchange, even when the two parties are predisposed to distrust one another, and impartial third party, known as the escrowholder, is commonly employed. The escrowholder receives instructions from the buyer and seller as to the conditions which must be met prior to the execution of the exchange. Fundamentally, the buyer will require that the funds placed on deposit with the escrowholder not be disbursed until a title search confirms that the property is unencumbered, and the seller will require that the deed transferring title to the buyer not be recorded until all funds have been received. Thus, the escrowholder is simply the individual who receives and distributes documents and funds to and from the parties involved in the transaction.

Among the specific purposes of escrow are the following:

☐ Facilitate the transaction in general and protect the interest of the buyer, the seller, and the lender, especially in the event of the death or withdrawal of a party to the escrow

☐ Facilitate financing arrangements

☐ Assure the collection and remittance of the real estate agent's commission

☐ Permit the holding of a transaction in abeyance while conditions are fulfilled and defects and encumbrances are removed

☐ Permit FHA insurance of a mortgage or a trust deed before and pending the completion of FHA requirements (if applicable)

☐ Permit the closing of a transaction at a convenient geographical location

☐ Permit the assimilation of several contiguous parcels, especially when the buyer cannot obtain all the deeds simultaneously

☐ Draft basic documents, such as conveyances and releases, and carry out the basic formalities requisite to a valid and expedient real estate transaction.

For an escrow to be considered operative, there must be a valid and enforceable contract between the parties. A contract sufficient to support and escrow must comply with the requirements of any valid contract, namely, competent parties, a valid consideration, a proper subject matter, and mutual agreement as to the terms and conditions of the contract. The contract may be evidenced by the purchase contract itself, by the escrow instructions prepared by the escrowholder pursuant to the direction of the parties, or by both.

Escrow services in the United States generally are provided by title companies, lending institutions, and individuals such as real estate brokers and attorneys. However, in California, there has emerged an additional form of escrow depository, known as the independent escrow company. Independent escrow companies are primarily located in Southern California and they provide only escrow services, while the other entities generally provide escrow services as either a secondary or incidental function.

In addition, there exists a distinction between escrow practices in Northern California and escrow practices in Southern California. In Northern California, escrows generally are processed at the end of the transaction. These escrows are referred to as *unilateral escrows*. In contrast, in Southern California, escrows generally are processed at the beginning of the transaction. These types of escrows are referred to as *bilateral escrows*. The differences between these two types of escrows are discussed in more detail in Section II—Profile of California's Escrow Industry.

The emergence of independent escrow companies in California during the late 1940s apparently prompted the California State Legislature to enact the *Escrow Law* in 1947. The *Escrow Law* has since become the primary source of law in California governing escrow service providers. It requires all corporations engaged in the escrow business as escrow agents to be licensed as independent escrow companies by the Department of Corporations. However, certain entities were *exempted* from the *Escrow Law*, including banks, trust companies, savings and loan associations, attorneys, insurance companies, title companies, and real estate brokers.[2]

Escrow-related regulations governing *exempted* escrow service providers are primarily the responsibility of the various State and federal agencies which traditionally have regulated them. For example, at the State level, the Department of Real Estate regulates real estate brokers, the Department of Insurance regulates title insurance companies, the Department of Banking regulates State-chartered banks, and the Department of Savings and Loan regulates State-chartered savings and loan associations. At the federal level, federally-chartered banks are regulated by the Federal Reserve and federally-chartered savings and loans are regulated by the Federal Home Loan Bank Board. A more detailed discussion of each of these agency's escrow-related regulations, as well as those of the Department of Corporations which regulates independent escrow companies in California, is provided in Section III—Summary of Federal and State Legislation and Regulations Governing California's Escrow Industry.

---

[2] Two of the *exempted* entities (trust companies and attorneys) are not significantly involved in providing escrow services in California and, therefore, were not included in the scope of this study.

PROBLEM STATEMENT

Real estate transactions involve an exchange of assets (usually real property is exchanged for money). It is the escrow agent's responsibility to hold the assets until all conditions requisite to the sale have been met. To protect the buyer, the seller, and the lender, regulations have been placed on escrow agents to mitigate the risk of escrow agents losing or absconding with trust monies deposited by consumers with the agent. However, these regulations have not eliminated all the problems in the escrow industry. This subsection describes five regulation-related problem areas in the escrow industry. The subsection is organized as follows:

- Competitive Equality

- Kickbacks and Rebates

- Adequacy of Consumer Protection Against Loss or Misuse of Escrow Trust Funds

- Competency of Escrow Officers

- Enforcement of Existing Regulations.

Competitive Equality

Due primarily to differences in the levels and types of regulation placed on escrow service providers, there exists the potential for *competitive inequality* within the escrow industry. Competitive inequality occurs when one or more entities providing essentially the same service are subject to relatively more or relatively less regulation than the other entities in the industry, thereby resulting in reduced service levels and/or increased costs for the more regulated entities. In California's escrow industry, the four major categories of escrow service providers (e.g., independent escrow companies, title companies, real estate brokers, and lending institutions), each re subject to different escrow-related regulations, However, only one of these entities (e.g., independent escrow companies) is required to be licensed under the *Escrow Law* and is required to bear all of the specific costs associated with complying with the *Escrow Law*. All of the other escrow industry participants are exempted from the provisions of this law, as well as associated regulations promulgated by the Department of Corporations. To the extent that the *Escrow Law* and associated regulations promulgated by the Department of Corporations results in relatively higher costs for independent escrow companies, these providers of escrow services could be at a competitive disadvantage.

Exempted escrow industry participants generally provide escrow services as an extension of their principal business. For example, title companies primarily perform title searches and issue title insurance, real estate brokers are primarily involved in listing and selling real estate, and banks and savings and loan associations offer consumers checking and savings accounts, loans, and various investment instruments. While both title companies and real estate brokers are expressly exempt from the *Escrow Law*, the *Escrow Law* also contain certain restrictive conditions associated with these exemptions. Title companies can only provide escrow services for transactions in which it is contemplated that a title policy will be issued. Real estate brokers can only provide escrow services for transactions that are incidental to their real estate business. Therefore, a competitive advantage could be afforded to independent escrow companies and lending institutions (relative to title companies and real estate brokers) with respect to the available market for which they can provide escrow services.

Finally, concerns have been expressed by segments of the escrow industry regarding the extent to which title companies lower their escrow fees for transactions that involve a large fee for providing title services. The escrow fee is allegedly hidden in the charge for title services, and may not adequately reflect actual cost incurred by the title company in providing the escrow services. By subsidizing escrow service costs through title service charges, title companies could potentially obtain a competitive advantage over other escrow service providers operating in the same market.

Kickbacks and Rebates

There exists within the escrow industry the potential for kickbacks or rebates offered by escrow service providers to real estate agents in order to obtain the real estate agents client's escrow business. In many real estate transactions, the seller chooses which escrow agent to use primarily based on a recommendation made by the real estate agent. Thus, escrow service providers primarily solicit their services to real estate agents. This can occur in different ways, some of which may be legal and some of which may be illegal. Several example cases are briefly described in the paragraphs below.

Case No. 1: *Real Estate Broker Opens and Holds Escrow, but Escrow Service Provider Provides Staff*

A real estate broker opens the escrow and acts as the escrowholder, but the escrow service provider provides all the staffing necessary to complete the escrow. The escrow service provider handles all details of the escrow and charges an escrow fee commensurate with the going rate in the area. However, a portion of this fee is then paid back to the real estate broker following close of escrow.

Case No. 2: *Real Estate Broker Enters Into Contract with Escrow Service Provider*

A real estate broker or group of brokers enters into an agreement with an escrow service provider to funnel escrow business to the escrow service provider in return for a fee (in accordance with the agreement) for directing escrow business to the escrow service provider.

Case No. 3: *Broker Escrow Divisions*

A real estate broker hires an employee (or employees) to process all of the broker's escrows under the broker's supervision However, the real estate broker is paid a fee for directing business to this employee. The escrow employee enters into a contract with the broker to perform the broker's escrows for a percentage of the escrow fee. Any amount paid back to the broker would be considered a fee paid for referring escrows to the employee. Also, the broker encourages their real estate salespeople to use this escrow service by offering the salespeople financial or other incentives.

The last case, according to some industry participants, is the most prevalent in the industry and is practiced under the protection of the real estate broker exemption from the *Escrow Law*.

3. Adequacy of Consumer Protection Against Loss or Misuse of Escrow Trust Funds

The Escrow Law was created to provide protection to the consumers against loss or misuse of escrow trust funds by independent escrow companies. The *Escrow Law* requires independent escrow companies to meet certain financial requirements, including minimum net worth, bonding, and auditing requirements. Also, regulations have been placed on title companies and lending institutions in order to provide an adequate level of consumer protection. However, real estate brokers generally do not have any rigorous regulations placed on them regarding the provision of escrow services (i.e., no bonding requirements, no auditing requirements, no minimum net worth requirements, etc.). The extent to which the public is protected against loss or misuse of escrow trust funds by real estate brokers is a continuing concern to some industry participants.

4. Competency of Escrow Officers

Concerns have been expressed by some industry participants regarding the competency of escrow officers working for the different types of escrow service providers. Managers of independent escrow companies (who are required by law to have a minimum of five years of responsible escrow experience prior to becoming a manager at the main office, or four years of responsible escrow experience before becoming a manager at a branch office) generally are not the subject of this concern. Also, until recently, the Department of Savings and Loan did not impose any escrow experience requirements on escrow officers at organizations under their jurisdiction. Other escrow service providers (e.g., title companies and real estate brokers) are not required to have any sort of experience with the provision of escrow services which could lead to an incorrect disbursement of funds from the escrow accounts. The amount of money lost due to an incorrect disbursement is usually negligible relative to the amount of money involved in the entire transaction. As a result, the buyer and seller may be either unaware of, or unconcerned with, the error even though one or more of the parties involved in the transaction is losing money.

5. Enforcement of Existing Regulations

Concerns have been expressed by some industry participants regarding the extent to which State and federal agencies adequately enforce existing escrow-related regulations. For example, the Department of Insurance's position regarding title company escrows is that the Department generally is not responsible for anything other than a "limited audit," which consists of making sure disbursements were made according tot eh escrow instructions and that the trust funds balance. Also, concerns have been expressed about the delineation of regulatory agency responsibilities with respect to regulation of the various categories of escrow service providers. For example, the Department of Real Estate's position is that brokers handling escrows that are not incidental to their business are in violation of the Escrow Law which is within the Department of Corporation's jurisdictional area of responsibility. However, the Department of Corporation's position is that generally the Department cannot take enforcement action against escrow service providers which are not licensed by the Department *unless they are violating the restrictive conditions of the exemption contained in the Escrow Law*. This delineation of responsibilities is somewhat confusing to some industry participants.

In summary, escrow services are provided by several different categories of escrow service providers subject to differing levels of regulation. These different levels of services. A study comparing the differing levels of regulation governing escrow service providers and evaluating the extent of the involvement of the different categories of escrow service providers performing escrow services has not previously been conducted. A change in the regulations governing escrow service providers could potentially provide a more adequate level of consumer protection, and/or reduce or eliminate any significant competitive inequalities which currently exist.

RECOMMENDATIONS

As a result of study efforts, including (1) dissemination of a major mail survey to 2,500 chief escrow officers, (2) conduct of interviews with representatives of independent escrow companies, title companies, realty firms, and mortgage lending institutions in California, and (3) review of federal and State legislation and regulations governing the escrow industry, we have concluded that:

☐ Independent escrow companies and lending institutions have a competitive advantage over title companies and real estate brokers with respect to the provision of escrow services in that there are no regulatory restrictions on the types of escrows they can process. In contrast, title companies can only act as an escrow agent in transactions where it is contemplated that a title insurance policy will be issued in connection with the escrow. Real estate brokers can only process escrows that are incidental to their real estate brokerage business.

☐ Firm financial soundness-related regulatory requirements placed upon independent escrow companies, title companies, and lending institutions provide a relatively high level of assurance to the public that escrow trust funds will not be lost due to escrow service provider incompetence, ineptitude, negligence, or misconduct. However, similar regulatory requirements generally do not apply to real estate brokers providing escrow services. Also, significant costs are incurred by independent escrow companies, title companies, and lending institutions to meet financial soundness-related regulatory requirements which generally are not imposed on real estate brokers providing escrow services. As a result of these differences in financial soundess-related regulatory requirements, real estate brokers have a competitive advantage over the other three categories of escrow service providers.

☐ Personnel qualification requirements placed on independent escrow companies and State-chartered savings and loan associations appear to afford a competitive advantage to the other escrow service providers (e.g., title companies, real estate brokers, State-chartered banks, and federally-chartered banks and savings and loans). However, this competitive advantage may not be significant because title companies and lending institutions generally already use experienced escrow officers to manage their escrow operations. Also, the level of competitive advantage placed on independent escrow companies and State-chartered savings and loans may not be significant because the personnel qualification requirements only apply to specified employees and not to all escrow staff.

☐ The extent to which escrow service providers (excluding independent escrow companies) are in compliance with existing statutes and regulations governing the provision of escrow services by these firms is not known because none of the responsible regulatory agencies regularly conduct thorough operational procedure reviews of the escrow service providers within their jurisdiction. Title companies, real estate brokers, and lending institutions have a competitive advantage over independent escrow companies because generally they are not subject to these types of reviews and they do not have to bear the additional costs of having the reviews performed or pay the annual assessment for enforcement actions.

☐ All of the California State Government agencies involved in enforcing existing statutes and regulations governing California's escrow service providers are part of the Business, Transportation, and Housing Agency. However, confusion among industry participants exists as to the scope and authority of each agency's jurisdictional responsibility. As a result, a need exists to better communicate to industry participants (particularly to complainants) each agency's scope of jurisdictional responsibility so that all complaints from the public and industry participants can be addressed.

As a result of these findings, we have developed several recommendations for consideration by government officials and industry participants. In the remainder of this section, we discuss each of these recommendations.

A. Real Estate Broker Compliance with Restrictions on the Types of Escrows They can Handle

Currently, the Department of Real Estate requests, as part of the annual license renewal process, that real estate brokers voluntarily provide the DRE with information regarding their involvement with the provision of escrow services. Also, the Department performs a limited number of random audits of real estate brokers involved in providing escrow services. However, the Department of Real Estate does not know with certainty how many real estate brokers are processing their own escrows or the volume of escrows being processed by these brokers. This information is necessary in order to evaluate whether brokers are abusing the broker exemption from the Escrow Law and which brokers need to be examined more frequently for compliance with the broker exemption.

Recommendation No. 1

Real estate brokers who are providing escrow services should be required to report to the Department of Real Estate on an annual basis (1) the number of escrow transactions processed during the preceding year and (2) the average monthly balance of the broker's escrow trust accounts over the preceding year.

B. Financial Soundness of Real Estate Brokerage Firms Handling Substantial Volumes of Escrows

Several real estate broker respondents to the Survey of Escrow Service Providers conducted as part of this study indicated that they handle substantial volumes of escrows (e.g., 860 residential home escrows in the last year) and that the average monthly balance of their escrow trust accounts is relatively high (e.g., greater than $1 million). However, real estate brokers do not have regulations placed on them assuring the public that they are (1) financially sound, or (2) using correct operational procedures handling escrows. The Department of Real Estate needs to determine if brokers currently providing escrow services on a large scale are adhering to applicable laws and regulations. Based on the results of these examinations, the Department of Real Estate needs to determine whether regulation is necessary for real estate brokers who are performing a substantial number of escrows in order to ensure the financial soundness of their firms.

Recommendation No. 2

The Department of Real Estate should conduct thorough operational procedure reviews of a sample of real estate brokers who are performing substantial numbers of escrows.

Recommendation No. 3

Based on the results of these operational procedure reviews, the Department of Real Estate should determine whether financial soundness-related regulations are necessary for real estate brokers who are performing substantial number of escrows.

C. **Escrow Service Provider Personnel Qualification Requirements**

The potential exists for incorrect disbursement of escrow trust funds due to incompetent or inexperienced escrow officers. The *Escrow Law* attempts to reduce the probability for incorrect disbursements of escrow trust funds by placing minimum escrow-related experience requirements on managers of independent escrow companies. Additionally, specified personnel at State-chartered savings and loan associations are required to meet minimum experience requirements. However, the other escrow service providers do not have any escrow-related personnel qualification regulatory requirements governing them.

Title companies and most lending institutions do not have any escrow-related experience and/or education requirements placed on them. However, title companies and lending institutions generally use experienced escrow officers to manage their escrow operations because of the potential liability they incur by providing escrow services. Incorrect disbursement of escrow trust funds could result in title companies or lending institutions having to pay for such errors from their profits. In order to avoid this, title companies and lending institutions generally use escrow manages who have escrow-related experience.

Finally, real estate brokers are not required to have any escrow-related experience when handling escrows and are not required to complete any escrow-related courses. Therefore, the potential exists for incorrect disbursements of escrow trust funds by real estate brokers. The extent to which real estate brokers are disbursing escrow trust funds incorrectly is not know by the Department of Real Estate but could be determined through the operational procedure reviews (Recommendation No. 2). If the Department of Real Estate finds that real estate brokers are disbursing escrow trust funds incorrectly, the Department could require brokers to meet minimum experience and/or education requirements in order to handle escrows, thus mitigating the problem.

> **Recommendation No. 4**
>
> **Based on the results of the operational procedure reviews, the Department of Real Estate should determine whether real estate brokers who handle substantial volumes of escrows need to have minimum escrow-related experience and/or education requirements placed on them.**

D. Escrow Service Provider Compliance with Existing Statutes and Regulations

The extent to which escrow service providers (excluding independent escrow companies) are in compliance with existing statutes and regulations governing the provision of escrow services by these firms is not known because none of the responsible regulatory agencies (excluding the Department of Corporation) regularly conduct thorough operational procedure reviews of the escrow service providers within their jurisdiction. The extent to which escrow service providers are in compliance with operational procedure guidelines needs to be determined so that these regulatory agencies can appropriately discipline escrow service providers who are in violation of the regulations, thus providing better public protection against fraudulent or dishonest escrow practices.

> **Recommendation No. 5**
>
> **Regulatory agencies governing the various escrow service providers (excluding the Department of Corporations) need to conduct more thorough operational procedure review of the escrow service providers they regulate.**

E. Regulatory Agency Scope of Jurisdictional Authority

In previous sections of this report (Section I and V), we have discussed the confusion surrounding the jurisdictional authority of various California State Government agencies responsible for investigating complaints against escrow service providers. Also discussed were the apparent reasons for this confusion among industry participants. The various California State Government agencies which regulate escrow service providers need to better inform and educate industry participants, especially when initially responding to complaints, as to how the determination of government agency jurisdictional authority is made.

> **Recommendation No. 6**
>
> **The scope of juridictional authority of each regulatory agency governing escrow service providers needs to be better communicated to industry participants and complainants.**

Glossary

Abstract of Judgment: Summary of a court's order. When recorded it creates a general lien upon real and personal property of a judgment debtor in the county where recorded.

Acceptance: The taking of the offer which, under the same conditions of the offer, becomes a contract when a lawful object, meeting of the minds, competent parties, and consideration are involved.

Accommodating Party: A party used as a catalyst to create an exchange when there may be reluctance of parties who would be the most logical choice to consummate the transaction. Accommodating parties serve as a transitional bridge.

Accounts Receivable: Accounts billed upon which payment has not been remitted.

Actual Notice: To inform or to express information of a fact.

Adjustment Slips: Input documents used to rectify incorrectly entered data in an accounting system.

Affidavit: A written statement of facts sworn to or affirmed before an authorized official (usually a notary public).

Agency: The relationship of trust in which one person (the agent) represents another (the principal) in dealing with third parties, as authorized by the principal.

Agent: A person who enters into a fiduciary relationship with another party and is authorized to act for that party.

Alcoholic Beverage Control Board: State agency which regulates liquor licenses, including transfer of licenses in connection with bulk sale of a business.

All-Inclusive Trust Deed: An obligation which not only encumbers equity financed, but also incorporates the amounts of senior obligations in the total indebtedness. Obligation to pay these senior liens is set forth in the all-inclusive documentation.

Amortization: The liquidation of a financial obligation on an installment basis. Also, recovery, over a period of time, of cost or value.

Annual Percentage Rate (APR): The rate of interest weighted by the effects of loan costs over time.

Assessment: An evaluation, specifically of property for tax purposes.

Appreciation: Increase in value due to any cause.

Assign: To transfer over to another a claim, right, or title to property or a contractual claim or right.

Assignee: The person receiving the right or property being assigned (transferred).

Assignment: Transfer of a party's rights under a contract.

Attorney-in-Fact: A person (real or artificial) appointed in writing to act on behalf of a principal within the powers conferred by the document.

Automation: The use of mechanical systems (computers) for processing data, text, etc.

Bailment: A delivery of personal property by one person to another in trust for the accomplishment of a certain purpose, such as taking a suit to the cleaners.

Balance Sheet: A financial statement showing assets, liabilities, and net worth as of a specific date.

Banker's Rule: A month consists of 30 days, and a year of 360 days, for proration and some other purposes.

Banking Commission: The state appointed agency whose director regulates banks under charter by the state.

Bankruptcy: A proceeding established by federal statute that allows debtors to resolve burdensome credit situations and make arrangements with creditors toward such resolution.

Barred (To Bar) : Obstructed by a barrier which will prevent legal recovery. Such as, barred by the Statute of Limitations since time has lapsed during which one may assert his or her legal rights.

Bar Treaty: A formal agreement between the bar association and representative employer groups (title insurers, realtors, independent escrow licensees, banks, savings and loans, etc.) relative to the conduct of employees in the escrow process in specific areas (giving of legal advice, preparation of documents, etc.). In 1979 the State Bar of California revoked all such agreements.

Basis: Property owner's "book value" for income tax purposes. Original cost plus capital improvements less depreciation.

Bilateral Instruction: An escrow contract in which both contracting parties are bound to fulfill obligations reciprocally towards each other.

Bill of Sale: A document used to transfer interest in personal property.

Bona Fide: In good faith, without fraud.

Borrower: The person obligated for the debt.

Borrower/Buyer Instructions: Unilateral escrow instruction stating requirements of a purchaser or borrower in a real estate transaction.

Bracketing: In appraisal, the selecting of a value that falls within the highs and lows of recent selling prices of comparable homes. Used in the market data approach.

Breach: Failure to perform a duty or promise.

Broker: A natural or legal person, who for compensation or in expectation of compensation, acts for another in a real estate or related transaction.

Broker Arranged Loans: Loans arranged by real estate licensees subject to the provisions of the Real Property Loan Brokerage Laws relative to terms and charges. With the passage of California's Proposition 2 in 1979, brokers received insulation from the state's usury law.

Builder: One who conducts a business that includes the subdivision and/or improvement of real property for resale.

Building Code: A state, city, or county law which sets forth minimum construction standards.

Bulk Sale Escrow: Sale of business personal property under the provisions of divisions 6 and 9 of the Uniform Commercial Code, State of California.

Bundle of Rights: The rights or interests that a person has in a thing; the exclusive right of a person to own, possess, use, enjoy, and dispose of real or personal property. The ownership of property.

Business and Professions Code: The title of the statute which contains the provisions of the California Real Estate Law.

California Escrow Association: A professional group composed of escrow managers and practitioners who are members of individual local escrow associations and by such membership enjoy membership in the statewide group.

Call Card: A means of developing customer profiles and frequency of contact within the market area.

Cal-Vet: Program under which the Department of Veterans Affairs of the State of California makes direct loans to eligible veterans through the use of a land contract.

Cancellation: A mutual instruction which is designed to cancel an escrow transaction by the principals and outlines the apportionment of the deposit and payment of charges.

Capacity: The legal ability of a person to perform certain civil acts.

Capitalization: The method of converting anticipated future income into value.

Cash or Cash Through Escrow: Where cash and/or its equivalent in loan proceeds provides all or a portion of the consideration to the seller.

Casualty Insurance Company: A company engaged in insuring against the possibility of a future event (loss by fire, improper title, accidental death, etc.) in return for a premium which is calculated on the probability of such an event happening.

Cash Receipts Journal: A record of all funds received. Record of trust funds received in the form of cash or checks.

Caveat Emptor: Latin term meaning "Let the buyer beware." The buyer must examine the purchase and buy at his or her own risk. No longer applicable to real estate transactions in California.

Certiorari: A writ issued by an appellate court calling for further information in a pending cause.

Chain of Title: An accumulation of instruments affecting the ownership of property over a stated period of time.

Chattel: An item of personal property.

Chattel Real: A personal property right in real estate, such as a lease.

Claim: The right of a creditor to compensation.

Closing: The process entailed in consummating a transaction that involves the encumbrance or sale of real or personal property.

Closing Statement: An itemized accounting for the respective parties in escrow indicating receipts and disbursements, various charges and credits, and appropriate prorations.

Cold Call: A visit to a prospect that has not been prearranged.

Collection Agent: One who collects and disburses payments on obligations as an agent of the party who is entitled to the collection proceeds after expenses are paid.

Commercial Bank: A commercial business which serves as custodian, lender, exchanger or issuer of money, for the extension of credit, and for facilitating the transmission of funds.

Commission: An agent's compensation (fee) for negotiating a real estate or loan transaction.

Commissioner's Regulation's: Regulations adopted by the Real Estate Commissioner to implement the administration and enforcement of the Real Estate Law. They have the force and effect of the law itself. Contained in the California Administrative Code.

Commodities Escrow: An escrow in which the subject matter is personal property whose value is usually established outside of escrow—a very dangerous situation.

Common Interest Development (CID): The form of ownership which includes condominiums, cooperatives, and planned developments. Characteristics include common ownership of certain areas, and governance by an owner's association.

Comptroller of Currency: The federally appointed regulator for national banks.

Computer: An electronic machine for performing mathematical calculations and accumulating and manipulating data.

Condition: A premise upon which the fulfillment of an agreement depends (e.g., a deed for money).

Consent: To agree to do something; give permission, approval or assent. Mutual consent of all parties is one of the essentials of a valid contract.

Consideration: Anything of value given by one person to another to induce a contractual relationship. A necessary condition for a legal contract.

Constructive Fraud: Any breach of duty which, without an actually fraudulent intent, gains an advantage to the person in fault by misleading another to his prejudice. What the law declares to be fraudulent, without respect to actual fraud.

Consumer Credit Protection Act: Legislation enacted in 1969 which initiated the first requirements for lending disclosure to actual or potential borrowers.

Constructive Notice: Notice given by the public records or by possession. Notice to the world.

Consumerism: The sensitivity of governing agencies and general public to consumer issues, and the imposition of regulations to protect public consumers of products and/or services.

Contingency: A condition of closing which may or may not be capable of performance (such as a buyer obtaining a new loan, a seller being able to obtain a new house, or a buyer being able to sell an existing house).

Contract: A deliberate agreement, based upon legal consideration, between two or more parties who have legal capacity, to perform or abstain from doing a legal act.

Conventional Loan: Any loan that is not insured or guaranteed by a government agency.

Conversion: Change from one character or use to another. As applied to trust funds, the unlawful appropriation of another's property.

Conveyance: A written instrument by which some estate or interest in real property is transferred from one person (real or artificial) to another.

Corporation: An artificial being created under state or national law which acts in accordance with its by-laws as interpreted by a board of directors and implemented by its officers.

Corporations Commissioner: The state appointed regulator for independent escrow licensees.

Cost Analysis: A study of the basic components of cost required to sustain an enterprise.

Covenant: A clause in a contract; a promise; an agreement contained in a deed for the performance or nonperformance of certain acts, or for the use or nonuse of the property.

Covenant Not to Compete: A protective agreement given by seller to buyer of a business that seller will not establish a competitive business operation within a certain radius of the business being transferred.

Covenants, Conditions, and Restrictions: Collectively called CC&Rs or "restrictions," which are private rights imposed by prior owners relative to the use and occupancy of the land and improvements thereon.

Credit Unions: State or federally chartered thrift institutions formed by various groups for the purpose of savings return based upon lending or investing funds on deposit.

Damages: Money payment ordered by a court to be paid to one whose property rights or personal rights have been violated.

Debt Service: Repaying a loan through regular payments on principal and interest.

Declaration of Merger: A definitive statement outlining the merger of two separate estates in real property (fee and leasehold, easement and fee, etc.).

Deed: The instrument designed to transfer title in real estate transactions. Two basic types are used in California. See Grant Deed and Quitclaim Deed.

Deed in Lieu of Foreclosure: A deed given by a defaulting borrower to a lender in consideration of foregoing the foreclosure process.

Deed of Trust: An instrument designed to secure the obligation of a note by affixing a lien to real property. Many times the word "mortgage" is used to describe this instrument.

Default: Failure to perform a duty or to discharge an obligation.

Default Judgment: A court order resulting from the failure of a defendant to answer a complaint in a lawsuit.

Delivery: The final and absolute transfer of a deed, properly executed, to the grantee or some person (title company, escrow company, or recorder) in such a manner that the deed cannot be recalled by the grantor.

Department of Real Estate: The governmental body that administers the provisions of the Real Estate Law.

Department of Veterans Affairs, State of California: See Cal-Vet.

Deposit Receipt: A written offer by a real estate purchaser, supported by consideration, to purchase under certain terms and conditions. If accepted by the seller, it becomes a contract of purchase.

Depository: The place where a deposit is placed and kept. The person or entity who holds a deposit of any kind, such as an escrowholder.

Diagramming: A method used to conceptualize the structure of an exchange escrow.

Disbursement: Payment of expenditure for which one is entitled to credit and proper accounting (statement).

Document: See Instrument.

Due on Sale: A clause designed to accelerate the maturity of an obligation upon sale of the property.

Due Process Law: Refers to exercise of governmental powers which essentially provide that "notice" of a charge and "an opportunity to be heard" be given the individual involved.

Duress: Unlawful force used to compel a person to do something against his or her will.

Easement: The right to use the land of another for a specified purpose (utilities, ingress and egress).

Eastern Closing: A closing process consummated at one sitting involving the principals, lenders, title insurers, and/or their representatives.

Emancipated Minor: A person under the age of 18 who is or has been married, or is serving in the Armed Forces, or has received a "Declaration of Emancipation" by court order.

Endorsement: Modification of standard title insurance to expand, modify, or delete specific coverages incorporated in the basic policy.

Enforceable: A contract or agreement which the party (parties) can be compelled to perform by a court of law or equity.

Entrepreneur: One who organizes, manages, and assumes the risk of a business or enterprise.

Equity: The value of an interest being sold, less existing debt and closing costs.

Escrow: A neutral depository for documents and/or funds to be exchanged on performance of a condition or conditions.

Escrow Administrator: One who supervises several escrow offices.

Escrow Agent or Escrowholder: The individual or firm responsible for the escrow documents and deposits.

Escrow Center: An escrow office that capitalizes upon the varied talents of its personnel to offer complete escrow services.

Escrow Certificate Program: A study course established by the California Escrow Association and approved community colleges within California to provide required escrow curricula and certificates of completion.

Escrow Checks: The basic input document for disbursement in an automated accounting system or ledger card system.

Escrow Information Sheet or Memorandum: A programmed interview form designed to extract sufficient information to prepare a proper escrow instruction.

Escrow Manager: The individual responsible for the direction or control of an escrow office or department.

Escrow Officer: The person to whom an escrow file is assigned for processing.

Escrow Receipt: Input document for money received and accounted for in an automated accounting system.

Escrow Secretary: One who performs clerical and stenographic duties in support of an escrow office.

Estate or Interest: The ownership interest that one holds in property.

Exchange: A mutual grant of interests in real property, where consideration could also comprise other than real property.

Exchange Agreement: A mutual purchase agreement executed by the parties to an exchange transaction.

Exchanger: The person who structures an exchange transaction.

Exculpatory: Language used to hold a person or firm harmless of the effect of certain events or actions.

Extended Coverage Survey: A special survey prepared by a civil engineer in conjunction with the issuance of an extended coverage title insurance policy.

Extended Title Insurance Coverage: Almost unlimited insurance as to coverage of ownership interest in real property.

Federal Home Loan Mortgage Corporation (FHLMC): A secondary financing source established by the Federal Home Loan Bank to create an orderly mortgage market for savings and loan associations and other eligible sellers.

Federal Housing Administration (FHA): An agency of the Department of Housing and Urban Development that insures loans originated by institutional lenders which fulfill their underwriting requirements.

Federal National Mortgage Association (FNMA): A private secondary market source for purchasing or selling loans initiated by eligible institutional lenders.

Fee Slips: Input documents for fee accrual in an automated accounting system.

FICA: Federal Insurance Contribution Act, better known as Social Security.

Fiduciary: A person holding a position of trust; agents, trustees, executors, administrators, and attorneys in fact.

Financing Statements: A method of filing a security interest with the Secretary of State or County Recorder, depending upon the type of personal property being secured.

Foreclosure: A legal process available to a lender to acquire an encumbered property from a defaulting borrower without court proceedings.

Forfeiture: Loss of anything of value due to failure to perform.

Forgery: The uttering, altering, or affixing of a signature to a document with intent to defraud.

General Index: An index by name, which may or may not be phonetically coded, that lists legal matters affecting parties to a real estate transaction.

Good Will: The value of the reputation and esteem of a business being purchased.

Government National Mortgage Association (GNMA): A government-owned secondary market source used as a credit vehicle by institutional lenders and as support for government subsidized housing programs.

Grant Deed: The grant deed conveys title and covenants no previous conveyance of the same estate by the grantor and freedom of the estate from any encumbrance placed thereon by the grantor. It also may convey after acquired title. Compare Quitclaim Deed.

Ground Lease: Lease of land only, sometimes secured by the improvements placed on the land by the user.

Guaranty: Special limited use coverage issued by title insurers to fill specific customer needs (foreclosure, condemnation, subdivisions, etc.).

Holding Escrow: Holding funds for distribution upon performance of certain conditions and/or delivery of documents.

Homeowners' Association: A structure for planned developments to administer the maintenance of common areas and enforce rules of conduct for the owners within the project to maintain uniformity.

HUD-1 Uniform Settlement Statement: A statement of closing costs rendered in accordance with the Real Estate Settlement Procedures Act.

Implied Warranties: The warranties, implied by law but not expressed, in a deed which uses the word "grant" to convey a fee estate.

Imputed Notice: Information as to a given fact charged (imputed) to a person, affecting his or her rights, on the ground that actual notice was given to some person whose duty was to report it to the person affected.

Income Analysis: A study or projection of fees earned or contemplated, to determine the profitability of a business.

Independent Escrow Company or Independent Escrow Licensee: An escrow practitioner who is licensed to operate under the State Division of Corporations.

Input: Information fed into a computing and/or word-processing device.

Insanity: An adjudication by the superior court that the party involved is not mentally capable of handling personal affairs, including contracts.

Institutional Lenders: Corporate lenders who operate under the supervision of one or more government agencies.

Institute of Real Estate Management (IREM): A professional association affiliated with the National Association of Realtors for persons who meet standards of experience, education, and ethics in property management.

Instrument: A formal legal document attesting to the rights of the parties specified therein.

Insurance: Coverage whereby one party guarantees to pay a sum of money for the other party's loss in exchange for the insured paying a premium.

Insurance Commissioner: The regulatory agency that supervises activity of insurance companies doing business or domiciling their home office within a state.

Insurance Companies: Companies that assume the risk of the happening or non-happening of an event in return for payment of a premium which is invested.

Interest: See Estate. Also, the percentage of a sum of money charged for its use.

Interpleader: A court action that may be initiated by an escrowholder to determine the ownership of funds on deposit or to settle a dispute of the parties in the transaction.

Inventory: A list of articles representing the effects of a business being transferred.

Joint Venture or Joint Adventure: A business organization composed of two or more persons to conduct a single enterprise (such as build a tract, develop and operate a shopping center, etc.).

Judgment: A general monetary obligation on all property of a debtor in the county in which an abstract is recorded which has been established by court adjudication. Unless renewed, it is effective for 10 years from date of entry.

Judgment Lien: A money claim against property established by recording an abstract of judgment.

Junior Lender: Any lender subordinate to a superior lien (such as a second or third mortgage).

Land Registration or Torrens Title: A method used in certain British jurisdictions and formerly in California to classify land ownership and assure owners of the efficacy of title and the burdens against it. Sometimes a fund for indemnification of defective title is established to protect owners against loss.

Land Sale Contract: A method of selling property on the installment plan which calls for delivery of a deed at a later prescribed date.

Lawful Object: An object of a contract which is permitted by law and possible of performance.

Lease: A contract by which one conveys real estate for a term of years, or at will, for a specified rent. Also the act of such conveyance, or the term for which it is made.

Leasehold Escrow: An escrow to transfer the ownership of a lease by assignment.

Legal Description: A method of describing real property by reference to record maps which can distinguish it with certainty from any other piece of real property.

Legal Person: A creature of law having certain powers and duties of a natural person; usually a corporation.

Lenders: Individuals or institutions who directly or indirectly provide the means of financing a transaction.

Less-Than-Freehold: An estate of certain duration which is limited in time or by desire of the parties; leasehold.

License: An authorization by law to do some specific thing. A personal, revocable, and nonassignable permission or authority to enter upon the land of another for a particular purpose.

Limited Partner: The member of a business arrangement whose liability is limited to the extent of his investment.

Liquidated Damages: A sum stipulated by the parties to the transaction as damages if the transaction fails to consummate.

Loan Administration: The duties involved in maintaining an existing loan (collection of payments, checking tax payment, maintaining insurance coverage, etc.).

Loan Escrow: Any escrow transaction that involves the lending process.

Loan Escrow Instructions: Instructions prepared by an escrowholder to assure borrower compliance with lender requirements.

Loan Escrow Officer: An escrow officer assigned principally to loan closing.

Loan Processing: The qualification process and, in some cases, document preparation for parties involved in a loan transaction.

Manual Bookkeeping: An accounting system that is maintained by hand entry or other than automated means.

Market: The defined area within which a business operates; also, the potential customers for a commodity or service, or network in which transactions take place.

Market Study: An economic analysis and survey of actual or potential customers within a given market area.

Marketing: The creation of a desire by the public to use a service or consume a product.

Marketing Plan: A plan to induce trade within the area of operation based upon data gathered from a market study.

Meeting of the Minds: The mutual understanding of contractual terms by the contracting parties.

Memo Box: That portion of the escrow instruction which summarizes the flow of consideration in a real estate or personal property transfer.

Memorandum: See Escrow Information Sheet.

Mineral Rights: The right to extract migratory substances such as oil, gas, asphaltum, and petroleum, or non-migratory minerals that may be on or below the surface of a property.

Minor: A person under 18 years of age; certain persons under 18 may be termed "emancipated minors."

Misrepresentation: A false, incorrect, or misleading statement, account, or explanation.

Mobilehome: A manufactured housing unit placed on a permanent or temporary foundation and connected to local utilities.

Mobilehome Dealer: A dealer licensed by the Department of Motor Vehicles to sell new or used mobilehomes.

Mobilehome Escrows: Disposition of delivery to purchaser of a mobilehome as described in the motor vehicle code, generated either by a mobilehome dealer or by a real estate licensee.

Mortgage Banker: One acting as a loan correspondent for one or more lenders who performs all phases from loan origination, submission, sale, to servicing of the loan for the ultimate lender.

Move-in Costs: For an unfurnished dwelling—three months' rent (first month's rent plus a deposit equal to two months' rent). For a furnished dwelling—four months' rent (first month's rent plus a deposit equal to three months' rent).

Multi-Unit Property: Properties with 5 or more units.

Mutual Consent: Both parties approve or assent to the terms of a contract.

Natural Person: A living person, as contrasted to a legal person (a corporation).

Negative Fraud: The withholding of a material fact from a buyer or lessee, thereby inducing the person to enter into a contract which causes him damage or loss.

Negotiating: Business dealings between parties to determine price, quantity, quality, etc.

Non-Cash Consideration: Various equities or other items such as personal property that may be used as a portion or all of the consideration.

Northern California Closing Procedure: The closing process characterized by later timing of instruction preparation as well as the use of the unilateral instruction in a majority of cases.

Note: A promise to pay.

Notice to Creditors: A published notice to claimants to make them aware of a pending transfer of the business to allow them time for filing of claims for payment.

Novation: The substitution of a new obligation for an old one.

Offer: A proposal tendered for the purpose of reaching agreement.

Open Housing Law: The federal law banning discrimination in the sale, use, or rental of housing based upon race, color, religion, sex, or national origin of the buyer or tenant. The two formal names are the Civil Rights Act, Title VIII and Public Law No. 90-284.

Operating Statement: A profit and loss statement for an enterprise over a specific period.

Operative Language: The words that serve as the moving force of a legal document, such as the granting clause in a deed, the promise in a note, let and demise in a lease, etc.

Option: An agreement supported by consideration to purchase in the future for a stipulated priced.

Oral Contract: An oral or spoken (parol) contract. One not reduced to writing.proprietary right in real or personal property.

Owner's Statement: Statement by an owner in conjunction with the issuance of extended coverage title insurance, relative to the use and occupancy of the premises being insured.

Partnership: An association of two or more competent persons as co-owners to carry on a business for profit.

Peer: One who is of equal standing with another.

Performance: To act in accordance with prior agreement.

Personal Property: All property that is not real property: usually movable, sometimes intangible.

"Pot" or "Melting Pot" Escrow: An exchange transaction wherein all parties and properties are gathered into one distribution point, and deeds to ultimate purchasers are prepared without regard to intermediary title transfers which proper form might dictate.

Police Power: The right of the state to regulate the use of private property for the protection of the health, safety, morals, or general welfare of the public.

Preliminary Interview: A fact-finding discussion with the principals by the escrowholder prior to preparing the escrow instruction.

Preliminary Title Report: A report on the condition of title prepared in anticipation of closing and prior to issuance of a title insurance policy.

Principals: The contracting parties in escrow (buyer-seller, borrower-lender, lessor-lessee).

Priority Distribution of Claims: The payment of creditors according to a ranking list set forth in the California Business and Professions Code and the Financial Code when escrow deposits are insufficient to pay all bulk sale claims.

Probate: Legal proceedings to distribute the assets of a deceased person and assume payment of required estate taxes. Executors or administrators are appointed by the court to manage the affairs of the deceased, dependent upon whether a will is involved.

Proceeds: The balance due to seller in excess of closing costs and refund of buyer's deposit less appropriate charges.

Product Mix: The variety of services and/or products offered by an enterprise.

Professional: One who is dedicated to high standards of conduct, education, and ethics.

Professional Designations: Titles conferred upon escrow licensees by the California Escrow Association upon applicants' meeting certain criteria of experience, education, or testing for a category.

Promise: A binding declaration by a party to do or not to do a certain act described in the language of a contract.

Proration: The proportional allocation of charges or credits in a real estate or personal property transfer.

Prospect: A potential customer.

Purchase Money Trust Deed: A trust deed contracted to effect the purchase of a property, no matter what the source of consideration (seller, institutional lender, etc.).

Quitclaim Deed: The quitclaim deed conveys present right, title, and interest of the grantor in the real property rather than conveying such property, and does not contain any implied warranties or after acquired title. Compare Grant Deed.

Real Estate Broker: One who is licensed under the provisions of the Real Estate Law to negotiate the purchase and sale of property.

Real Estate Licensee: One who is licensed by the Department of Real Estate to represent a principal in a real estate transaction.

Real Estate Settlement Procedures Act (RESPA): A law that requires the disclosure of the costs charged to the principals in a real estate transfer by institutional first trust deed lenders or their agents.

Real Property: The land, that which is affixed to the land, and that which is immovable by law.

Reciprocal Closing: Mutual closing of two or more property transfers.

Reconciliation: A balancing of two or more accounts, e.g. the balancing of a broker's trust account record to the bank balance.

Record: To file for record in the office of the county recorder. Gives constructive notice to the world of the contents of the document.

Referral: Obtaining new business as the result of recommendations from satisfied customers and clients.

Regulator: One who fixes, establishes, or controls; adjusts by rule, method, or established mode; directs by rule or restriction; subjects to governing principles of laws.

Rescind (Rescission): To cancel a contract from the beginning, restoring the parties to their original positions. Also referred to as annulment.

Rescindable Transaction: For example, an extension of credit that can be cancelled in three business days under the terms of the Consumer Credit Protection Act.

Sale: The transfer of ownership and title to a property from one entity (real or artificial) to another for a consideration.

Sale of a Trust Deed: An escrow transaction involving the transfer of the beneficial interest in a loan that is secured by deed of trust.

Sale-Leaseback: A transaction in which at the time of sale the seller retains occupancy by concurrently agreeing to lease the property from the purchaser. The seller receives cash while the buyer is assured a tenant and a fixed return on the investment.

Savings and Loan Association: A business that solicits savings in the form of share capital, and invests those funds principally in real estate and consumer loans.

Security Agreement: A written instrument created in accordance with the Uniform Commercial Code to secure an interest in personal property; a chattel mortgage.

Seller's Instruction: A unilateral escrow instruction stating the requirements of the transferor in a real estate sale.

Service or Product Mix: The variety of services or goods offered for sale by an enterprise.

Shareholders: Owners of stock in a corporation or depositors in a savings and loan or credit union—those who hold partial interest in a business.

Software: Electronic information used to instruct a computer to perform particular tasks. Physically, software comes in the form of small, flat disks. When the software is run, the information on the disk is copied into the computer's memory.

Southern California Closing Procedure: Usually entails preparation of bilateral escrow instructions, initiated upon completion of a deposit receipt by the parties or by the broker.

Specific Performance: A doctrine of contract law by which a party can be compelled by the court to perform his agreement.

Stakeholder: Holder of documents and/or money in which no interest is claimed by this party; an escrowholder.

Standard Title Insurance Coverage: Limited insurance coverage of an ownership interest in real property.

Start Card: The basic input document for automated accounting systems.

State Board of Equalization: The agency that administers the sales and use taxes required from business collections.

State Housing Law: The state law which sets minimum building standards throughout the state of California.

Statute of Frauds: Law which requires certain contracts to be in writing.

Statement of Identity: A form designed to provide information about parties in ownership which serves as a means of identification in general index search and legal and/or tax matters.

Stockholding Escrows: The conditional delivery of shares of corporate stock from a depository upon performance of a condition.

Structural Pest Control Operator: See Termite Companies.

Subdivided Lands Act: Prescribes the disclosures required from a subdivider via a public report to purchasers of such real property.

Subdivision Escrow: An escrow involved with land developers selling parcels of property under a permit issued by the Real Estate Commissioner's Office.

Subdivision Map Act: Prescribes the requirements for filing maps in conjunction with land being subdivided.

Sublease: A lease given by a lessee for part of the premises or less than the remaining term.

Syndicate: An association of two or more persons formed to accomplish an investment objective.

Tax Lien: A general tax obligation against all property of the person assessed. The lien may be imposed by a state or federal agency.

Tenancy: The mode of holding, such as a joint tenancy, tenancy in common, etc.

Tender: The offer of performance, not performance itself. When unjustifiably refused, places another party in default and permits party making tender to exercise remedies for breach of contract. An offer of money.

Tenure: The term or length of time. For example, the tenure of a lease may be definite or indefinite.

Termite Companies: Structural pest control operators licensed by the state to perform inspections and provide corrective or preventive work to reduce deterioration of a structure caused by pests and/or dry rot.

Third Party Instruction: Instructions relative to money and/or documents and their use by parties who are not principals to the transaction, such as brokers, lender, etc.

Title Insurance: Insurance of ownership interests in the title or encumbrance of real property.

Torrens: See Land Registration.

Transaction: The entire series of acts and conduct between parties in pursuit of some end or agreement.

Transfer: A conveyance of right, title, and interest in real or personal property from one entity to another.

Transferee: The buyer of personal property.

Transferor: The seller of personal property.

Trust Account: A special account into which money is deposited by an agent for the account of a principal, to be kept intact and not commingled.

Trust Accounting Systems: Services designed to provide individual escrow file accounting with supportive management and marketing reports.

Trust Relationship: An implied pledge to act in good faith imposed upon a trustee or custodian.

Trustee: A person appointed or required by law to administer a trust.

Underwriting: The decision-making process based on evaluation of risk, leading to the granting of real estate credit.

Unilateral Instructions: An escrow contract in which one undertakes a performance without receiving in return a promise of performance from the other (each party's promise is separate and distinct from the other).

Unlawful Detainer: Lawsuit to evict a tenant who unlawfully remains in possession of real property rightfully obtained.

Unruh Civil Rights Act: Law which prohibits discrimination by agents or business establishments because of race, color, creed, or national origin.

U.S. Department of Veterans Affairs (USDVA): A government agency established to guarantee loans by lenders for eligible veterans. Formerly called Veterans Administration.

Usury: An excessive and unlawful interest rate charged on a loan. Considerable liberalization of California's usury law has taken place since 1979.

Valuation: The total price in dollars affixed to a parcel in an exchange transaction.

Vesting: The manner in which title to real property is held (A and B as joint tenants, etc.).

Voidable: That which is capable of being made void, but is not void unless action is taken to make it so.

Waiver: The intentional or voluntary relinquishment of a known right, essentially a unilateral act.

Zoning Report: A report prepared by a local agency or planning department describing the zoning of a property, the structures permitted, and any permits issued after the original building permit.

Index